CONTENTS

GCSE

English

CLASSBOOK

Ian Barr
David Bazen

Every effort has been made to trace copyright holders and to obtain their permission for the use of copyright material. The author and publishers will gladly receive information enabling them to rectify any error or omission in subsequent editions.

First published 1996

Letts Educational
Aldine House
Aldine Place
London W12 8AW
0181 740 2266

Text: © Ian Barr and David Bazen 1996

Design and illustrations © BPP (Letts Educational) Ltd 1996

Design and page layout: Ken Vail Graphic Design

Shakespeare illustrations: Hugh Marshall

British Library Cataloguing-in-Publication Data

A CIP record for this book is available from the British Library

ISBN 1 85758 410 4

Printed and bound in Great Britain by Ashford Colour Press

Letts Educational is the trading name of BPP
(Letts Educational) Ltd

INTRODUCTION

The Letts GCSE English Classbook has been developed against the background of the new GCSE syllabuses. The various approaches and techniques used by all of the Examining Boards are covered within the book.

The classbook is designed for use in the classroom, providing stimulus material and tasks to be worked through. There is also an accompanying homework book, containing stimulus material and exercises for you to do at home; plus a teacher's guide, which offers advice and further ideas for teachers.

This GCSE English classbook is divided into ten chapters. Each chapter is designed to provide enough classwork to cover half a term. The classbook will, therefore, take you from the beginning of Year 10 to the end of the Easter term in Year 11.

Each chapter explores a theme – such as 'courage' – by drawing on a wide range of stimulus material and setting associated tasks. The stimulus material is taken from both non-literary and media sources, such as newspapers, magazines, adverts, as well as literary sources. Some material is deliberately taken from different cultures and reflects different customs and ways of life.

The literary stimulus material includes extracts from significant pre-twentieth century literature, as well as modern works. Each chapter contains a section on Shakespeare, with extracts drawn from his plays and tasks designed to explore his use of language and ideas.

At the start of each chapter there is a checklist of Key National Curriculum Skills covered by the chapter in question.

The wide variety of tasks throughout the book are designed to cover all three National Curriculum Attainment Targets as follows:

- **Speaking and Listening** – there are tasks to encourage discussion, speech and formal debate, as well as play- and poetry-reading.

- **Reading** – the wide range of stimulus material provides plenty of opportunity to extend reading skills. There are many tasks which are designed to test whether the stimulus material has been read carefully and with understanding. These tasks include writing summaries; comprehension-style questions, which progress systematically through the stimulus material; character studies and the analysis of writing style.

- **Writing** – there are many opportunities to develop different writing styles and tackle different mediums, such as narrative; poetry writing; script- and dialogue-writing. The importance of 'audience' is continually addressed.

Each chapter contains three 'Time Out Tasks'. These are free-standing exercises which are designed to improve the standard of written English. They are called Time Out Tasks because they step outside the chapter's exploration of a theme to address a specific grammatical point, or deal with a particular requirement of GCSE English, such as letter-writing.

ACKNOWLEDGMENTS

p2 from *A Question of Courage* by Marjorie Darke, Copyright © Marjorie Darke 1975, reproduced by permission of the author c/o Rogers, Coleridge & White Limited, 20 Powis Mews, London W11 1JN; **p4** from *The Health of the Army* by Phoebe Hesketh; **p7** 'Scott Who Challenged the Tobacco Giants', by Jacqui Marson, reprinted with permission from the June 1994 *Reader's Digest*, Copyright © The Reader's Digest Association Limited; **p14** 'For the Fallen', by Laurence Binyon; **p17** 'The Hero', by Siegfried Sassoon, reprinted by permission of George Sassoon; **p23** from *Seize the Moment*, by Helen Sharman and Christopher Priest, published by Victor Gollancz, reprinted with permission; **p25** 'Goliath', by Walter de la Mare; **p28** 'Hero', by Mike Gowar; **p30** from April Fool's Day, by Bryce Courtenay, published by William Heinemann, Sydney, reprinted with permission; **p34** from *Pole to Pole*, by Michael Palin, reprinted by permission of BBC Worldwide Limited; **p36** from *The Beauty of Kenya*; **p39** *Opportunity for Adventure with Oxventure*, reproduced by permission of Oxventure, Oxford; **p43** from *The Life and Times of Henry V*, by Peter Earle; **p46** from *Fair Stood the Wind for France*, by H E Bates, published by Michael Joseph Limited, reproduced by permission of the estate of H E Bates and Laurence Pollinger Limited; **p48** from *A Year in Provence*, by Peter Mayle; **p50** 'He Paints the Heroes of Dreamtime', by Paul Raffaele, reprinted with permission from the July 1995 *Reader's Digest*, Copyright © The Reader's Digest Association Limited; **p56** from *Spring and Port Wine*, by Bill Naughton, Copyright © 1958 under the title *My Flesh, My Blood*, revised and rewritten 1967, reproduced with permission. All rights whatsoever in this play are strictly reserved and application for performance etc. must be made before rehearsal to Casarotto Ramsay Limited, National House, 60-66 Wardour Street, London W1V 4ND. No performance may be given unless a licence has been obtained; **p58** from *The Virgin in the Ice*, by Ellis Peters; **p59** from *The Unpleasantness at the Bellona Club*, by Dorothy L Sayers, published by New English Library, reproduced with permission from David Higham Associates Limited; **p60** from 'The Pinnacle of Achievement' by Chris Bonington, published in the *Geographical* magazine, December 1993, reprinted by permission of The Royal Geographical Society; **p68** from *After the First Death*, by Robert Cormier; **p72** from *Return with Honour*, by Scott O'Grady, published by Bloomsbury Publishing Plc in London in 1995, reprinted with permission; **p75** reproduced by arrangement with Watts Books, a division of the Watts Publishing Group, London from *Life Guides: The Environment and Health*, by Brian Ward, published by Franklin Watts; **p77** from *Journey's End*, by RC Sherriff, Copyright © R C Sherriff, reproduced by permission of Curtis Brown Group Limited, London; **p79** 'Nervous Prostration' from *The Writings of Anna Wickham Free Woman and Poet*, by Anna Wickham, published by Virago, reprinted with permission; **p80** 'The Farmer's Bride' from *Collected Poems*, by Charlotte Mew, published by Carcanet Press Limited, reprinted with permission; **p84** 'Star crossed lovers', by Sarah Cunningham, reprinted with permission, Copyright © Sarah Cunningham/ Marie Claire/ Robert Harding Syndication; **p94** from 'Can the Tiger Survive?', by Eugene Linden, from Time magazine, 28 March 1994, reprinted with permission, Copyright © Time Inc., New York; **p97** from *Lord of the Flies*, by William Golding, published by Faber and Faber Limited, reprinted by permission of Faber and Faber Limited; **p100** from *The Diary of Anne Frank*; **p103** from *1984*, by George Orwell, Copyright © The estate of the late Sonia Brownell Orwell and Martin Secker and Warburgh Limited, reprinted with permission; **p106** 'A Face for David', by Jim Hutchison, reprinted with permission from the November 1994 *Reader's Digest*, Copyright © The Reader's Digest Association Limited;

p109 'Secrets of A-Grade Pupils', by Edwin Kiester and Sally Valentine Kiester reprinted with permission from the November 1994 *Reader's Digest*, Copyright © The Reader's Digest Association Limited; **p113** 'Beautiful Old Age', by DH Lawrence from *The Complete Poems of DH Lawrence*, reprinted with permission from Laurence Pollinger Limited and the estate of Frieda Lawrence Ravagli; **p113** 'In Oak Terrace' from *New and Selected Poems*, by Tony Connor, published by Anvil Press Poetry, 1982, reprinted with permission; **p114** from *A Message for the Pig-Man*, © The Estate of John Wain reproduced with permission of Curtis Brown Ltd; **p116** 'Little City', by Robert Horan, published in the *Criterion Book of Modern American Verse*, Criterion Books, 1956; **p117** 'The Wasps' Nest', by James L Rosenberg; **p118** from *Winnie-the-Pooh*, by AA Milne, published by Methuen Children's Books, reprinted with permission; **p120** from *Watership Down* by Richard Adams; **p124** from *Constant Glory* by Chandan Mitra, reprinted by permission of Oxford University Press, New Delhi; **p126** 'Mapping for Pleasure', by Tony Seaton and Fiona McWilliam, published in the *Geographical* magazine, February 1995, reprinted by permission of The Royal Geographical Society; **p129** 'Death of a Slave', by Jonathan Silvers, published in *The Sunday Times*, 15 October 1995, Copyright © Jonathan Silvers, reprinted with permission; **p133** 'Executive', from *Collected Poems*, by John Betjeman, reprinted by permission of John Murray (publishers) Limited; **p134** 'Vital', from *Collected Poems 1952-1983*, by Alan Brownjohn, Copyright © Alan Brownjohn 1983,1988, reprinted by permission of Rosica Colin Limited; **p136** 'Feminine Advice', from *True Confessions and New Clichés*, by Liz Lochhead, Polygon Books, reprinted with permission; **p137** 'Maintenance Engineer', by Sandra Kerr; **p139** from *Appointments Magazine*, 7 November 1995, Copyright © Oxford and County Newspapers; **p142** from *Hobson's Choice*, by Harold Brighouse; **p143** 'Talking Dirty', by Jenny Deeprose from *The Grocer*, 4 November 1995, Copyright © William Reed Publishing Limited, reprinted with permission; **p149** 'Do you have a disability?', from *Positive About Disabled People*, Employment Department Group; **p151** from 'Shooting an Elephant', by George Orwell, Copyright © The estate of the late Sonia Brownell Orwell and Martin Secker and Warburgh Limited, reprinted with permission; **p152** from *Cannery Row*, by John Steinbeck, published by William Heinemann, reprinted permission; **p154** from *A Kestrel for a Knave*, by Barry Hines, reprinted by permission of Penguin Books; **p157** from *Positive Action: Promoting Racial Equality in Employment*, Employment Department Group; **p159** from 'Every day friends ask for money', by David Cohen, *Independent Magazine*, 4 November 1995, reprinted by permission of The Independent Newspaper Plc.; **p161** from 'A Drink in the Passage', from *Debbie Go Home*, by Alan Paton, published by Jonathan Cape, reprinted by permission of the estate of Alan Paton and Jonathan Cape; **p165** from *Roll of Thunder, Hear My Cry*, by Mildred Taylor, published by Victor Gollancz, reprinted with permission; **p166** 'Ninetieth Birthday', from *R S Thomas Collected Poems 1945-1990*, by R S Thomas, published by J M Dent, reprinted by permission of The Orion Publishing Group Limited; **p167** 'Aunt Julia', from *Collected Poems*, by Norman MacCaig, published by Chatto & Windus, reprinted with permission; **p168** 'The Hunchback in the Park', from *The Poems*, by Dylan Thomas, published by J M Dent, reprinted by permission of David Higham Associates; **p170** from 'Stone Cold', by Robert Swindell; **p172** 'Telephone Conversation', by Wole Soyinka; **p175** from an article published in *The Independent*, 28 September 1991, by Martin Amis, reprinted by permission of Aitken, Stone & Wylie; **p177** from *Animal Farm*, by George Orwell, Copyright © The estate

Acknowledgements

of the late Sonia Brownell Orwell and Martin Secker and Warburg Limited, reprinted with permission; **p180** from *Stephen Hawking: A Life in Science*, by Michael White and John Gribbin, published by Viking, reprinted with permission; **p191** from 'Don't Waste your Time with those Kids', by Janice Anderson Connolly, from *The First Year of Teaching*, edited by Pearl Rock Kane, published by Walker and Company, New York; **p205** from 'The National Trust Lake District Appeal', Copyright © National Trust, reprinted with permission; **p211** from 'We must end this war of town v country', by Ken Warpole from *The Independent*, 23 October 1995, reprinted by permission of The Independent Newspaper Plc.; **p213** 'The Kite', by W Somerset Maugham; **p216** from *Touch and Go*, by Elizabeth Berridge, published by Transworld Books, reprinted by permission of David Higham Associates; **p219** 'Wind', from *The Hawk in the Rain* by Ted Hughes, published by Faber and Faber Limited, reprinted by permission of Faber and Faber Limited; **p221** 'The Horses' by Ted Hughes, reprinted by permission of Faber and Faber Limited; **p223** from *The AA Book of the British Countryside*, Copyright © Reader's Digest Association Limited, reprinted with permission; **p225** 'The Man by the Fountain', by George Hebbelinck; **p228** 'Follower', from *Death of a Naturalist*, by Seamus Heaney, published by Faber and Faber, reprinted by permission of Faber and Faber Limited; **p228** 'My Grandmother', from *Collected Poems*, by Elizabeth Jennings, published by Carcanet, reprinted by permission of David Higham Associates; **p229** 'Twelve Songs, IX ("Stop all the clocks...'), from *Collected Poems*, by W H Auden, published by Faber and Faber Limited, reprinted with permission; **p230** 'Heaven preserve the family from teenage girls', by Jonathan Miller, from *The Sunday Times*, 1 January 1995; **p233** 'Ray of Hope for destitute parents', from Reuters, published in *The New Straits Times*, 7 July 1994, reprinted by permission of The New Straits Times Sdn Berhad, Kuala Lumpur and Reuters; **p234** 'Lament of a 65-year-old man', by Ahmad Ari Eckhardt, published in *The New Straits Times*, 8 July 1994, reprinted by permission of The New Straits Times Sdn Berhad, Kuala Lumpur; **p235** 'Memorable moments of school life', by Oh Teik Theam, published in *The New Straits Times*, 8 July 1994, reprinted by permission of The New Straits Times Sdn Berhad, Kuala Lumpur; **p239** 'Rising Five', from *Collected Poems*, by Norman Nicholson, published by Faber and Faber Limited, reprinted by permission of David Higham Associates; **p241** 'My Daughter, My Friend', by Patricia Lorenz, from *Working Mother*, New York, March 1993; **p250** from 'David and Broccoli' (play), by John Mortimer, reprinted by permission of the Peters Fraser & Dunlop Group Limited; **p251** 'Mother in half a million', by Reva Klein, from Times Educational Supplement, 25 February 1994; **p255** from *Animal Farm*, by George Orwell, Copyright © The estate of the late Sonia Brownell Orwell and Martin Secker and Warburg Limited, reprinted with permission; **p257** from 'Odour of Chrysanthemums', by D H Lawrence, from *The Complete Short Stories of D H Lawrence*, reprinted by permission of Laurence Pollinger Limited and the estate of Frieda Lawrence Ravagli; **p261** from *Cider With Rosie*, by Laurie Lee, published by Chatto & Windus, reprinted with permission; **p264** from 'Supernova! A Star Explodes', by John Tierney, from *Discover*, New York, July 1987; **p267** 'Did Comets Kill The Dinosaurs?', by Richard Muller, from *New York Times Magazine*, 24 March 1985; **p269** 'Design', by Robert Frost from *The Poetry of Robert Frost*, edited by Edward Connery Lathem, published by Jonathan Cape, reprinted by permission of the estate of Robert Frost and Jonathan Cape; **p270** 'The Kaleidoscope', from *Elegies*, by Douglas Dunn, published by Faber and Faber Limited, reprinted by permission of Faber and Faber Limited; **p275** from *Cromwell: Our Chief of Men*, by Antonia Fraser; **p279** from 'Let The Children Live!', reprinted by permission of Let The Children Live! Care For The

Children Of The Streets, registered charity; **p281** 'Death in Leamington', from *Collected Poems*, by Jonathan Betjeman, published by John Murray Limited, reprinted with permission; **p283** 'Do not go Gentle into that Good Night', from *The Poems*, by Dylan Thomas, published by J M Dent, reprinted by permission of David Higham Associates; **p284** from *Writing Home*, by Alan Bennett, published by Faber and Faber Limited, reprinted by permission of Faber and Faber Limited; **p286** from *Of Mice and Men*, by John Steinbeck, published by William Heinemann, reprinted with permission; **p290** from *The Children of Men*, by P D James, published by Faber and Faber Limited, reprinted by permission of Faber and Faber Limited; **p292** from *The Day of the Triffids*, by John Wyndham, published by Michael Joseph; **p294** from *Hi-Fi News and Record Review*; **p296** from 'Life - Don't Keep it to Yourself', published by the Department of Health; **p297** from "You too could save a life...", published by permission of the Anthony Nolan Bone Marrow Trust; **p299** 'Prayer before Birth', by Louis MacNeice, reprinted by permission of Faber and Faber Limited; **p301** '5 Ways to kill a man', by Edwin Brock, reprinted by permission of Edwin Brock; **p302** 'Horoscopes', by Tanya Obreza, from *Company*, April 1995, reprinted by permission of Company Magazine/ © National Magazine Company; **p304** 'Horoscopes', from *Elle*, April 1995, reprinted by permission of Elle and Bernard Fitzwalter; **p305** 'Debbie pulls it off', by Jessica Berens, from the *Independent Magazine*, 7 October 1995, reprinted by permission of the Independent Newspaper Plc.; **p311** 'Your Attention Please', by Peter Porter, reprinted by permission of Oxford University Press; **p312** 'The Horses', from *Collected Poems* by Edwin Muir, published by Faber and Faber Limited, reprinted by permission of Faber and Faber Limited; **p314** from *Brother in the Land*, by Robert Swindell; **p315** from *Z for Zachariah*, by Robert O'Brien, reprinted by permission of Victor Gollancz Limited.

Photographs

p18 *The Martyrdom of St. Sebastian*, by Andrea Mantegna, reproduced by courtesy of the Louvre, Paris, Copyright © Photo R.M.N.; **p19** *Christ driving the traders from the temple*, by El Greco, reproduced by courtesy of the Trustees, The National Gallery, London; **p19** *The Third of May, 1808*, by Francisco Goya, reproduced by courtesy of the Prado, Madrid, Copyright © Museo del Prado, Madrid; **p21** *Aftermarth at Ypres, 1917*, © The Hulton Deutsch Collection; **p22** *The raft of the Medusa*, by Theodore Gericault, reproduced by courtesy of the Louvre, Paris, Copyright © Photo R.M.N.; **p22** *Breezing Up*, by Winslow Homer, reproduced with permission, Copyright © Board of Trustees, National Gallery of Art, Washington DC; **p39** Photograph supplied by John Havens, reproduced by permission of Oxventure, Oxford; **p52** Budapest, © Tony Stone Images; **p53** Anchorage, © The Image Bank; **p53** Bled, © Spectrum Colour Library; **p61** Iditarod musher, Alaska, © Tony Stone; **p92** Iditarod musher, Alaska, © Tony Stone; **p93** Alaska, © Tony Stone; **p93** Denali National Park, © Tony Stone; **p94** Young Male Tiger, © Bruce Coleman Collection; **p96** Caribou, Alaska, © Tony Stone; **p96** Alaska, © Tony Stone; **p171** Homeless Man, © Photofusion; **p173** Mods, © The Hulton Deutsch Collection; **p173** Football Fans, © The Hulton Deutsch Collection; **p174** Welcoming Mandela Home, © The Hulton Deutsch Collection; **p198** from *Tolkein: The Illustrated Encyclopaedia*, by David Day, published by Mitchell Beazley, reproduced with permission; **p242** Manchester S.I., © The Hulton Deutsch Collection; **p243** Ethiopia, © The Hulton Deutsch Collection; **p243** Deep in Thought, © The Hulton Deutsch Collection; **p243** Whiskers, © The Hulton Deutsch Collection; **p244** Skins S.I., © The Hulton Deutsch Collection; **p244** Watcher, © The Hulton Deutsch Collection.

For each chapter of this book we have chosen a topic which will allow you to think and develop your ideas coherently. In doing so, we do not want the topic to become a straitjacket but we want you to be able to develop your ideas in a wide variety of ways. We want you to explore English!

So 'courage', our first topic, can mean many different things to different people. Some of you will think of the courage people show in war; some of you will think much more generally of the courage people show in fighting, in a variety of ways, for causes in which they believe; some of you may know people who show courage simply by living from day to day and coping with immense personal problems.

No one type of courage is greater than another – so let's begin exploring!

ENGLISH IN THE NATIONAL CURRICULUM:

Key Skills you will cover in this chapter

- ✓ You will be asked to think widely about issues and, in arriving at your judgements, react both to what you feel and to what you believe is right or wrong.
- ✓ You will consider how we all live and work in a number of different groups and these, together with the wider society in which we live, all affect our lives in different ways.
- ✓ You will talk about ideas and experiences which are presented to you and think about how you are putting your ideas across (you're going to speak a little differently with a group of adults rather than a group of your own friends).
- ✓ You will be presented with all different types of writing and you should be able to understand the different ways in which ideas and subjects are put across.
- ✓ You must understand how clear, factual and argumentative writing is used to convey ideas and information and need to show that you can write in the appropriate style.

A Question of Courage is the title of a book by Marjorie Darke. The book is concerned with the campaign for women's rights before the First World War – 'Votes for Women'.

Emily Parker is seventeen, she works long hours sewing garments by hand for low wages. At home she is expected to do her share of chores – unlike her two brothers and her father.

However, she is a strong-willed and independently-minded young woman. Attracted to the campaign to get voting rights for women, she and Louise Marshall decide to make a splash.

A Question of Courage

'I met someone,' Louise replied to her unformed question. 'Mary Grant. She came up from London to speak at one of our drawing-room meetings. It was incredible listening to her. She has been in Holloway prison four times and she described the way she was forcibly fed. Oh – it is monstrous – disgusting! I don't know how she could have borne it, she is so frail and delicate, like a tiny bird. But she's got the courage of a lion.'

Emily shivered, recognising the undercurrent of violence in Louise's voice again.

'Those prison doctors are brutes. Some of the things Mary said made me want to vomit …'

Emily was afraid Louise was going to describe the scenes in detail and hastily interrupted. 'She must be brave.'

'She is … but there are many others and they're all prepared to go back again and again even though it means going through the whole ghastly business once more.' Louise sounded almost as if she were enjoying the horror.

'Would you do it? Go on hunger strike, I mean?' asked Emily.

Louise did not answer straight away and when she did, sounded uncertain.

'I believe I could. Thinking about it now, in the open air, it would be easy to say "Of course". But it's when you are there, shut away inside the prison that counts. It will all be different then.'

Will be? She made it sound as if this was waiting for them just round the corner, an inevitable happening. 'Yo really mean that,' Emily said slowly. The implications were enormous. 'Are yo going to keep on doing things like tonight?'

'This is just the beginning. You'll see!'

'Mary Grant must have been a real soul-mover,' Emily said with conviction.

'She is. Hearing her tipped the scales.'

So there *was* something else. Before she could probe further Louise touched her arm.

'There's a cart track here. If we go up it there are two gates, one on each side. They lead on to the golf course. It spreads out either side. Used to be farm land, you see. The farmhouse is still there just at the top of this track.'

'Does anyone live there?'

'Oh yes. The farmer has land the other side of the course.'

Then there were people near by; dogs perhaps. Emily tied up the remains of her courage. She'd come this far. It was no use getting cold feet now. Cold feet? Hers were freezing! 'Let's get a move on, before we turn into snowmen. Yo go first and tell me what to do.' It occurred to her that she had no idea what a green was, had never seen a golf course. All she knew of golf were some strange pictures she had seen in a magazine.

They left the track, edging through the swing gate into rough grass. The ground was hard and lumpy beneath their feet. The full moonlight revealed the land falling away into a shallow valley, to rise against a horizon that was broken by the dark bunching of trees and bushes.

'Down here,' Louise whispered.

Rime flicked from long grass blades as they tramped downhill to a flat, closely-mown lawn which had a flag on a pole sticking out of the ground. So *that* was the purpose of the flags she had stitched. Eighteen! They'd have to work fast or it would be daylight before they finished.

'Here!' Louise handed her a pair of scissors. 'Cut off the old flags and tie on one of ours. I'll start painting.'

Emily moved towards the flag. Never in her life had she done anything remotely outside the law. 'Keep your nose clean,' Dad always said. 'Steer clear of them bobbies. They'll as soon nick yo as look' – and here she was about to destroy something belonging to someone else … deliberately! She glanced at Louise and saw she had already finished the first long white stroke of her V. Emily tightened her hold on the flag bunting, closed the scissors and hacked. Then crouching down, she untied her bundle, selected a new flag and tied it to the pole with the four stout tapes May had sewn on. Louise had painted VOTES FOR W … The letters gleamed clearly in the moonlight. They would be seen for miles, Emily felt sure, if anyone was looking.

'There!' Louise finished the N with a flourish. 'Mind

where you walk.'

Emily took her bundle and picked her way over the whitewash. Now she was a *law-breaker* ... a *criminal*. She'd burned her boats ... cut her flag! There was something oddly exciting about demonstrating her decision. The martyr part was there in the background, an unsolved dilemma, but it was too distant to worry about. What was happening now reminded her of Vic's Penny Dreadfuls. All wild adventure. Blood and thunder ... only it was quiet as anything except for the rustle made by the two of them walking.

The next green was farther down the slope over to their left. Emily pushed through clumps of scutch grass.

'There's a great pit of sand here,' she said.

'Bunker,' Louise corrected. 'A sort of trap to catch the golf balls.'

Emily attached her second flag, puzzling over the odd hazards of this strange game. 'What made yo pick on a golf course?'

'Private property. Owned by wealthy men, like my father. They don't like their property damaged. It's sacred. They will take a lot of notice when it's spoiled, much more than listening to reasonable argument.' There was a hardness to Louise's voice.

Her father? Was that the other reason ... the deeper one? 'Your father will be furious.'

Louise did not answer directly, but muttered threats under her breath, one to each brushstroke. Emily caught broken phrases.

'... Being pig-headed ... can't stop me ... won't give in ... it's my life ... I'm not his property ...'

So it was a twofold thing after all. One blow for Women's Rights, the other directed at her father! Which mattered most? Emily felt let down, as if this personal feud had tarnished her golden image of Louise. But perhaps the two things were connected anyway. Fathers were men and both were trouble! If anger at that final row in the kitchen had pushed her into coming, then Louise had just as much right to be forced on by her emotions. You could love and detest people at the same time, be driven to all sorts of rash acts, but it didn't mean those acts weren't *right*.

'Why did you ask *me* to come? There's all them ladies at the drawing-room meetings like Una and Maude Holiday ... or there's Vera.'

'Ladies!' The amount of scorn Louise put into the word was remarkable. 'Meek creatures. They wouldn't say boo to a goose, let alone approve. As for Vera ... I don't know; there's something sort of *closed*. I'd never be certain.'

'But me ... why me?' Emily insisted.

'Because you are a fighter, like me. Nerve, courage, call it what you like. You are reliable. Besides, I like you.' She paused in mid-stroke. Emily thought she was smiling. Whitewash, dripping off her brush, made a thin white line down her skirt. 'Oh, now look what I've gone and done!'

'Here, mop it up with the matching bit on this flag.'

Emily was all concern in the middle of her joy. Another link had been forged between them. Louise's pedestal, in shrinking a little, had brought friendship closer.

An owl hooted with startling clarity. Farther off came an answering call and a great white bird sailed out from a clump of skeleton trees.

'It'll be witches on broomsticks next,' Emily said shakily.

'If they do I shall rapidly paint VOTES FOR WOMEN on our remaining flags and persuade the old dears to tie them on their broomhandles. It'd be the best bit of advertising the Cause has ever had. Just think of the newspaper headlines – SUFFRAGETTES HARNESS THE SUPERNATURAL ... CAN PARLIAMENT WITHSTAND THIS ATTACK?'

The idea wasn't really funny, but they found themselves giggling on the way to the next green and the next. Emily fumbled with the tapes, all thumbs, pulling hard, tearing the stitching. 'Oh, blast it!'

'Tell you what, we could change over next time if you like,' Louise offered.

'All right.'

The walking was rough. They crossed a small brook by way of a flat wooden bridge, the noise of their footsteps shatteringly loud. Over a ridge into a second valley and back again. Surely someone must hear? But it seemed they had the night to themselves.

'We have to cross the farm track to the other part of the course now,' Louise said.

They could see the farmhouse black and silver against a quiet sky. Nine greens done, another nine and they would be finished.

And then the dog barked. Not a single enquiring sound, but on and on with the rattle of his chain as he ran backwards and forwards. He knew they were there.

'It's all right, he's tied up,' Louise whispered.

'But we ain't finished.'

'We've done enough. Come on!'

They were coming out of the valley with the gate in sight when the farmhouse door banged. A man's voice called out:

'All right, Tiger. Down boy!' Metal chinked on stone.

'The dog's free,' Louise hissed. 'Run!' She spurted forward, Emily close on her heels. Suddenly Emily saw Louise spread her arms, body twisting, but there was no time to take evasive action. As Louise sprawled full length on the turf, Emily tripped helplessly over her legs. The remaining whitewash splashed from the can over them both. Louise curled up, clutching her ankle. Boots crunched over the stony track. The barking closed in.

'Go, can't you ... run!' Louise was almost sobbing with pain and frustration.

Emily said nothing, but moved up close to her friend, crouching as if to shield her from attack. The dog was on them now with growls and panting breath. Too terrified to move, they waited for him to charge, but he stood, hackles raised, daring them to try.

'Sit, Tiger! And you ... don't try anything or I'll pepper you good and proper!' The voice changed from threat to astonishment. 'Well I'll be danged ... a couple of gels!'

But still they didn't move. Looking up, they found themselves staring into the menacing barrels of a shotgun.

MARJORIE DARKE

TASKS

1. Emily and Louise talk about other people's bravery. What are their opinions? Summarise what they say about the courage of others.
2. Explain in your own words what sort of courage is needed to do the things Emily and Louise do.
3. Discuss in small groups what you really think of Emily and Louise. You might find for instance, that boys in your group have different views from girls; you might find everyone thinks the same way. Whatever the case, discuss the reasons for the opinions held. Then move onto the next written task.
4. Do you admire Emily and Louise? Explain your reasons for what you think.

You will find that we have reprinted this article in your homework book with some further tasks, which will take your thinking forward.

'Votes for Women' got under way because many women had proved that they were capable of fine and heroic deeds. One of the best-known of these is Florence Nightingale. Her work in the Crimean War (1853–1855) won her a place in history. She became known as 'the Lady with the Lamp' as she helped and comforted wounded soldiers night after night.

However, it is important to remember that Florence Nightingale did not give up when the war was over. She wanted to reform the whole medical system in the army. Here is an extract from Phoebe Hesketh's biography of Florence Nightingale.

The Health of the Army

'The diamond has shown itself,' wrote Sidney Herbert, 'and it must not be allowed to return to the mine.' It had no intention of so doing. There was work to be done, a pledge to be redeemed. 'I stand at the altar of the murdered men and while I live I shall fight their cause,' she wrote. Those men had been murdered by a system – a system deeply entrenched, immensely powerful, hallowed by tradition and essentially masculine. It was this system she now set herself to change.

Within a day or two of her arrival at Lea Hurst, ill and emaciated as she was, nauseated by the sight of food, she wrote to Lord Panmure and to Sidney Herbert asking for interviews. It was August. Panmure was in Scotland shooting grouse, Herbert in Ireland catching salmon. Panmure replied that she must surely be in need of rest, Herbert passed on the advice of his Carlsbad doctor: '*Ni lire, ni écrire, ni reflechir* [Don't read, write or think]'. No advice could have been more unacceptable.

Florence did all three with unremitting industry, and Sidney Herbert wrote expressing concern about her overwrought state of mind.

Invitations poured in entreating her to address meetings, accept tributes, attend functions; she refused them all. The showiness, 'fuz-buz about my name', she despised. She was 'as merry about little things as ever', Parthe wrote, but in private notes she poured out her frustrations, and to Colonel Lefroy, now back at the War Office, she wrote of the 'detestation with which I am regarded by the officials'. Her chief enemy was Sir Benjamin Hawes, Permanent Under-Secretary at the War Office and an implacable opponent of reform.

Then, quite unexpectedly, came an opportunity to state her case at the highest level of all. The Queen wanted to hear of her experiences at first hand. The royal physician, Sir James Clark, invited Florence to stay at his Scottish home near Balmoral. She set to work with enormous thoroughness to prepare her case. Sir John McNeill lived in Edinburgh and she arranged to stay with him *en route*, and summoned thither Colonel Tulloch.

One of the reasons for Florence's success was that she knew exactly what she wanted to achieve. She never waffled. She wanted the root-and-branch reform of the army medical services and knew that the way to go about it, for a start, was to have a Royal Commission. Both its composition and the gist of its recommendations were already clear in her mind. Four days were spent in Edinburgh in conclave with McNeill and Tulloch. Florence was still weak, food still nauseated her, but she spent what little free time she had inspecting barracks and hospitals. On 15 September 1856 she arrived at Sir James Clark's home, Birk Hall, and two days later her first interview with the Queen and the Prince Consort took place.

It was a crucial interview, and a complete success. Florence was a woman after the Queen's own heart. Prince Albert's, too. 'She put before us all the defects of our present military hospital system, and the reforms that are needed. We are much pleased with her; she is extremely modest.' A few days later the Queen drove over to Birk Hall and they had 'tea and a great talk'. Other visits followed; she had conquered the Queen, who wrote to her cousin the Duke of Cambridge, the Commander-in-Chief: 'I wish we had her at the War Office.' No wonder Florence's 'hopes were somewhat raised'. But only somewhat; she knew quite well the limits of the royal powers. Lord Panmure was the man who really mattered. Panmure was due to pay a visit to Balmoral, and the Queen thought it would help Florence's cause if she were to meet the Minister under the royal roof. 'I don't,' Florence wrote bluntly, 'but I am obliged to succumb.' The Queen attempted a little softening up in advance. 'Lord Panmure', she wrote, 'will be much gratified and

struck with Miss Nightingale – her powerful, clear head, and simple, modest manner.' But Sidney Herbert was 'not sanguine: for, tho' he [Panmure] has plenty of shrewd sense, there is a *vis inertiae* in his hesitance which is very difficult to overcome'.

Panmure was a past master in the art of ignoring or avoiding trouble. Anything in the nature of what we now call a confrontation was anathema, and work, Herbert wrote, 'he found easy through the simple process of never attempting to do it.' He had been angry with McNeill and Tulloch for writing such a harmful report, and did his best to smother it. A Royal Commission that would stir up even murkier waters was clearly the last thing to be desired. He was altogether a much tougher proposition than the Queen.

Widely experienced as he was in resisting pressure, knowing as he did that Florence's iron will and relentless perseverance would be sure to create trouble, he allowed himself to be beguiled. 'You fairly overcame Pan,' Sir James Clark's son wrote to her. 'We found him with his mane absolutely silky, and a loving sadness pervading his whole being.' Sidney Herbert wrote that 'he was very much surprised at your physical appearance, as I think you must have been with his.' Panmure had probably expected a hatchet-faced amazon, instead of this demure, frail, soft-spoken modest lady – everyone stressed her modesty. By the end of their talks, she had won every point. There was to be a Royal Commission; she was to be invited to submit a full report with her recommendations; her proposal that an Army Medical School should be set up was well received; and finally 'the Bison', on his own initiative, offered to submit to her the plans of the first General Military Hospital to be built in Britain, at Netley, for her comments. It seemed to be a total victory.

PHOEBE HESKETH

TASKS

5 Describe in your own words the sort of person which you think Florence Nightingale was.
6 How was she different from Lord Panmure?
7 Explain how she overcame his resistance to her proposals.
8 In the extract which you have read there is a reference to Florence Nightingale's letter to her cousin, the Duke of Cambridge. Put yourself in her shoes and write the letter in full, as you think she might have written it. (Think about style and remember that Florence Nightingale lived in the middle of the nineteenth century – this means, for instance, you need to consider the vocabulary you might use in the letter.)

TIME OUT TASK!

Punctuation

Throughout your years in school you will have learnt about punctuation. Everything you have read has been punctuated. As your own writing has developed, so has your punctuation.

You know what commas, fullstops, question marks, exclamation marks and so on are. You use punctuation in your writing every day of your school life. But do you use it correctly?

What is printed below is a passage where we have taken all the punctuation out. Can you put it back in? There might not always be just one right answer but remember that the job of the punctuation you put in is to clarify meaning and to make the passage easier to read. We have also taken out the capital letters to make it a little more difficult.

Remember that as you write this passage out with the punctuation put in, you should also paragraph it. Remember especially the punctuation and paragraphing of speech. Inverted commas around the words which are actually said and a new paragraph every time we move from one speaker to the next.

The passage fits in well with this chapter's theme of 'courage'. It is about Marti Caine, the comedienne who bravely fought cancer for a long time. Marti Caine's married name was Mrs Ives.

kenneths driving hes whistling in four years of marriage ive never heard him whistle before hes nervous four years the 6th of february my god its our wedding anniversary wed both forgotten in no time at all were fighting for a parking space outside the cromwell then striding purposefully through its wide corridored opulence to our duly appointed reception area ah mrs ives a beautiful filipino nurse with a smile come with me and ill take a little blood no need to take your blouse off just roll up your sleeve kenneth started to whistle again why dont you go now love come and see me later bring me some grapes in an air sickbag i think he was grateful to be let off the hook and backed out waving saying good luck enjoy it now one little prick and its all over and it was she skilfully inserted a thin tube into my forearm attached to a multiheaded nozzle affair called a cannula which would accomodate various syringes and drips with no need to stick anything else into me thats a relief she taped the cannula snugly to my arm and i forgot it was there as i scooped up my jacket and collected my bags ill be up later to give you your treatment im scared

END OF TIME OUT!

Printed opposite is an article entitled 'Scot who challenged the Tobacco Giants'. Alfred McTear was an ordinary man who led a very ordinary life but, when the moment came, he was ready to show immense courage as he decided to help other people, while all the time knowing that it was too late for himself.

Scot who Challenged the Tobacco Giants

When Alfred McTear learned he had lung cancer, he made a hero's vow: to spend his dying days bringing to justice the industry he held responsible

Net curtains twitched in Cherrywood Drive in the little Scottish town of Beith, near Glasgow, as the cul-de-sac began to fill up with gleaming Mercedes and BMWs. Well-groomed men in expensive over-coats picked their way up the garden path to number 20. Inside they squashed themselves on to a three-piece suite or perched on kitchen chairs, files resting on a fold-down dining-table.

They had come to take part in a rare legal event – a court hearing held in a private house. Because the key witness was too ill to travel, the judge, court clerk, lawyers and company executives had left behind the pomp of the Edinburgh court-house to hear Alfred McTear's evidence, under oath, in his own front room.

Everyone knew Alfred had only a short time to live as he walked slowly into the makeshift court that morning of March 16, 1993, and lowered him-self carefully into an armchair. Each breath was drawn in pain, rasping up from cancer-ridden lungs; his best suit hung in folds off his emaciated body; the bones of his face were visible through papery skin. Yet his eyes shone with vitality and determina-tion. 'Alfred showed fantastic guts, energy and enthusiasm,' recalls solicitor John Carruthers. 'He was even cracking jokes.'

Giving court evidence had been a looming hur-dle since Alfred, a 48-year-old retired telephone engineer, volunteered to sue the Bristol based Imperial Tobacco company on behalf of the anti-smoking lobby. His case, that Imperial Tobacco was selling a dangerous product which caused his lung cancer, would be the first of its kind to go to court in Britain.

If successful, the case would mean tobacco companies could be held liable for the effects of their product, which kills an estimated 110,000 people every year in the UK alone. Such a legal ruling would open the floodgates to claims against tobacco companies, weakening their business and perhaps saving thousands of lives.

Margaret McTear, married to Alfred for 28 years, was apprehensive about the onslaught of attention.

A shy, self-contained woman with greying hair and baby-soft skin, she didn't know how to answer jour-nalists' insistent questions. What she did know was that she would continue the battle after his death.

Because she was going to give evidence later in the case, Margaret was not allowed to hear her husband's testimony, and she waited anxiously in the kitchen. 'Freddie was so weak he could hardly speak,' she recalls.

'The reporters kept asking questions – before the hearing, in the break, at lunchtime – when he should have been resting. I could see he was get-ting exhausted.'

Sure enough, by lunchtime on Wednesday, the second day of the hearing, Margaret had to call the doctor, who declared that Alfred was not strong enough to continue his evidence that day.

On Thursday and Friday morning the expensive cars once more rolled up to 20 Cherrywood Drive. But Alfred's GP, the stern, no-nonsense Dr Sheila McCarroll, said he was again too ill to continue. He died on the following Tuesday.

Ten months earlier, Alfred had gone to see Dr McCarroll at her surgery. He had been so off-colour for about a month that he had finally given up cigarettes, after almost 30 years of smoking between 20 and 60 a day. A bronchoscope exami-nation confirmed a cancerous tumour on Alfred's lung. The optimism of the man who woke the family every morning singing Scottish folk songs in the bathroom was suddenly extinguished. 'He became quite down,' recalls Margaret. 'I couldn't mention the subject to him because I couldn't believe it was happening myself.'

A few weeks later, Alfred read a short article in the Scottish *Daily Record* reporting a partial victo-ry for the family of Rose Cipollone, who was suing several US tobacco manufacturers for causing her death. The US Supreme Court ruled that govern-ment health warnings on cigarette packets did not automatically protect the company against such legal claims. Even though the Cipollone family could not afford to continue the case, it was a breakthrough for the anti-smoking lobby.

Reading on, Alfred saw that the charity Action on Smoking and Health (ASH) in Scotland was seeking anyone who thought they might have a strong case against a tobacco manufacturer.

Next morning he rang ASH and volunteered him-self. Says Alison Hillhouse, director of ASH Scotland, 'I got a stream of calls, but Alfred was the person who stood out. He made a deep impression on me.'

Ross Harper & Murphy, a large firm of Glasgow solicitors who had offered their services for free, agreed with her. 'I felt that here was a genuine, caring man who wanted to send a warning about smoking before he died,' says solicitor John Carruthers.

While there has been talk of damages of up to £500,000, Alfred dismissed suggestions that he was in it for financial gain. 'I'm doing this because I believe smoking is evil and I'd like to put a stop to it once and for all. A lot of people think of me as fighting a losing battle, but some day the common man must win.'

As the self-appointed small man in a classic David-and-Goliath battle, he captivated the media. And he handled them with masterly assurance. At a press conference to announce the legal action, a journalist shouted, 'How does it feel to be dying of lung cancer, Alfred?' McTear paused, then said softly in his strong Glaswegian accent: 'I am a dying man. I haven't got a future. But that's why I'm doing this. So that other people might have.'

The room went silent. ASH's Alison Hillhouse was moved to tears. 'His sincerity touched everyone. It was extraordinary to see the effect he had on those case-hardened hacks.'

But it takes more than a sympathetic personality to win a complex legal case. Solicitors John Carruthers and Cameron Fife believe that Alfred's smoking history provides winning legal arguments.

First there is the timing. Alfred started smoking in 1964, long before the Government put health warnings on packets, and when smoking was openly advertised as desirable and glamorous. As Alfred said, everyone smoked, from cinema matinée idols to sports stars. 'I just went along with the crowd. I hadn't the slightest idea it was bad for your health.'

But at least some of the tobacco companies knew. As far back as the 1940s they had commissioned their own research in the US into the effects of tobacco smoke. The Cipollone evidence included a 1946 letter from a company chemist of the Lorillard Tobacco Company to the manufacturing committee. It analysed a media report about animal experiments that had revealed a cancer-causing chemical 'presumed to be a combustion product of burning tobacco'. Internal memos from the mid-1950s and early 1960s, generated by Lorillard and some other tobacco companies, also confirm their awareness of the growing evidence of a link between smoking and cancer. But none of these companies released findings of their own investigations to the public.

Though Imperial Tobacco deny that the link between smoking and lung cancer has been conclusively proved, they maintain that by the time Alfred started smoking, doctors had already publicised the dangers. However, in Britain health warnings did not appear on cigarette packets until 1971.

Once Alfred realised how dangerous his habit was, he tried repeatedly to give up, but by then he was strongly addicted to nicotine. Although he sought help from Dr McCarroll and another GP in the same practice, every attempt failed. 'Whenever he gave up for a few days', recalls Margaret, 'he was like a bear with a sore head.'

Nicotine is a powerfully addictive substance. A 1988 report by the US Surgeon General concludes that the chemical processes that determine tobacco addiction are similar to those that mark addiction to drugs such as heroin and cocaine. Says Cameron Fyfe: 'Alfred became addicted to a dangerous substance before the manufacturers were willing to tell him how potentially damaging it was.'

The second strong legal argument, say his lawyers, is Alfred's brand loyalty to John Player's cigarettes, manufactured by Imperial Tobacco. According to medical evidence 90 per cent of lung cancer cases are caused by smoking. On that basis, his lawyers claim Imperial Tobacco's product almost certainly caused the lung cancer which killed him. Says Cameron Fyfe, 'Numerous expert medical witnesses will testify that in this case smoking was the cause beyond all reasonable doubt.'

The firm is so confident of success that when its legal-aid application was turned down last year, it decided to finance the case itself.

Alfred both inspired, and was buoyed up by, this optimism. He campaigned on behalf of ASH, he wrote to people in the news who had cancer, or who had lost loved ones through the disease. And along one side of his bedroom he created a morbid yet fascinating 'wall of death', covering it with newspaper cuttings about cigarettes, lung cancer and death.

Margaret knew this calm exterior masked a devastated man who discovered by chance that he had only months left. 'None of the doctors had ever given him a time limit,' explains Margaret. 'Then in November we saw a copy of a solicitor's letter, saying that Freddie was not expected to see another summer. It was like receiving his death sentence through the post.'

In February, Alfred and Margaret went away to Malta. It was unseasonably cold but, despite the chill wind and rain and his own increasing frailty, he was determined to make the most of his final holiday. 'You see things you think you'll never see again,' he explained, 'so everything has an added urgency.'

Two weeks back from Malta, he went to see his specialist, Anna Gregor, at Edinburgh's Western General Hospital. she showed him his X-ray. One lung was completely filled with tumour, making him breathless and compressing his windpipe. 'I'm sorry, Alfred,' Anna had to tell him, 'we can help control the pain but we have nothing to shrink the tumour, stop it growing or make it go away.'

By now Alfred was often in such excruciating pain that 11 different drugs scarcely contained it. Conversation tired him within minutes, and he would slump back on his pillows, sweat trickling down his ashen forehead. Margaret nursed him patiently, and his solicitors worked desperately to organise a court hearing in the McTears' home.

Cameron Fyfe was only too aware of the delaying tactics used by tobacco companies in the US. Lawyers there have engineered to keep cases like Alfred's going through various courts for years wearing the plaintiff down financially until he drops the case.

The US tobacco companies have also employed researchers and lawyers to muckrake for something damaging, like a venereal disease or family suicide, that will intimidate the plaintiff into giving up. In 40 years of lawsuits, the US tobacco industry has never paid out a cent in damages or settlement for smoking-related claims.

However, Scottish law allows only two appeals, one to the Inner House of the Court of Session, and finally to the House of Lords. And, says Cameron Fyfe: 'Anything about Alfred's family or marriage would be ruled irrelevant.'

In any case, Alfred was a devoted family man. Back in the 1960s when their three children were small, he worked nights and looked after them during the day while Margaret was out at her job as a coupon checker for Littlewoods Pools. He changed nappies, read stories, helped with homework, baked bread, did the washing and ironing.

The hardest part of accepting his imminent death was the prospect of leaving his adored grandchildren, four-year-old Joe, Cheryl and Gemma, both two, and baby Graeme, who came to the house every day. 'It really hurts me to think I'll never see them grow up, because I love them so deeply.'

After the supreme effort of giving his evidence, Alfred spent his final days drifting in and out of consciousness. Holding his hand not long before he died, Margaret broke down for the first time. 'He saw me crying and said, "Has my time come?" I said, "No". Now I wonder if I let him down . He wanted to talk to me about death all the time, but I couldn't face it.'

Today it is left to Margaret to carry on the battle. This 49-year-old widow, still working as a coupon checker, is an unlikely champion of the anti-smoking cause. But she has blossomed under the responsibility. She now answers reporters' questions with measured confidence and is passionately articulate in her condemnation of the tobacco industry. She patiently awaits the date of the final hearing, which will take place later this year or in early 1995.

The eyes of the western world will be on its outcome. Alfred's solicitors already have 30 similar cases on their books, and London solicitors Leigh, Day another 300. Meanwhile, Cameron Fyfe is confident that Alfred gave sufficient evidence before he died, and Margaret is determined to see the legal action through to the final appeal. It is what Alfred wanted.

'People still don't realise the damage that smoking does,' she says. 'I feel that if one person stops smoking because of this publicity, then my husband's death was not in vain. This became his purpose. I hope it will become his great achievement.'

JACQUI MARSON

TASKS

9   When you have read this article, in groups discuss the content. Do you agree that it is the tobacco company's fault or do you think it is the smoker's own responsibility? Should the government take action? You undoubtedly have a number of friends who smoke (you may smoke yourself). Will any story like this deter them or you?

As a group, prepare a presentation to a teenage audience (i.e. the rest of the class!) stating your views.

10   The class is going to have a formal debate. Prepare a speech either for or against the motion:
'This house believes that the government should pass a law banning smoking in all public places.'

We have reprinted this passage in your homework book together with one further task, which we hope will give you food for thought.

Shakespeare makes us think a lot about courage in *Macbeth*. Many students doing English courses for GCSE will study this play in full. Some of the tasks after the extracts that follow will assume that you know the play well.

At the start of the play there is none more brave than Macbeth.

Macbeth

Act 1 Scene 2

MALCOLM:
  Say to the King the knowledge of the broil,
  As thou didst leave it.

CAPTAIN:
  Doubtful it stood,
  As two spent swimmers, that do cling together
  And choke their art. The merciless Macdonwald
  (Worthy to be a rebel, for to that
  The multiplying villainies of nature
  Do swarm upon him) from the western isles
  Of Kernes and Gallowglasses is supplied;
  And Fortune, on his damnèd quarrel smiling,
  Showed like a rebel's whore: but all's too weak;
  For brave Macbeth (well he deserves that name),
  Disdaining Fortune, with his brandished steel,
  Which smoked with bloody execution,
  Like Valour's minion, carved out his passage,
  Till he faced the slave;
  Which ne'er shook hands, nor bade farewell
    to him,
  Till he unseamed him from the nave to the chaps,
  And fixed his head upon our battlements.

DUNCAN:
  O valiant cousin! worthy gentleman!

CAPTAIN:
  As whence the sun 'gins his reflection,
  Shipwracking storms and direful thunders break,
  So from that spring, whence comfort seemed
    to come,
  Discomfort swells. Mark, King of Scotland, mark:
  No sooner justice had, with valour armed,
  Compelled these skipping Kernes to trust
    their heels,
  But the Norweyan lord, surveying vantage,
  With furbished arms, and new supplies of men,
  Began a fresh assault.

DUNCAN:
  Dismayed not this
  Our captains, Macbeth and Banquo?

CAPTAIN:
  Yes;
  As sparrow eagles, or the hare the lion.
  If I say sooth, I must report they were
  As cannons overcharged with double cracks;
  So they
  Doubly redoubled strokes upon the foe:
  Except they meant to bathe in reeking wounds,
  Or memorise another Golgotha,
  I cannot tell –
  But I am faint; my gashes cry for help.
                              WILLIAM SHAKESPEARE

Macbeth's wife knows that his bravery could be turned to his (and her) own advantage if he murdered King Duncan and seized the crown. Macbeth, however, is not so sure.

Macbeth
Act 1 Scene 7

MACBETH:
  We will proceed no further in this business:
  He hath honoured me of late; and I have bought
  Golden opinions from all sorts of people,
  Which would be worn now in their newest gloss,
  Not cast aside so soon.

LADY MACBETH:
  Was the hope drunk,
  Wherein you dressed yourself? hath it slept since,
  And wakes it now, to look so green and pale
  At what it did so freely? From this time
  Such I account thy love. Art thou afeared
  To be the same in thine own act and valour,
  As thou art in desire? Wouldst thou have that
  Which thou esteem'st the ornament of life,

And live a coward in thine own esteem,
Letting 'I dare not' wait upon
   'I would,'
Like the poor cat i' the adage?

MACBETH:
   Pr'ythee, peace.
   I dare do all that may become a man;
   Who dares do more is none.

LADY MACBETH:
   What beast was't then
   That made you break this enterprise to me?
   When you durst do it, then you were a man;
   And, to be more than what you were, you would
   Be so much more the man. Nor time nor place
   Did then adhere, and yet you would make both:
   They have made themselves, and that their
      fitness now
   Does unmake you. I have given suck, and know
   How tender 't is to love the babe that milks me:
   I would, while it was smiling in my face,
   Have plucked my nipple from his boneless gums,
   And dashed the brains out, had I so sworn as you
   Have done to this.

MACBETH:
   If we should fail, –

LADY MACBETH:
   We fail?
   But screw your courage to the sticking-place
   And we'll not fail. When Duncan is asleep
   (Whereto the rather shall his day's hard journey
   Soundly invite him), his two chamberlains
   Will I with wine and wassail so convince,
   That memory, the warder of the brain,
   Shall be a fume, and the receipt of reason
   A limbeck only: when in swinish sleep
   Their drenchèd natures lie, as in a death,
   What cannot you and I perform upon
   Th' unguarded Duncan? What not put upon
   His spongy officers, who shall bear the guilt
   Of our great quell?

MACBETH:
   Bring forth men-children only!
   For thy undaunted mettle should compose
   Nothing but males. Will it not be received,
   When we have marked with blood those
      sleepy two
   Of his own chamber, and used their
      very daggers,
   That they have done't?

LADY MACBETH:
   Who dares receive it other,
   As we shall make our griefs and clamour roar
   Upon his death?

MACBETH:
   I am settled, and bend up
   Each corporal agent to this terrible feat.
   Away, and mock the time with fairest show:
   False face must hide what the false heart
      doth know.

Exeunt
WILLIAM SHAKESPEARE

Macbeth does murder his king. It brings him the throne but
not peace of mind. Other murders follow; Lady Macbeth dies
(she may have committed suicide); Macbeth is a changed man.

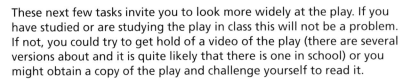

Macbeth
Act 5 Scene 5

MACBETH:
  She should have died hereafter:
  There would have been a time for such a word. –
  Tomorrow, and tomorrow, and tomorrow,
  Creeps in this petty pace from day to day,
  To the last syllable of recorded time;

And all our yesterdays have lighted fools
The way to dusty death. Out, out, brief candle!
Life's but a walking shadow, a poor player
That struts and frets his hour upon the stage,
And then is heard no more: it is a tale
Told by an idiot, full of sound and fury,
Signifying nothing.

WILLIAM SHAKESPEARE

TASKS

11 Judging from the first extract, describe in your own words the sort of courage which Macbeth shows.
12 In the second extract Lady Macbeth uses the fact that her husband is 'brave' to persuade him to kill the king. She succeeds! Explain how her words (and actions) influence Macbeth.
13 By the end of the play (third extract) Macbeth is alone, but he hasn't quite given up. What are his feelings now? To help you write your answer, look at the mood, tone and feelings in his speech.

These next few tasks invite you to look more widely at the play. If you have studied or are studying the play in class this will not be a problem. If not, you could try to get hold of a video of the play (there are several versions about and it is quite likely that there is one in school) or you might obtain a copy of the play and challenge yourself to read it.

14 Compare the bravery Macbeth shows at the start of the play with his actions in killing Duncan.
15 Is Macduff a brave man or not?
16 Lady Macbeth claims to be brave; she wants to be like a man. What evidence is there that she is brave? What effects do her actions have on her life?

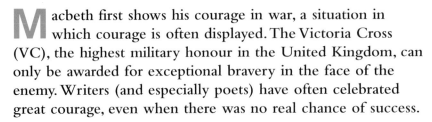

Macbeth first shows his courage in war, a situation in which courage is often displayed. The Victoria Cross (VC), the highest military honour in the United Kingdom, can only be awarded for exceptional bravery in the face of the enemy. Writers (and especially poets) have often celebrated great courage, even when there was no real chance of success.

Alfred Lord Tennyson wrote about a famous incident during the Crimean War.

The Charge of the Light Brigade

I

Half a league, half a league,
Half a league onward,
All in the valley of Death
Rode the six hundred.
'Forward, the Light Brigade!
Charge for the guns!' he said:
Into the valley of Death
Rode the six hundred.

II

'Forward, the Light Brigade!'
Was there a man dismay'd?
Not tho' the soldier knew
Some one had blunder'd:
Theirs not to make reply,
Theirs not to reason why,
Theirs but to do and die:
Into the valley of Death
Rode the six hundred.

III

Cannon to right of them,
Cannon to left of them,
Cannon in front of them
Volley'd and thunder'd;
Storm'd at with shot and shell,
Boldly they rode and well,
Into the jaws of Death,
Into the mouth of Hell
Rode the six hundred.

IV

Flash'd all their sabres bare,
Flash'd as they turn'd in air
Sabring the gunners there,
Charging an army, while
All the world wonder'd:
Plunged in the battery-smoke
Right thro' the line they broke;
Cossack and Russian
Reel'd from the sabre-stroke
Shatter'd and sunder'd.
Then they rode back, but not
Not the six hundred.

V

Cannon to right of them,
Cannon to left of them,
Cannon behind them
Volley'd and thunder'd';
Storm'd at with shot and shell,
While horse and hero fell,
They that had fought so well
Came thro' the jaws of Death,
Back from the mouth of Hell,
All that was left of them,
Left of six hundred.

VI

When can their glory fade?
O the wild charge they made!
All the world wonder'd.
Honour the charge they made!
Honour the Light Brigade,
Noble six hundred!

ALFRED LORD TENNYSON

Later, in 1915, Rupert Brooke published a poem called *The Soldier*. It sums up his view of the possibility of dying in battle. He died, a member of the Royal Navy Volunteer Reserve, later that same year.

The Soldier

If I should die, think only this of me:
That there's some corner of a foreign field
That is for ever England. There shall be
In that rich earth a richer dust concealed;
A dust whom England bore, shaped, made aware,
Gave, once, her flowers to love, her ways to roam.
A body of England's, breathing English air,
Washed by the rivers, blest by suns of home.

And think, this heart, all evil shed away,
A pulse in the eternal mind, no less
Gives somewhere back the thoughts by England
  given;
Her sights and sounds; dreams happy as her day;
And laughter, learnt of friends; and gentleness,
In hearts at peace, under an English heaven.

RUPERT BROOKE

Laurence Binyon looks back in his poem, *For the Fallen*, on the contribution made by those who die for their country. The fourth verse is used every year in November on Remembrance Day.

For the Fallen

With proud thanksgiving, a mother for her children
England mourns for the dead across the sea.
Flesh of her flesh they were, spirit of her spirit,
Fallen in the cause of the free.

Solemn the drums thrill: Death august and royal
Sings sorrow up into immortal spheres.
There is music in the midst of desolation
And a glory that shines upon our tears.

They went with songs to the battle, they were young,
Straight of limb, true of eye, steady and aglow.
They were staunch to the end against odds uncounted,
They fell with their faces to the foe.

They shall grow not old, as we that are left grow old:
Age shall not weary them, nor the years condemn.
At the going down of the sun and in the morning
We will remember them.

They mingle not with their laughing comrades again;
They sit no more at familiar tables at home;
They have no lot in our labour of the day-time;
They sleep beyond England's foam.

But where our desires are and our hopes profound,
Felt as a well-spring that is hidden from sight,
To the innermost heart of their own land they are known
As the stars are known to the Night.

As the stars that shall be bright when we are dust,
Moving in marches upon the heavenly plain,
As the stars that are starry in the time of our darkness,
To the end, to the end, they remain.

LAURENCE BINYON

TASKS

17   Explain in your own words as fully as you can:

   a   What does Tennyson admire about the men in *The Charge of the Light Brigade*?

   b   Rupert Brooke is looking to the future. What 'ambition' does he have for himself?

   c   When Lawrence Binyon writes about those who have died, what is his opinion? Do you think he conveys this view appropriately in his poem?

   d   You have studied three poems celebrating courage in war. Some of you may well choose a career in the armed forces. In some countries in the world a compulsory period of service in the armed forces is part of the lives of all young people. Imagine this was the case for you. Discuss in groups what your feelings would be when your call-up papers arrive.

Rupert Brooke would probably have approved of an old latin slogan 'Dulce et Decorum Est, Pro Patria Mori.' (It is good and fitting to die for your country.) The saying is used by Wilfred Owen as the title of a poem of his own.

Dulce et Decorum Est

Bent double, like old beggars under sacks,
Knock-kneed, coughing like hags, we cursed through sludge,
Till on the haunting flares we turned our backs,
And towards our distant rest began to trudge.
Men marched asleep. Many had lost their boots,
But limped on, blood-shod. All went lame, all blind;
Drunk with fatigue; deaf even to the hoots
Of gas-shells dropping softly behind.

Gas! GAS! Quick, boys! – An ecstasy of fumbling,
Fitting the clumsy helmets just in time,
But someone still was yelling out and stumbling
And floundering like a man in fire or lime. –
Dim through the misty panes and thick green light,
as under a green sea, I saw him drowning.

In all my dreams before my helpless sight
He plunges at me, guttering, choking, drowning.

If in some smothering dreams, you too could pace
Behind the wagon that we flung him in,
And watch the white eyes writhing in his face,
His hanging face, like a devil's sick of sin;
If you could hear at every jolt, the blood
Come gargling from the froth-corrupted lungs,
Bitter as the cud
Of vile, incurable sores on innocent tongues, –
My friend, you would not tell with such high zest
To children ardent for some desperate glory,
The old Lie: Dulce et decorum est
Pro patria mori.

WILFRED OWEN

Wilfred Owen was a soldier in the First World War; he saw at first hand what was happening and it made him wonder about the cause he was fighting for. In *Disabled* he shows us what happens to men who go to war.

Disabled

He sat in a wheeled chair, waiting for dark,
And shivered in his ghastly suit of grey,
Legless, sewn short at elbow. Through the park
Voices of boys rang saddening like a hymn,
Voices of play and pleasure after day,
Till gathering sleep had mothered them from him.

About this time Town used to swing so gay
When glow-lamps budded in the light blue trees,
And girls glanced lovelier as the air grew dim, –
In the old times, before he threw away his knees.
Now he will never feel again how slim
Girls' waists are, or how warm their subtle hands;
All of them touch him like some queer disease.

There was an artist silly for his face,
For it was younger than his youth, last year.
Now, he is old; his back will never brace;
He's lost his colour very far from here,
Poured it down shell-holes till the veins ran dry,
And half his lifetime lapsed in the hot race,
And leap of purple spurted from his thigh.

One time he liked a blood-smear down his leg,
After the matches, carried shoulder-high.
It was after football, when he'd drunk a peg,
He thought he'd better join. – He wonders why.
Someone had said he'd look a god in kilts,

That's why; and may be, too, to please his Meg:
Aye, that was it, to please the giddy jilts
He asked to join. He didn't have to beg;
Smiling they wrote his lie; aged nineteen years.
Germans he scarcely thought of; all their guilt,
And Austria's, did not move him. And no fears
Of Fear came yet. He thought of jewelled hilts
For daggers in plaid socks; of smart salutes;
And care of arms; and leave; and pay arrears;
Esprit de corps; and hints for young recruits.
And soon, he was drafted out with drums
 and cheers.

Some cheered him home, but not as crowds
 cheer Goal.
Only a solemn man who brought him fruits
Thanked him; and then inquired about his soul.

Now, he will spend a few sick years in Institutes,
And do what things the rules consider wise,
And take whatever pity they may dole.
To-night he noticed how the women's eyes
Passed from him to the strong men that
 were whole.
How cold and late it is! Why don't they come
And put him into bed? Why don't they come?

WILFRED OWEN

At the time Owen was writing it was thought 'cowardly' not to go to war and it was thought 'cowardly' to show fear in battle. You will have your own view on whether being 'courageous' means you are not afraid. The following poem is about 'fear' and 'cowardice'.

The Hero

'Jack fell as he'd have wished,' the Mother said,
And folded up the letter that she'd read.
'The Colonel writes so nicely.' Something broke
In the tired voice that quavered to a choke.
She half looked up. 'We mothers are so proud
Of our dead soldiers.' Then her face was bowed.
Quietly the Brother Officer went out.
He'd told the poor old dear some gallant lies
That she would nourish all her days, no doubt.
For while he coughed and mumbled, her weak eyes
Had shone with gentle triumph, brimmed with joy,
Because he'd been so brave, her glorious boy.

He thought how 'Jack', cold-footed, useless swine,
Had panicked down the trench that night the mine
Went up at Wicked Corner; how he'd tried
To get sent home, and how, at last, he died,
Blown to small bits. And no one seemed to care
Except that lonely woman with white hair.

SIEGFRIED SASSOON

TASKS

18 Describe Owen's experiences in war. What has he seen and been involved with?

19 Owen creates vivid word pictures in his poems. Describe in your own words what he has conveyed to you.

20 Contrasts – of ideas or scenes – are also important in poetry. What contrasting ideas or images are to be found in Owen's poems, or between the poems of Owen and Brooke?

21 In your own words explain *The Hero* by Siegfried Sassoon.

'The Hero' has been printed again in your homework book as a stimulus for some personal writing.

Courage in the face of adversity has always been a theme frequently explored by great painters. Look at the five pictures in this chapter (p18, p19 and p22) which explore this theme in different ways and use one, or even all of them as the basis for some personal writing. Or you could use the World War 1 photograph on p21.

The martyrdom of St Sebastian, by Andrea Mantegna

Sebastian was a Roman soldier who was sentenced to death by the emperor because of his belief in Christianity.

Christ driving the traders from the temple, by El Greco

This is a representation from the story in the New Testament when Jesus showed his anger and courage in driving the traders out of the temple, saying that they had turned a holy place into a den of thieves.

The third of May 1808, by Francisco Goya

On May 3 1808 the people of Madrid rose up against the forces of the French Emperor Napoleon. They never stood a chance and this painting shows a number of them being shot by the French soldiers.

TASKS

22 In groups discuss the effectiveness of each of the six pictures in conveying the idea of courage.

23 Choose one of the pictures and use it as the basis for a piece of personal writing. You may choose to write either a story or a poem.

24 For a second piece of writing you may either choose one of the other pictures, or you may choose to do some research either in the library or in the Art Department of your school and find a painting of your own to use as a basis.

Advice on creative writing

You are often asked to write imaginatively. This gives you a chance to explore your own ideas and thoughts, and to express them in any way you like.

You should consider the titles (or pictures) available to you and choose the one that immediately sparks a thought or an idea. Let that idea head off in any direction you like. Initially you might have a muddle of ideas, however, you must plan and draft carefully to produce a logically constructed story which a reader can follow.

TIME OUT TASK!

Think about adjectives

The quality and breadth of vocabulary which you use in your writing is a good indicator of the general quality of your writing.

In this chapter you have already read several pieces of stimulus material and have written several pieces of your own.

Take one piece of writing, either a piece of stimulus or a piece of your own writing and underline or write down all the adjectives (words which describe nouns) which you can identify.

Then experiment with replacing each one with a different adjective. Don't be satisfied with your first attempt.

Remember that adjectives should make nouns more vivid, more precise, more exciting. Simply ask yourself, 'Is this new adjective making the sentence better?'

END OF TIME OUT!

The aftermath at Ypres, 1917

This photograph captures the horror faced by soldiers in the trenches during World War 1.

The raft of *The Medusa*, by Theodore Gericault

In 1816 a French military transport frigate, *The Medusa*, laden with settlers and soldiers for Senegal, had been wrecked off the coast of West Africa. One hundred and fifty passengers and crew were crammed onto a makeshift raft, but two weeks later only fifteen of them were alive to tell the tale.

Breezing up, by Winslow Homer

Three boys are out fishing under the guidance of an older man. We can sense the power of the sea as the boys control the little boat.

Helen Sharman was the first British woman to travel in space, as a crew member on a Russian flight. Printed below is the part of her story which deals with the take off.

Seize the Moment

MAY 18, 1991. My training as Britain's first astronaut was over, Now, in the warm midmorning at Baikonur Cosmodrome, deep in the south of the then Soviet Union, I was about to be launched into space with two soviet cosmonauts – but not before a traditional ceremony.

Ungainly in our stiff, padded spacesuits we walked out on to the parade-ground, where three white squares were painted to show us where to stand. It was here that Yuri Gagarin received his official send-off before his momentous launch in 1961, when he became the first man in space. Russians cherish his memory; they love their hero. So, like all Soviet cosmonauts since, we followed the ritual set for Gagarin.

Flight engineer Sergei Krikalev and I stood on either side of our commander, Anatoly ('Tolya') Artsebarski. Tolya saluted the Soviet general in charge of the ceremony and announced: 'We are ready to fly the Soyuz TM–12 mission.'

The general saluted back. 'I give you permission to fly. I wish you a successful flight and a safe return.'

A great cheer went up from the hundreds of onlookers as we turned to board the long blue and silver bus waiting to take us to the launch site. My father and mother, sister Andrea and brother Richard had flown from Sheffield to see the launch, and Mum managed to push through the crowd to the bus door. We stole a quick hug.

Then, preceded and followed by police cars, their lights flashing, the bus headed into Kazakhstan's desolate scrubland beyond the main cosmodrome complex. The atmo-sphere on board was cheerful: we had astronauts from earlier missions for company. Alexei Leonov, the first man to walk in space, stood beside my seat, grinning mischievously.

'Ilenechka,' he said using the Russian diminutive of my name, 'on the space station it's traditional for everyone to eat a dinner together. The two guys already on Mir won't have had a meal with a lady for six months. I thought you might like to dress for dinner, so I bought you something.' He produced from his jacket pocket a pink chiffon jumpsuit, with elasticised bits to go round my knees and a wonderfully frilly front and billowing sleeves. 'Just for fun!' he said. I was delighted. I undid the zips of my spacesuit and pushed the garment inside the chest piece before Tolya and Sergei could see it.

The mood on the bus now suddenly became serious. Ahead lay the launch pad. Nothing in training can prepare you for the prospect of your own rocket, the actual one that will blast you into the sky. There was ours: grey, solid and dauntingly huge. I stared at it in awe. Close to the top they had painted the Soviet flag and, for the first time in manned space travel, the Union Jack.

As Tolya, Sergei and I stood in the cage lift that took us up to the spacecraft part of the rocket, white vapour rolled down over us, condensed out of the atmosphere against the bitterly cold fuel tanks.

The crew area consisted of the orbital capsule – an elongated sphere the size of a tiny boxroom, which was our living quarters – and below it the command capsule (also used for re-entry), where the main controls were located. Both cap-sules were slightly larger than eight feet in diameter. I hauled myself into the orbital capsule head first and went feet first down into the command capsule. It was so crammed with equipment we had to ease ourselves into the seats, bumping elbows. As soon as Tolya and Sergei weren't looking I slipped the chiffon jumpsuit out of my chest piece and quickly pushed it into the space beneath my chair.

With a clang the orbital capsule hatch was closed by a technician on the launch-gantry platform outside. We glanced at each other, the same feeling sweeping across us. No more lectures, no more salutes and smiles. This was it. We were sealed away from the world, isolated, the rocket swaying perceptibly in the wind.

I thought of the tension my family on the spectators' platform little more than a mile away, would be experiencing; the wait for ignition seemed interminable. I thought of the similarities between me and the US astronaut Christa McAuliffe, who died in the Shuttle Challenger launch explosion. We were both civilian women. She, like me, had sat high inside a space vehicle, waiting for the torch to be lit beneath her. I thought, too, of the unimaginable energy pent up in this rocket's tanks. It couldn't happen twice, could it?

In our earphones, a voice from the bunker said, 'Five minutes to go.' 'Two minutes.' Then, 'One minute.' Deep below, there came a rumbling as the rocket engines ignited. Two seconds, three – the rumbling grew louder. The four arms of the launch-gantry swung away. I could feel vibration and knew we must be in that momentary limbo where the rocket seems to balance precariously on its thrust, surely destined to topple.

But as the engines continued to roar, we could feel the pressure of g-forces growing steadily. After 40 seconds the bunker confirmed a successful launch. At 115 seconds came a bump and a loud bang; the escape rocket, designed to snatch us clear and parachute us to safety if the launch had failed, was jettisoned. We were 28.5 miles from the ground. Three seconds later, there was another big jolt and a bang from below as the first-stage booster rockets separated from us.

We passed the 31–mile mark. Now we were using the second-stage engine. Golden sunlight streamed in through the window beside me.

The second stage separated after 288 seconds; then the third stage fired ferociously. At 530 seconds the third stage cut out and was jettisoned. One moment we were being pressed hard into our seats, thrilled with the sensation of tremendous acceleration, the next we were not. Quite involuntarily, all of us exclaimed, 'Uhh!'

I looked out of the window again. We were already over the Pacific! Just nine minutes ago I had been bound to the Earth's surface. Now I could see the curvature of the Earth and speckly white clouds. I was weightless. I was in space. Dreams sometimes do come true.

HELEN SHARMAN
CHRISTOPHER PRIEST

TASK

25 Answer the following questions carefully in your own words.
  a Explain both the 'traditional ceremony' which is referred to in the first paragraph and the reason for it.
  b There are quite a lot of details about the rocket itself given in this extract. Write your own detailed description of the rocket.
  c Inevitably Helen Sharman felt some apprehension as she was waiting for the take off. Explain the reasons for this apprehension.

This article has been reprinted in your homework book, with another task to do in connection with Helen Sharman's experience.

TIME OUT TASK!

Reading

Do you read a newspaper?

Do you read a teenage magazine?

Do you read technical magazines – computer magazines, fishing magazines, fashion magazines?

Do you read novels?

Do you read non-fiction books?

I wonder how many of those questions you could answer with a positive 'yes'. You will find that, throughout this book, we will be asking you to read different things and to demonstrate that you have read them with understanding.

In order to help you develop your reading it doesn't matter what you read, so long as it is written in sustained sentences and uses a reasonable range of vocabulary.

Be honest with yourself in answering these next questions.

What was the last novel that you read by yourself? What was it about? What did you think of it?

When did you last read a newspaper – not just the sports' page but the whole thing? When did you last consult a technical magazine or a non-fiction book and what was your purpose in doing so?

- Go to your school library, or your local library. Take out a book, either fiction or non-fiction and challenge yourself to read it from beginning to end.
  Then write a few paragraphs (no more than a side) about the book which would be suitable to print on the cover of the book. Remember that the purpose of such a piece of writing would be to persuade people to buy the book.

- Read two newspapers, preferably of the same date, of different types. One might be a tabloid and the other a broadsheet for instance. Which one would you recommend people to buy on a regular basis?
  Write a paragraph explaining your recommendation.

- Choose a magazine. You might find one in the library which you can read. You might choose one which you read regularly anyway. You might go to the newsagents and buy one.
  Write a letter to the editor saying what you think of the magazine.

Make a resolution to read something each week which you have chosen yourself and not had chosen for you. It can be a book, a magazine or a newspaper. That is up to you!

END OF TIME OUT!

Some stories have been part of our culture for a very long time. This is one such story. Read the following poem by Walter de la Mare, entitled *Goliath*.

Goliath

Still as a mountain with dark pines and sun
He stood between the armies, and his shout
Rolled from the empyrean above the host:
'Bid any little flea ye have come forth,
And wince at death upon my finger-nail!'
He turned his large-boned face; and all his steel
Tossed into beams the lustre of the noon;
And all the shaggy horror of his locks
Rustled like locusts in a field of corn.
The meagre pupil of his shameless eye
Moved like a cormorant over a glassy sea.
He stretched his limbs, and laughed into the air,
To feel the groaning sinews of his breast,
And the long gush of his swollen arteries pause:

And, nodding, wheeled, towering in all his height.
Then, like a wind that hushes, he gazed and saw
Down, down, far down upon the untroubled green
A shepherd-boy that swung a little sling.

Goliath shut his lids to drive that mote
Which vexed the eastern azure of his eye
Out of his vision; and stared down again.
Yet stood the youth there, ruddy in the flare
Of his vast shield, nor spake, nor quailed, gazed up,
As one might scan a mountain to be scaled.
Then, as it were, a voice unearthly still
Cried in the cavern of his bristling ear,
'His name is Death!'... And, like the flush
That dyes Sahara to its lifeless verge,
His brow's bright brass flamed into sudden crimson;
And his great spear leapt upward, lightning-like,
Shaking a dreadful thunder in the air;
Span betwixt earth and sky, bright as a berg
That hoards the sunlight in a myriad spires,
Crashed: and struck echo through an army's heart.

Then paused Goliath, and stared down again.
And fleet-foot Fear from rolling orbs perceived
Steadfast, unharmed, a stooping shepherd-boy
Frowning upon the target of his face.
And wrath tossed suddenly up once more his hand;
And a deep groan grieved all his strength in him.
He breathed; and, lost in dazzling darkness, prayed—
Besought his reins, his gloating gods, his youth:
And turned to smite what he no more could see.

Then sped the singing pebble-messenger,
The chosen of the Lord from Israel's brooks,
Fleet to its mark, and hollowed a light path
Down to the appalling Babel of his brain.
And like the smoke of dreaming Souffrière
Dust rose in cloud, spread wide, slow silted down
Softly all softly on his armour's blaze.

WALTER DE LA MARE

Walter de la Mare's poem is based on a story to be found in the Bible. Here is the story from the Authorised Version or King James's Bible, a translation into English made in 1611.

1 SAMUEL 17

32 And David said to Saul, Let no man's heart fail because of him; thy servant will go and fight with this Philistine.

33 And Saul said to David, Thou art not able to go against this Philistine to fight with him: for thou *art but* a youth, and he a man of war from his youth.

34 And David said unto Saul, Thy servant kept his father's sheep, and there came a lion, and a bear, and took a lamb out of the flock;

35 And I went out after him, and smote him, and delivered it out of his mouth: and when he arose against me, I caught *him* by his beard, and smote him, and slew him.

36 Thy servant slew both the lion and the bear: and this uncircumcised Philistine shall be as one of them, seeing he hath defied the armies of the living God.

37 David said moreover, The LORD that delivered me out of the paw of the lion, and out of the paw of the bear, he will deliver me out of the hand of this Philistine. And Saul said unto David, Go, and the LORD be with thee.

38 And Saul armed David with his armour, and he put an helmet of brass upon his head; also he armed him with a coat of mail.

39 And David girded his sword upon his armour, and he assayed to go; for he had not proved *it*. And David said unto Saul, I cannot go with these; for I have not proved *them*. And David put them off him.

40 And he took his staff in his hand, and chose him five smooth stones out of the brook, and put them in a shepherd's bag which he had, even in a scrip; and his sling *was* in his hand: and he drew near to the Philistine.

41 And the Philistine came on and drew near unto David; and the man that bare the shield *went* before him.

42 And when the Philistine looked about, and saw David, he disdained him: for he was *but* a youth, and ruddy, and of a fair countenance.

43 And the Philistine said unto David, *Am* I a dog, that thou comest to me with staves? And the Philistine cursed David by his gods.

44 And the Philistine said to David, Come to me, and I will give thy flesh unto the fowls of the air, and to the beasts of the field.

45 Then said David to the Philistine, Thou comest to me with a sword, and with a spear, and with a shield: but I come to thee in the name of the LORD of hosts, the God of the armies of Israel, whom thou hast defied.

46 This day will the LORD deliver thee into mine hand; and I will smite thee, and take thine head from thee; and I will give the carcases of the host of the Philistines this day unto the fowls of the air, and to the wild beasts of the earth; that all the earth may know that there is a God in Israel.

47 And all this assembly shall know that the LORD saveth not with the sword and spear: for the battle *is* the LORD'S, and he will give you into our hands.

48 And it came to pass, when the Philistine arose, and came and drew nigh to meet David, that David hasted, and ran toward the army to meet the Philistine.

49 And David put his hand in his bag, and took thence a stone, and slang *it*, and smote the Philistine in his forehead, that the stone sunk into his forehead; and he fell upon his face to the earth.

50 So David prevailed over the Philistine with a sling and with a stone, and smote the Philistine, and slew him; but *there was* no sword in the hand of David.

51 Therefore David ran, and stood upon the Philistine, and took his sword, and drew it out of the sheath thereof, and slew him, and cut off his head therewith. And when the Philistines saw their champion was dead, they fled.

52 And the men of Israel and of Judah arose, and shouted, and pursued the Philistines, until thou come to the valley, and to the gates of Ekron. And the wounded of the Philistines fell down by the way to Shaaraim even unto Gath, and unto Ekron.

53 And the children of Israel returned from chasing after the Philistines, and they spoiled their tents.

54 And David took the head of the Philistine, and brought it to Jerusalem; but he put his armour in his tent.

TASKS

26   Write in your own words the story of David and Goliath.
27   The Bible story tells us mainly about David. What view of him do you get?
28   De la mare writes about Goliath. In what ways does he present his character?

Concentrate on language

29   In the poem there are many words and phrases ('images' or 'word pictures') used to describe Goliath. Choose at least five of them and write about why they are effective ways of describing him.
30   The Bible story gradually builds up a picture of David. What are the stages this goes through? What impression do you have of the boy David? Pick out the words which are used to describe David, and Goliath's feelings about him and say how effective you think the words are.
31   Compare the two versions of the story. Remember to consider:
     ▨ the story and the order of events,
     ▨ the characters,
     ▨ the settings,
     ▨ the language used.

Y ou have been thinking about being 'courageous' or 'heroic'. Here is a poem called *Hero* which is about a modern situation but an old problem.

Hero

'Of course I took the drugs. Look son,
there's no fair play, no gentlemen,
no amateurs – just winning.
No one runs for fun – well, not beyond
the schoolboy stuff – eleven or twelve years old.
I'd been a pro, for years,
My job – to get that Gold.

Mind you, we English are an odd lot
like to believe we love the slob that fails,
the gentlemanly third: so any gap-toothed yob who
gets the glory
also gets some gentlemanly trait: helps cripples get
across the street, nice to small animals. You know the
kind of thing,
it helps the public feel it's
all legit; that sportsmanship is real and that
its all clean fun –
the strongest, bravest, fittest
best man WON.

Yeah, Steroids ... Who do you think? ... Oh, don't be wet –
My coach, of course, he used to get them
through this vet ... The side effects? Well, not so bad
as things go – for eighteen months or so
I didn't have much use for girls. But, by then
I was training
for the Big One – got to keep the body pure,
not waste an ounce of effort!

He gives a great guffaw –
a chain of spittle
rattles down the front of
his pyjamas jacket.
He wipes his mouth;
his eyes don't laugh at all.

' ... Do it again? Of course I would –
I'd cheat, I'd box, I'd spike, I'd pay the devil's price
to be that good again
for just one day. You see, at twenty-three
I peaked – got all I ever wanted:
All anyone would ever want from me.
After the race this interviewer told me
50 million people's hopes and dreams had been
fulfilled – A GOLD!
How many ever get that chance – I did.
Would you say No to that!
Of course not.

Damn the bell. You'd better go, they're pretty strict.
Yeah, leave the flowers there – on the top,
the nurse'll get some water and a vase.'

MIKE GOWAR

TASKS

32 Answer all the following questions, which will test that you have read with understanding.
   a What has the adult in this poem done?
   b How does he justify his actions to his son?
   c What ideas about behaviour does he reject?
   d Do you think the poet has a point of view about this? Is he trying to influence the reader? How does he do this?
   e What are your reactions to the situation?

Your own writing tasks
33 Write a story of your own using one of the following titles:
   ▪ My hero!
   ▪ I never thought he or she was capable of that!
   ▪ I was afraid but ...
   ▪ A cause worth fighting for
   ▪ A land fit for heroes

What is printed below is the last part of a story entitled 'April Fool's Day'.

When Damon was born it was quickly discovered that he was a haemophiliac, which meant that every cut or bruise he suffered, however trivial, was potentially fatal and, on numerous occasions, he was only saved by blood transfusions.

With great courage he fought his way through to young adulthood and fell in love with Celeste. However, before they had the chance of a life together, it was discovered that he had contracted AIDS through infected blood, used for one of his 'routine' blood transfusions.

April Fool's Day

How our Mighty Damon survived was a mystery; why he continued to want life was even more bewildering. The need to live is a tenacious instinct, yet how could this horror be called living? Where did his strength come from? Was it love? Celeste still believed with all her soul that Damon was going to make it.

It came as an enormous surprise when Benita told me he wanted to take a trip to Europe and see his brother Adam, now working in London. 'He's missing Adam terribly,' Benita told me.

At this point there was nothing I would deny Damon. Yet how would he be treated in a foreign land if he fell ill? It was taking a huge chance. But his doctor at the AIDS unit agreed it might be possible. 'Sometimes these things hold patients together, give them a reason for continuing. It could be a good thing for Damon,' he concluded.

Damon, Celeste and Benita left for London in October 1990. The first day there he must have covered almost two miles, walking very slowly but refusing to stop. Occasionally Adam would catch him gritting his teeth from sudden pain, but mostly he showed nothing. Instead, he asked questions all the time. Damon was the most naturally curious person I've ever known.

After a week they moved on to Paris, where Damon seemed to lose some of his energy. They continued through France to a marvellous hotel overlooking the Mediterranean, and he was able to rest for a few days. He simply loved it, with coffee and fresh croissants every morning on the balcony overlooking the sparkling sea. After one night at an Italian seaside resort, they headed for Florence.

They arrived at sunset, just after a rainstorm, and as they drove into the city, Celeste started to weep. She pointed to the sky. The sun's rays were stabbing through the clouds. 'Look, Damon, the fingers of God!'

By the time they reached Rome a week later, it was clear that Damon had had enough. They returned to London, where I went to meet them for Christmas. The weather was turning cold, and with it, Damon seemed to be fading. Most days he spent in an exhausted, troubled sleep, rising only in the late afternoon without the will or strength to go out. By mid-evening he was ready to go to bed again.

My memory of this time is warped. I would rise at 4am and begin work on my book, a novel that was overdue to my London publisher, and sometimes I'd hear Damon getting up. At first I went to him offering help, but he didn't want me.

Damon, my beautiful boy, had become like a ghost. I wrote, and he died slowly in the room next door. Each day a little more went out of him, and each day my book moved closer to its inevitable end.

We were determined to make his last Christmas with us a joyous, laughing day. We decorated the flat we had rented in London, and put lights and tinsel on the tree, with presents piled underneath. The Christmas table groaned with goodies, a golden-brown turkey and all the traditional fare.

Silver gleamed and crystal sparkled, as we toasted one another with champagne in fragile, long-stemmed glasses. The dinner was superb, and we had a perfectly splendid time. When, at 4pm, Damon was too exhausted to remain on his feet, he went back to bed, announcing that it was the nicest Christmas he could remember.

A few days later, Damon declared that he wanted to go home. By the time we arrived in Sydney, the Damon we knew was gone. There was nothing left, and it was agony seeing him every day.

In mid-March, Damon suffered a massive seizure. Sitting with him in the back of the ambulance, Celeste took his hand as he returned to consciousness. Fighting back her tears, she said, 'Hello, Damon. We're taking you to hospital. You're going to be alright.' He stared blankly at her, with no sign of comprehension or recognition.

Until then, the two of them had always been able to cling together. For six years, Celeste had been Damon's devoted nurse. She dressed his bedsores, swabbed the crusted thrush from his lips and the pus from his eyes. She washed him when he was incontinent and dressed his shingles. She had administered his morphine and the drugs that kept his heart pumping.

All this time, Damon insisted that Celeste take precautions so she wouldn't be exposed to the deadly virus. She had to wear surgical gloves when she transfused him. Where his beloved Celeste was concerned, he wasn't taking any chances.

Celeste was not prepared to let death into Damon's room and so she beat it back, threatened it with laughter and sheer, desperate bluff. But now, in the ambulance with him, for the first time the person she loved most in the world didn't know who she was. And for the first time Celeste began to embrace the possibility of Damon's death.

Damon made me promise that, if he should die, he would do so at home, in his own bed. Now, just before he was released from the AIDS ward, a male nurse asked be if I had a moment to talk. 'There are some things you are going to have to know.'

My mind went numb, and it must have been a few moments before I collected my thoughts. 'He won't be back here? This is it?' I asked, my heart starting to pound.

He spoke as gently as he could. 'Bryce, Damon is going home for the last time.'

Later I was sitting with Damon, holding his hand, unable to face him. In a quiet voice he told me it was time to call Adam in London and bring him home.

I could feel the tears running down my cheeks, and all I could do was squeeze his hand to tell him I understood. 'It's OK, Dad,' Damon said. We sat there for a long time and said nothing. There was nothing more to say. The Mighty Damon had come to terms with his sweet, sad life.

Adam arrived from London, and Celeste went to the airport to pick him up. Then they both went directly to see Damon. Both brothers cried a bit, Adam holding the tiny Damon in his arms like a child. Damon came home the following day.

By Saturday he was in such pain that the liquid morphine was not sufficient to mask it. We got on the phone and started to call his friends, his schoolmates, those people who had been close to Damon all his life. Finally, on Sunday afternoon, Toby came to say goodbye – Toby, who had introduced Damon to Celeste, who had been such a part of Damon's young life, whom Damon loved so very much. Now each said his own quiet goodbye.

On April Fool's Day, 1991, I woke very early and went for a run along the coastline. An hour before dawn, the sky began to glow. Perhaps volcanic dust in the atmosphere or some trick of temperature was bending the sun's rays to create a false dawn. I stood on the rocks and watched the sky grow lighter.

On his last day, Damon will have two sunrises and no sunset, I thought, trying to grin through my tears. That's just like him, all start and no finish.

Attempting to hold back my tears, I ran hard, until I felt my lungs would burst. Then I turned and started back in the smooth, cold dawn.

I got home and sat on the terrace and wept and wept as a beautiful Sydney autumn day arrived blazing over the harbour. Then I put on the coffee and phoned our eldest son Brett, and woke Benita.

We all had time to say goodbye. Brett, silent and big as a barn door, and Adam, soft big-hearted Adam, stood around, gentle and a bit clumsy as they tried to help the smoothly functioning Celeste, who still spoke to Damon with a clear, laughing indulgent voice.

On this day that began with unexpected colour, there was no colour left in Damon. His eyes, once a clear hazel, had changed to a mottled brown. It was a great effort for him to talk, and we took turns moving up close.

I leaned over and kissed him, and he stretched out and took my hand. 'Thanks, Dad, thanks for everything'. Then in a voice hardly above a whisper, 'I love you very much, Dad.'

Celeste was with Damon when he died – the Mighty Damon once more in Celeste's arms. This time she had to let him go.

Benita and I have a picture of Damon and Celeste taken inside the British Museum. They are standing within a great basalt gateway built by the ancient Assyrians. The photo is a telling reminder that nothing lasts as long as we want it to, neither the monuments we build to our arrogance nor the careful building of a single life. He looks so frail in that photo, yet he could still get excited. He was so courageous, using up the very last bit of life in him.

Damon was not a saint, and yet he gave us all a sense of living beyond ourselves. He heightened our awareness of life and taught us all the meaning of love. He showed us how important it is to squeeze the essence from the hours we are given. The Mighty Damon was completely alive every day of his life.

Months after it was all over, I went for a run with one of Damon's doctors, who had become a friend of the family. 'You know, Damon wasn't just an ordinary young man,' he told me. 'He had more heart, more guts, more character and more courage than any patient I've ever treated. He taught me a great deal. As far as I'm concerned, he died absolutely covered in glory.'

BRYCE COURTENAY

TASKS

34 Virtually everyone mentioned in the story shows an enormous amount of courage.
Explain the courage shown by Damon's father, his mother, Benita, and his brothers, Adam and Brett.

35 Celeste was clearly a very special person. Write briefly about her, explaining what you have learnt from her about courage.

36 At the end of the story the doctor says, 'He taught me a great deal.' What do you think Damon taught the doctor? What has the story taught you?

TRAVEL AND ADVENTURE

Nearly everyone dreams of travelling to far-off places and having amazing adventures, but the nearest the majority of us get to it is in our imagination – while we are watching a film or a television programme or reading a book.

In this chapter we are going to explore our theme by reading about people who have dared to set off into the unknown, by thinking about how we might plan to follow them, and inviting you to use your imagination and to dream a little.

ENGLISH IN THE NATIONAL CURRICULUM:

Key Skills you will cover in this chapter

- ☑ You will demonstrate your knowledge about the different ways in which you might organise your ideas and put them into words.
- ☑ You will be asked to think of the audiences you are writing for or talking to and to make sure that your presentation is right for that audience.
- ☑ You will be presented with more than one text to look at and be asked to compare these texts and make connections between them.
- ☑ You will be asked to think about the writers and the ways in which they present their ideas, the ways in which they create their characters and make them behave, and the ways in which they develop their stories; in short every aspect of the writing which makes an impact on you.
- ☑ You will be expected to make good use of the information which you are given when producing your personal writing.

A few years ago Michael Palin set off from the North Pole on a great adventure. His aim was to leave the North Pole and to travel in a straight line to the South Pole, not using an aircraft except as a last resort. He didn't manage to travel in an exactly straight line, and he found himself using some quite extraordinary means of transport, but he kept going and, miraculously, in the end, he made it.

He stopped in a huge number of places, one of which was Luxor in Egypt. We have printed below his enthusiastic report of Day 56 of his journey, his day in the city of Luxor.

Several people are mentioned in the extract, including Joseph the attendant on the train, Basil, who was one of the BBC crew who accompanied Michael Palin on the journey and Tadorus (or Peter), who was the guide to the city.

Day 56–Luxor

My sleeping-car berth is comfortable but the ride is ferocious. For the last two hours to Luxor the train seems possessed by devils, and Joseph has no need to knock so hard at my door. I'm awake and hanging on for dear life.

'It's 4.45 …,' he announces, and he lays a tray of unidentifiable cling-wrapped things beside me, '… nice breakfast sir.'

At 5.35 in the morning the train pulls into Luxor, known by the Greeks as Thebes, 420 miles south of Cairo, in Upper Egypt. I cannot conceal my excitement at being here for the first time in my life. Basil, never even in Africa before, is finding the whole journey beyond description: 'This is a great picnic …,' he raves, '…this is the Mother of Picnics.'

Luxor Station is tastefully monumental in decoration, with tall columns, gilded details on the doors, eagle heads and a hieroglyphic design somehow incorporating power stations, railways and ancient history.

Opposite this grand façade there is a bicycle leaning against a wall and lying in the dust between the bike and the wall is its owner, who hasn't had to get up as early as we have. Figures materialise from the pre-dawn gloom to offer us taxi rides. You will never stand on your own for long in Egypt.

We shall be joining a Nile cruise for the next leg of our journey, and as we drive along the river to find our boat – the *Isis* – I can see serried ranks of chunky four-storeyed vessels, maybe 100 in all, lined up along the riverbank, awaiting the day the tourists come back.

My guide to Luxor is a tall, straight, matchstick-thin aristocrat of the business whose name is Tadorus but who asks me to call him Peter … 'It's easier'. I would rather call him Tadorus, but he doesn't look the sort you argue with. He wears a white djellabah and cap and carries with him a Chaplinesque walking stick which he often rests across his shoulders. An enormous pair of Esprit sunglasses almost obscures his striking but emaciated face, and when he removes them they reveal a pair of moist, sad eyes. He is 83 years old, and as a boy of 14 was present when the archaeologist Howard Carter first pushed open the door of Tutankhamun's tomb.

Peter takes me across on the Nile ferry to a cluster of mud buildings on the West Bank opposite the city. We are driven past fields of sugar cane and alongside an irrigation canal financed by the Russians in 1960. The greenery ends abruptly as we climb a winding road up into barren, rubble-strewn desert. We pass an ostentatious modern cafeteria. 'The Temple of Coca-Cola,' Peter announces, permitting himself a shade of a smile. Then we are into the Valley of the Kings, which resembles a gigantic quarry, littered with rock debris, bleached white by the sun. We leave the bus and walk up towards the tombs in dry and scorching heat. Peter estimates the temperature at 40 Celsius, 104 Fahrenheit. I ask him if it's usually like this.

'No ... no ...,' he shakes his head dismissively, 'last month was hot!'

This vast necropolis contains the remains of 62 Pharaohs of the New Kingdom, established in Thebes 3,000 to 3,500 years ago. It was discovered – 'rediscovered', as Peter corrects me – in 1892. Only 40 of the tombs have been found, and all, bar one, had been emptied by robbers. That's why Howard Carter's discovery of Tutankhamun's burial chamber was of such significance. Because it had been built beneath another tomb (that of Rameses VI) the rubble left by the robbers had helped to hide the entrance and what Peter saw with Carter, that day in 1922, was Tutankhamun's treasure exactly as it had been sealed in the tomb 3,300 years earlier. I asked him what he could remember of the moment of discovery.

'We find all the beds and the chairs and the statues ... stacked one on top of the other up to the ceiling.'

'What was Howard Carter's reaction?'

'He became crazy ... when he have a look at the state coffin, which it is made of solid gold, that thick gold, not like our gold, 24 carat gold, he became crazy, you know ... hitting like that.' Here Peter slapped at the sides of his face with his long bony hands in a passable imitation of a Pools winner, 'Unbelievable, unbelievable.'

I asked him about the curse that was supposed to have been visited on anyone who opened the tomb.

'No curse ... no curse at all.'

'It was said that a mosquito flew from the tomb as it was opened.'

'No mosquito. They say there is a mosquito came out of the tomb and bite him and he died ... he discovered the tomb in 1922, he's still inside the tomb up to 1927 ... he died in 1939, he died a very very old man.' And not from a mosquito bite apparently.

We walk down into the tomb of Rameses III. The walls are covered in rich paintings and complex inscriptions illustrating the progress of the Pharaoh on his journey through the underworld, filled with wicked serpents, crocodiles and other creatures waiting to devour him. Because of the dry desert air, they are well preserved, an extraordinary historical document.

The sun is setting behind the Valley of the Kings when we return on the ferry. At this indescribably beautiful time of day, when the rich golden brown of the lower sky spills onto the surface of the Nile, turning it an intense amber, and the palm trees along the bank glow for a few precious minutes in the reflection, it is not difficult to imagine the power and spectacle of a funeral procession bearing the God-King's body across this same river, three and a half thousand years ago, at the beginning of his last and most important journey.

MICHAEL PALIN

TASKS

1 Michael Palin is not writing a guidebook but an account of his exciting journey from his point of view. Make a list of the personal touches in his writing which wouldn't belong in a guidebook.

2 Tadorus (or Peter) is clearly a fascinating character.
Firstly, in your own words, write a brief description of him.
Secondly, imagine that you are him at the age of 14 and, in your own words, describe the day when the archaeologist discovered Tutankhamun's tomb.

In your homework book we have printed a short extract from the next day of the journey, Day 57, and have suggested another task for you to tackle.

We are going to stay in Africa and you will find printed below an extract entitled 'Green City in the Sun' which is from a guidebook entitled *The Beauty of Kenya*. This extract is written in a descriptive style which a number of guidebooks use to try to give the reader a real feel of a place.

Green City in the Sun

At the centre of harp-shaped Kenya is the capital, Nairobi, a city of about a million people. Despite Nairobi's size and modernity, however, it is the pungent smell of earth and flowers and the extraordinary clarity of light which first strikes the visitor here on the Equator, a mile (1,670 metres) above sea level.

This 'green city in the sun' is a mosaic of woodland and pleasant parks, winding lanes and broad highways, mansions and shanties, industrial sites and well-kept lawns.

The trees of the outer suburbs clothe the city in a luxuriant green shawl, patterned by houses of many styles and vintages, with gardens ablaze with the colour of shrubs and flowers that thrive in the year-round equable, temperate climate. Trees and green spaces in the city centre soften the harsh concrete outlines of modern hotels and geometric office buildings, cinemas, night clubs, art galleries and government buildings. Among Nairobi's groves and forest patches are open golf courses, the testing chicanes of a motor race track, the green oblong of the city's Ngong horse-racing course, a polo ground and the show stands and arena of Jamhuri Park. This agricultural and industrial display park, set amidst indigenous forest, is often described as the world's most beautiful showground. Annually it presents the Nairobi International Show – shop-window for Kenya's long-established agriculture and mushrooming industry.

Dinghies and sailboats glide across the dark, reed-fringed waters of Nairobi Dam, a postwar man-made lake, flanked on one side by new middle-class housing estates and the tin-and-wood shanty town of Kibera. And on yet another side is Wilson Airport, base for hundreds of Kenya's light aircraft, mostly owned by charter firms which do a booming business to destinations within Kenya and far beyond. In terms of its take-offs and landings, it is one of Africa's busiest airfields. Beyond Wilson Airport, to the south-east of the city's urban sprawl, is a triangular wedge of wilderness – Nairobi National Park. It is made up of 110 square kilometres (42 square miles) of plains and forest with its eastern apex touching the satellite town of Athi River. Home for many forms of wildlife, the park is separated from the bustle of Nairobi's flour mills, tyre plants, vehicle assembly shops, breweries, plastics factories and pharmaceutical enterprises by a mere wire fence.

Near the city centre, rail tracks loop and curve into a great maze of marshalling yards. It was here, on 30 May, 1899, that Nairobi was born on a bare flat plain at the edge of a papyrus swamp, when the builders of the Uganda Railway – 'The Lunatic Line' – paused to establish a supply depot before embarking on the difficult climb to the edge of the Great Rift Valley's eastern wall, nearly 8,000 feet (2,438 metres) above sea level.

Nairobi soon became a sprawling, squalid, fever-ridden bazaar shanty of hovels and lean-tos, frenetic with 24-hour-a-day activity. But that temporary railhead base now is an elegant capital city covering 698 square kilometres (269 square miles). From its beginning, Nairobi always contained a polyglot, cosmopolitan community. The thousands of immigrants who flocked to Kenya in the wake of the railway's arrival brought with them their own cultures, a heritage that has helped to make today's Kenya truly multi-racial. As recently as September 1983 an African electorate overwhelmingly returned a white Kenyan as their Member of Parliament for Nairobi's Langata constituency – and a large proportion of Asian Kenyans voted for a veteran African politician in the city's Parklands constituency.

Nairobi has become known world-wide as the gateway to adventure and safaris. In English, the word safari originally meant 'a hunting expedition'. Its contemporary usage, however, goes far beyond the Oxford English Dictionary's generic definition. The word has come to suggest the romance and excitement of leaving city and towns far behind, of entering virgin bush crowded with animals of all shapes and descriptions under an azure-blue sky, flecked with cotton-wool clouds. It no longer means only killing wild animals; most visitors are now content with photographing them.

Yet a safari in most senses of the word is possible without even leaving Nairobi. Only eight kilometres (five miles) from Parliament Buildings and the Kenyatta International Conference Centre lies Nairobi National Park, the country's first wildlife reserve, which opened in 1946. (Fifty years after all of what was then 'Kenia District' had been proclaimed a game reserve.) At night the Park's lions break the stillness with their sonorous roars. Small game and monkeys frequently raid vegetable patches and poke around the shrubs and compost heaps of homes in Nairobi's outskirts. Occasionally larger animals stray from the Park; in 1984 a leopard was seen in a crowded modern Nairobi estate close to the city centre, sneaking round the walls of a maisonette. In 1956 a lion had to be shot when it strayed out of the Park and finally ended up in the garden of a private residence less than a mile from the heart of Nairobi. Inside the Park gates the transition from today to the former wild Africa is sudden: a journey back in both time and space. The Park is unchanged by man's forces, its seasons recurring in a pageant of primal and pristine Africa as it has for thousands of years. Yet clearly visible from within the park is Nairobi's familiar serried skyline.

The only major wildlife species the Park does not contain is elephant. Buffalo and rhino disappeared after the turn of the century – the plains on which the Park stands provided an ideal location for the new town's hunting buffs to indulge in blood-letting. However, the two species were re-introduced successfully in the 1960s.

At the Park's main entrance is the Nairobi Animal Orphanage, established as a rehabilitation and rescue centre for orphans from the wild. Some animals that cannot be returned to their natural homes have become permanent residents. Sebastian, its greatest character, is a chain-smoking chimpanzee whose antics over the years have entertained thousands. He has a renowned temper, especially if deprived of his beloved nicotine. On many occasions he has outwitted his captors and escaped into the nearby forests, disappearing up the tallest trees. The only way to capture him is with an anaesthetic dart but once he went to sleep before the safety net was strung up beneath him. He thumped to the ground with a bone-jarring jolt, fortunately without damage.

TASKS

3   Imagine you are on holiday in Kenya. Write a vivid description of one day of your holiday, basing it on the information in the article.
4   Imagine that you have been asked to write a guidebook about the area in which you live. Carry out the following tasks in groups:
  - research a variety of guidebooks to give you an idea of what the writers tend to say;
  - discuss the purpose of your guidebook – your answer will probably be that you are trying to interest people and persuade them to visit your area, but there may be other motives as well;
  - discuss what places in your local area you would refer to;
  - discuss what you would say about these places.

When you have finished your discussion write a section of your guidebook. Then read each other's entries and decide which is the best (that is, which one you think would bring in the crowds of visitors).

W e started off this chapter in Africa and now we are going to head deeper into the world of adventure. Printed below is an advertisement headed 'Opportunity for Adventure with Oxventure'.

Read the advertisement carefully and then do the tasks which follow.

Opportunity for Adventure with Oxventure

John Havens (who organises the operations of Oxventure) is looking for people to join him in three special projects to the forests and jungles of remote west Nepal.

John wants to open up adventure trips to all types of people, including the disabled.

He is using this trip, in conjunction with the last two trips, as an exercise to assess how much of an adventure could be adapted for the disabled. This trip will be a mixed ability trip.

The two week trip will include: Tiger tracking, white water rafting and wildlife safaris on the back of elephants. John and Dr Hilary Jones (from TV AM), will analyse the activities in Nepal to see how they can be carried out involving some disabled people. The group size will be quite small, with a maximum of 17, including John, the Doctor and two disabled people.

Oxventure's Jungle Survival Course

With a team of instructors headed by Lofty Wiseman (Author of 'The S.A.S. Survival Handbook') to be held at Tiger Tops Jungle Lodge, Royal Chitwan Park.

I could make a large list of different emergencies that we hope we will never find ourselves in, but with today's thirst for more adventurous travel, more and more of us are placing ourselves

(and others if you are the team leader) nearer these situations.

It is not just the knowledge of how to cope, it is a combination of the knowledge and some experience of what to do, that turns an emergency into a story that you can tell your friends around the dinner table.

Oxventure's Everest Trek

The Everest Trek is a three week trek up to Base Camp. No climbing experience is needed, you just need to be fit enough to walk for 18 days (with a day here and there, with no walking, for rest and altitude acclimatisation), in the most powerfully scenic mountain range in the world. This trip is also mixed ability. Departure date is mid-November for four weeks, back just in time for Christmas!

The cost of the Adventure and Everest trip is £1,535.00. The cost of the Survival Course is £1,495.00 which is the subsidised price. The actual cost per person is £2,300.00. As you can see everyone on the trip has been subsidised to the tune of £765.00 each, thanks to John's links with the airlines and the different expedition organisers in Nepal.

The prices quoted above include all hotels, transport, International return flights, tentage, sleeping bags, all food when we are out of Kathmandu, river guides, jungle guides and naturalists, boats and all safety equipment, and an elephant or two. The price does not include insurance, personal spending money, meals while in Kathmandu (we are in Kathmandu for one and a half days at the beginning, and two days at the end). Also departure tax when leaving Nepal (this was £7.89 at the time of print).

The air tickets are open for three months, sometimes for as much as a year, which means, subject to extending your visa in Kathmandu, you can travel to Nepal with us, then stay for as long as your ticket and visa allow.

Oxventure is a charitable organisation, and any surplus funds help towards an annual trip taking handicapped people to Everest Base Camp.

For details please ring John Havens on 018677 3598 or write for details enclosing your telephone number and a stamped, addressed envelope, 9" x 7" to

Oxventure, 28 Beech Road, Wheatley,
Oxford OX9 1UR.

TASKS

5 Write a letter asking for details of the adventures, as mentioned at the bottom of the advertisement.

6 Write a series of letters to local firms asking for sponsorship to allow you to join the expedition. You will need to use information from the advertisement to clarify the kind of expedition you are writing about and you may well want to write different kinds of letters to different types of firms.

7 Imagine that you are on one of the trips with a disabled friend. Write about your adventures.
(Before you begin writing, you might swap ideas with others in the class about the problems and challenges of such a holiday and how you might help make sure that your friend has a great time.)

You will find that, in your homework book, we have used again the idea of an advertisement for adventure for you to respond to.

TIME OUT TASK!

Drafting and re-drafting

When you are writing what you mustn't do is be satisfied with the first thing that comes into your head or your first effort at putting it down on paper.

The first thing that you must do is plan and the second thing is draft. What we are concentrating on here is drafting and re-drafting.

When you have finished the first draft of your writing read it through and ask yourself some questions and answer them honestly.

- Will it interest a reader?
- Have I said what I want to say?
- Is the writing well-balanced or should I give more emphasis to an important point and reduce a rather unimportant point which is coming over too strongly at the moment?
- Have I checked my spelling?

- Are my sentences grammatically correct?
- Have I paragraphed properly?

and if it's a story …

- Do my characters seem real?
- Have I described things well with good adjectives?

and so on …

At this stage, if you have been honest with yourself, you can probably write a second draft improving on the first.

Now you might ask someone to read through what you have written and to ask them if they think you can improve it.

The sort of advice you might receive includes:

- I don't really understand that point – try to make it more clear.
- Your conclusion needs 'beefing up'.
- You've made rather a lot of spelling mistakes – check them through.
- That character didn't seem real – have another look.
- Whatever you do, don't change that superb bit.

and so on …

Remember that someone reading a draft will come back to you with comments but it is not their job to correct everything for you. After all, it's your work, not theirs – and you don't have to accept their advice!

Now we suggest that you produce a piece of writing and put the above guidelines into practice. Here are a couple of titles:

The family goes out

The importance of family life

END OF TIME OUT!

For the next part of this chapter we are going to imagine that we are travelling to the north of France. We are visiting the area which, in the 15th century, was invaded by the English under the leadership of King Henry V.

First of all a little historical background. In the year 1415 King Henry V set out for France. His intention was to conquer lands which he believed belonged to the English crown. In his play about Henry V, written about 180 years later, Shakespeare celebrated Henry's great victories, first at Harfleur, then at Agincourt. The young king is a hero, courageous and worthy of admiration.

The first extract you find printed below is the words of a speech made by the Chorus in Shakespeare's play *Henry V*, who transport us, the audience of the play, on 'imagin'd wing' to France.

Henry V

Act 2
Enter Chorus

CHORUS:
   Thus with imagin'd wing our swift scene flies,
   In motion of no less celerity
   Than that of thought. Suppose that you have seen
   The well-appointed king at Hampton pier
   Embark his royalty; and his brave fleet
   With silken streamers the young Phœbus fanning:
   Play with your fancies; and in them behold
   Upon the hempen tackle ship-boys climbing,
   Hear the shrill whistle which doth order give
   To sounds confus'd; behold the threaden sails,
   Borne with the invisible and creeping wind,
   Draw the huge bottoms through the furrow'd sea,
   Beasting the lofty surge: O, do but think
   You stand upon the rivage and behold
   A city on the inconstant billows dancing;
   for so appears this fleet majestical,
   Holding due course to Harfleur. Follow, follow!
   Grapple your minds to sternage of this navy;
   And leave your England, as dead midnight still,
   Guarded with grandsires, babies, and old women,
   Either past or not arrived to pith and puissance;
   For who is he, whose chin is but enrich'd
   With one appearing hair, that will not follow
   These cull'd and choice-drawn cavaliers to France?
   Work, work your thoughts, and therein see a siege;
   Behold the ordnance on their carriages,
   With fatal mouths gaping on girded Harfleur,
   Suppose the ambassador from the French comes back;
   Tells Harry that the king doth offer him
   Katharine his daughter; and with her, to dowry,
   Some petty and unprofitable dukedoms.
   The offer likes not: and the nimble gunner
   With linstock now the devilish cannon touches,
   {*Alarum, and chambers go off, within*}
   And down goes all before them. Still be kind,
   And eke out our performance with your mind.
              Exit

The next scene opens with the king addressing his soldiers as they attack Harfleur.

Henry V
Act 3
SCENE 1. – FRANCE. *Before Harfleur.*
Alarums. Enter KING HENRY, EXETER, BEDFORD, GLOSTER, *and* soldiers, *with scaling ladders.*

K. HENRY:
>Once more unto the breach, dear friends, once more;
>Or close the wall up with our English dead!
>In peace there's nothing so becomes a man
>As modest stillness and humility:
>But when the blast of war blows in our ears,
>Then imitate the action of the tiger;
>Stiffen the sinews, summon up the blood,
>Disguise fair nature with hard-favour'd rage;
>Then lend the eye a terrible aspect;
>Let it pry through the portage of the head
>Like the brass cannon; let the brow o'erwhelm it
>As fearfully as doth a galled rock
>O'erhang and jutty his confounded base,
>Swill'd with the wild and wasteful ocean.
>Now set the teeth and stretch the nostril wide;
>Hold hard the breath, and bend up every spine
>To his full height! – On, on, you noble English,
>Whose blood is fet from fathers of war-proof!
>Fathers that, like so many Alexanders,
>Have in these parts from morn till even fought
>And sheath'd their swords or lack of argument:–
>Dishonour not your mothers; now attest
>That those whom you call'd fathers did beget you!
>Be copy now to men of grosser blood,
>And teach them how to war! – And you, good yeomen.
>Whose limbs were made in England, show us here
>The mettle of your pasture; let us swear
>That you are worth your breeding: which I doubt not;
>For there is none of you so mean and base,
>That hath not noble lustre in your eyes.
>I see you stand like greyhounds in the slips,
>Straining upon the start. The game's afoot:
>Follow your spirit; and upon this charge
>Cry – God for Harry! England! and Saint George!
>>*Exeunt. Alarum, and chambers go off, within.*

Having looked at the extracts from Shakespeare we will now look at a modern account of the siege of Harfleur by Peter Earle.

As the great armada approached the shores of Normandy, it was a relief to find that the initial problem of landing a great army on a hostile shore would be comparatively easy. There was virtually no resistance to Henry's disembarkation at the Clef de Caus on the north side of the Seine estuary, some three miles from the reputedly impregnable walled trading city of Harfleur, now little more than a suburb of the modern port of Le Havre. The beach was rough, with large stones which made movement difficult, and smaller stones fit for slinging, but by 16 August the army and all its stores had been unloaded with virtually no loss.

The next stage was likely to be more difficult. Little progress could be made without first capturing Harfleur, well-protected by its situation and its fortifications, and considered to be the key to Normandy. Set astride a small tributary of the Seine, which provided a constant supply of water, and was dammed by the defenders to flood the surrounding countryside and fill the moats, the city was completely surrounded with massive walls in which 26 towers with such delightful names as the Dragon and the Tin Pot were set, some of them 'with narrow chinks and places full of holes through which they might annoy us with their tubes, which we in English call "gunnys".' Undeterred, Henry entered into that business of siege which was to keep him busy for the rest of his life. His brother Clarence was sent round to the other side of the town to prevent the arrival of a relieving army, while he himself, having laid his great guns within range of the walls, retired to the comparative comfort of a neighbouring hill to watch progress.

Progress was slow. Mining operations were checked by successful countermining and vigorous hand-to-hand fighting underground. The damage done by the King's guns, even the great gun known as the King's Daughter, was repaired in the night by the desperate townsmen. The moat was too wide to use a ram. Efforts to climb the walls were met with showers of sulphur and lime poured into the faces of the grappling English, or by the tipping of great buckets of heated earth and oil. Communications between the King and Clarence were made difficult by the flooded lands, and worst of all the English found the salt-marshes that formed their camp to be a pestilential death trap. Soon men were dying in scores from the bloody flux.

The position of the besieged was no better. Week after week there was no sign of the relieving army which might have been expected to arrive from Paris or Rouen, where the chivalry of France were rather dilatorily assembling to repulse the invader. Stores were running low and time was clearly running out, despite all the heroic efforts of the garrison. On 16 September an English division under the Earl of Huntingdon at last managed to seize one of the main bulwarks of the fortifications. Henry's subsequent summons to surrender having been refused, he decided to storm the town. He kept his guns firing at night to deny the garrison sleep and planned to storm the walls at dawn, but in fact he had already done enough. At midnight the garrison asked to treat, and eventually it was agreed that if they had not been relieved by the following Sunday they would surrender the town, which they duly did.

The actual surrender, as Henry entered into possession of one of the great towns of his duchy, was attended with considerable pomp. Clad in gold, Henry ascended his royal throne which had been placed at the top of the hill opposite the town, and here received the keys of the city from the officers of the garrison, who were dressed in shirts of penitence with ropes about their necks. Well might they have feared their reception from the man who had just proved in the most effective way that he was their lawful Duke, but in fact Harfleur was spared the horrors of a medieval sack and, though the leading prisoners were held for ransom, they were treated with respect. Here as later, Henry was keen to appease the citizens of his duchy.

PETER EARLE

N ow we are going to travel on to visit one of the battlefields we have mentioned, the battlefield of Agincourt.

Battlefields are places which people still visit. Below is part of a leaflet which was produced by the museum at Agincourt and which is designed to give visitors a little information and, with the plan, to help visitors find their way around the battlefield site and to understand how the battle was fought. (Part of the leaflet is, unsurprisingly, in French and the English is not a direct translation of the French. For instance, the French section tells us that at Harfleur there were 200 men at arms and 6000 archers and they had marched on to Agincourt.)

Historique

Au XVe Siècle, la FRANCE subissait alors une de ses crises qui font craindre pour l'avenir d'une nation. Son Roi CHARLES VI était en état de démence. Les factions d'Orléan et de Bourgogne avaient naître une guerre civile. Ce fut alors que HENRY V Roi d'Angleterre depuis 1413, résolut de profiter de ces discordes. Mettant à profit cette guerre civile qui, après le meutre de LOUIS D'ORLEANS en 1407 oppose Armagnacs et Bourguignons, HENRY V tente d'obtenir par la voie diplomatique, sinon le titre de Roi de France, qu'il revendique toujours, du moins une part toujours plus large du royaume français et surtout la riche Normandie dont la possession lui permettrait de surveiller PARIS et de mettre ainsi en tutelle la dynastie rivale. Au début de 1415, le parti des Armagnacs, alors au pouvoir, refuse de consentir à cette concession exhorbitante, c'est la rupture. La parole est désormais aux armes.

Le mardi 13 août 1415, HENRY V d'Angleterre débarque à Chef-en-Caux (Sainte-Adresse) dans l'estuaire de la Seine. Le 18 août, avec 2000 hommes d'armes et 6000 archers, il entreprend le siège de HARFLEUR. Après un mois de rudes combats, le Sire de GAUCOURT capitule et rend la ville meutrie aux Anglais. HENRY V décide de laisser sur place une garnison ayant pour mission de veiller sur ce 'Calais Normand' et quitte HARFLEUR le 7 Octobre avec le reste de son armée en vue de regagner Calais en longeant la côte. HENRY V décide de remonter la rive gauche de la Somme afin de trouver un gué ou un pont mal défendu. Cette recherche d'un point de passage pour franchir la Somme puis la Canche et la Ternoise va conduire l'armée anglaise sur le plateau où est situé le village d'AZINCOURT? L'armée français sous les ordres du Connétable d'ABRET, n'a jamais perdu le contract et barre la qu'il ne peut plus éviter l'affrontement. Il ne lui reste plus qu'à combattre et à défendre chèrement l'honneur anglais à un contre trois.

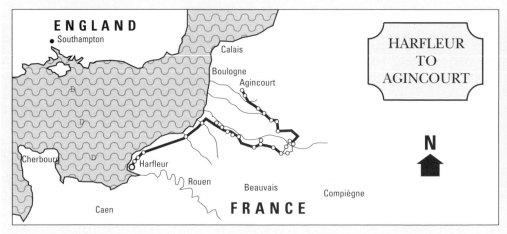

Two Kings Face To Face: Henry V And Charles VI

France was suffering one of those crises which gave cause for concern for the future of the country. Its king – CHARLES VI – was insane. The factions of ORLEANS and BURGUNDY provoked a civil war. Then HENRY V, King of England since 1413, a devious politician and clever general, decided to take advantage of all these problems. HENRY V, turning this civil war to good account (after LOUIS OF ORLEANS was murdered, the Armagnacs were against the Burgundys) tried to obtain if not the title 'King of France' at least a large part of the kingdom.

In particular he wanted the rich area of Normandy, the ownership of which would enable him to oversee PARIS and to keep the rival dynasty in his power. At the beginning of 1415, the faction of Armagnacs, at that time in power, refused this big concession. This was a disaster and arms were taken up.

Without delay, HENRY V decided to wage war on the continent. A classic campaign, with limited targets, would enable him to dishearten his opponents. In ROUEN, CHARLES VI was eager to show his ability and would have led his army into a serious conflict with disastrous consequences but for the DUKE OF BERRY. He was respected by the army as its leader and requested the king not to command his troops personally. As has been previously said: 'It is better to lose a battle rather than the war'. The conduct of the operation was given to the Chief Constable of France ALBRET.

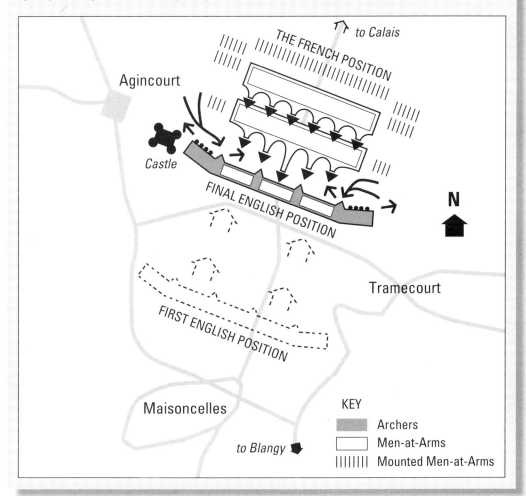

KEY

▨	Archers
☐	Men-at-Arms
|||||||	Mounted Men-at-Arms

TASKS

8 Exchange ideas in small groups about what it must have been like to be a soldier in Henry's army.

9 It is said in the play that going to France with Henry is an opportunity not to be missed. Work out with your group the pros and cons of going or staying at home.

10 Imagine you are a soldier at Harfleur. You hear Henry's speech. Write about your feelings and reactions.

11 Do you agree that both the Chorus and Henry himself make this expedition sound exciting? Explore how this is achieved.

12 Now work by yourselves. You are a guide to a coachload of English tourists who are visiting the area, including the battlefield at Agincourt. Use the material at your disposal, the extracts, the plans, the Shakespeare speeches, to make notes. You could even carry out additional research in the library. Refer to these notes to give a commentary as you visit the battle site. Remember that you want to make the visit as exciting for the tourists as possible. You also want the tourists to go away with a clear impression of King Henry V and his army.
Use the members of your class as the tourists and give your commentary.

We are going to stay in France but the next extracts bring us up to date.

H E Bates also wrote about travelling to France to wage war. He wrote about the Second World War (1939–45) and about a British airman, John Franklin, whose plane crashed in enemy-occupied territory. John Franklin is fortunate to be helped by the family of a French farmer. However, it is not easy for them.

Fair Stood the Wind for France

The doctor went on speaking. Franklin realised that what he was saying was of immense importance, but he did not care. For some moments his mind did not respond in French, then it cleared and he grasped that the doctor was talking about a hospital.

'Hospital?' he said.

'I have to tell you that at this time the record of French hospitals is not good.'

'Hospital?'

'For such an arm as yours there is no course but hospital.'

Franklin did not speak. Why can't you stand still? he thought. Please stand still. Now what? What hospital?

'You yourself have to make the choice of course.'

Franklin struggled into a moment of coherent response.

'Between what?'

'Between going to the hospital as a prisoner and remaining here.'

There's only one answer to that, he thought. Why trouble to put it like that?

'For hiding an escaping airman the complications would be very serious?' he said.

'As you know.'

'No complications.' he said. 'Please. I want to stay here.'

It seemed a long time before the doctor spoke again.

'There is the other side of the picture,' he said at last.

'Yes?'

He saw the face of the doctor blown slowly forward into focus, out again, and then once more in towards him, this time to remain, grey and fixed and living.

'You must be fully aware of what it means to remain here.'

I am aware, he thought. No one is more aware. I know what it means for you.

'I find it difficult to tell you,' the doctor said.

'I am fully aware,' he said. 'There is no need.'

'It is not quite that,' the doctor said.

He retreated again, blown out of focus, and then came back, to be fairly steadfast once more.

'No,' he said. 'This is what you must understand.' The voice was kindly, distant, almost a whisper. 'If you remain here it will be necessary to take off the arm.'

The words hit him and then were swept far away, part of all the bad dreams of his sickness, as if blown on a wind of terror. This terror was a single violent emotion that came burning out of all his flying life. It was the biggest horror he had ever known. Jesus, he thought; please! Jesus! The terror seemed to career furiously round the whole world, like a terrific living comet of protest, and then complete its crazy circumnavigation in his face. It broke its motion against his eyes and became instantly a single and more terrible thought. 'I'll never fly again, I'll never fly again. Jesus, I'll never fly again, I'll never fly again! I'll never fly again!'

'You would like a few moments alone?' the doctor said.

'No.'

What can I do? he thought. If this is it, this is it. There's nothing for it now.

'The complications for you remain,' he said to the doctor.

'We will take care of that. A few more complications in France will hardly be noticed.'

'Be frank with me,' he said.

Franklin held the grey kindly face in focus, as he might have held the sight of a gun.

'I will be frank,' the doctor said. 'If you go to hospital they will take off the arm. There is no choice. If the operation is done now I have complete confidence. I will bring my brother from the hospital itself. He is a surgeon. Very competent. He needs some fishing, too.'

'When will you do it?'

'I hope to-night. There is no need to worry.'

Franklin, not answering at once, suddenly remembered Sandy and O'Connor.

'What time to-night?'

'It will probably be late. I have to get word to my brother. He has to get here. Don't worry.'

'I am not worrying for myself,' Franklin said.

'Don't worry for us, either.'

'It is the other two,' Franklin said. 'They are going to-night. I don't want them to know.'

'It will be all right,' the doctor said.

Franklin saw him recede for the final time out of focus. He felt very tired. He tried to say something to the doctor, but the words never came and, in any case, he thought, he isn't there to listen. There was nothing there at all now except the lightly blowing curtains moving in the wind coming up from the sunny evening plain, far away on the edge of the world. He wanted the girl very badly to be near him because he knew now, for a small moment of relief in a long obscure dream, that she had not really been there all the afternoon.

Her absence flung him down into a final moment of despair. 'I'll never fly again,' was all he could think now. 'Jesus! I'll never fly any more.'

H E Bates

TASK

13 Look at three of the extracts which we have just used:
   – the speeches from *Henry V*;
   – the piece by Peter Earle;
   – the extract from *Fair Stood the Wind for France*.

An important skill in writing about literature is to be able to make comparisons between two or more pieces.

Identify as many similarities or differences as you can in these three different pieces. Think about:

▦ the purpose of the writing;

▦ the feelings it arouses;

▦ the ways in which characters are presented;

▦ the mood of the scene;

▦ the writer's choice of words.

Record your thoughts in a piece of extended writing.

Finally in France we head south to enjoy some French cooking. *A Year in Provence* is the story of a year in France. Peter Mayle and his wife moved into an old farmhouse in Provence and had a year full of adventure. In this extract he talks about them being in France out of the tourist season and a meal they had in winter.

A Year in Provence

The well-known food of Provence is summer food – the melons and peaches and asparagus, the courgettes and aubergines, the peppers and tomatoes, the *aioli* and bouillabaisse and monumental salads of olives and anchovies and tuna and hard-boiled eggs and sliced, earthy potatoes on beds of multicoloured lettuce glistening with oil, the fresh goats' cheeses – these had been the memories that came back to torment us every time we looked at the limp and shrivelled selection on offer in English shops. It had never occurred to us that there was a winter menu, totally different but equally delicious.

The cold weather cuisine of Provence is peasant food. It is made to stick to your ribs, keep you warm, give you strength and send you off to bed with a full belly. It is not pretty, in the way that the tiny and artistically garnished portions served in fashionable restaurants are pretty, but on a freezing night with the Mistral coming at you like a razor there is nothing to beat it. And on the night one of our neighbours invited us to dinner it was cold enough to turn the short walk to their house into a short run.

We came through the door and my glasses steamed up in the heat from the fireplace that occupied most of the far wall of the room. As the mist cleared, I saw that the big table, covered in checked oilcloth, was laid for ten; friends and relations were coming to examine us. A television set chattered in the corner, the radio chattered back from the kitchen, and assorted dogs and cats were shooed out of the door as one guest arrived, only to sidle back in with the next. A tray of drinks was brought out, with pastis for the men and chilled, sweet muscat wine for the women, and we were caught in a crossfire of noisy complaints about the weather. Was it as bad as this in England? Only in the summer, I said. For a moment they took me seriously before someone saved me from embarrassment by laughing. With a great deal of jockeying for position – whether to sit next to us or as far away as possible, I wasn't sure – we settled ourselves at the table.

It was a meal that we shall never forget; more accurately, it was several meals that we shall never forget, because it went beyond the gastronomic frontiers of anything we had ever experienced, both in quantity and length.

It started with home-made pizza – not one, but three: anchovy, mushroom and cheese, and it was obligatory to have a slice of each. Plates were then wiped with pieces torn form the two-foot loaves in the middle of the table, and the next course came out. There were pâtés of rabbit, boar and thrush. There was a chunky, pork-based terrine laced with *marc*. There were *saucissons* spotted with peppercorns. There were tiny sweet onions marinated in a fresh tomato sauce. Plates were wiped once more and duck was brought in. The slivers of *magret* that appear, arranged in fan formation and lapped by an elegant smear of sauce on the refined tables of nouvelle cuisine – these were nowhere to be seen. We had entire breasts, entire legs, covered in a dark, savoury gravy and surrounded by wild mushrooms.

We sat back, thankful that we had been able to finish, and watched with something close to panic as plates were wiped yet again and a huge, steaming casserole was placed on the table. This was the speciality of Madame our hostess – a rabbit *civet* of the richest, deepest brown – and our feeble requests for small portions were smilingly ignored. We ate it. We ate the green salad with knuckles of bread fried in garlic and olive oil, we ate the plump round *crottins* of goat's cheese, we ate the almond and cream gâteau that the daughter of the house had prepared. That night, we ate for England.

With the coffee, a number of deformed bottles were produced which contained a selection of locally-made *digestifs*. My heart would have sunk had there been any space left for it to sink to, but there was no denying my host's insistence. I must try one particular concoction, made from an eleventh-century recipe by an alcoholic order of monks in the Basses-Alpes. I was asked to close my eyes while it was poured, and when I opened them a tumbler of viscous yellow fluid had been put in front of me. I looked in despair round the table. Everyone was watching me; there was no chance of giving whatever it was to the dog or letting it dribble discreetly into one of my shoes. Clutching the table for support with one hand, I took the tumbler with the other, closed my eyes, prayed to the patron saint of indigestion, and threw it back.

Nothing came out. I had been expecting at best a scalded tongue, at worst permanently cauterised taste buds, but I took in nothing but air. It was a trick glass, and for the first time in my adult life I was deeply relieved not to have a drink. As the laughter of the other guests died away, genuine drinks were threatened, but we were saved by the cat. From her headquarters on top of a large *armoire*, she took a flying leap in pursuit of a moth and crash-landed among the coffee cups and bottles on the table. It seemed like an appropriate moment to leave. We walked home pushing our stomachs before us, oblivious to the cold, incapable of speech, and slept like the dead.

PETER MAYLE

TASKS

14 If you enjoyed this description it may have been because it reminded you of a special meal you have had. Write about such a meal in a lively and enjoyable way.

15 Peter Mayle describes this meal using words which you would find in recipe books. Make a list of the terms and find out what they mean. Now re-write his description of the meal replacing the special vocabulary with ordinary everyday words.
Compare the two versions. Which do you prefer and why?

TIME OUT TASK!

Think about verbs

You may well have learnt at some stage, 'verbs are doing words'. Well, they are – they express actions. But they also say what the state of things are – for instance something is ...

In this Time Out we are going to concentrate on verbs which express actions. Nearly every time you write a sentence you will use one of these verbs and you can get in a rut with the choice of verb. The most obvious example is when you are writing a story and people are speaking to each other. You carry on and on using the word 'said', when there are dozens of other words which you might use.

- Write the word 'said' at the top of a page.
- Now write down as many alternative words as you can think of in just a few minutes.
- Compare your list with those of your friends, and extend your list.
- Now resolve that, in your next few stories, you will not use the word 'said' at all, but will always use an effective alternative.

You could try the same exercise with a number of over-used verbs:
– went
– walked
– got
and so on ...

Remember the National Curriculum Key Skill which encourages you to extend your vocabulary and to use the most effective vocabulary you can.

END OF TIME OUT!

Travel and adventure sometimes take people very far away, to experience things which are fascinatingly different from their everyday lives. Printed below is an account written by Paul Raffaele of a time when he was in Australia and had the privilege of meeting an Aborigine painter.

He Paints the Heroes of Dreamtime

I had been admiring the works of French Post-Impressionists Gaugin and Bonnard at the Art Gallery of New South Wales in Sydney, when I wandered away from the main exhibit – and into another world.

I found myself in front of a slab of bark, tall as a man. On it was painted a serpent, with the head of a crocodile, its eyes glaring malevolently like the embers of a dying fire.

Australian Aborigines began to make these extraordinary paintings thousands of years ago. The art is still created today in the remotest reaches of Arnhem Land in northern Australia.

'It's mostly just the old men like me who paint on bark in the true way,' says 60-year-old Thompson Yulidjirri, one of the finest bark painters alive. 'Our old ways could soon be lost for ever.'

* * *

Two thousand feet above the forests of Arnhem Land, where a few hundred Aborigines of the Kunwinjku tribe inhabit thousands of square miles of wilderness, our six-seater Cessna approaches Mamadawerre, a tiny settlement some 190 miles east of Darwin. A landscape of sandstone hills and lush, forested valley stretches below.

At the end of the red, dusty runway, a slight, white-bearded man greets me after we land. He wears only a broad smile and skimpy shorts; ceremonial scars circle his ebony chest. 'Welcome,' he says. 'I am Yulidjirri.'

That night, as I lie on a bunk, monsoonal rain drumming on the roof, I dream about Kinga, the salt-water crocodile.

I'm woken at sunrise by the cackle of kookaburras in a gum tree outside my window. 'We'll fetch the bark now, while it's cool,' Yulidjirri says. Smoke rises from an outdoor fireplace as we head out of the settlement and into the monsoon forest.

'Why not take the bark from one of these trees?' I ask as we pass a grove of woollybutt eucalypts.

'The Creators said that it can only be taken from the stringybark,' he explains. Aborigines believe that when the Creator Spirits roamed Arnhem Land at the beginning of time, they set a strict code of behaviour. Known by most Australians as the Dreamtime, it's called Djang, or The Law, by tribesmen, and its commandments are as rigid as biblical dictates.

After three hours we are among giant stringybark trees that obscure the sun, creating a cathedral-like gloom. 'I've been coming here since my father showed me this place as a child,' Yulidjirri says. 'My ancestors have been coming here for thousands of years.'

At last he stops at a perfectly straight stringybark, cuts into the trunk and feels the oozing sap with his fingers. 'This one,' he murmurs.

Yulidjirri cuts out a six-foot by three-foot section, then tears away the inch-thick covering as if peeling an orange. 'That was the easiest part,' he says. 'The rest of it takes weeks.'

Back at his home, Yulidjirri sits on the grass outside, trimming the edges with his curved bush knife. For the rest of the afternoon, he patiently planes the moist yellow inside of the bark. Finally he rubs the surface vigorously with fig leaves: their prickly texture is as effective as fine sandpaper. As the sun drops below the jungle line, Yulidjirri places four stones at the bark's corners to ensure it stays flat when it dries.

The next day we wade across a creek, then battle up a slope to a sacred cave. When my eyes grow accustomed to the gloom, the hair rises on the back of my neck. On the back wall, wrapped in paperbark and pushed into a recess, is a skull, stark-white in the gloom. 'It's the burial place of ancestors,' Yulidjirri says.

The themes of his paintings have powerful spiritual significance: his pictures represent tales of the Creator heroes, from the beginning of time, handed down through his ancestors' paintings. Yulidjirri had come to the cave for inspiration.

On a boulder near the entrance is a 12-foot-long picture of a salt-water crocodile – a much-used motif in Aboriginal art. It's painted in the X-ray style unique to western Arnhem Land. Clearly visible are the monster's heart, liver, stomach and spine. Yulidjirri sits cross-legged, closes his eyes and murmurs the words of a Kunwinjku song. Eventually he stirs and says, 'I'll paint a Kinga like the one on the rock.'

Meanwhile the bark has dried and is now bone-hard. Yulidjirri can begin painting. First, to make the brush, he deftly cuts off a piece of discarded bark the size of his hand, then chops energetically at one edge to fray it like the bristles of a brush. Like all Kunwinjku painters, Yulidjirri uses four natural pigments – red and yellow ochre, white clay and charcoal. He then grinds a chunk of red ochre on a flat rock, mixing the small pile of dust with water and fixing agent. He colours the entire bark with swift strokes of red, which represent blood, the painter's life source.

Yulidjirri sketches the basic shape of the crocodile with the jet-black paint. Hours pass and ths sun beats down pitilessly, but the painter is lost in concentration, sometimes putting aside the brush to visualise the composition.

By nightfall a black crocodile more than three feet long has come alive on the bark. A goanna lizard perches above its head. Floating round it are canoes and water birds. It depicts an important Creation myth that Yulidjirri inherited from his ancestors.

'No one can paint this story without my permission,' he says. 'When I was a child, if a man painted someone else's story, he'd be killed.' He paints more than 15 stories about Creation and has the right to paint many plants and animals.

The tale is about two brothers who want to cross the ocean to an island but arrive to find others have taken their canoes. Angry, they dive into the water and overturn them. The men paddling the canoes emerge as the first water birds, while the brothers transform themselves into the first salt-water crocodile and goanna.

Dipping into a pot of white clay, Yulidjirri carefully paints the crocodile's teeth and eyes, then etches its internal organs, finishing with a large, empty stomach. 'This Kinga's hungry,' he says with a grin.

PAUL RAFFAELE

TASKS

16　When you have read the passage, answer the following questions.

   a　Describe Thompson Yulidjirri and his Aboriginal beliefs.

   b　Explain in your own words how Thompson Yulidjirri prepares the bark before painting.

   c　In your own words explain the painting which Thompson Yulidjirri painted for the writer.

17　Sometime later a parcel containing the painting arrives at the writer's house. By chance he has some visitors staying with him at the time who react to the painting in different ways.

Write the conversation which Paul Raffaele has with his visitors.

On these two pages you will find some photographs from three travel books. The people who have taken the photographs have chosen to use different techniques, but they all have the same intention of persuading you to visit their town.

Budapest is the capital city of Hungary, standing on both banks of the River Danube.

Anchorage is the main city of Alaska, the northernmost state of the United States of America.

Bled is a lakeside town in the small country of Slovenia.

TASKS

18 Discuss in groups which technique you think is the most effective and successful in persuading you to visit the town.
19 Write a brief commentary to accompany each photograph in a guidebook.
20 Imagine you are on holiday in one of these places. Write about one day of your holiday.

We are now going to set off into the fictional world of travel and adventure.

A famous book concerned with adventure in far-off and unknown lands is *Gulliver's Travels* by Jonathan Swift. Lemuel Gulliver travels first to Lilliput, a land inhabited by very small people indeed. Gulliver is shipwrecked but manages to reach land. Exhausted, he falls asleep but a surprise is awaiting him when he wakes.

Gulliver's Travels

I lay down on the Grass, which was very short and soft; where I slept sounder than ever I remember to have done in my Life, and as I reckoned, above Nine Hours; for when I awaked, it was just Day-light. I attempted to rise, but was not able to stir: For as I happened to lie on my Back, I found my Arms and Legs were strongly fastened on each Side to the Ground; and my Hair, which was long and thick, tied down in the same Manner. I likewise felt several slender Ligatures across my Body, from my Armpits to my Thighs. I could only look upwards; the Sun began to grow hot, and the Light offended my Eyes. I heard a confused Noise about me, but in the Posture I lay, could see nothing except the Sky. In a little time I felt something alive moving on my left Leg, which advancing gently forward over my Breast, came almost up to my Chin; when bending my Eyes downwards as much as I could, I perceived it to be a human Creature not six Inches high, with a Bow and Arrow in his hands, and a Quiver at his Back. In the mean time, I felt at least Forty more of the same Kind (as I conjectured) following the first. I was in the utmost Astonishment, and roared so loud, that they all ran back in a Fright; and some of them, as I was afterwards told, were hurt with the Falls they got by leaping from my Sides upon the Ground. However, they soon returned; and one of them, who ventured so far as to get a full Sight of my Face, lifting up his Hands and Eyes by way of Admiration, cryed out in a shrill, but distinct Voice, *Hekinah Degul*: The others repeated the same Words several times, but I then knew not what they meant. I lay all this while, as the Reader may believe, in great Uneasiness: At length, struggling to get loose, I had the Fortune to break the Strings, and wrench out the Pegs that fastened my left Arm to the Ground; for, by lifting it up to my Face, I discovered the Methods they had taken to bind me; and, at the same time, with a violent Pull, which gave me excessive Pain, I a little loosened the Strings that tied down my Hair on the left Side; so that I was just able to turn my Head about two Inches. But the Creatures ran off a second time, before I could seize them; whereupon there was a great Shout in a very shrill Accent; and after it ceased, I heard one of them cry aloud, *Tolgo Phonac*; when in an Instant I felt above an Hundred Arrows discharged on my left Hand, which pricked me like so many Needles; and besides, they shot another Flight into the Air, as we do Bombs in *Europe*; whereof many, I suppose, fell on my Body, (though I felt them not) and some on my Face, which I immediately covered with my left Hand. When this Shower of Arrows was over, I fell a groaning with Grief and Pain; and then striving again to get loose, they discharged another Volley larger than the first; and some of them attempted with Spears to stick me in the Sides; but, by good

Luck, I had on me a Buff Jerkin, which they could not pierce. I thought it the most prudent Method to lie still; and my Design was to continue so till Night, when my left Hand being already loose, I could easily free myself: And as for the Inhabitants, I had Reason to believe I might be a Match for the greatest Armies they could bring against me, if they were all of the same Size with him that I saw. But Fortune disposed otherwise of me. When the People observed I was quiet, they discharged no more Arrows: But by the Noise increasing, I knew their Numbers were greater; and about four Yards from me, over against my right Ear, I heard a Knocking for above an Hour, like People at work; when turning my Head that Way, as well as the Pegs and Strings would permit me, I saw a Stage erected about a Foot and a half from the Ground, capable of holding four of the Inhabitants, with two or three Ladders to mount it: From whence one of them, who seemed to be a Person of Quality, made me a long Speech, whereof I understood not one Syllable. But I should have mentioned, that before the principal Person began his Oration, he cryed out three times *Langro Dehul san*: (these Words and the former were afterwards repeated and explained to me.) Whereupon immediately about fifty of the Inhabitants came, and cut the Strings that fastened the left Side of my Head, which gave me the Liberty of turning it to the right, and of observing the Person and Gesture of him who was to speak. He appeared to be of a middle Age, and taller than any of the other three who attended him; whereof one was a Page, who held up his Train, and seemed to be somewhat longer than my middle Finger; the other two stood one on each side to support him. He acted every part of an Orator; and I could observe many Periods of Threatnings, and others of Promises, Pity, and Kindness. I answered in a few Words, but in the most submissive Manner, lifting up my left Hand and both my Eyes to the Sun, as calling him for a Witness; and being almost famished with Hunger, having not eaten a Morsel for some Hours before I left the Ship, I found the Demands of Nature so strong upon me, that I could not forbear shewing my Impatience (perhaps against the strict Rules of Decency) by putting my Finger frequently on my Mouth, to signify that I wanted Food. The *Hurgo* (for so they call a great Lord, as I afterwards learnt) understood me very well: He descended from the Stage, and commanded that several Ladders should be applied to my Sides, on which above an hundred of the Inhabitants mounted, and walked towards my Mouth, laden with Baskets full of Meat, which had been provided, and sent thither by the King's Orders upon the first Intelligence he received of me. I observed there was the Flesh of several Animals, but could not distinguish them by the Taste. There were Shoulders, Legs, and Loins shaped like those of Mutton, and very well dressed, but smaller than the Wings of a Lark. I eat them by two or three at a Mouthful; and took three Loaves at a time, about the bigness of Musket Bullets. They supply me as fast as they could, shewing a thousand Marks of Wonder and Astonishment at my Bulk and Appetite. I then made another Sign that I wanted Drink. They found by my eating that a small Quantity would not suffice me; and being a most ingenious People, they slung up with great Dexterity one of their largest Hogsheads; then rolled it towards my Hand, and beat out the Top; I drank it off at a Draught, which I might well do, for it hardly held half a Pint, and tasted like a small Wine of *Burgundy*, but much more delicious. They brought me a second Hogshead, which I drank in the same Manner, and made Signs for more, but the had none to give me.

JONATHAN SWIFT

TASKS

21 Imagine that you are one of the small people who found Gulliver. What would be your version of this discovery?

22 *Gulliver's Travels* was published in 1726. What do you notice about the way the story is written? Try to write an account of another adventure Gulliver might have had, using the same style of writing.

TIME OUT TASK!

Styles of writing

When any author is writing she or he must always be conscious of their writing style. Some styles are right for some subjects and not for others. Styles need to be varied depending on who is being written for.

Earlier in this chapter you looked at an extract from *A Year in Provence*. Peter Mayle was writing in an amusing way and he was probably writing for an audience with a fondness for France.

To bring you down to earth read the following extract from the play *Spring and Port Wine* by Bill Naughton. It is Friday night and the Cromptons, Rafe (the father), Daisy (the mother) and their grown-up children are having tea.

Spring and Port Wine

Act 1

DAISY: Come on, Hilda love, sit in.

HILDA: I'm not that hungry.

HAROLD: No, but we are. Come on.

HILDA: *hesitates, then slowly walks to her place, at the table.* WILFRED: *moves to his place, below Harold.* DAISY: *regards the table, which is now laid.*

DAISY: Oh, Florence, before I forget I must give you that pound you lent me.

WILFRED: You're doing a lot of money juggling, Mum.

DAISY: Ssh! (*She takes a note and hands it to Florence.*) Ta very much.

FLORENCE: Oh, thanks, Mother. (*She takes the note.*)

RAFE *enters spotting* DAISY's *guilty movement. They all sit down to tea:* RAFE *is at the head of the table,* FLORENCE *left of him, and* HAROLD *on his right.* WILFRED *sits on Harold's right, and* DAISY *below Harold.* HILDA *is down left of* FLORENCE, *where she is conspicuous to the audience.*

RAFE: What was that, Mother.

DAISY: A little something I borrowed off our Florence.

RAFE (*quoting*): 'Neither a borrower nor a lender be ...'

HAROLD: Hey, Wilf, pass the tartar sauce.

WILFRED: The what?

FLORENCE: Sauce tartare. (*She picks it up.*) Here you are.

HAROLD: Ta ta. 'For loan oft loses both itself and friend'. Do you fancy some, Dad?

RAFE: I prefer the natural taste of the herring.

HAROLD: I find this sauce quite piquant. How much a jar is it, Mum?

DAISY: I don't know – oh, one-and-ninepence. I knew there was something I didn't write down. (*She starts to rise, then sits.*) I'll do it later.

RAFE *looks at her.*

HAROLD: What about you, Florence?

FLORENCE: I'll give it a miss. These taste lovely as they are.

HILDA: I say, Mum, I really don't fancy my herring – if you don't mind.

DAISY: No, of course not, love! What would you like instead? I've got some nice fresh eggs.

HAROLD: Aye, with some streaky rashers.

HILDA: No, just an egg.

HAROLD: Sunny side up?

HILDA: Done on both sides. But wait till you're finished, Mum.

DAISY: It's all right, love – won't take me a minute. (*Rising.*) You must be ready for it after a day's work ....

They think they have got away with it, but Rafe quietly beckons Daisy to sit.

RAFE: Hold on a minute, Mother. (*To Hilda.*) Is there something wrong with your herring?

HILDA: No, nothing wrong with it – only I don't feel like it.

RAFE: That's a lovely fresh herring, it's been done in best butter, and yet you have the nerve to sit there and say you don't feel like it.

HILDA:	What else can I say if I don't?
RAFE:	You can eat it and say nothing.
HAROLD:	Well, that's asking a bit much, Dad!
HILDA:	I'll just go and fry myself an egg, Mum.
RAFE:	No, you won't.
HILDA:	Why not?
RAFE:	Because this is a home, not a cafeteria.
HILDA:	I'm entitled to some choice over what I have for my tea – I'm bringing my share of money into the home.
RAFE:	You don't think I thought less of you over all the years you never brought in a ha'penny? I'd as soon see the smiling face you had in them days than you were bringing twenty pounds a week home today.
WILFRED:	Here, dad, to save any bother, I'll eat our Hilda's herring.
RAFE:	You'll do nothing of the sort. You get on with your own tea.

DAISY (*not put out*): Dad – it wouldn't take a second to fry an egg.

RAFE:	There's no fried eggs coming on the scene.
HILDA:	Then there's no point in my waiting here. (*Rising.*) Excuse me, everybody – I'll just go upstairs …
RAFE:	No you won't. Sit down.
HILDA:	What?

HILDA *is undecided.* DAISY *gives her a pleading look.* Pigs leave their troughs when it suits – but not civilised human beings.

WILFRED *gives* Hilda *a look of sympathetic support,* FLORENCE *gives her a reproving glance.* HAROLD *continues to eat with an air of detached interest about the outcome.* DAISY *does not want trouble, but gives Hilda a comforting, motherly look.*

DAISY:	Dad – I'll just …

RAFE *remains oddly above it all, continuing to eat naturally as he talks.* HILDA *catches Daisy's look and sits down, but away from the table.*

RAFE:	No, you won't Mother. They were never spoilt when young – it 'ud be a pity to start now. One day, young woman, you may realise what words like home and family mean. A man and a woman marry, they have children, feed and tend 'em, work for 'em, guide, aye, an 'love 'em.
HILDA:	Just as they ought.
RAFE:	Aye, I agree – as they ought. Over the years they try to make a home for those children, not just a furnished place to live in, but a home, mark you, with some culture. But do those children thank you? Well, perhaps some do – mostly they don't. They take you an' your home for granted. Well, there's nobody taking me for granted.
HILDA:	I don't see why I should eat that herring if I don't want it …

BILL NAUGHTON

- Clearly Bill Naughton's style of writing is very different from Peter Mayle's because his purpose and audience are different. What is his purpose and what is the mood he is trying to create?
- Remember that we are examining style. Try your hand at using the style of the two writers and write two passages about school dinners. The first will be trying to amuse, the second will treat the meal as a dour and rather sombre affair. Think of vocabulary, exaggeration, character, imagery (similes and metaphors) and so on.

END OF TIME OUT!

A particular type of adventure people like reading about is to be found in detective stories. A typical story would involve the uncovering of a crime, the finding of clues and the identification of the criminal. Surprise is often the most important element.

In the following extract from *The Virgin in the Ice* the experienced detective is Brother Cadfael. He is a twelfth-century Benedictine monk.

The Virgin in the Ice

They went briskly wherever the forest thinned and the lingering light showed their way clearly. The first floating flakes of new snow drifted languidly on the air as they came down to the Hopton brook, and crossed it on solid ice, Cadfael lighting down to lead the horse over. From that point they bore somewhat to the left, though veering gradually away from the course of the brook, and came to the first of the little tributaries that flowed down into it, from the long, gentle slope on their right hand. Every stream was still, frozen now for many days. The sun was gone, only an angry glow remained in the west, sullen under leaden greyness. The wind was rising, the snow beginning to sting their faces. Here the forest was broken by scattered holdings and fields, and occasionally a sheep shelter, roughly propped with its back to the wind. Shapes began to dissolve into a mere mottle of shadows, but for fugitive gleams of reflected light from surfaces of ice, and the bluish mounds where untrodden snow had drifted deep.

The second brook, still and silent like the rest, was a shallow, reed-fringed, meandering serpent of silver. The horse disliked the feel of the ice under him, and Cadfael dismounted again to lead him over. The wide, glassy surface shone opaque from every angle, except when looking directly down into it, and Cadfael was watching his own foothold as he crossed, for his boots were worn and smooth. Thus his eye caught, for a moment only, the ghostly pallor beneath the ice to his left, before the horse slithered and recovered, hoisting himself into the snowy grass on the further side.

Cadfael was slow to recognise, slower to believe, what he had seen. Half an hour later, and he would not have been able to see it at all. Fifty paces on, with a thicket of bushes between, he halted, and instead of remounting, as Yves expected, put the bridle into the boy's hands, and said with careful calm: 'Wait a moment for me. No, we need not turn off yet, this is not the place where the tracks divide. Something I noticed there. Wait!'

Yves wondered, but waited obediently, as Cadfael turned back to the frozen brook. The pallor had been no illusion from some stray reflected gleam, it was there fixed and still, embedded in the ice. He went down on his knees to look more closely.

The short hairs rose on his neck. Not a yearling lamb, as he had briefly believed it might be. Longer, more shapely, slender and white. Out of the encasing, glassy stillness a pale, pearly oval stared up at him with open eyes. Small, delicate hands had floated briefly before the frost took hold, and hovered open at her sides, a little upraised as if in appeal. The white of her body and the white of the torn shift which was all she wore seemed to Cadfael to be smirched by some soiling colour at the breast, but so faintly that too intent staring caused the mark to shift and fade. The face was fragile, delicate, young.

A lamb, after all. A lost ewe-lamb, a lamb of God, stripped and violated and slaughtered. Eighteen years old? It could well be so.

By this token Ermina Hugonin was at once found and lost.

ELLIS PETERS

TASK

23 There are clues in this piece of writing which prepare us for the discovery of the body. Looking through the extract, what are the clues you can find?
How does the writer make the extract mysterious and exciting?

H ere is a rather different piece of writing also involving a body. At the start of *The Unpleasantness at the Bellona Club* Dorothy L Sayers begins with the finding of a body.

The Unpleasantness at the Bellona Club

'What in the world, Wimsey, are you doing in this Morgue?' demanded Captain Fentiman, flinging aside the *Evening Banner* with the air of a man released from an irksome duty.

'Oh, I wouldn't call it that,' retorted Wimsey amiably. 'Funeral Parlour at the very least. Look at the marble. Look at the furnishings. Look at the palms and the chaste bronze nude in the corner.'

'Yes, and look at the corpses. Place always reminds me of that old thing in *Punch*, you know – "Waiter, take away Lord Whatsisname, he's been dead two days." Look at Old Ormsby there snoring like a hippopotamus. Look at my revered grandpa – dodders in here at ten every morning, collects the *Morning Post* and the armchair by the fire, and becomes part of the furniture till the evening. Poor old devil! Suppose I'll be like that one of these days. I wish to God Jerry had put me out with the rest of 'em. What's the good of coming through for this sort of thing? What'll you have?'

'Dry Martini,' said Wimsey. 'And you? Two dry Martinis, Fred, please. Cheer up. All this remembrance-day business gets on your nerves, don't it? It's my belief most of us would only be too pleased to chuck these community hysterics if the beastly newspapers didn't run it for all it's worth. However, it don't do to say so. They'd hoof me out of the Club if I raised my voice beyond a whisper.'

'They'd do that anyway, whatever you were saying,' said Fentiman gloomily. 'What *are* you doing here?'

'Waitin' for Colonel Marchbanks,' said Wimsey. 'Bung-ho!'

'Dining with him?'

'Yes.'

Fentiman nodded quietly. He knew that young Marchbanks had been killed at Hill 60, and that the Colonel was wont to give a small, informal dinner on Armistice night to his son's intimate friends.

'I don't mind old Marchbanks,' he said, after a pause. 'He's a dear old boy.'

Wimsey assented.

'And how are things going with you?' he asked.

'Oh, rotten as usual. Tummy all wrong and no money. What's the damn good of it, Wimsey? A man goes and fights for his country, gets his inside gassed out, and loses his job, and all they give him is the privilege of marching past the Cenotaph once a year and paying four shillings in the pound income tax. Sheila's queer, too – overwork, poor girl. It's pretty damnable for a man to have to live on his wife's earnings, isn't it? I can't help it, Wimsey. I go sick and have to chuck jobs up. Money – I never thought of money before the War, but I swear nowadays I'd commit any damned crime to get hold of a decent income.'

Fentiman's voice had risen in nervous excitement. A shocked veteran, till then invisible in a neighbouring armchair, poked out a lean head like a tortoise and said 'Sh!' viperishly.

* * *

'Here's Colonel Marchbanks,' broke in Wimsey, 'we'll talk about it another time. Good evening, Colonel.'

'Evening, Peter. Evening, Fentiman. Beautiful day it's been. No – no cocktails, thanks, I'll stick to whisky. So sorry to keep you waiting like this, but I was having a yarn with poor old Grainger upstairs. He's in a baddish way, I'm afraid. Between you and me, Penberthy doesn't think he'll last out the winter. Very sound man, Penberthy – wonderful, really, that he's kept the old man going so long with his lungs in that frail state. Ah, well! It's what we must all come to. Dear me, there's your grandfather, Fentiman. He's another of Penberthy's miracles. He must be ninety, if he's a day. Will you excuse me for a moment? I must just go and speak to him.'

Wimsey's eyes followed the alert, elderly figure as it crossed the spacious smoking-room, pausing now and again to exchange greetings with a fellow-member of the Bellona Club. Drawn close to the huge fireplace stood a great chair with ears after the Victorian pattern. A pair of spindle shanks with neatly-buttoned shoes propped on a footstool was all that was visible of General Fentiman.

'Queer, isn't it,' muttered his grandson, 'to think that for Old Mossy-face the Crimea is still *the* War, and the Boer business found him too old to go out. He was given his commission at seventeen, you know – was wounded at Majuba – '

He broke off. Wimsey was not paying attention. He was still watching Colonel Marchbanks.

The Colonel came back to them, walking very quietly and precisely. Wimsey rose and went to meet him.

'I say, Peter,' said the Colonel, his kind face gravely troubled, 'just come over here a moment. I'm afraid something rather unpleasant has happened.'

Fentiman looked round, and something in their manner made him get up and follow them over to the fire.

Wimsey bent down over General Fentiman and drew the *Morning Post* gently away from the gnarled old hands, which lay clasped over the thin chest. He touched the shoulder – put his hand under the white head huddled against the side of the chair. The Colonel watched him anxiously. Then, with a quick jerk, Wimsey lifted the quiet figure. It came up all of a piece, stiff as a wooden doll.

Fentiman laughed. Peal after hysterical peal shook his throat. All round the room, scandalised Bellonians creaked to their gouty feet, shocked by the unmannerly noise.

'Take him away!' said Fentiman, 'take him away. He's been dead two days! So are you! So am I! We're all dead and we never noticed it!'

DOROTHY L SAYERS

TASKS

24 Compare the way in which the body is discovered here with the approach used by Ellis Peters in the previous extract.
25 Discuss the mood in this extract.
26 The opening of the book leads us to expect the finding of a dead body. How does the writing raise our expectations?
27 Try your own hand at writing about the discovery of a serious crime.

The most famous answer ever given to the question, 'Why do you want to climb a mountain?' was 'Because it's there!'

Chris Bonington has travelled all over the world climbing mountains 'because they are there'. The article below tells the story of one of his expeditions, an expedition to Greenland's Lemon Mountains.

You will find that the article contains some technical terms to do with climbing and it will be useful to have a dictionary at hand to look up these words – unless you're a climber yourself, of course!

The Pinnacle of Achievement

Scrabbling frantically for footholds on a smooth rock face with a 200-metre drop below you is not everyone's idea of pleasure. But when Chris Bonington got into this situation while exploring Greenland's Lemon Mountains, he found the effort was amply rewarded by the incredible views from the summits.

The groove soared above me, bristling in small overhangs, which faded into an overlapping curtain of smooth rock. Each move was taxing. From below, it looked impossible, and yet somehow the holds materialised. But poised under the final overhang, some 40 metres above Graham Little, I ran out of holds.

My arms ached and my fingers were going into involuntary cramp, curling into a rigid claw. I could only straighten them out with my teeth.

There was a rounded foothold on the crest of a prow out to my left. I pulled on the edge of the prow above the foothold and eased myself across. Below was a sheer drop of almost 200 metres. There was another small

finger scrape just above me and I pulled up on this. I was now arched back, out of balance, panting, fingers weakening. But the angle dropped back onto a kind of gangway that reached up to the left. I eased myself over the bulge. Another rounded scrape to pull on, step up and I was on the gangway, balanced at last, but without any positive holds or cracks to slot in a nut (for a running belay).

By this time, the rope, clipped through a dozen karabiners and rubbing over rocky edges, was dragging me back. Graham was no longer in sight and an overhanging 'V' chimney loomed above. I edged my way into it and, at the full stretch of the rope, reached a tiny ledge with a good belay point. I yelled and whooped with absolute euphoria. It was the most challenging yet aesthetically pleasing rock pitch I

had climbed for years. I had been unsure whether there was a way at all. Yet as I had made each move, I had felt in control. Our isolation, the fact that we were on an unclimbed peak on the edge of the Greenland Ice Cap, almost 500 kilometres from the nearest human, made the sense of achievement all the more powerful.

There were just four of us: Graham, with whom I had made the first ascent of the west ridge of Panch Chuli II in the Kumaon Himalaya the previous year, and the two encamped on the glacier below, Jim Lowther and Rob Ferguson, both of whom were experienced Greenland hands.

We were exploring and climbing the peaks around this isolated glacier on the east coast of Greenland just above the Arctic circle. This range has some of the steepest peaks in

Greenland and yet had only been visited on four previous occasions. Gino Watkins' 1931 British Arctic Air Route Expedition (BAARE) was largely responsible for engendering British interest in the area. It was its aerial surveying work which led to the discovery of two striking mountain ranges. The higher of these became known as the Watkins Mountains, and the smaller, but more spectacular, as the Lemon Mountains – so named because the pilot of the survey plane was Sir Percy Lemon. The first visit was in 1931, when Lawrence Wager, who was to reach 8,475 metres on Everest two years later, sledged up the Frederiksborg Glacier. The next visit was in 1974 by a party led by Stan Woolley, who made the first ascent of a peak they named Mitivangkat.

The range was then left until

1991 when Jim Lowther and I had sailed with Robin Knox-Johnston in the *Suhaili*, the boat in which he completed the first non-stop, single-handed circumnavigation of the world. We had to thread our way through the ice that guards the east coast to make a landing at Watkins Fjord, then sledge inland up the Frederiksborg Glacier to attempt the Cathedral, the highest mountain in the range. However, we discovered that the map was incorrect and that the peak marked on the map as the Cathedral was in fact not this peak at all. The following year, another British expedition flew in, landed on the ice cap near 'the Cathedral' and climbed this and several other peaks.

This year, we also chartered a plane, and landed on the Chisel Glacier, a tributary of the Frederiksborg Glacier just to the south of the Cathedral. It had never been explored and appeared to have some of the range's steepest and most challenging peaks around it. We had with us a hand-held GPS (global positioning system) with which we could set positional and altitude fixes, both on the summits we reached and on other features, to check the accuracy of the map and where necessary redraw it. Our means of transport were Nordic skis and pulks – plastic sledges with alloy shafts that enable the traveller to haul loads of 100 kilos with amazingly little effort. On this expedition we were to shift camp three times.

As the plane vanished over the immensity of the Frederiksborg Glacier, it was difficult to believe that only 30 hours earlier we had been in the busy departure lounge of Glasgow Airport, on our way to Iceland. A scheduled flight from Keflavik airport had taken us to Akureyri

on the north coast of Iceland. From there we flew by charter to Constable Point off Scoresby Sound to be picked up by a twin-engined Otter fitted with skis that took us down to the Lemon Mountains.

There can be few wild places in the world that are so accessible and yet so remote and unspoilt. Once the plane had vanished there was absolute silence, no sound of wind or running water. We had three weeks to climb and explore this amazing array of mountains and glaciers. Immediately opposite was Mejslen (Chisel). It was aptly named, soaring to a sharp chisel-like rock summit from a plinth of complex ice falls and hanging glaciers divided by rocky walls. It had caught our imagination when we sledged past it in 1991. Phil Bartlett and Luke Hughes had attempted it from the other side in 1992, and now we resolved to make it our first objective.

There was no obvious route to its summit. That first afternoon, having pitched our tents, we skied up the glacier in the hope of spying an easy line. But we could see none and finally decided on a tortuous route up a series of linked snow gullies, gangways and ledges through its complex rocky defences.

It was alpine in scale. Although only 2,430 metres above sea level, with our camp on the glacier at 1,170 metres, it meant a height gain of 1,260 metres to the summit. Having a full 24 hours of daylight each day made the decision about when to start our climb more, rather than less, difficult. We wanted the snow to be as hard as possible, which entailed working out the times when the face of Mejslen would be in the shade. We finally decided to set out at 1pm the

following day, as the face went into the shade in the late morning and came into the sun again around the middle of the night.

A short walk up to the bergschrund (the crevasse between the moving glacier and the static ice slope of the mountain face), and then across a series of snow slopes and ridges, alternating with stretches of bare ice, led to the rocky wall we had to cross to reach the next large snow patch. Time to put on the rope. Graham and I were out in front, alternating leads as we picked our way through the rocky maze and up to the open slopes of a hanging glacier on the upper part of the north face.

There was one more rocky barrier between us and the summit, but this was also broken by a tenuous snow line. We reached its foot at around 7pm that evening. We had been on the go for six hours and it seemed high time for a break. Having 24 hours of daylight removes some of the time constraints, but it has its hazards. There is a temptation to keep going for as long as the climb lasts without any rest.

We set out refreshed, climbing sugary, insubstantial snow on top of hard ice, weaving our way between bulging granite walls. A final snow slope, stretching up into steep ice, led towards the summit ridge. Another rope length and we were on the summit – a dramatic little rock spire with scarcely enough room for the four of us to cling to. It was just after midnight and the sun, lying low on the rocky horizon to the north, still lit the sky. It was a superb viewpoint. We could see the Cathedral about 24 kilometres to the north. We could also see the Coxcomb rock peak we had mistaken for the Cathedral.

Beyond was the great white sweep of the ice cap and below us the huge expanse of the Frederiksborg Glacier, reaching down to the ocean.

It took us longer to get down than it had to make the ascent. We rested for several hours on the way, while we waited for the snow slope to come into the shade. We had been away for 30 hours when we finally returned to our camp.

It had been a good start. The next day we packed our pulks and set out on skis for a new base at the head of the Chisel Glacier. We wanted to look at the array of jagged peaks that ringed the top of the glacier. I sat out the next climb. I had a bad cold and was tired. The other three climbed a peak they called Beacon, while I went on a gentle exploration of the glacier just above our camp. I spied a route up an elegant blade of rock that we eventually called the Ivory Tower, after the ivory gulls that we assumed had their home somewhere on its flanks.

We now had three days of bad weather, and to pass the time we settled down to some serious bridge. Once the weather improved we returned to the fray, with three successful ascents and four attempts on the peaks around the glacier basin. Jim and Rob made a challenging first ascent of an ice and rock peak they named the Trident, while Graham and I turned our attention to the spectacular rock spires that are such a feature of these mountains. We travelled light, wearing rock shoes rather than boots, and reached the top of the Ivory Tower in just under 12 hours.

The focus of our attention was a magnificent peak we called the Needle. It reminded me of the famous Southwest Pillar of the Drus above Chamonix in the Alps – about 700 metres of soaring granite with hardly a snow patch on it. We spent an afternoon running out three of our ropes, the top rope length being the superb pitch I have already described, before abseiling down and then skiing to our camp.

We returned the following morning, quickly jumaring (using special ratchet-like clamps) up the ropes we had left in place to continue the climb. The rock now became more broken, with a loose section that led up to a shoulder on the crest of the pillar. A fault line we had picked out from the bottom stretched up towards a deep-cut chimney capped with an arch of snow. Our route lay through the eye of the needle. I sat belayed to the rock while Graham led the next pitch and I wondered at the fragile life that existed in this harsh environment. Green tendrils of dwarf willow reached over the ledge; purple saxifrage clung to a sheltered cranny. A butterfly flitted past.

On the north side of the Needle we were faced with snow-covered ledges and snow-jammed grooves that we hadn't been able to see from below. Climbing these in rock shoes was cold and frightening. I belayed Graham as he pulled over a final bulge to complete one of the finest rock routes I have ever climbed. In the midnight sun the view from the top was superb. But the descent was far from enjoyable – it was more nerve-racking than the climb itself. On the more broken pitches, it was impossible to abseil and we had no choice but to climb back down the steep and difficult sections. We had been on the go for almost 23 hours by the time we reached the camp.

Meanwhile, Rob and Jim had been attempting the highest peak of the cirque, which we had named the Citadel. It was a massive, fortress-like mountain of around 2,500 metres. They had made fast initial progress, climbing a series of snow ramps and gullies to just below the summit ridge, but then Jim was hit by a falling stone and broke his collar bone. Fortunately, helped by Rob, he was able to make it down. It brought home how potentially dangerous climbing is in the Lemon Mountains. We had a radio alarm beacon which we could have activated, but there was no means of knowing if any passing aircraft would pick up the signal, or how long help would be in coming. We had to get Jim down off the mountain without outside help anyway.

We still had to sledge out from the mountains to the coast, involving seven days hard work, the last four backpacking loads over a shoulder at the foot of the Frederiksborg Glacier. Our plane arrived at the air strip at Sødalen within minutes of the arranged time to take us back to civilisation. It had been a profoundly satisfying expedition. Between us we had completed five challenging first ascents and had explored and remapped an untouched glacier basin in a period of only four weeks. But many superb unclimbed rock and ice summits remain.

TASKS

28   Various details and hints, together with the language which is used, help
us to understand the fascination climbing holds for Chris Bonington.
In groups or as a class, discuss these details and the language
of the article.
During your discussion make notes and then, by yourself, write a short
article of your own entitled 'The Fascination of Climbing'.

29   Now move on to a far more practical point and, using material from the
passage, explain the dangers which the climbers on this expedition faced.

30   In the introduction to these tasks you were reminded that the article
contains technical terms to do with climbing. Make a list of all these
terms with a brief explanation of what they mean beside each one.

31   Using information from the passage, write a brief guide suitable for a
young person who wants to take up climbing.
In your guide you will need to give advice about equipment, safety etc.

SURVIVORS

3

The word 'survival' suggests many things. Living through a disaster, staying alive in very difficult circumstances, overcoming adverse conditions – these ideas will be behind many of our thoughts. And if people are to survive, what characteristics will they show? Courage, staying-power, stamina, determination, obstinacy? All of these and many more!

The reading in this chapter will reflect a very wide range of ways in which people survive. You will be able to consider for yourself what you understand and think about surviving.

ENGLISH IN THE NATIONAL CURRICULUM:

Key Skills you will cover in this chapter

- ☑ You will be asked to consider how the writer has presented his or her ideas and to appreciate the impact that the text has on you while you are reading it.
- ☑ You will be looking at some literature of high quality and will see how the writers have succeeded.
- ☑ You will be engaging with the ideas of the passages and will be able to analyse them.
- ☑ You will be developing your ability to write narrative.
- ☑ You will be encouraged to think of the vocabulary which is used both by others and by yourself.

To start off we are going to look at a short story by a French writer, Guy de Maupassant, called *A Vendetta*. This story describes a particular kind of survival; the mother has to survive so that she can carry out what she has sworn to do ...

A Vendetta

Paolo Saverini's widow lived alone with her son in a tiny cottage on the ramparts of Bonifacio. The town, built on a mountain spur, in some places actually overhanging the sea, faces the low-lying coast of Sardinia across the strait with its bristling reefs. At its foot on the other side it is almost entirely enclosed by a gash in the cliff like a gigantic passage, which serves as its harbour. The little Italian or Sardinian fishing-boats and once a fortnight the old puffing steamer, which runs to and from Ajaccio, come up as far as the first houses, after threading their way between two precipitous walls of rock.

On the white mountain-side the collection of houses makes a whiter patch. They look like the nests of wild birds clinging to the rock looking down on this dangerous channel, into which few ships venture. The wind harasses the sea remorselessly, sweeping the barren coast sparsely covered with coarse grass; it roars down the strait, stripping the land bare on both sides. Patches of whitish foam round the black tips of the countless reefs, which pierce the waves in every direction, look like torn sheets floating and drifting on the surface of the water.

The widow Saverini's house, clinging to the very edge of the cliff, had three windows opening on to this wide desolate view.

She lived there alone with her son, Antoine, and their dog, Frisky, a great raw-boned bitch, with a long rough coat, of the sheep-dog breed. The young man used her as a gun-dog.

One evening, after a quarrel, Antoine Saverini was treacherously knifed by Nicolas Ravolati, who escaped to Sardinia the same night.

When the old woman received her son's body, brought to her house by the passers-by, she shed no tears, but stood motionless for a long while, gazing at it; then, stretching out her wrinkled hand over the corpse, she vowed vengeance. She refused to let anyone stay with her, and shut herself up with the body and the howling dog.

The animal never stopped howling, standing at the foot of the bed, with head stretched out towards her master and tail between her legs. She stood as still as the mother, who bent over the body with staring eyes, now weeping silently, as she looked at him.

The young man, lying on his back, wearing his home-spun tweed jacket, with holes and rents in the breast, seemed to be asleep; but there was blood everywhere – on his shirt, which had been torn for first-aid dressings, on his waistcoat, on his trousers, on his face and on his hands. There were clots of dried blood on his beard and hair.

His aged mother began to speak to him; at the sound of her voice the dog stopped howling.

'Don't worry, my boy, my poor child, I will avenge you. Do you hear me? It's your mother's promise, and your mother always keeps her word, you know that.'

And slowly she bent over him, pressing her cold lips against the dead man's lips. Then Frisky began howling again, uttering a long-drawn-out moan, monotonous, piercing, sinister.

They stayed there, the two of them, the woman and the dog, till morning.

Antoine Saverini was buried next day, and he was soon forgotten in Bonifacio.

He had left neither brother nor near relative, so there was no one to take up the vendetta on his behalf.

His old mother was the only person who never forgot.

Across the strait all day long she could see a white speck on the coast. It was the little Sardinian village of Longosardo, where Corsican bandits took refuge when hard pressed by the police. They were almost the only inhabitants of the hamlet, facing the coast of their own country, and they waited there till it was safe to come back and return to the 'maquis'. It was in this village, she knew, that Nicolas Ravolati had taken refuge.

Entirely alone she sat all day long at her window and gazed at this village, dreaming of her vengeance. How was she to carry it out? She was a weak woman, with not much longer to live, but she had promised it, she had sworn it on the body. She could not forget or put it off. What was she to do? Now she would not sleep at night; she had no rest, no peace of mind, obstinately determined to find a way.

The dog dozed at her feet and at intervals raised her head and howled into space. Since her master's death, she often howled in this way, as if calling him; she would not be comforted, as if her animal soul also carried an indelible memory.

One night, as Frisky began to howl, the mother had a sudden inspiration, the fierce vindictive inspiration of a savage. She pondered over it all night, and, getting up at daybreak, she went to the church. There she prayed, bowed down on the stone floor, humbling herself before God, seeking help and support, praying that her poor worn-out body might have the strength to avenge her son.

Then she went home. She had in her back yard an old stove-in barrel, which collected the rain-water from the gutters; she turned it upside down, emptied it and fixed it on the ground with stakes and stones; next she chained Frisky in this kennel and went into the house.

That day she spent hours walking up and down restlessly in her room, her gaze always fixed on the coast of Sardinia, the refuge of the assassin.

The dog howled all day and all night. In the morning the old woman took her a bowl of water, but nothing else – no bread or soup.

Another day passed. Frisky slept, weak with hunger. Next day her eyes were shining, her coat bristling and she was tugging furiously at the chain.

Still the old woman gave her no food. The animal, by now maddened with hunger, kept up her hoarse barking, Another night passed. At dawn the widow Saverini went to a neighbour's house and begged two trusses of straw. She took some of her late husband's clothes and stuffed them with the straw to resemble a human body.

Having fixed a stake in the ground in front of Frisky's kennel, she fastened the dummy to it, so that it looked like a man standing there, and made a head out of a roll of old linen.

The dog looked at the straw in surprise, and stopped howling, in spite of her hunger.

Next the old woman went to the pork-butcher's and bought a long piece of black blood-sausage. Returning home, she lit a wood fire in the yard near the kennel and grilled the sausage. Frisky, maddened, leapt about and foamed at the mouth, her eyes fixed on the grilling meat, the smell of which sharpened her appetite.

At last the old woman made this steaming savoury mess into a scarf round the dummy's neck. She tied it there with string, leaving it for some time, so that it soaked well into the straw. This done, she untied the dog.

With one terrific bound the animal leapt at the dummy's throat, and with her paws on the shoulders began to tear at it. She dropped to the ground with some of the meat in her mouth; then she returned to the attack, burying her teeth in the string, and tore out more bits of sausage, dropped once more to the ground, and again attacked with mad fury. She tore the face to pieces and reduced the whole throat to ribbons.

The old woman, motionless and silent, watched the dog with tense excitement. Then she chained her up again, kept her without food for another two days and repeated the strange performance.

For three months she trained the dog to this kind of fight, making her use her teeth to get her food. Now she no longer chained her up, but set her on the dummy with a gesture.

She had taught her to go for the figure and tear it to pieces, even when there was no food hidden in the neck. Afterwards she rewarded the animal with the sausage she had grilled for her.

Whenever the dog saw the dummy, she immediately quivered all over, and looked towards he mistress, who cried in a shrill voice, pointing: 'At him!'

* * *

When she thought the time had come, she went to Confession and received the Sacrament one Sunday morning with ecstatic fervour; then, dressing in man's clothes to look like an old ragged beggar, she struck a bargain with a Sardinian fisherman, who took her, together with the dog, across the strait.

She carried a big piece of sausage in a canvas bag. Frisky had had nothing to eat for two days. The old woman kept making her smell the savoury food to excite her.

They reached Longosardo, and the old Corsican woman hobbled along to the baker's and enquired for Nicolas Ravolati's house. He had resumed his old trade as a joiner, and was working alone at the back of his shop.

The old woman pushed open the door and shouted: 'Hullo! Nicolas!' He turned round; then, slipping the dog's lead, she cried: 'At him! Go for him, tear him to pieces!'

The starving animal leapt at him and seized his throat. The man, throwing out his arms, grappled with the dog and fell to the ground. For a few seconds he writhed, kicking the ground with his heels. Then he lay still, while Frisky wrenched at his throat, tearing it to ribbons. Two neighbours, sitting at their doors, remembered distinctly seeing an old beggar come out of the shop with an emaciated black dog; as it walked, it was eating something brown, which its master gave it.

The old woman returned home in the evening. That night she slept soundly.

GUY DE MAUPASSANT

TASKS

1 Discuss the character of the widow Saverini. What are the qualities which she possesses?
2 What exactly is a vendetta? Talk about how it is portrayed in this story.
3 Imagine you are the widow Saverini at the end of the story. Write down your thoughts about yourself and your actions.

TIME OUT TASK!

Using a dictionary

Be honest with yourself. Do you use a dictionary? How often do you use a dictionary? What do you use a dictionary for?

The probable answer is that you use a dictionary sometimes to find out the meaning of a word or because you are checking your spelling. It is just possible that you might be hoping to find out how to pronounce a word.

Printed below is a list of words. There's nothing special about this list, look up the words and see if you can write down the following.

- Where did the word come from?
- What are its meanings?
- What is the plural of the word if it has a plural?
- Is there a synonym (a word which means the same)?
- Is the word a noun, a verb, an adjective, or what is it?

FATIGUE

ARTICULATE

COMPILE

STRESS

RAGE

Always have a dictionary by you.

END OF TIME OUT!

In *After the First Death* Robert Cormier has created a story about the hijacking of a school bus. The children on the bus are hostages and the hijackers have many demands. The driver of the bus is a young woman. When she has driven the bus, following the hijackers' orders, on to a high bridge she is able to think again …

After the First Death

Okay. She wasn't panicky. She listened to the boy, telling herself to be sharp, alert, on her toes, cheerleading herself onward. She knew the boy's name was Miro and the man was Artkin. She'd heard them exchanging names a few moments age, and somehow the realisation that they had names restored a sense of normality to the situation, reduced the degree of terror that had engulfed her during the bus ride to the bridge. *Miro, Artkin* was much better then *the boy, the man*, rendering them human. And yet what this boy named Miro was telling her now was inhuman, a horror story. The child was dead.

'Murdered,' she said, the word leaping to her lips, an alien word she had never uttered before in its real meaning.

'Not murder, miss,' the boy said. 'It was an accident. We were told the drugs were safe, but this boy died.'

'Does this mean the other kids are in danger, too?'

'No. We have checked them all – you can see for yourself – and they are normal. Perhaps this boy had a weak heart. Or he was allergic to the drugs.' He pronounced 'allergic' as three separate words.

Kate turned to look at the children. They were still subdued, although some yawned and stirred restlessly in their seats.

'We want you to help us with the children,' the boy said. 'Take care of them. See to their needs. This will convince you that we mean them no harm.'

'How long are we going to be here?' she asked. She nodded towards the man, who was going from seat to seat, touching the children, their foreheads, their cheeks, speaking to them gently and soothingly. 'He said it would be all over when we reached the bridge.'

Miro thought fast. 'We have had a change of plans. Because of the death of the boy. We will be here a bit longer.'

'How long?' she asked, pressing on, sensing a sudden uncertainty in the boy.

He shrugged. 'No one knows, really. A few hours …'

At that moment, a noise at the door claimed her attention. The big lumbering man who had forced open the door with a crowbar was back at the door again. He shattered the windows in the door with a rock.

'What's he doing?' she asked.

The man broke the glass with a glowering intensity, looking neither at the girl nor the Miro.

'He is breaking the glass to put a lock on the door so that it cannot be opened with the handle there,' Miro said.

Her glance went automatically to the emergency door on the left halfway down the bus. The boy did not miss the direction her eyes had taken. He did not smile; he seemed incapable of smiling. But his eyes brightened. 'The emergency door will be locked with a clamp,' he said. 'And the windows – we will seal the windows shut. It is useless to think of escaping.'

She felt mildly claustrophobic and also transparent, as if the boy could see right into her mind. Turning away, she saw the man standing now at the seat where the dead boy lay. She wondered which child was dead and yet, in a way, she didn't want to know. An anonymous death didn't seem so terrible. She didn't really know any of the children, anyway, although their faces were familiar from the few times she'd substituted for her uncle. She'd heard them call each other by name – Tommy, Karen, Monique. But she couldn't place names with faces.

'May I see the child?' she asked. And realised she didn't really want to see the child. Not a dead child. But she felt it was her responsibility to see him, to corroborate the fact of his death.

Miro paused.

'What is your name?' he asked.

'Kate. Kate Forrester.'

'My name is Miro,' he said. He realised that this was perhaps the first time he had ever introduced himself to anyone. Usually, he was anonymous. Or Atkin would say 'The boy's name is Miro' when they encountered strangers.

Kate pretended that she hadn't learned his name earlier. 'And your friend's name?' she asked.

'Artkin,' he said.

The huge man outside the bus was now testing the lock. Kate didn't care to know *his* name. His name would only establish his existence in her life, and he was so ugly and menacing that she didn't want to acknowledge him at all. She glanced at the van and saw the black fellow at the wheel, staring into space, as if in a dream world of his own, not really here in the van, on the bridge.

'Please,' Kate said. 'May I see the child?'

Miro shrugged. 'We are going to be together for a while on this bus. You should call me Miro and I should call you Kate.' Miro found the words difficult to say, particularly to a girl and an American girl at that. But Artkin had told him to win her confidence.

The girl didn't answer. Miro, flustered, turned away and then beckoned her to follow him. He led her to the centre of the bus. 'She wants to see him,' he told Artkin.

Kate drew a deep breath and looked down. The child lay still, as if asleep. His pallor had a bluish tint. Miro also looked, seeing the child from the girl's viewpoint, wondering what she thought. Had she ever seen a dead person before? Probably not; not in her well-scrubbed American world. The girl shuddered slightly. 'Come,' Miro said. She looked grateful as she turned away from the child. At least she had not fainted. Her flesh was pale, however, and this somehow made her blond hair more pronounced, more radiant. He realised that American boys would consider her beautiful.

Artkin accompanied them to the front of the bus.

'What happens now?' Kate asked. Would she ever forget that blue child on the bus seat?

'As far as your part is concerned, miss,' Artkin said, 'it will consist mostly of waiting. For a few hours. We have sent messages and are waiting for a reply. Meanwhile, you will care for the children. They will be awakening soon. I want you to reassure them. Most of all, keep them in control, keep them quiet.'

ROBERT CORMIER

TASKS

4 On the bus are children, the driver, the hijackers. What would be the different attitudes of these three groups of people? Write your answer in three short paragraphs.

5 Make a close study of this passage:
- what does it tell you about Kate?
- what do you learn about Miro?

■ does the passage hint that things could turn out well or badly?
For a few pages write your own continuation of the story.

You will find that we have reprinted this passage in your homework book together with a further task which will give you a chance to develop your own writing.

Our next stimulus involves a fight for survival not against other people but against nature. In chapter 37 of *Far From the Madding Crowd* Thomas Hardy writes about a fight against the horrors of nature. The story is set in the Wessex countryside: it is the nineteenth century. In this extract Gabriel Oak is fighting to secure the recently harvested corn: only one person is available to help.

Far From the Madding Crowd

'Is that you, ma'am?' said Gabriel to the darkness.

'Who is there?' said the voice of Bathsheba.

'Gabriel. I am on the rick, thatching.'

'O, Gabriel! – and are you? I have come about them. The weather awoke me, and I thought of the corn. I am so distressed about it – can we save it anyhow? I cannot find my husband. Is he with you?'

'He is not there.'

'Do you know where he is?'

'Asleep in the barn.'

'He promised that the stacks should be seen to, and now they are all neglected! Can I do anything to help? Liddy is afraid to come out. Fancy finding you here at such an hour! Surely I can do something?'

'You can bring up some reed-sheaves to me, one by one, ma'am; if you are not afraid to come up the ladder in the dark,' said Gabriel. 'Every moment is precious now, and that would save a good deal of time. It is not very dark when the lightning has been gone a bit.'

'I'll do anything!' she said resolutely. She instantly took a sheaf upon her shoulder, clambered up close to his heels, placed it behind the rod, and descended for another. At her third ascent the rick suddenly brightened with the brazen glare of shining majolica – every knot in every straw was visible. On the slope in front of him appeared two human shapes, black as jet. The rick lost its sheen – the shapes vanished. Gabriel turned his head. It had been the sixth flash which had come from the east behind him, and the two dark forms on the slope had been the shadows of himself and Bathsheba.

Then came the peal. It hardly was credible that such a heavenly light could be the parent of such a diabolical sound.

'How terrible!' she exclaimed, and clutched him by the sleeve. Gabriel turned, and steadied her on her aerial perch by holding her arm. At the same moment, while he was still reversed in his attitude, there was more light, and he saw, as it were, a copy of the tall poplar tree on the hill drawn in black on the wall of the barn. It was the shadow of that tree, thrown across by a secondary flash in the west.

The next flare came. Bathsheba was on the ground now, shouldering another sheaf, and she bore its dazzle without flinching – thunder and all – and again ascended with the load. There was then a silence everywhere for four or five minutes, and the crunch of the spars, as Gabriel hastily drove them in, could again be distinctly heard. He thought the crisis of the storm had passed. But there came a burst of light.

'Hold on!' said Gabriel, taking the sheaf from her shoulder, and grasping her arm again.

Heaven opened then, indeed. The flash was almost too novel for its inexpressibly dangerous nature to be at once realised, and they could only comprehend the magnificence of its beauty. It sprang from east, west, north, south, and was a perfect dance of death. The forms of skeletons appeared in the air, shaped with blue fire for bones – dancing, leaping, striding, racing around, and mingling altogether in unparalleled confusion. With these were intertwined undulating snakes of green, and behind these was a broad mass of lesser light. Simultaneously came from every part of the tumbling sky what may be called a shout; since, though no shout ever came near it, it was more of the nature of a shout than of anything else earthly. In the meantime one of the grisly forms had alighted upon the point of Gabriel's rod, to run invisibly down it, down the chain and into the earth. Gabriel was almost blinded, and he could feel Bathsheba's warm arm tremble in his hand – a sensation novel and thrilling enough; but love, life, everything human, seemed small and trifling in such close juxtaposition with an infuriated universe.

Oak had hardly time to gather up these impressions into a thought, and to see how strangely the red feathers of her hat shone in this light, when the tall tree on the hill before mentioned seemed on fire to a white heat, and a new one among these terrible voices mingled with the last crash of those preceding. It was a stupefying blast, harsh and pitiless, and it fell upon their ears in a dead, flat blow, without that reverberation which lends the tones of a drum to more distant thunder. By the lustre reflected from every part of the earth and from the wide domical scoop above it, he saw that the tree was sliced down the whole length of its tall, straight stem, a huge riband of bark being apparently flung off. The other portion remained erect, and revealed the bared surface as a strip of white down the front. The lightning had struck the tree. A sulphurous smell filled the air; then all was silent, and black as a cave in Hinnom.

'We had a narrow escape!' said Gabriel hurriedly. 'You had better go down.'

Bathsheba said nothing; but he could distinctly hear her rhythmical pants, and the recurrent rustle of the sheaf beside her in response to her frightened pulsations. She descended the ladder, and, on second thoughts, he followed her. The darkness was now impenetrable by the sharpest vision. They both stood still at the bottom, side by side. Bathsheba appeared to think only of the weather – Oak thought only of her just then. At last he said –

'The storm seems to have passed now, at any rate.'

'I think so too.' said Bathsheba. 'Though there are multitudes of gleams, look!'

The sky was now filled with an incessant light, frequent repetition melting into complete continuity, as an unbroken sound results from the successive strokes on a gong.

'Nothing serious, ' said he. 'I cannot understand no rain falling. But Heaven be praised, it is all the better for us. I am going up again.'

'Gabriel, you are kinder than I deserve! I will stay and help you yet. O, why are not some of the others here!'

'They would have been here if they could,' said Oak, in a hesitating way.

'O, I know it all – all,' she said, adding slowly: 'They are all asleep in the barn, in a drunken sleep, and my husband among them. That's it, is it not? Don't think I am a timid woman and can't endure things.'

'I am not certain,' said Gabriel. 'I will go and see.'

He crossed to the barn, leaving her there alone. He looked through the chinks of the door. All was in total darkness, as he had left it, and there still arose, as at the former time, the steady buzz of many snores.

He felt a zephyr curling about his cheek, and turned. It was Bathsheba's breath – she had followed him, and was looking into the same chink.

He endeavoured to put off the immediate and painful subject of their thoughts by remarking gently, 'If you'll come back again, miss – ma'am, and hand up a few more, it would save much time.'

The Oak went back again, ascended to the top, stepped off the ladder for greater expedition, and went on thatching. She followed, but without a sheaf.

THOMAS HARDY

TASKS

6 What worries and fears would Gabriel have as he worked on the ricks?

7 How does the description of the storm add to the sense of drama here? It will help plan your answer if you list the different sights and sounds which are mentioned.

8 Bathsheba is the owner of the farm and she has recently married. Things aren't exactly perfect with her marriage; we are told her husband is asleep in the barn and he is blind drunk. The marriage is causing other problems though. How can you tell from the passage that it is causing difficulties between herself and Oak?

9 Storms of all kinds can be terrifying. Write a description of your own about a storm which you have experienced.

Some of the most extraordinary stories of survival are associated with war. What is printed below is an extract adapted from a book called *Return with Honour* by Captain Scott O'Grady, an american pilot who was shot down when working for NATO during the Bosnian conflict.

Return with Honour

It was 1.15pm as I moved the throttle to max, kicked in the afterburner, and took off at 200mph. Wilbur and I flew a standard formation, 'tactical line abreast': a mile-and-a-half apart, with an altitude stack of 1,000 to 2,000ft.

He established an oval pattern for our patrol. We would fly the first leg of the oval, 25 miles long, about three minutes' travel, then bank in tandem and do the three-minute return leg back to where we'd started.

Back and forth we went that day – with no reason to suspect that a Bosnian Serb outfit had secretly moved an SA-6 battery south of its normal position. Or that it had lined up its missiles within easy range, poised to pounce – to down the first American pilot in the course of this long and ugly war.

Suddenly Wilbur's warning system told him he was 'spiked' – that an enemy radar on the ground might be looking at him. This didn't mean they were actually shooting at him, but they sure might be thinking about it. After 10 tense seconds, the equipment registered it as a false alarm. Full speed ahead.

Shortly after, at 3.03pm precisely, *my* radar warning receiver sounded. I felt uneasy. I didn't like being stared at – especially when the staring might preface a missile aimed straight at my gut. I gazed out through the canopy, looking for the telltale white smoke plume of a rocket motor. Nothing.

Six seconds after the spike, I heard a new signal, louder, like a car alarm. Heart sinking, I realised I'd been locked on. This was no false alarm. Somebody was shooting at me. The missile might already be in the air. I began to duck and manoeuvre in three dimensions, pushing the F-16 to its limit. Three seconds went by and in a brilliant red flash to my right, a missile exploded in the air between my plane and Wilbur's.

We weren't safe yet – SA-6s came packaged in threes. A second later, a murderous *bang* swallowed me whole. The missile soared up from my blind spot and struck square in the belly of the fuselage. For the briefest instant I felt pitched up, as if uppercut by a giant fist, and then savagely down as the plane sheared in two, the nose and cockpit breaking away.

My console was disintegrating before my eyes.

Fire was all around me. Flames found the space between my oxygen mask and visor and I felt the heat and pain on my neck. My end had come. A fraction later I looked down, through the blaze, to the yellow handle under my seat and saw the words: 'PULL TO EJECT'. I reached down. And pulled.

The good news was that the plane had by now slowed to about 350mph, moderating the force of the wind as I was blasted up and out. The bad news was that I was five miles high and plunging to the earth and had no idea whether my parachute would work. I was falling face down, my eyes staring at the Bosnian countryside coming at me, as through a slow zoom lens. Falling and falling, and I knew I'd be conscious to the end. Of all the ways to die, this would be one of the very bad ones.

Seconds later, I jerked as the parachute billowed out like somebody shaking a gigantic bed sheet. I abruptly found myself descending at a new angle, perpendicular to the ground, the way it was supposed to be. For the first time, it occurred to me that my main problem now was on the war-torn land to which I was swirling, ready or not.

As my parachute descended to 1,000ft, a highway lay dead ahead; I could see a lorry with a canvas top – the type used to carry soldiers – and a car stopped a mile or two up the road. Under my candy-coloured, 28ft canopy, I was as conspicuous as the Goodyear blimp. I could almost feel the sets of eager eyes boring in at me. Was I a curiosity? A target? A hostage-to-be?

I recalled what I'd been told many times by the intelligence people back at base: there were no friendly forces in Bosnia, no safe areas, nobody you could count on.

I had already spotted a dense wood that rose into a hill – ideal ground for evasion. But could I steer myself there? I made one last effort to direct the chute but it was no use: I was at the mercy of the wind. I made myself stop staring at the watchers gathered below, and prepared to land.

Right at the end, the wind took mercy. I cleared the road with a stone's throw of height to spare and landed just 50 yards beyond. Better still, I wasn't stuck in a tree or exposed in some farmer's back yard. I'd skimmed into a small, empty clearing of foot-high grass, with woods all around. It wasn't paradise, but it would do.

My landing was textbook; there was no chute drag, and I stopped clean. Now I was in a race – I had to make cover before my watchers reached the clearing. I quick-released the clips but wasted seconds recovering my radio, which had slipped from my pocket and become snarled in the parachute lines. And I didn't have seconds to spare. The hunters from the highway were coming closer with each breath.

I grabbed my survival rucksack, wedged its 20lb under my arm like a football, and I ran. In my haste, I made a mistake, forgetting to pick up the auxiliary survival kit with a back-up radio and half my ration of water inside.

I bolted out of the clearing and into a maze of low bushes and short, skinny trees. I'd thought I could run a marathon, that my determination would carry me for ever, but after 30 seconds my legs were lead pipes.

This whole impossible afternoon suddenly caved in on me, and my body broke down. I had to stop.

I flung myself into a clump of trees. The undergrowth wasn't as dense as I'd hoped for, but I wasn't feeling choosy. I lay down, propping myself behind a tree root. The dirt was dark, almost black. Drenched with the sweat of fear and exertion, I could hear vehicles near the point where I'd ditched my parachute – one, two, three of them. The last one rumbled to a stop with the unmistakable, grinding groan of a lorry.

The people would be here soon, but I had to try and make contact with the other F-16, miles overhead. If I was going to be captured – and the odds of that seemed pretty fair just now – it was crucial for the airforce to know I was alive. I grabbed the radio, pushed a button to transmit over the emergency channel and whispered as clearly as I could: 'Hey, Wilbur, this is Zulu.'

No sooner was my nickname out of my mouth than I heard voices by my parachute, and the grass rustled with footsteps, coming my way. Coming with the careless noise of men who know their prey is cornered. I shut off the radio and burrowed by face into the dirt, but the tree root made poor cover. I froze, barely breathing, willing myself into invisibility.

Within five minutes two men, one white-haired, the other young, maybe 18, had arrived. They wore rough country clothes and appeared unarmed. They were five yards off and closing. My face pitched back into the dirt. My heart was thumping in my ears. They came louder with each step. I thought

they were sure to see me – how could they miss? – and I knew they had reinforcements behind them.

My brain skittered off to what I'd do when I was caught – the best time to escape, I knew, was right after you'd been captured – and then to what *they* might do to me. The armies down here played by their own rules – I had a shattered airplane as proof of that. If I was lucky, I'd get off with a beating, till somebody in authority reached the scene and claimed his pawn for the next round of negotiations. And if I wasn't …

I held my breath; I imagined myself blending into the dirt. I wouldn't do their work for them. If they wanted me, they'd have to grab me; they'd have to peel me from the ground.

The two men walked to the edge of my hiding spot, five feet from my burrowed head … and kept going straight down the path, without a hitch in stride or conversation. I don't know why they missed me, can't explain it, except that God veiled me from them.

My relief was short-lived. Minutes later I heard new stirrings, male voices on both sides. I was surrounded. Through the low-hanging branches, I glimpsed backs and legs. They were in groups of two and three, poking about the brush, calling out to one another. At times they were no more than 10ft away from me. Over the next hour I counted 15 of them and heard dozens more rushing around.

Like the first pair, these men wore civilian clothes, but they'd brought along something extra: each one of them had a rifle. I stopped worrying about becoming a hostage, about torture or solitary confinement. These men were out to kill me.

That's when I heard the first rifle shot, much too close, echoing through the woods. I was more frightened than I'd ever been in my life. I believed I was about to die. The Lord's Prayer came into my mind.

Our Father, who art in heaven hallowed be Thy name …

Another shot and a pinging ricochet. Were they trying to flush me out? Or just shooting at the slightest quiver of a branch or bush, hoping to find me behind it?

I heard more rifle shots throughout that first afternoon and men passing about me for two hours. The miracle is that not one of them spotted me. After a time the voices grew fainter. I dared not stir.

By six o'clock I felt bold enough to try my radio again. 'Anyone – Basher Five-Two,' I said, using my call-sign. Static was my answer. I knew I wouldn't be rescued that day.

My stress found a release. My bowels gave way and flooded my trousers. I'd have to live with it for now. I wondered about the burns on my face. Using a blade from my Swiss army knife as a mirror, I saw my cheeks had blistered, and the fire had singed off my eyelashes and part of my eyebrows. I felt relieved – I'd been worried that half my face had melted off.

I stayed stock-still behind my tree root well into darkness, long after I'd heard the last searcher leave the area. Noise carries farther in the dark; a dry twig can crack like a cherry bomb. I watched a few lights in the distance, staring at them long enough so that they seemed to move. Were they house lights? Searchlights? Flashlights? Were they coming back to look for me?

It was midnight before I decided to move on. There were risks, but it was out of the question to stay so close to the road. I would go south, towards the higher ground, as I'd planned while coming down in my parachute.

The night was silent and dark as a tomb as I walked, one step at a time, always careful: stop, look, listen. Perhaps there were soldiers out there with night-sights.

After 20 minutes I found myself in a small clearing. I zipped open my rucksack. Inside were eight flexipacks of water, a total of two pints; an empty plastic water pouch; a woollen ski hood; a pair of socks; a pair of green mittens; a floppy orange and green hat; a thin vinyl tarpaulin, green on one side, silver on the other; a square of black and brown camouflage netting; a foil space blanket; a pair of sun goggles and a bottle of sunblock lotion; a 5in knife; and a 121-page booklet entitled Aircrew Survival.

It was a mixed bag. I could use the water, tarp, and clothing; the rest of it was excess baggage. I was unlikely to snuggle up with Aircrew Survival; my common sense and training would have to guide me for now.

In my survival vest, I had my radio and medical kit, a variety of flares, a compass, a whistle, a tourniquet, a wire snare, and a GPS navigational receiver which can fix your position to within 100ft. I took out the GPS; I needed to be sure where I was before I could do much good on the radio. Within 15 minutes I had my latitude and longitude to three decimal places: a major triumph. I might be in the middle of no-man's-land, but at least I could tell people how to get there.

I was ready to broadcast again. 'Anyone. Basher Five-Two.' I'd rehearsed my brief message in my head. It *had* to be brief; any hostile party with the proper equipment could track me after 10 seconds of transmission.

'Anyone, Basher Five-Two.' Once again I got static as reply. My ordeal showed no signs of ending. No one knew where I was or even whether I'd survived.

For all that, I felt calm, even content. I wasn't quite the same person who'd taken off from base 12 hours before. I'd been through the crucible, through terror and the smell of death, and come through in one piece. There would be scares ahead, no doubt, but somehow I sensed that I'd never be afraid in that same, stark way again – not in Bosnia, not anywhere.

I knew, also, that I'd never again feel so alone. I'd had a revelation that afternoon. While I'd found peace with God long before, my belief had never been put to so hard a test. Those rifle shots had tempered my faith, like strokes from a blacksmith's hammer; those trembling hours in the woods had cemented it. I'd learned that I could turn to God at the very worst times and that He would never desert me.

Time was on my side as long as it stayed dark, and I used it to scout for somewhere to hole-up. From the clearing I walked into the forest, wincing at the noise of my footsteps. Some trees slightly thicker than the rest offered concealment if I got in tight against them. I pulled the tarpaulin over me with the green side showing and the netting on top of that. It was all too small; my feet stuck out at the end. I tried more radio calls – no go. I broke out a flexipack of water, my first liquid in 17 hours. Should I have one more? No, I'd wait.

It wasn't till dawn broke that I saw how the night had tricked me. In the light of day I realised I had little cover from the trees after all. I needed a new hole-up, and fast. Collecting my gear, I headed to where the undergrowth was denser and dug in at the edge of a clearing. I broke a branch off a tree and placed it over me for extra camouflage.

When I finished, I lay with my head propped up so that I could just see out. Sleep was hopeless. My mind spun like a racing engine; it wouldn't shut off.

It was time to take a good look at my evasion chart, a topographical map of Bosnia, which was made out of a heavy-duty, waterproof material and could be used as a blanket, a bag or even a splint for a broken wrist. But it had two drawbacks: it was huge, about 5ft by 3ft, and it was about 50 times as loud to handle as a newspaper unfolding.

From it, I worked out that the big hill I'd targeted was two miles away – a healthy hike, given the likely pitfalls along the way. I had no lack of incentive to be careful. I'd heard the nightmare stories about American prisoners of war in Vietnam. Capture led to any number of things, most of them ugly. I would do anything I could to avoid it.

Later that morning I heard two male voices – in casual conversation. They grew more distinct, and then I knew they were headed towards my position. I turned my face toward the ground. My nose flat, my eyes clamped shut. I pressed my feet flush to the ground, curled my legs to my chest. The steps came nearer, the voices ever louder, until the men were 5ft from my head.

Hail Mary, full of grace. The Lord is with thee …

They didn't stop. I heard them trail away from me. I'd been expecting the hunt to continue but I was still at large. Still alive.

Later, I heard the whir of a helicopter flying low. One of ours? But that was wishful thinking; Nato couldn't know where to begin to look for me. As the chopper skimmed the trees I saw it was a Gazelle, the bad guys' brand. That meant the Bosnian Serbs had raised the ante. I was an important person in these parts. They were tracking me. I felt shaken by all this attention, by the forces out there pursuing me.

But I had to hold out, to stay free. I knew it would take time to be rescued. When your airplane is shot down, you naturally land on top of the shooters, which means there is a strong possibility that anybody coming in for you will be shot down as well. If all broke right, I might get picked up tomorrow. But I thought a week's wait was more likely, and I decided, then and there, to steel myself to evade for as much as 45 days if necessary.

SCOTT O'GRADY

TASKS

10 In your own words, summarise exactly what happened to Scott O'Grady from the moment when he took off, to the moment when he landed in the small empty clearing.

11 What were Scott O'Grady's feelings during the first few minutes after he hit the ground? Look at what he says; put yourself in his shoes; and write about your feelings.

12 At one point Scott O'Grady describes the contents of his rucksack and of his survival vest. It is quite clear that he regards some things as useful but others as totally useless. He is quite sarcastic, for instance, about the 121-page survival guide.

   a Look at the list of items and, taking each one, say whether you think it would be useful and briefly give your reason.

   b Imagine that you have to put a survival pack together. You can put 10 items in and no more.
      What would you put in the pack? List the items and give your reasons for your choice.

13 Write a character study of Captain Scott O'Grady.

In our modern world it sometimes seems that we are warned about the dangers of so many things that it is a miracle that any of us survive. Read the following two extracts from *The Environment and Health*, a book which briefly analyses some of the common risks to health.

The Air We Breathe

Because the air we breathe is invisible, it is difficult to think of it as a possible risk to health. Yet because of the tremendous amount of air which passes in and out of our lungs every day, even small amounts of air pollution can eventually cause health problems. The nostrils and trachea are very efficient at cleaning the air we breathe and filtering out particles of dust and soot but sometimes, pollutants damage the cleaning mechanism or are still present in large amounts when they reach the lungs.

Throughout the world, lung diseases like bronchitis can occur wherever factories and power stations discharge smoke into the atmosphere. If the smoke cannot easily blow away, as happens in some sheltered valleys, then air pollution builds up and the health risk is increased.

In Tokyo, where the problem of air pollution is particularly severe, many people wear smog masks to filter out the worst of its effects. However, these masks cannot remove the smallest particles and irritating gases which can damage health.

Although most people think of air pollution as being an industrial problem, many of us suffer from the effects of a form of natural pollution. In spring and summer, huge amounts of microscopic pollen grains are blown in the wind. When these are inhaled, they can cause hay fever.

The air we breathe contains many forms of contamination, mostly in the form of tiny particles of dust, soot and pollen, all of which can collect in the lungs and cause health problems. The lungs normally clean themselves of this material, when tiny, beating hairs called cilia pump a stream of sticky mucus up out of the lungs, carrying the trapped dirt with it. But some substances in smoke paralyse these beating cilia, so dirt and mucus accumulate, causing an irritating cough and sometimes leading to lung infection.

Smoke and Fumes

When fuels such as coal, oil and petrol burn, they produce a whole range of gases, together with solid materials such as soot and tar particles which are a threat to health. When coal fires were widely used in homes, these materials frequently produced thick, evil-smelling, smoky fogs called 'smogs' which killed many people. In a four-day smog in London in 1952, there were 4,000 more deaths than normal. In most places, the use of smoky fuel is now forbidden.

Los Angeles, on the west coast of America, is well known for its smogs. These are produced when chemicals from car exhausts react with light. The thick haze that results can last for several days, causing breathing problems especially among old people.

Car exhausts and power stations produce sulphur dioxide and nitrogen oxides, gases which irritate the lungs, causing coughing and watering eyes. In large amounts they can cause permanent lung damage. Another product of burning oil or petrol is carbon monoxide, which interferes with the body's proper use of oxygen.

Bronchitis is a lung disease which is closely related to the amount of pollution in the air we breathe. As the amount of smoke in the air is reduced, due to restrictions on burning smoky fuel, so the number of deaths from bronchitis falls.

TASK

14 You have read the information in the extracts and have decided that you want to persuade your friends and others that they should wear smog masks when cycling around town streets.
You decide that you are going to produce a leaflet which you will deliver to all the households in your area.
Prepare your leaflet using material from the extracts.
Remember that your leaflet needs to be

■ eye-catching;   ■ accurate;   ■ persuasive.

Pressure on people can be caused by many things. War puts people under pressure. Surviving can be difficult – often unlikely. *Journey's End* is a play set in World War I (1914–18). The action takes place in the British trenches in France.

In the extract which we have printed opposite some officers are discussing their next move.

Journey's End

OSBORNE: The colonel came here while you were asleep.

TROTTER: Oh?

OSBORNE: We've got to make a raid tomorrow afternoon.

TROTTER: Oh, Lord! What – all of us?

OSBORNE: Two officers and ten men.

TROTTER: Who's got to do it?

OSBORNE: Raleigh and I.

TROTTER: Raleigh!

OSBORNE: Yes.

TROTTER: But 'e's only just come!

OSBORNE: Apparently that's the reason.

TROTTER: And you're going too?

OSBORNE: Yes.

TROTTER: Let's 'ear all about it.

OSBORNE: I know nothing yet. Except that it's got to be done.

TROTTER: What a damn nuisance!

OSBORNE: It is, rather.

TROTTER: I reckon the Boche are all ready waiting for it. Did you 'ear about the raid just south of 'ere the other night?

OSBORNE: Nothing much.

TROTTER: The trench-mortars go and knock an 'ole in the Boche wire to let our fellers through – and in the night the Boche went out and tied bits o' red rag on each side of the 'ole!

OSBORNE: Yes. I heard about that.

TROTTER: And even then our fellers 'ad to make the raid. It was murder. Doesn't this tea taste of onions?

OSBORNE: It does a bit.

TROTTER: Pity Mason don't clean 'is pots better.
    MASON *brings some bread on a plate.*
    This tea tastes of onions.

MASON: I'm sorry, sir. Onions do 'ave such a way of cropping up again.

TROTTER: Yes, but we 'aven't 'ad onions for days!

MASON: I know, sir. That's what makes it so funny.

TROTTER: Well, you better do something about it.

MASON: I'll look into it, sir.
    He goes out.
OSBORNE *and* TROTTER *prepare themselves slices of bread and jam.*

TROTTER: Joking apart. It's damn ridiculous making a raid when the Boche are expecting it.

OSBORNE: We're not doing it for fun.

TROTTER: I know.

OSBORNE: You might avoid talking to Raleigh about it.

TROTTER: Why? How do you mean?

OSBORNE: There's no need to tell him it's murder—-

TROTTER: Oh, Lord! no. (*He pauses.*) I'm sorry 'e's got to go. 'E's a nice young feller—-
    OSBORNE *turns to his book. There is silence.*
    What are you reading?

OSBORNE (*wearily*): Oh, just a book.

TROTTER: What's the title?

OSBORNE (*showing him the cover*): Ever read it?

TROTTER (*leaning over and reading the cover*):
    Alice's Adventures in Wonderland – why, that's a kid's book!

OSBORNE: Yes.

TROTTER: You aren't *reading* it?

OSBORNE: Yes.

TROTTER: What – a *kid's* book?

OSBORNE: Haven't you read it?

TROTTER (*scornfully*): No!

OSBORNE: You ought to. (*Reads*):
    'How doth the little crocodile
    Improve his shining tail,
    And pour the waters of the Nile
    On every golden scale?

    'How cheerfully he seems to grin
    And neatly spread his claws,
    And welcomes little fishes in
    With gently smiling jaws!'

TROTTER (*after a moment's thought*): I don't see no point in that.

OSBORNE (*wearily*): Exactly. That's just the point.

TROTTER (*looking curiously at Osborne*): You *are* a funny chap!
    STANHOPE *returns.*

STANHOPE: The sergeant-major's getting volunteers.

OSBORNE: Good!

TROTTER: Sorry to 'ear about the raid, skipper.

STANHOPE (*shortly*): So am I. What do you make the time?

TROTTER: Just on four.
    MASON *brings in more tea.*

STANHOPE (*taking the mug of tea*): Was Hibbert asleep when you came out of there?

TROTTER: No. 'E was just lying on 'is bed, smoking.

STANHOPE (*going to the sleeping dug-out*): Hibbert!

HIBBERT (*coming out*): I'm ready, Stanhope.

STANHOPE: Had some tea?

HIBBERT: Yes, thanks.

TROTTER: I reckon Raleigh'll be glad to be relieved. Rotten being on dooty for the first time alone.

OSBORNE: I don't think he minds.

STANHOPE: I shall be up there some time, Uncle.

OSBORNE: I say, why don't you have a rest? – you've been on the go all day.

STANHOPE: There's too much to do. This raid's going to upset the arrangements of the wiring party tonight. Can't have men out there while the toch-emmas are blowing holes in the Boche wire. (*He drinks up his tea.*) Ready, Hibbert? Come on, my lad.

STANHOPE *and* HIBBERT *leave the dug-out together.* TROTTER *looks after them curiously, and turns to* OSBORNE.

TROTTER: Can't understand that little feller, can you?

OSBORNE: Who?

TROTTER: Why, 'Ibbert. D'you see 'is eyes? All red. 'E told me in there 'e'd got 'ay-fever.

OSBORNE: Rotten thing, hay-fever.

TROTTER: If you ask me, 'e's been crying —-

OSBORNE *is writing at the table.*

OSBORNE: Maybe.

TROTTER: Funny little bloke, isn't 'e?

OSBORNE: Yes, I say – d'you mind? I just want to get a letter off.

TROTTER: Oh, sorry. They 'aven't collected the letters yet, then?

OSBORNE: Not yet.

TROTTER: I'll get one off to my old lady. (*He goes towards his dug-out.*) She's wrote and asked if I've got fleas.

OSBORNE: Have you?

TROTTER (*gently rotating his shoulders*): I wish it *was* fleas.

TROTTER *goes into his dug-out;* OSBORNE *continues his letter.*

RALEIGH *comes down the steps from the trench.*

RALEIGH (*excitedly*): I say, Stanhope's told me about the raid.

OSBORNE: Has he?

RALEIGH: Just you and me, isn't it – and ten men?

OSBORNE: Yes, tomorrow. Just before dusk. Under a smoke cloud.

RALEIGH: I say – it's most frightfully exciting!

OSBORNE: We shall know more about it after Stanhope sees the colonel tonight.

RALEIGH: Were you and I picked – specially?

OSBORNE: Yes.

RALEIGH: I say!

THE CURTAIN FALLS

R C SHERRIFF

TASKS

15 Discuss in groups the different attitudes to war that are to be found here.

16 What, according to the extract, are the chances of Osborne, Raleigh and the ten men of surviving the raid?

17 Imagine that Raleigh is going to speak to the ten men before the raid. Work out what you think he will say.

18 Now imagine that Raleigh is making the speech which you have just written for him. Write down what you think Osborne's thoughts might be while Raleigh is speaking.

You will find that we have reprinted this extract from 'Journey's End' in your homework book with an additional task, which will give you a chance to use your imagination.

TIME OUT TASK!

The argumentative essay

You are quite frequently asked to write what is called an argumentative essay. What this means is that the title of the essay is such that different views can be expressed on the topic.

Your aim should be to consider the title from all angles and to present a balanced argument.

A very typical essay title of this type is, 'Should the death penalty be reintroduced?' You may have a strongly held view on the subject. However, in your essay you should not just present your own point of view but should put forward the arguments on both sides before drawing a conclusion.

The theme of this chapter of your classbook is 'Survivors'.
Choose one of the following essay titles:

- Trade in live animals is cruel and should be banned.
- People should be able to choose whether or not to be kept alive by machine.
- The government should decide on a minimum wage on which a person can survive.

Divide your planning page into two columns and list arguments for and arguments against as part of your planning of the essay.

Decide which column contains the strongest arguments and plan your essay conclusion.

Finally, plan your introduction in which you will state what you will be doing in the essay.

You should then have a balanced essay plan.

END OF TIME OUT!

You don't necessarily need war or violence to demonstrate survival. The following poems are about people living in difficult and frustrating circumstances: 'surviving' rather than living and enjoying life.

Nervous Prostration

I married a man of the Croydon class
When I was twenty-two.
And I vex him, and he bores me
Till we don't know what to do!
It isn't good form in the Croydon class
To say you love your wife,
So I spend my days with the tradesmen's books
And pray for the end of life.

In green fields are blossoming trees
And a golden wealth of gorse,
And young birds sing for joy of worms:
It's perfectly clear, of course,
That it wouldn't be taste in the Croydon class
To sing over dinner or tea:
But I sometimes wish the gentleman
Would turn and talk to me!

But every man of the Croydon class
Lives in terror of joy and speech.
'Words are betrayers', 'Joys are brief' –
The maxims their wise ones teach –
And for all my labour of love and life
I shall be clothed and fed,
And they'll give me an orderly funeral
When I'm still enough to be dead.

I married a man of the Croydon class
When I was twenty-two.
And I vex him, and he bores me
Till we don't know what to do!
And as I sit in his ordered house,
I feel I must sob or shriek,
To force a man of the Croydon class
To live, or to love, or to speak!

ANNA WICKHAM

The Farmer's Bride

Three Summers since I chose a maid,
Too young maybe – but more's to do
At harvest-time than bide and woo.
When us was wed she turned afraid
Of love and me and all things human;
Like the shut of a winter's day.
Her smile went out, and 'twasn't a woman –
More like a little frightened fay.
One night, in the Fall, she runned away.

'Out 'mong the sheep, her be,' they said,
Should properly have been abed;
But sure enough she wasn't there
Lying awake with her wide brown stare.
So over seven-acre field and up-along across
    the down
We chased her, flying like a hare
Before our lanterns. To Church-Town
All in a shiver and a scare
We caught her, fetched her home at last
And turned the key upon her, fast.

She does the work about the house
As well as most, but like a mouse:
Happy enough to chat and play
With birds and rabbits and such as they,
So long as men-folk keep away

'Not near, not near!' her eyes beseech
When one of us comes within reach.
The woman say that beasts in stall
Look round like children at her call
I've hardly heard her speak at all.

Shy as a leveret, swift as he,
Straight and slight as a young larch tree,
Sweet as the first wild violets, she,
To her wild self. But what to me?

The short days shorten and the oaks are brown,
The blue smoke rises to the low grey sky,
One leaf in the still air falls slowly down,
A magpie's spotted feathers lie
On the black earth spread white with rime,
The berries redden up to Christmas-time.
What's Christmas time without there be
Some other in the house than we!

She sleeps up in the attic there
Alone, poor maid. 'Tis but a stair
Betwixt us. Oh! my God! the down,
The soft young down of her, the brown,
The brown of her – her eyes, her hair, her hair!

CHARLOTTE MEW

TASKS

19 These are very personal poems. In a short piece of writing put each of the speaker's feelings into your own words.

20 Compare your version with the original poems. What advantages do the poems have in conveying ideas vividly?

A sixteen-year-old GCSE student has written about these two poems. Read what she has written, noting the advice given by her teacher.

(i)

Nervous Prostration

"Nervous Prostation" by Anna Wickham is about a woman who married a man of the "croydon class". Anna Wickham in this poem may be writing of her own experiences. This "croydon class" seems to be an upper class group of businessmen. The poem describes how this woman who married at twenty two is bored ✓ and seems to be frustrated ✓ with the way she is supposed to act. It seems the men of the croydon class don't or are not supposed to show love or affection to their wives. Her husband doesn't seem to acknowledge her. ✓ She seems to be very unhappy ✓ with her life married to this cold man. ✓ She seems to regret ✓ her marriage to him at the young age of twenty two. She talks about the birds being able to sing for joy of worms but she would never be able to sing over dinner or tea. I think Anna would like to shout out at the top of her voice "Look I am here please notice me". I like this poem as it has rhythm and some of the poem rhymes. I feel this poem has a lot of power. ✓ I can feel ✓ that she is angry. I also think she feels that because her husband is feeding and clothing her, he thinks that it is enough and that he doesn't have to pay attention to her.

Opportunity to show contrast in the poem

Consider: mood, language of poem. Three well organised paragraphs better than rather rushed one long para.

The Farmer's Bride

This poem is by Charlotte Mew and I thought was very sad. It is about a woman who married a farmer and after the marriage the wife totally shut out her husband as well as other men. Charlotte Mew describes it "like the shut of a winter's day". This poem also has rhyme and rhythm and I think the writer gets the message through about the husband being stunned by her turning against him. Charlotte Mew compared her to a fairy, she says "twasn't a woman - more like a frightened fay". This comes across as if the woman is really a girl who is innocent who married too young. I think an experience since her marriage has turned her against men we don't know what this experience is. Maybe the girl is feeling left out because the farmer leaves her out when he is working.

It says in the poem:

"Too young maybe but more's to do at harvest time than bide and woo".

This sounds as if he can't mess about getting married because at harvest time there is lots to do. It also says that she ran away but they "chased" after her and "fetched her home at last and turned the key upon her fast". It seems they have to lock her in to stop her going, so there must be something really wrong for this girl to want to run away all the time.

③

She seems to get on with women well and children and she is

"Happy enough to chat and play
With birds and rabbits and such as they"

This implies that it is just men with whom she feels ill-at-ease. The writer compares her to a mouse so we then get the picture of her being timid and small. I think her husband is very confused, he thinks she is so beautiful and he talks of her brown eyes and her hair and he is probably frustrated that he just can't go near her. He also talks of Christmas time saying what is Christmas time if it is just going to mean both of them being alone.

I think this poem is well written because it is by a female writer who places herself into a mans point of view and I feel she does this well and gets the message through of how the male feels in this situation. I felt sad at the end of reading this poem especially for the male when he says "the berries redden up to christmas time" it seems as if he is saying everyone is getting ready for christmas and he has this annoying, frustrated upsetting problem. I think that they should talk about this problem that exists in their new marriage.

Good point to pick up

Good point

Mood of poem too

TASK

21 Now that you have studied the poems and have read one student's essay, write a commentary on the essay. Consider the student's ideas and the teacher's comments and in each case say what you think are their strengths and weaknesses.

Before tackling this task draw up a list of things you would expect to be commented on in an essay about these poems.

Romeo and Juliet, Shakespeare's famous young lovers, failed to survive but they have inspired many people struggling with the problems of being in love. In Shakespeare's play Romeo and Juliet live in Verona in Italy. The following article tells how a letter written in 1937 started the 'Juliet Club'.

★ Star-Crossed Lovers ★

Every year over 3,000 heartbroken men and women from around the world write to Juliet in Verona, seeking comfort and advice.

Crammed into a tiny office in the heart of Verona, 60-year-old Giulio Tamassia struggles through his daily paperwork and, together with his 29-year-old daughter Giovanna and a team of helpers, begins to compose the first letter of the day. Whether he is responding to tales of heartbreak or infidelity, comforting star-crossed lovers or congratulating those for whom the course of true love is running smoothly, as President of the Juliet Club, Tamassia plays confessor, friend or confidant to more than 3,000 people a year.

It all began in 1937 when a lovesick Englishman addressed a letter to 'Juliet, Verona'. The letter has since been lost, but its contents prompted a kind-hearted Signor Solimani, guardian of Juliet's tomb, to write back as if he were the dead girl's secretary. So began a tradition of writing to Juliet that is now used by lovers from all over the world, particularly America, Italy, France, Turkey, China and Russia. The Germans and British rarely write.

The club has been passed down through various like-minded romantics, with former confectionery manager Giulio Tamassia taking on the job of secretary six years ago. Partly funded by the council (whose staff answered the letters until they found they hadn't enough time to soothe international heartache) and partly by Tamassia himself, the club answers every letter personally. Tamassia searches high and low for

helpers; he once persuaded a Turkish airforce officer at a nearby NATO base to provide translations. 'Letters from Turks are often straightforward,' he explains. 'They complain that they can't get a bus to the next village to see their boyfriend or girlfriend – that sort of thing. The French always seem to have the most complex problems. Many women in their mid-to-late twenties write to Juliet about their complicated private lives, with both a husband and a lover, or even two lovers. They are difficult letters to reply to. Like the Frenchwoman who wrote saying, 'I am married to a charming man who showers me with gifts and looks after me wonderfully. But my problem is that I just don't love him and, in fact, I've never loved him.' She went on to explain how much she loves her young daughter, who she doesn't want to lose, and she pleaded, 'Juliet, please tell me what to do. Should I choose the stability of being with my husband and daughter, or the adventure of being with my beloved?'

Juliet's secretary offered this reply: 'Your problem is very serious and I really don't know how I should advise you. I can hardly believe that your husband has never known the truth. Why have you never told him that you do not love him? Has he never guessed a thing? Are you sure this is your great love, your real love? Or is it just a passion, an entirely physical love?' The letter continues: 'If you are sure this is real love and that you want to spend the rest of your life with this man, I think you must tell your husband and explain your decision. You will have to reach some agreement so that you can share your little girl.'

One wonders whether this was news to the Frenchwoman, who may or may not have been heartened by the conclusion: 'Love is very important, it is necessary for life, but in your case you need a lot of courage. I hope you make the right decision and I wish you a happy future.'

Are the moral judgements as broad as the advice? Well, they were fairly stern with 60-year-old Franco, a widower who had fallen in love with a nun, only to be told by her that she would never give up her vows. 'Our reply was that he must learn to accept her decision and that if he is strong, there is no reason why they should not maintain their friendship,' says Giovanna.

'Sometimes we have to tell people that what they are doing is wrong. It's nice to say "Everything's fine, carry on, you're right", but sometimes we have to say "You're wrong". Basically we do the job for the pleasure it brings, but we have no doubt that we help people because quite a few write back and thank us, saying they were desperate when they wrote and that we offered some relief.'

Tamassia's daughter Giovanna is a language graduate. She used to help out part time but has been writing letters full time for the past six months. 'To read, translate and reply to all these letters requires a lot of time and commitment,' she says. 'I decided to help my father because so many letters – thousands – were arriving for Juliet and the club really needed a hand.

'At first it was hard to work out how to reply as Juliet. Now when I read a letter and write a reply, I obviously say what I think myself, but I also try to imagine what Juliet would say because people are really writing to her. They know she doesn't exist, but they see her as the symbol of true love.'

There are no solutions to some of the problems posed by women across the world. From Beirut a young Lebanese woman complained (in faultless Italian): 'I'm at the end of my tether. I am a 27-year-old upper middle-class Lebanese woman who cannot seem to meet her Romeo. The problem is that, with the wars and the economic problems, all the ambitious men have left for America or Europe. I am not the only Juliet who is waiting – there are twelve women for every man in the Lebanon.'

Some of the most-heart rending letters come from teenagers, especially in America. 'I'm fourteen and pregnant,' wrote one girl. 'My boyfriend lives thousands of miles away … When I found out I was pregnant, I wrote and told him this. When he wrote back he informed me he was infected with the HIV virus. The worst part is, we're keeping this a secret … My mom doesn't like him at all, and if I tell her she might kick me out. I'm really scared. Please help me, I don't know what to do.' Juliet's secretary wrote back immediately and told the girl she must tell her parents everything, straight away.

People write describing their feelings of despair and thoughts of suicide – a psychologist friend helps with those. The only guarantees the club can give are that they will always respond, even if someone strikes up a regular correspondence. 'We always reply if people write, however often, even if it's just a postcard,' says Tamassia. 'It would be nasty to stop writing suddenly. We get letters from lots of prisoners, and they write to us over and over again – we are probably the only ones who write to these people.'

Tamassia and his daughter have no regrets at taking on the club and plan to expand Juliet's role in Verona. 'We'd really like to be able to do something to restore her house; apart from the balcony, there's little to see of it at the moment,' he says. But for the time being it is time to reply to the 43-year-old married woman from Florence who is obsessed with a brief failed affair with a younger man; the young girl from Rome who sees her boyfriend only at weekends and is desperate for the day 'when we can open our eyes and see each other there'; and the 22-year-old girl from France who wonders if it is normal to find her boyfriend desperately boring and wants to know what true love actually feels like. She thought Juliet must know the answer.

SARAH CUNNINGHAM

TASKS

22 Jot down your ideas about the following things and then hold a class discussion:
  ■ do you think it is a good idea to take the letters seriously and reply to them?
  ■ judging from the article, are the writers serious?
  ■ why do you think people write to this club and to other magazines?

23 Bring into school some examples of letters which you have found in
'agony columns'. You may well find examples in your own magazines or
those of your mother; you may find examples in tabloid newspapers.
Discuss the letters in small groups and then, as a group, present your
opinions to the class.

24 In your group write some letters as if to an 'agony column' and
exchange them with another group. Then write replies to the letters
you have received. Remember that people who write these letters are
hoping to receive serious answers which will help them to 'survive'.

In Jane Austen's novel *Pride and Prejudice* Elizabeth Bennet
is the second oldest of five daughters. She has many difficulties,
struggles and disappointments to overcome in the course of the
story. Towards the end of the novel, however, it seems likely that
she will win through to be married to Mr Darcy. Not, however, if
Lady Catherine de Bourgh (Darcy's aunt) has her way!

Pride and Prejudice

'Let me be rightly understood. This match, to which you have the presumption to aspire, can never take place. No, never. Mr. Darcy is engaged to *my daughter*. Now what have you to say?'

'Only this; that if he is so, you can have no reason to suppose he will make an offer to me.'

Lady Catherine hesitated for a moment, and then replied, 'The engagement between them is of a peculiar kind. From their infancy, they have been intended for each other. It was the favourite wish of *his* mother, as well as of hers. While in their cradles, we planned the union: and now, at the moment when the wishes of both sisters would be accomplished, in their marriage, to be prevented by a young woman of inferior birth, of no importance in the world, and wholly unallied to the family! Do you pay no regard to the wishes of his friends? To his tacit engagement with Miss de Bourgh? Are you lost to every feeling of propriety and delicacy? Have you not heard me say, that from his earliest hours he was destined for his cousin?'

'Yes, and I had heard it before. But what is that to me? If there is no other objection to my marrying your nephew, I shall certainly not be kept from it, by knowing that his mother and aunt wished him to marry Miss de Bourgh. You both did as much as you could, in planning the marriage. Its completion depended on others. If Mr. Darcy is neither by honour nor inclination confined to his cousin, why is not he to make another choice? And if I am that choice, why may not I accept him?'

'Because honour, decorum, prudence, nay, interest, forbid it. Yes, Miss Bennet, interest; for do not expect to be noticed by his family or friends, if you wilfully act against the inclinations of all. You will be censured, slighted, and despised, by every one connected with him. Your alliance will be a disgrace; your name will never even be mentioned by any of us.'

'These are heavy misfortunes,' replied Elizabeth. 'But the wife of Mr. Darcy must have such extraordinary sources of happiness necessarily attached to her situation, that she could, upon the whole, have no cause to repine.'

'Obstinate, headstrong girl! I am ashamed of you! Is this your gratitude for my attentions to you last spring? Is nothing due to me on that score?

'Let us sit down. You are to understand, Miss Bennet, that I came here with the determined resolution of carrying my purpose; nor will I be dissuaded from it. I have not been used to submit to any person's whims. I have not been in the habit of brooking disappointment.'

'*That* will make your ladyship's situation at present more pitiable; but it will have no effect on *me*.'

'I will not be interrupted. Hear me in silence. My daughter and my nephew are formed for each other. They are descended on the maternal side, from the same noble line; and, on the father's, from respectable, honourable, and ancient, though untitled families. Their fortune on both sides is splendid. They are destined for each other by the voice of every member of their respective houses; and what is to divide them? The upstart pretensions of a young woman without family, connections, or fortune. Is this to be endured!

But it must not, shall not be. If you were sensible of your own good, you would not wish to quit the sphere, in which you have been brought up.'

'In marrying your nephew, I should not consider myself as quitting that sphere. He is a gentleman; I am a gentleman's daughter; so far we are equal.'

'True. You *are* a gentleman's daughter. But who was your mother? Who are your uncles and aunts? Do not imagine me ignorant of their condition.'

'Whatever my connections may be' said Elizabeth, 'if your nephew does not object to them, they can be nothing to you.'

'Tell me once for all, are you engaged to him?'

Though Elizabeth would not, for the mere purpose of obliging Lady Catherine, have answered this question; she could not but say, after a moment's deliberation,

'I am not.'

Lady Catherine seemed pleased.

'And will you promise me, never to enter into such an engagement?'

'I will make no promise of the kind.'

'Miss Bennet I am shocked and astonished. I expected to find a more reasonable young woman. But do not deceive yourself into a belief that I will ever recede. I shall not go away, till you have given me the assurance I require.'

'And I certainly *never* shall give it. I am not to be intimidated into anything so wholly unreasonable. Your ladyship wants Mr. Darcy to marry your daughter; but would my giving you the wished-for promise, make *their* marriage at all more probable? Supposing him to be attached to me, would *my* refusing to accept his hand, make him wish to bestow it on his cousin? Allow me to say, Lady Catherine, that the arguments with which you have supported this extraordinary application, have been as frivolous as the application was ill-judged. You have widely mistaken my character, if you think I can be worked on by such persuasions as these. How far your nephew might approve of your interference in *his* affairs, I cannot tell; but you have certainly no right to concern yourself in mine. I must beg, therefore, to be importuned no farther on the subject.'

'Not so hasty, if you please. I have by no means done. To all the objections I have already urged, I have still another to add. I am no stranger to the particulars of your youngest sister's infamous elopement. I know it all; that the young man's marrying her, was a patched-up business, at the expense of your father and uncles. And is *such* a girl to be my nephew's sister? Is *her* husband, is the son of his late father's steward, to be his brother? Heaven and earth! – of what are you thinking? Are the shades of Pemberley to be thus polluted?'

'You can *now* have nothing farther to say,' she resentfully answered. 'You have insulted me, in every possible method. I must beg to return to the house.'

And she rose as she spoke. Lady Catherine rose also, and they turned back. Her ladyship was highly incensed.

'You have no regard, then, for the honour and credit of my nephew! Unfeeling, selfish girl! Do you not consider that a connection with you, must disgrace him in the eyes of everybody?'

'Lady Catherine, I have nothing farther to say. You know my sentiments.'

JANE AUSTEN

TASKS

25 This interview is very tense but very polite. Discuss how Lady Catherine puts Elizabeth under pressure. The following points will help you to form your answer:
  ■ Lady Catherine's reasons for opposing the marriage;
  ■ the ways in which Jane Austen makes Lady Catherine look and sound ridiculous here;
  ■ the ways in which we are made to admire Elizabeth.

26 Write your own interview between two people in which you include the following ideas:
  ■ one of your characters disapproves of something the other has done;
  ■ each is trying to be controlled and confident;
  ■ they are both very determined.

We have reprinted this extract in your homework book and have set another task for you to do by yourself.

TIME OUT TASK!

Think about adverbs

We have already suggested that you should develop your vocabulary by thinking about adjectives and verbs. Now we are going to look at adverbs.

An adverb is a word which adds to the meaning of a verb in the same way as an adjective adds to the meaning of the noun.

You can recognise the majority of adverbs because they end with the letters 'ly'. You will immediately think of some which don't – words like 'fast' – but there are always exceptions to rules.

When you are reading something, pick out some sentences which contain adverbs and write them down. In each case underline the adverb. Now write out the sentence several more times using different adverbs and see how you can change either the meaning or the emphasis of the sentence.

In your next piece of writing accompany as many as possible of the verbs you use with an adverb which improves or clarifies the verb.

END OF TIME OUT!

In this chapter the Shakespeare play we are looking at is *The Taming of the Shrew*. Baptista is the father of two daughters, Kate and Bianca. Everyone would say that Bianca is a charming girl but Kate is not so. She is so sharp-tongued and difficult that no one can get on with her.

Baptista wants Kate to marry, but who will take her on? The man who is prepared to have a go is Petruchio – but he finds that it is a terrific struggle. They are both determined to get the upper hand. Here is what happens on their wedding day. Read the extract carefully in class or in a group and discuss it to make sure that you understand what is happening.

The Taming of the Shrew

Act 3 Scene 2

TRANIO:
   Signior Gremio, came you from the church?
GREMIO:
   As willingly as e'er I came from school.
TRANIO:
   And is the bride and bridegroom coming home?
GREMIO:
   A bridegroom say you? 'Tis a groom indeed,
   A grumbling groom, and that the girl shall find.

TRANIO:
   Curster than she? Why, 'tis impossible.
GREMIO:
   Why, he's a devil, a devil, a very fiend.
TRANIO:
   Why, she's a devil, a devil, the devil's dam.
GREMIO:
   Tut, she's a lamb, a dove, a fool to him.
   I'll tell you, Sir Lucentio, when the priest
   Should ask, if Katherine should be his wife,
   'Ay, by goggs woones!' quote he and swore so loud

That, all amazed, the priest let fall the book.
And as he stopped again to take it up,
This mad-brained bridegroom took him such a cuff
That down fell priest and book and book and priest.
'Now, take them up,' quoth he, 'if any list.'

TRANIO:
What said the wench when he rose again?

GREMIO:
Trembled and shook, for why he stamped and swore
As if the vicar meant to cozen him.
But after many ceremonies done
He calls for wine. 'A health!' quoth he as if
He had been aboard, carousing to his mates
After a storm; quaffed off the muscadel
And threw the sops all in the sexton's face,
Having no other reason
But that his beard grew thin and hungerly,
And seemed to ask him sops as he was drinking.
This done, he took the bride about the neck
And kissed her lips with such a clamorous smack
That at the parting all the church did echo,
And I, seeing this, came thence for very shame.
And after me, I know, the rout is coming.
Such a mad marriage never was before.
Hark, hark, I hear the minstrels play. *Music plays.*
Enter Petruchio, Kate, Bianca, Hortensio (as
Litio), Baptista (with Grumio and others).

PETRUCHIO:
Gentlemen and friends, I thank you for your
pains.
I know you think to dine with me today
And have prepared great store of wedding cheer,
But so it is, my haste doth call me hence
And therefore here I mean to take my leave.

BAPTISTA:
Is't possible you will away tonight?

PETRUCHIO:
I must away today, before night come.
Make it no wonder; if you knew my business,
You would entreat me rather go than stay.
And honest company, I thank you all
That have beheld me give away myself
To this most patient, sweet, and virtuous wife.
Dine with my father, drink a health to me,
For I must hence, and farewell to you all.

TRANIO:
Let us entreat you stay till after dinner.

PETRUCHIO:
It may not be.

GREMIO:
Let me entreat you.

PETRUCHIO:
It cannot be.

KATE:
Let me entreat you.

PETRUCHIO:
I am content.

KATE:
Are you content to stay?

PETRUCHIO:
I am content you shall entreat me stay,
But yet not stay, entreat me how you can.

KATE:
Now if you love me, stay.

PETRUCHIO:
Grumio, my horse!

GREMIO:
Ay, sir, they be ready; the oats have eaten the horses.

KATE:
Nay then,
Do what thou canst, I will not go today,
No, nor tomorrow, not till I please myself.
The door is open, sir, there lies your way.
You may be jogging whiles your boots are green;
For me, I'll not be gone till I please myself.
'Tis like you'll prove a jolly surly groom,
That take it on you at the first so roundly.

PETRUCHIO:
O Kate, content thee; prithee, be not angry.

KATE:
I will be angry. What hast thou to do?
Father, be quiet; he shall stay my leisure.

GREMIO:
Ay, marry, sir, now it begins to work.

KATE:
Gentlemen, forward to the bridal dinner.
I see a woman may be made a fool
If she had not a spirit to resist.

PETRUCHIO:
They shall go forward, Kate, at thy command.
Obey the bride, you that attend on her.
Go to the feast, revel and domineer,
Carouse full measure to her maidenhead,
Be mad and merry, or go hang yourselves.
But for my bonny Kate, she must with me.
Nay, look not big, nor stamp, nor stare, nor fret;
I will be master of what is mine own.
She is my goods, my chattels; she is my house,
My household stuff, my field, my barn,
My horse, my ox, my ass, my anything,
And here she stands. Touch her whoever dare,
I'll bring mine action on the proudest he
That stops my way in Padua. Grumio,
Draw forth thy weapon, we are beset with thieves.
Rescue thy mistress, if thou be a man.
Fear not, sweet wench; they shall not touch
thee, Kate.
I'll buckler thee against a million.
Exeunt Petruchio, Kate (and Grumio).

WILLIAM SHAKESPEARE

TASKS

27 Write about Petruchio's treatment of Kate here. What is he trying to do? Do you think he will succeed?

28 Write briefly explaining what you find amusing about this scene.

29 Describe Kate's reactions to what is happening.

At the end of the play Kate makes a speech acknowledging her husband's authority over her. Again, read the speech carefully and discuss it in class or in a group to make sure that you understand it.

The Taming of the Shrew

Act 5 Scene 2
KATE:

Fie, fie, unknit that threatening unkind brow
And dart not scornful glances from those eyes
To wound thy lord, thy king, thy governor.
It blots thy beauty as frosts do bite the meads,
Confounds thy fame as whirlwinds shake fair buds,
And in no sense is meet or amiable.
A woman moved is like a fountain troubled,
Muddy, ill-seeming, thick, bereft of beauty,
And while it is so, none so dry or thirsty
Will deign to sip or touch one drop of it.
Thy husband is thy lord, thy life, thy keeper
Thy head, thy sovereign – one that cares for thee,
And for thy maintenance commits his body
To painful labour both by sea and land,
To watch the night in storms, the day in cold,
Whilst thou li'st warm at home, secure and safe;
And craves no other tribute at thy hands
But love, fair looks, and true obedience:
Too little payment for so great a debt.
Such duty as the subject owes the prince,
Even such a woman oweth to her husband,
And when she is froward, peevish, sullen, sour,
And not obedient to his honest will,
What is she but a foul contending rebel
And graceless traitor to her loving lord?
I am ashamed that women are so simple
To offer war where they should kneel for peace,
Or seek for rule, supremacy, and sway,
When they are bound to serve, love, and obey.
Why are our bodies soft and weak and smooth,
Unapt to toil and trouble in the world,
But that our soft conditions and our hearts
Should well agree with our external parts?
Come, come, you froward and unable worms,
My mind hath been as big as one of yours,
My heart as great, my reason haply more,
To bandy word for word and frown for frown.
But now I see our lances are but straws,
Our strength as weak, our weakness past compare,
That seeming to be most which we indeed least are.
Then vail your stomachs, for it is no boot,
And place your hands below your husband's foot,
In token of which duty, if he please,
My hand is ready, may it do him ease.

WILLIAM SHAKESPEARE

TASK

30 In small groups discuss the following subjects:
   ▪ modern audiences can find this play rather difficult. Judging from the extracts, why do you think this is the case?
   ▪ what are your views about marriage? Should women 'love, honour, and obey' their husbands?

We have reprinted the second extract from 'The Taming of the Shrew' in your homework book and have set a task to allow you to explore a similar idea for yourself.

On these two pages and page 96 there are five photographs of the desolate wastes of Alaska and of one of the men who fights to survive and make a living by trading in the region. He is behind his team of huskies.

Look at the five photographs and imagine yourself with your team of huskies in that desolation.

TASK

31   Use the photographs and your own imagination to write your own story entitled 'Survival'.

So far in this chapter we have concentrated on the survival of humans in a variety of situations, but we must also be concerned with the survival of wild creatures which are threatened with extinction. One such animal is the tiger. One of the main problems is that in the Far East various parts of the tiger's body are meant to have medicinal properties, making the tiger trade big business.

Read the article printed below.

Can the Tiger Survive?

The great beast materialises out of the dusk – a striped vision of might and mystery. Emerging from a thicket in southern India's Nagarahole National Park, the Bengal tigress is hungry and ready to hunt. To nourish her 23-stone body, she must kill a deer, a boar or some other large animal every week. Her massive shoulders and forelimbs can bring down a wild ox that may weigh more than half a ton, and her powerful jaws and dagger-like teeth make quick work of a kill.

But there will be no killing for now. After briefly padding along a park road, the tigress abruptly melts into the brush. Watching her disappear, Indian biologist Ullas Karanth of New York's Wildlife Conservation Society breaks into a knowing smile. 'When you see a tiger,' he muses, 'it is always like a dream.'

All too soon dreams may be the only place where tigers roam freely.

No more than 5,000 to 7,500 of the majestic carnivores remain on the entire planet – a 95 per cent decline in this century. Unless something dramatic is done soon, tigers will be seen only in zoos or circuses.

Officials only recently realised the scale of the slaughter of tigers. A sting operation by the Indian government and TRAFFIC, an organisation that monitors the wild-life trade, uncovered a vast poaching network centred in New Delhi. One raid alone, in August 1993, yielded 617 pounds of tiger bone (equivalent to 20 tigers) and eight pelts.

The operation also discovered more than a dozen families in squalid tenements, engaged in illicit wild-life trade. There tigers are skinned, their prized parts dried and packaged, their bones cleaned and bleached. The skins, which can bring as much as £9,500, travel west, often to the homes of wealthy Arabs, while the bones move east, sometimes on the backs of Tibetans across mountainous terrain to the Chinese border.

Indian conservationists watch with dismay as this new round of poaching unravels the work of decades. Sanjoy Debroy, a wildlife officer who directed a tiger reserve in Assam for more than 12 years, has heard that 30 to 40 of the park's estimated 90 tigers were killed in just four months.

'I thought I had done something to restore the tiger,' Debroy says, 'but now I watch my life's work go down the drain.'

The situation is even worse in eastern Russia's taiga. The Amur tiger that inhabits this 800-mile stretch of evergreen forest nearly disappeared during the 1930s, when Communist bigwigs would bag up to 10 cats in a single hunt. When the state decided to protect the tigers, their population recovered from roughly 30 to as many as 400 by the late 1980s – but then tiger prices surged just when the fall of the Soviet Union led to economic chaos, leaving local wildlife departments broke and officials susceptible to bribes.

The losses have been staggering. In the winter of 1992–93, some 90 tigers were killed in the taiga. Unless the Russian government controls hunting, the Amur tiger could face extinction within two or three years.

The crisis exposes the shortcomings of old-line conservation efforts. Says Samuel LaBudde of the Endangered Species Project in San Francisco: 'The failure to address market demand – which drives poaching – means that millions invested to save the tiger have amounted to little more than a subsidy for the Chinese traditional-medicine market.'

But Western publicity campaigns, which helped reduce the demand for ivory, may have less effect on the demand for tiger bone in China, Korea and Taiwan. And tiger-bone remedies are so ingrained in these cultures that their governments have been slow to control the trade. In fact, all three countries have long paid lip service to agreements protecting endangered species while continuing to do business as usual.

In September 1993 the Convention on International Trade in Endangered Species of Wild Fauna and Flora (CITES) warned China and Taiwan to stop their illicit trade in tiger and rhino parts, and in April 1994 the US announced limited trade sanctions against Taiwan for its failure to do so. But investigations by environmental groups suggest that potions made from endangered species are still readily available.

Even if international pressure eliminated poaching, the tiger would still be in trouble. Its habitat and food supply are shrinking as the territory claimed by humans expands. Says Geoffrey Ward, co-author of *Tiger-Wallahs*: 'Poaching is murder, but crowding is slow strangulation.'

For the majority of tigers, India is where the battle for survival will be won or lost. It is not the best place to make a stand, given the pressures of human population growth. Kamal Nath, the country's environment minister, says, 'The threat to the tiger has never been so real.' However, India has invested some £18 million in the 20 years of Project Tiger and still has a culture which respects nature.

Humans and tigers have coexisted for hundred of thousands of years. Until now the cat has been highly adaptable and resilient. But the tiger has finally run foul of man, who has proved the more resourceful killer.

'What will it say about the human race if we let the tiger become extinct?' asks Ashok Kumar, vice president of the Wildlife Protection Society of India. 'What can we save? Can we save ourselves?'

EUGENE LINDEN

TASKS

32 The Tiger Trust is a charity devoted to tiger conservation. You have decided that you want to help the cause and you have persuaded your Year Head to let you speak in an assembly to encourage support.
You have two aims: you want to persuade your fellow pupils that the issue is important; you want to persuade them to help you publicise the cause and to raise money.
Draft your speech.

33 At the beginning of this article the writer wants to create the impression that the tiger is a truly magnificent animal.
Re-read the first paragraph to see how he does this.
Now write a paragraph of your own about a wild animal of your own choice – try to create your own impression of that animal.

WORLDS APART

4

In this chapter we shall be concentrating on the experiences of different people in different, and sometimes strange, places. We shall also look at people who for one reason or another feel themselves to be worlds apart from others. One of the things you will be asked to do is spot differences and make comparisons.

As an approach to English literature, understanding different cultures and making comparisons are very important skills.

ENGLISH IN THE NATIONAL CURRICULUM:

Key Skills you will cover in this chapter

☑ You will have further opportunities in this chapter to analyse and become involved with writers' ideas, how characters are developed to behave in the ways they do and how writers choose to develop their plots. You will also be invited to make judgements of texts as a whole.

☑ You will be invited to look at how language is used and how different styles of writing produce different effects.

☑ You will be looking at extracts which are drawn from a whole range of different cultures.

☑ You will be asked to make comparisons between different texts and to draw conclusions.

As a starting point let us look at William Golding's novel *Lord of the Flies*. The novelist imagines that a group of boys is being evacuated to safety after an atomic explosion. The aeroplane in which they are travelling crashes: only the boys survive. They find themselves on an uninhabited island in the Pacific Ocean. The boys are aged from 6 or 7 to 12.

You will find below and overleaf two extracts, one from the beginning and one from towards the end of the novel.

Lord of the Flies

Here the beach was interrupted abruptly by the square motif of the landscape; a great platform of pink granite thrust up uncompromisingly through forest and terrace and sand and lagoon to make a raised jetty four feet high. The top of this was covered with a thin layer of soil and coarse grass and shaded with young palm trees. There was not enough soil for them to grow to any height and when they reached perhaps twenty feet they fell and dried, forming a criss-cross pattern of trunks, very convenient to sit on. The palms that still stood made a green roof, covered on the underside with a quivering tangle of reflections from the lagoon. Ralph hauled himself on to this platform, noted the coolness and shade, shut one eye, and decided that the shadows on his body were really green. He picked his way to the seaward edge of the platform and stood looking down into the water. It was clear to the bottom and bright with the efflorescence of tropical weed and coral. A school of tiny, glittering fish flicked hither and thither. Ralph spoke to himself, sounding the bass strings of delight.

'Whizzoh!'

Beyond the platform there was more enchantment. Some act of God – a typhoon perhaps, or the storm that had accompanied his own arrival – had banked sand inside the lagoon so that there was a long, deep pool in the beach with a high ledge of pink granite at the further end. Ralph had been deceived before now by the specious appearance of depth in a beach pool and he approached this one preparing to be disappointed. But the island ran true to form and the incredible pool, which clearly was only invaded by the sea at high tide, was so deep at one end as to be dark green. Ralph inspected the whole thirty yards carefully and then plunged in. The water was warmer than his blood and he might have been swimming in a huge bath.

Piggy appeared again, sat on the rocky ledge, and watched Ralph's green and white body enviously.

'You can't half swim.'

'Piggy.'

Piggy took off his shoes and socks, ranged them carefully on the ledge, and tested the water with one toe.

'It's hot!'

'What did you expect?'

'I didn't expect nothing. My auntie—'

'Sucks to your auntie!'

Ralph did a surface dive and swam under water with his eyes open; the sandy edge of the pool loomed up like a hillside. He turned over, holding his nose, and a golden light danced and shattered just over his face. Piggy was looking determined and began to take off his shorts. Presently he was palely and fatly naked. He tip-toed down the sandy side of the pool, and sat there up to his neck in water smiling proudly at Ralph.

'Aren't you going to swim?'

Piggy shook his head.

'I can't swim. I wasn't allowed. My asthma—'

'Sucks to your ass-mar!'

Piggy bore this with a sort of humble patience.

'You can't half swim well.'

Ralph paddled backwards down the slope, immersed his mouth and blew a jet of water into

the air. Then he lifted his chin and spoke.

'I could swim when I was five. Daddy taught me. He's a commander in the Navy. When he gets leave he'll come and rescue us. What's your father?'

Piggy flushed suddenly.

'My dad's dead,' he said quickly, 'and my mum—'

He took off his glasses and looked vainly for something with which to clean them.

'I used to live with my auntie. She kept a sweet-shop. I used to get ever so many sweets. As many as I liked. When'll your dad rescue us?'

'Soon as he can.'

Piggy rose dripping from the water and stood naked, cleaning his glasses with a sock. The only sound that reached them now through the heat of the morning was the long, grinding roar of the breakers on the reef.

'How does he know we're here?'

Ralph lolled in the water. Sleep enveloped him like the swathing mirages that were wresting with the brilliance of the lagoon.

'How does he know we're here?'

Because, thought Ralph, because, because. The roar from the reef became very distant.

'They'd tell him at the airport.'

Piggy shook his head, put on his flashing glasses and looked down at Ralph.

'Not them. Didn't you hear what the pilot said? About the atom bomb? They're all dead.'

Ralph pulled himself out of the water, stood facing Piggy, and considered this unusual problem.

Piggy persisted.

'This is an island, isn't it?'

'I climbed a rock,' said Ralph slowly, 'and I think this is an island.'

'They're all dead,' said Piggy, 'an' this is an island. Nobody don't know we're here. Your dad don't know, nobody don't know—'

His lips quivered and the spectacles were dimmed with mist.

'We may stay here till we die.'

With that word the heat seemed to increase till it became a threatening weight and the lagoon attacked them with a blinding effulgence.

'Get my clothes,' muttered Ralph. 'Along there.'

WILLIAM GOLDING

Lord of the Flies

Jack broke out of his gyration and stood facing Ralph. His words came in a shout.

'All right, all right!'

He looked at Piggy, at the hunters, at Ralph.

'I'm sorry. About the fire, I mean. There. I—'

He drew himself up.

'– I apologise.'

The buzz from the hunters was one of admiration at this handsome behaviour. Clearly they were of the opinion that Jack had done the right thing, had put himself in the right by his generous apology and Ralph, obscurely, in the wrong. They waited for an appropriately decent answer.

Yet Ralph's throat refused to pass one. He resented, as an addition to Jack's misbehaviour, this verbal trick. The fire was dead, the ship was gone. Could they not see? Anger instead of decency passed his throat.

'That was a dirty trick.'

They were silent on the mountain-top while the opaque look appeared in Jack's eyes and passed away.

Ralph's final word was an ungracious mutter.

'All right. Light the fire.'

With some positive action before them, a little of the tension died. Ralph said no more, did nothing, stood looking down at the ashes round his feet. Jack was loud and active. He gave orders, sang, whistled, threw remarks at the silent Ralph – remarks that did not need an answer, and therefore could not invite a snub; and still Ralph was silent. No one, not even Jack, would ask him to move and in the end they had to build the fire three yards away and in a place not really as convenient. So Ralph asserted his chieftainship and could not have chosen a better way if he had thought for days. Against this weapon, so indefinable and so effective, Jack was powerless and raged without knowing why. By the time the pile was built, they were on different sides of a high barrier.

When they had dealt with the fire another crisis arose. Jack had no means of lighting it. Then to his surprise, Ralph went to Piggy and took the glasses from him. Not even Ralph knew how a link between him and Jack had been snapped and fastened elsewhere.

'I'll bring 'em back.'

'I'll come too.'

Piggy stood behind him, islanded in a sea of meaningless colour, while Ralph knelt and focused the glossy spot. Instantly the fire was alight Piggy held out his hands and grabbed the glasses back.

Before these fantastically attractive flowers of violet and red and yellow, unkindness melted away. They became a circle of boys round a camp fire and even Piggy and Ralph were half-drawn in. Soon some of the boys were rushing down the slope for more wood while Jack hacked the pig. They tried holding the whole carcass on a stake over the fire, but the stake burnt more quickly than the pig roasted. In the end they skewered bits of meat on branches and held them in the flames: and even then almost as much boy was roasted as meat.

Ralph dribbled. He meant to refuse meat but his past diet of fruit and nuts, with an odd crab or fish, gave him too little resistance. He accepted a piece of half-raw meat and gnawed it like a wolf.

Piggy spoke, also dribbling.

'Aren't I having none?'

Jack had meant to leave him in doubt, as an assertion of power; but Piggy by advertising his omission made more cruelty necessary.

'You didn't hunt.'

'No more' did Ralph,' said Piggy wetly, 'nor Simon.' He amplified. 'There isn't more than a ha'porth of meat in a crab.'

Ralph stirred uneasily. Simon, sitting between the twins and Piggy, wiped his mouth and shoved his piece of meat over the rocks to Piggy, who grabbed it. The twins giggled and Simon lowered his face in shame.

Then Jack leapt to his feet, slashed off a great hunk of meat, and flung it down at Simon's feet.

'Eat! Damn you!'

He glared at Simon.

'Take it!'

He spun on his heel, centre of a bewildered circle of boys.

'I got you meat!'

Numberless and inexpressible frustrations combined to make his rage elemental and awe-inspiring.

'I painted my face – I stole up. Now you eat – all of you – and I—'

Slowly the silence on the mountain-top deepened till the click of the fire and the soft hiss of roasting meat could be heard clearly. Jack looked round for understanding but found only respect. Ralph stood among the ashes of the signal fire, his hands full of meat, saying nothing.

WILLIAM GOLDING

TASKS

1 Look at the first extract and describe what is happening. How are the boys behaving? What are they interested in?

2 Work in groups and put yourselves in the position of the boys in the novel. Discuss how you would feel about being stranded on a desert island, thousands of miles from home.

- What would be your priorities?
- What would you miss most?
- Would you want to be rescued?
- If you weren't rescued, what would you do?
- Do you think you would change as time went on?

3 Compare the two extracts. What signs are there to indicate changes in the boys?

You will find the first extract reprinted in your homework book with another task for you to do.

In another world entirely lived a real person, Anne Frank. For two years Anne and her family hid from the Nazis. The Franks were Jews. After Anne's capture and death the diary she had kept was published. It records her thoughts and feelings during the two years when she was in hiding.

The first extract describes how and where the Frank family hid in Amsterdam; the building can still be visited today.

The Diary of Anne Frank

Thursday, 9 July, 1942

Dear Kitty,

So we walked in the pouring rain, Daddy, Mummy, and I, each with a school satchel and shopping bag filled to the brim with all kinds of things thrown together anyhow.

We got sympathetic looks from people on their way to work. You could see by their faces how sorry they were they couldn't offer us a lift; the gaudy yellow star spoke for itself.

Only when we were on the road did Mummy and Daddy begin to tell me bits and pieces about the plan. For months as many of our goods and chattels and necessities of life as possible had been sent away and things were sufficiently ready or us to have gone into hiding of our own accord on 16th July. The plan had had to be speeded up ten days because of the call-up, so our quarters would not be so well organised, but we had to make the best of it. The hiding-place itself would be in the building where Daddy has his office. It will be hard for outsiders to understand, but I shall explain that later on. Daddy didn't have many people working for him: Mr Kraler, Koophuis, Miep, and Elli Vossen, a 23-year-old typist, who all knew of our arrival. Mr Vossen, Elli's father, and two boys worked in the warehouse; they had not been told.

I will describe the building. There is a large warehouse on the ground floor which is used as a store. The front door to the house is next to the warehouse door, and inside the front door is a second doorway which leads to a staircase (A). There is another door at the top of the

---

1ST FLOOR · **2ND FLOOR** · **3RD FLOOR**

stairs, with a frosted-glass window in it, which has 'Office' written in black letters across it. That is the large main office, very big, very light and very full. Elli, Miep, and Mr Koophuis work there in the daytime. A small dark room containing the safe, a wardrobe, and a large cupboard leads to a small, somewhat dark second office. Mr Kraler and Mr Van Daan used to sit here, now it is only Mr Kraler. One can reach Kraler's office from the passage, but only *via* a glass door which can be opened from the inside, but not easily from the outside.

From Kraler's office a long passage goes past the coal store, up four steps and leads to the show-room of the whole building: the private office. Dark, dignified furniture, linoleum and carpets on the floor, radio, smart lamp, everything first-class. Next door there is a roomy kitchen with a hot-water geyser and a gas stove. Next the W.C. That is the first floor.

A wooden staircase leads from the downstairs passage to the next floor (B). There is a small landing at the top. There is a door at each end of the landing, the left one leading to a store-room at the front of the house and to the attics. One of those really steep Dutch staircases runs from the side to the other door opening on to the street (C).

The right door leads to our 'Secret Annexe'. No one would ever guess that there would be so many rooms hidden behind that plain grey door. There's a little step in front of the door and then you are inside.

There is a steep staircase immediately opposite the entrance (E). On the left a tiny passage brings you into a room which has to become the Frank family's bed-sitting room, next door a smaller room, study and bedroom for the two young ladies of the family. On the right a little room without windows containing the washbasin and a small W.C. compartment, with another door leading to Margot's and my room. If you go up the next flight of stairs and open the door, you are simply amazed that there could be such a big light room in such an old house by the canal. There is a gas stove in the room (thanks to the fact that it was used as a laboratory) and a sink. This is now the kitchen for the Van Daan couple, besides being general living-room, dining-room, and scullery.

A tiny little corridor room will become Peter Van Daan's apartment. Then, just as on the lower landing, there is a large attic. So there you are, I've introduced you to the whole of our beautiful 'Secret Annexe.'

Yours, ANNE

ANNE FRANK

The second extract, two years later, was written shortly before the family was arrested.

The Diary of Anne Frank

Thursday, 15 June, 1944

Dear Kitty,

I wonder if it's because I haven't been able to poke my nose outdoors for so long that I've gone so crazy about everything to do with nature? I can perfectly well remember that there was a time when a deep blue sky, the song of the birds, moonlight and flowers would have never kept me spellbound. That's changed since I've been here.

At Whitsun, for instance, when it was so warm, I stayed awake on purpose until half-past eleven one evening in order to have a good look at the moon for once by myself. Alas, the sacrifice was all in vain, as the moon gave far too much light and I didn't dare risk opening a window. Another time, some months ago now, I happened to be upstairs one evening when the window was open. I didn't go downstairs until the window had to be shut. The dark, rainy evening, the gale, the scudding clouds held me entirely in their power; it was the first time in a year and a half that I'd seen the night face to face. After that evening my longing to see it again was greater than my fear of burglars, rats, and raids on the house. I went downstairs all by myself and looked outside through the windows in the kitchen and the private office. A lot of people are fond of nature, many sleep outdoors occasionally, and people in prisons and hospitals long for the day when they will be free to enjoy the beauties of nature, but few are so shut away and isolated from that which can be shared alike by rich and poor. It's not imagination on my part when I say that to look up at the sky, the clouds, the moon and the stars makes me calm and patient. It's a better medicine than either valerian or bromine; Mother Nature makes me humble and prepared to face every blow courageously.

Alas, it has had to be that I am only able – except on a few rare occasions – to look at nature through dirty net curtains hanging before very dusty windows. And it's no pleasure looking through these any longer, because nature is just one thing that really must be unadulterated.

Yours, ANNE

ANNE FRANK

TASKS

4   Imagine the situation and describe how you think it would feel to be in hiding in such cramped conditions for this length of time. (Make sure that you have studied the plan of their hiding place which consists of the two small sections top centre and top right of the plan. The hiding place is reached by moving a bookcase which you can see on the landing of the centre section.)

5   Using evidence from the passages, describe what Anne's feelings were at the time.

6   Anne's last entry is for 1 August 1944. On August 4 she and her family were arrested to be sent to Nazi concentration camps. Imagine that she was able to snatch a few moments to write a hurried diary entry for 4 August 1944. Write her diary entry for that day.

There have been many dreadful things in human history. In the twentieth century Naziism and Communism were responsible for unjust persecutions and hideous executions. Some writers have produced stories about the future designed to warn us about the present. George Orwell published a book in 1949 which he called *1984*.

Here is an extract which shows what this imaginary world was like.

1984

The Ministry of Truth – Minitrue, in Newspeak – was startlingly different from any other object in sight. It was an enormous pyramidal structure of glittering white concrete, soaring up, terrace after terrace, 300 metres into the air. From where Winston stood it was just possible to read, picked out on its white face in elegant lettering, the three slogans of the party:

WAR IS PEACE

FREEDOM IS SLAVERY

IGNORANCE IS STRENGTH

The Ministry of Truth contained, it was said, 3,000 rooms above ground level, and corresponding ramifications below. Scattered about London there were just three other buildings of similar appearance and size. So completely did they dwarf the surrounding architecture that from the roof of Victory Mansions you could see all four of them simultaneously. They were the homes of the four Ministries between which the entire apparatus of government was divided. The Ministry of Truth, which concerned itself with news, entertainment, education, and the fine arts. The Ministry of Peace, which concerned itself with war. The Ministry of Love, which maintained law and order. And the Ministry of Plenty, which was responsible for economic affairs. Their names, in Newspeak: Minitrue, Minipax, Miniluv, and Miniplenty.

The Ministry of Love was the really frightening one. There were no windows in it at all. Winston had never been inside the Ministry of Love, nor within half a kilometre of it. It was a place impossible to enter except on official business, and then only by penetrating through a maze of barbed-wire entanglements, steel doors, and hidden machine-gun nests. Even the streets leading up to its outer barriers were roamed by gorilla-faced guards in black uniforms, armed with jointed truncheons.

Winston turned round abruptly. He had set his features into the expression of quiet optimism which it was advisable to wear when facing the telescreen. He crossed the room into the tiny kitchen. By leaving the Ministry at the time of day he had sacrificed his lunch in the canteen, and he was aware that there was no food in the kitchen except a hunk of dark-coloured bread which had got to be saved for tomorrow's breakfast. He took down from the shelf a bottle of colourless liquid with a plain white label marked VICTORY GIN. It gave off a sickly, oily smell, as of Chinese rice-spirit. Winston poured out nearly a teacupful, nerved himself for a shock, and gulped it down like a dose of medicine.

Instantly his face turned scarlet and the water ran out of his eyes. The stuff was like nitric acid, and moreover, in swallowing it one had the sensation or being hit on the back of the head with a rubber club. The next moment, however, the burning in his belly died down and the world began to look more cheerful. He took a cigarette from a crumpled packet marked VICTORY CIGARETTES and incautiously held it upright, whereupon the tobacco fell out on to the floor. With the next he was more successful. He went back to the living-room and sat down at a small table that stood to the left of the telescreen. From the table drawer he took out a penholder, a bottle of ink, and a thick, quarto-sized blank book with a red back and a marbled cover.

For some reason the telescreen in the living-room was in an unusual position. Instead of being placed, as was normal, in the end wall, where it could command the whole room, it was in the longer wall, opposite the window. To one side of it there was a shallow alcove in which Winston was now sitting, and which, when the flats were built, had probably been intended to hold bookshelves. By sitting in the alcove, and keeping well back, Winston was able to remain outside the range of the telescreen, so far as sight went. He could be heard, of course, but so long as he stayed in his present position he could not be seen. It was partly the unusual geography of the room that had suggested to him the thing that he was now able to do.

But it had also been suggested by the book that he had just taken out of the drawer. It was a peculiarly beautiful book. Its smooth creamy paper, a little yellowed by age, was of a kind that had not been manufactured for at least 40 years past. He could guess, however, that the book was much older than that. He had seen it lying in the window of a frowsy little junk-shop in a slummy quarter of the town (just what quarter he did not now remember) and had been stricken immediately by an overwhelming desire to possess it. Party members were supposed not to go into ordinary shops ('dealing on the free market', it was called), but the rule was not strictly kept, because there were various things, such as shoelaces and razor blades, which it was impossible to get hold of in any other way. He had given a quick glance up and down the street and then had slipped inside and bought the book for two dollars fifty. At the time he was not conscious of wanting it for any particular purpose. He had carried it guiltily home in his brief-case. Even with nothing written in it, it was a compromising possession.

The thing that he was about to do was to open a diary. This was not illegal (nothing was illegal, since there were no longer any laws), but if detected it was reasonably certain that it would be punished by death, or at least by 25 years in a forced-labour camp. Winston fitted a nib into the penholder and sucked it to get the grease off. The pen was an archaic instrument, seldom used even for signatures, and he had procured one, furtively and with some difficulty, simply because of a feeling that the beautiful creamy paper deserved to be written on with a real nib instead of being scratched with an ink-pencil. Actually he was not used to writing by hand. Apart from very short notes, it was usual to dictate everything into the speak-write which was of course impossible for his present purpose. He dipped the pen into the ink and then faltered for just a second. A tremor had gone through his bowels. To mark the paper was the decisive act. In small clumsy letters he began to write.

GEORGE ORWELL

TASKS

7   Read through the passage carefully and answer the following questions quite briefly.

- Make a list of all the strange things there are in *1984*.
- What do you notice about the three slogans at the beginning of the extract?
- Look closely at the paragraph about the Ministry of Love. What are the ways in which it makes an impression on you?
- Judging from the extract, what sort of life was Winston leading?

8   Would you have liked to live in the world described in *1984*? Give your answer and explain your reasons for it.

You will find that the extract is reprinted in your homework book, together with a task which will allow you to write imaginatively in response to it.

TIME OUT TASK!

Think about Shakespeare

Everyone now studies Shakespeare, or at least some of his plays. We become accustomed to reading his plays in the classroom, watching them on video and, sometimes, going to the theatre.

Here are some points to consider which may help you to understand the plays you read a little better.

- Shakespeare wrote his plays for ordinary people.
- Shakespeare wrote his plays to help earn his living.
- His plays were designed to entertain and to make people think.
- He often used other people's stories but wrote them in his own way.
- People in the audience had all sorts of feelings as they watched the play – they were excited, frightened, angry, amused, upset, to mention only a few emotions.
- Shakespeare knew the best way for him to succeed was in his choice and arrangement of words.

Things to do

- Using the Shakespeare play you know best, work out the ways in which it holds an audience's attention.
- Check through and remind yourself – are there amusing moments in the play?
- What ideas does the play make you have?
- Are there some speeches you regard as very successful? Why are they so good?

Something which could help younger students

Prepare for a younger pupil some tips for reading and understanding Shakespeare, to take away the worry that some young pupils feel that Shakespeare is going to be impossibly difficult.

You might do a little research and explain something about how the plays would have worked on the Elizabethan stage. You might want to tell them that the stories of the plays are exciting and sometimes fun. You might want to try to convince them that you don't have to worry about the vocabulary and the poetry.

You could design a leaflet to convey the information.

END OF TIME OUT!

Printed below is an article entitled *A Face for David*. It is a remarkable story of a boy who was born in Peru and who had lost a large section of his face because he had been bitten by a sandfly and contracted a dreadful disease called leishmaniasis.

Not only had David started his life a world apart from the majority of us in geographical terms, but what had happened to him had set him so far apart from other people that, without help, he would have become just a grotesque beggar.

A Face for David

In Operating Room Four, at Providence Hospital in Southfield, near Detroit in the United States, Dr Ian Jackson stands with scalpel poised, intently studying the face of a 17-year-old boy. It's a face the grey-haired 57-year-old plastic surgeon from Glasgow knows far better than his own.

A curving incision across the upper lip begins the latest of more than 80 operations Jackson has performed on the boy since he was 2 years old. The normal banter of the five surgical team members fades as he takes tissue from the bottom lip to enlarge the boy's upper lip. There is breathtaking confidence in the precise strokes of his scalpel, no hint on that day in July 1992 that he is slicing into the face of his own son.

* * *

A pioneer in his field, Ian Jackson set up one of Britain's first craniofacial surgical teams at Canniesburn Hospital in Glasgow in 1959. He had often felt frustrated when he saw patients with severe facial deformities. 'They are just ordinary people trapped behind their disfigurement,' he told his wife Marjorie, 'yet society treats them as freaks.' Now he could offer them some hope.

In November 1976 Ian and Marjorie began a two-week charity mission at the Clinica San Felipe in Lima, Peru. From early morning to late at night, Jackson performed free of charge what seemed miracles to the people jamming the corridors. When Martine, a 20-year-old Swiss volunteer with a charity in Lima, saw Jackson interviewed on television, she thought he might help David.

David was a two-year-old she'd found sitting alone at the crowded Hospital del Nino. The centre of the little boy's face was missing. Apart from being cleaned and fed, he was virtually abandoned within the hospital by overworked staff who had no idea what to do about him.

The morning after the interview, Martine took David to the packed waiting room at San Felipe. Told the doctor was fully booked, she stubbornly sat down in a stairwell to wait.

It was late by the time Jackson finished his last operation and strolled through the clinic to examine more patients. Suddenly Martine stepped out in front of him. Jackson stopped in his tracks when he saw the boy she held by the hand. *I can't believe what I'm seeing*, he thought. The stick of the lollipop David was sucking protruded from near his eyes. 'Will you examine him, please?' Martine asked.

'Bring him tomorrow, and I'll take a look,' Jackson promised.

The next morning the toddler with a mop of jet-black hair gazed quietly at Jackson as he poked and prodded, evaluating each defect. Where David should have had a mouth, nose and upper jaw with teeth, there was only a gaping hole; he could actually bring his lower lip up to touch his forehead.

'All we know', Martine said, 'is that his name is David Lopez.' Later, the Jacksons learned that his father, a Campa Indian, had brought him to a Catholic mission in the jungle.

Never had Jackson seen such massive loss of bone and tissue. Much of the surgery needed just to give David a jaw – never mind a nose and mouth – had never been performed before. 'I can do nothing for him in Peru,' he told Martine; he was going home the next day. But in his heart, he dreaded the existence David was condemned to. *If he survives, he'll be a beggar. He'll be ridiculed as a monster*.

Ian said it would be easier to find help for David in Mexico or even in the US, but Martine was determined. Finally he told her that if she could get permission for David to leave the country and bring him to Glasgow, he would do what he could.

On the long flight home, Jackson and his wife

discussed the child's plight. If David ever came to Glasgow, Jackson had some of the surgical answers to help him, but the task would be enormous. And how would they pay for everything? He was sure other doctors would donate their services, but medical bills and lengthy stays in hospital would still run into tens of thousands of pounds.

Two months later on a February morning in 1977, as Marjorie got their four children ready for school and Ian prepared for a day of surgery, a startling telegram was delivered: *Arriving tomorrow. Love Martine*. She'd managed to wheedle airline passes that had to be used right away.

The Jacksons hadn't expected David until money was raised and a foster home found. Driving to the airport, Marjorie had no clear idea of what she would do once she got there, nor where David would stay.

At the terminal, she soon spotted Martine towing a pathetic little figure in scruffy boots and poncho. A bright knitted Peruvian Indian hat pulled down over his forehead left only his wide-eyed confusion and the awful hole in his face visible. As people stared and pointed, Marjorie scooped the child up in her arms. For now, David would stay with them.

When the children came home that day, Marjorie asked them to be quiet because David was asleep upstairs. As Susan 12, and Sarah, 10, sat quietly chatting in their room, they saw a pair of big brown eyes, filled with apprehension, peeping from the doorway. Slowly David's curiosity got the better of him, and he came in and silently took their hands. Delighted, the girls brought him downstairs to meet Linda, 15 and Andrew, 7.

The Jacksons' first meal with David was an event they will never forget. He not only gobbled up his own food, he grabbed scraps of chicken skin from the girls' plates and wolfed them down as they all looked on. They quickly realised he was half-starved. Ian was amazed by how well David managed to eat without a palate or upper jaw, pushing food around under his tongue until he could swallow it. To drink his milk, he simply tipped his head back and poured it down his throat.

At night he cried and cried if he was left alone. As she had done when her own children were ill or frightened, Marjorie sat stroking his head and singing to him until he fell asleep. Soon, however, he was picking up the household routine. Within a few days he was watching for the children to come home from school, running to greet them, eager to play. When Ian came home from work, David cuddled up in his lap.

Marjorie had tried to get funds from children's aid organisations, but none would help, so Ian wrote to Thomas Winning, the Roman Catholic archbishop of Glasgow. The cleric spread word of David's plight to priests and parishioners, and donations began to come in. Thanks to Edward Miller, director of education for western Scotland, teachers and pupils from the region also raised thousands of pounds.

Media stories about David began to appear, which would culminate in Desmond Wilcox's stunning series of six TV documentaries, broadcast between June 1983 and November 1994. Glaswegians opened their hearts and wallets. Within a month the 'David fund' had raised enough money for his treatment.

As the time drew near for the first operation, the Jacksons wondered if David was aware of how he looked. 'I can't put him through all this pain without him knowing why,' Ian told Marjorie. So one day she gently held David up to a mirror. He screamed.

By that time Martine had returned to Switzerland, and Mary Rodriguez, who had studied Spanish at the University of Glasgow, volunteered to interpret. The Jacksons now asked her to explain to David what Ian was going to do. 'Dr Jackson is going to try to make you a new nose,' Mary told him.

'A real nose?' he asked slowly. 'Like everyone else?'

'Yes, David.'

The boy rushed to Ian, hugged him hard, then danced and laughed. Mary tried to tell him he would be in hospital many times, but nothing could mar his happiness. His next question was 'Will it be a big nose?'

Early one morning that March, David was wheeled into the operating theatre at Canniesburn Hospital. Once the child was anaesthetised, Jackson released the tight scarring around the hole in his face, then cut a skin graft from his leg to suture into the raw area, minor procedures to gauge how well he would react to surgery. However, Jackson was dismayed to find bone and tissue loss worse than he'd imagined; so much so that he suspected some sort of disease as having been the cause.

The next day David lay listless. As the hours passed and the boy's temperature rose, Jackson was even more concerned. By the third day, even the small skin graft stitched to his upper face was not taking, and David was losing weight. *He's going to die*, the surgeon feared.

After six days David was no worse but no better, and Marjorie took him home; perhaps familiar surroundings would lift his spirits. David did begin to improve, but he was a long way from his old self. It was Easter, and the Jacksons went to the family cottage on Loch Long. To Marjorie and Ian's relief, soon David was happily throwing stones into the water with Andrew, as if the sickness had suddenly been lifted from him.

Several weeks later, with David healthy and strong, Jackson was eager to begin surgery in earnest. Using skin from David's forehead, he lengthened the middle of the boy's face. For the nose, he raised a length of flesh and hipbone, still attached at both ends, from David's groin and sewed the rolled edges together, creating a sausage-shaped pedicle. Over the next two months, Jackson delicately moved the pedicle, one end at a time, first to David's wrist, then to the top of his head. Once the rest of David's face was ready, Jackson shifted the pedicle into position.

* * *

At first, the nose looked like a lumpy potato, but gradually Jackson would trim and straighten it. David was delighted. His life became one operation after another, but he bore his pain stoically, drawing strength from his new family.

During this time, Marjorie never hid David, but when people stared at him she couldn't understand how they could be so insensitive. Once a woman walked up to the three-year-old in a supermarket and shouted, 'With a face as horrible as yours, you should stay inside till Halloween!' When he started nursery school, a few children were afraid of him, but as he scrambled up trees and played, they forgot about his deformity.

By now, with ribs taken for a jawbone and skin and tissue from the chest to form the bulk of his cheeks and upper lip, David's new face was slowly taking shape.

His most excruciating operation came when Jackson took part of his tongue to fashion a pink upper lip. For ten agonising days, the little boy's tongue was sewn to his upper face. But when the stitches were finally removed, he exclaimed happily, 'I can give real kisses now!'

In 1979, three years after David's arrival, Jackson accepted a position with the Mayo Clinic in Rochester, Minnesota, in the US. Since newly transplanted tissue was more susceptible to cold, David had to spend the next three winters with Mary Rodriguez, now living in southern Spain, but he came back to Minnesota for the summers and for surgery.

The summer when he was nine, David suffered a major setback. The upper jaw Jackson had built up over the years became infected during an attempt to prepare it for anchors for a permanent denture. David, who longed to have teeth there, would lose some bone, and progress would be put back at least two years.

As Marjorie phoned the bad news to Ian, operating in the British Virgin Islands, David asked her, 'Am I going to lose my nose?'

'No,' Marjorie replied.

'Then tell Dad it's OK. Don't tell him we were crying.'

For some time now, Marjorie and Ian had known they would legally adopt the boy who'd become part of their lives. Consent was needed from the child's natural parents, as well as a record of birth or baptism. In October 1982 Marjorie returned to Peru to search for David's parents.

With the help of Desmond Wilcox's team, she flew over the Andes in a small plane, landing near the Catholic mission at Puerto Ocopa. Father Teodorico Castillo, who ran the mission, knew of the family and offered his help as translator and guide. The padre took Marjorie down a small river in a motor-powered canoe in search of Santos Ramirez, David's father. Enquiring after the family as they went, they found them in four hours.

The family greeted Marjorie, and the father told David's story. When he was about three months old, he had been bitten by a sandfly. He soon became very ill, and his father took him to the mission seeking help. The Jacksons deduced that David's face had been eaten away by leishmaniasis, a ravaging disease carried by sandflies. When Marjorie showed the family recent pictures of David, they were astonished.

'Do they want him back?' Marjorie asked Father Castillo. Agonising moments ticked by before he turned back to her and said: 'They ask you to tell Ian how they admire his skill and are proud for David to be with him. They wish you joy.' A wave of relief swept over Marjorie as she thanked Ramirez.

On 14 November, 1984, only a day before a new Peruvian law would have barred the adoption, the magic piece of paper that made David officially one of the family was signed. The Jacksons gathered to celebrate the event. Tears of joy shone in David's eyes as he said to Marjorie, 'I'm safe now, Mum.'

* * *

It is 11.30am when Ian Jackson finishes the surgery on David's mouth at Providence Hospital, where he founded the Institute for Craniofacial and Reconstructive Surgery in 1989. As David stirs from his sedation, he asks his father, 'How did it go?'

'Looks very good,' Jackson says as David is wheeled outside the operating room to where, as always, his mother waits anxiously. 'Thanks, Dad,' David says. Well adjusted and popular, David looks like the victim of a bad car accident. But he knows how far he and his father have come. 'Dad's my hero,' he says simply.

JIM HUTCHISON

TASKS

9 In groups, discuss honestly how you would have reacted to David's physical deformity. Can you honestly say that you would have been able to ignore it?

10 Describe in detail all the operations which are referred to in the passage and analyse the purpose of each of them. (You will need to read the story with care and it might help you to draw an outline picture to make things clear.)

11 Imagine that you were David and that no one had come to help you. Use information from the passage and expand on it imaginatively to write the story of your life.

David's own determination was important but so was the determination of his adoptive parents.

We cannot pretend that the world is not competitive and possibly all of us spend part of our time making as sure as we can that we deserve to occupy a special place in it.

Printed below is an article which we can probably all learn something from. It tells us why some students are a world apart from the majority of us.

Secrets of A-Grade Pupils

Everyone knows about super-achieving pupils. They get excellent grades all right, but only by becoming boring swots, their noses always stuck in a book. They're useless at sport and failures when it comes to the opposite sex.

How, then, do we account for Alex Rodgers or Amanda Parr?

Alex, now a first-year student in natural sciences at Magdalene College, Cambridge, played rugby for William Hulme's Grammer School in Manchester and Wilmslow Rugby Club. In the lower-sixth form he directed the school production of a Dylan Thomas radio play which he'd adapted for the stage. Alex left school with five A-level grade As.

Amanda, reading English at Bristol University, acted in plays at the Weald of Kent Grammar School for Girls in Tonbridge, played badminton and did aerobics regularly. Yet she still managed to get nine grade As in her GCSEs and three As at A level. The orchestral piece she composed as part of her A-level course was short-listed for the prestigious Boosey and Hawkes music prize.

Both she and Alex won coveted medals awarded to outstanding students by the Associated Examining Board (AEB).

How do super-achievers like these do it? Brains aren't the only answer. 'The most academically gifted pupils do not necessarily perform best in exams,' says George Turnbull, senior administrator at the AEB. Knowing how to make the most of your innate abilities counts for much more. Sometimes learning comes too easily for high-IQ pupils and they never find out how to buckle down.

Hard work isn't the whole story either. 'It's not

how long you sit there with the books open,' said one of the high-achieving pupils we interviewed. 'It's what you do while you're sitting.' Some of these pupils actually put in fewer hours than their lower-scoring classmates. The kids at the top of the class get there by mastering a few basic techniques that others can readily learn. Here, according to education experts and students themselves both in this country and the US, are the secrets of A-grade pupils.

1 Set priorities. Top students brook no intrusions on study time. Once the books are open, phone calls go unanswered, TV unwatched, snacks ignored. Study is business; business comes before recreation.

2 Study anywhere – or everywhere. Claude Olney, a university business professor in Arizona assigned to tutor underachieving college athletes, recalls a cross-country runner who exercised daily. Olney persuaded him to use the time to memorise biology terms. Another student stuck a vocabulary list on the bathroom cabinet. He learned a new word every day while brushing his teeth.

Among the students we spoke to, study times were strictly a matter of personal preference. Some of them worked late at night when the house was quiet. Others woke early. Still others studied as soon as they came home when the day's work was fresh in their minds. All agreed, however, on the need for consistency. 'Whatever I was doing, I kept a slot free every day for studying,' says New Jersey college student Ian McCray.

3 Get organised. At school, Ian did athletics, played rugby and was in the band and orchestra. 'I was so busy, I couldn't waste time looking for a pencil or missing paper. I kept everything just where I could get my hands on it,' he says.

Paul Melendres, a student in New Mexico, maintains two folders –one for the day's assignments, another for homework completed and marked. High-achieving pupil Traci Tsuchiguchi has another system. She immediately files the day's school work in colour-coded folders by subject so they'll be available for review at exam time.

Even pupils who don't have a private study area remain organised. A rucksack or drawer keeps essentials together and cuts down on time-wasting searches.

4 Learn how to read. 'I used to wade through heaps of irrelevant material,' remembers Amanda Parr. 'But then I got used to reading quickly; if the first sentence of a paragraph wasn't relevant, I'd move on to the next paragraph.'

'The best course I ever took', says Oklahoma student Christopher Campbell, 'was speed-reading.

I not only increased my words per minute but also learned to look at a book's table of contents, graphs and pictures first. Then, when I began to read, I had a sense of the material and I retained a lot more.'

In his book *Getting Straight As*, Gordon Green says the secret of good reading is to be 'an active reader – one who continually asks questions that lead to a full understanding of the author's message'.

5 Schedule your time. When a teacher set a long essay, Alex Rodgers would spend a couple of days reading round the subject and making notes, then he'd do a rough draft and write up the essay. He would aim to finish a couple of days before the assignment was due in so that if it took longer than anticipated, he'd still make the deadline.

When preparing for exams, both Alex and Amanda handled revision in manageable blocks. 'Give yourself about eight weeks,' recommends Amanda. 'Set a small amount each day. If you just sit down to a huge file, you'll never get through it.'

Of course, even the best students procrastinate occasionally. But when that happens, they face up to it. 'Sometimes it comes down to late nights,' admits Christi Anderson, a pupil from South Dakota. 'Still, if you want good grades, you have to make the deadline.'

6 Take good notes. 'Before writing anything, I divide my page into two columns,' says Amanda. 'the left section is about a third of the page wide; the right, two-thirds. I write my notes in the wider column, and jot down the significance of each point on the left. During revision, this is very useful because you can see immediately why the material is relevant, rather than being daunted by great chunks of information.'

Just before the end-of-lesson bell rings, most pupils close their books, put away papers, talk to friends and get ready to leave. Christi Anderson uses those few minutes to write a two- or three-sentence summary of the lesson's principal points, which she scans before the next day's class.

7 Clean up your act. Neat papers are likely to get higher marks than sloppy ones. 'The student who hands in a tidy essay,' says Professor Olney, 'is on the way to an A grade.'

8 Speak up. 'If you ask questions, you know immediately whether you have grasped the point or not,' states Alex Rodgers. Being sure that you understand everything throughout the year makes preparing for exams easier, he says. Class participation goes beyond merely asking questions, though. It's a matter of showing intellectual curiosity.

In a lecture on economics, for example, Paul Melendres asked how the Chinese economy could be both socialist and market-driven, without incurring some of the problems that befell the former Soviet Union. 'I don't want to memorise information for tests only,' he says. 'Better grades come from better understanding.'

9 Study together. The value of working together was shown in an experiment at the University of California at Berkeley. While a postgraduate there, Uri Treisman observed a first-year calculus course in which Asian-Americans on average did better than other minority students from similar academic backgrounds. Treisman found that the Asian-Americans discussed homework, tried different approaches and explained their solutions to one another.

The others, by contrast, studied alone, spent most of their time reading and rereading the text, and tried the same approach time after time even if it was unsuccessful. On the basis of his findings. Treisman suggested teaching group-study methods in the course. Once that was done, the groups performed equally well.

10 Test yourself. Domenica Roman, at school in West Virginia, highlights any points she thinks may be covered in the exam as part of her note-taking. During revision she frames tentative test questions based on those points and gives herself a written examination. 'If I can't answer the question satisfactorily, I go back and review,' she says.

Experts confirm what Domenica has worked out for herself. Pupils who make up possible test questions often find many of them come up in the real exam and thus do better.

11 Do more than you're asked. If her maths teacher sets five problems, Christi Anderson does ten. If the history teacher assigns 8 pages of reading, she reads 12. 'Part of learning is practising,' advises Christi. 'And the more you practise, the more you learn.'

The most important 'secret' of superior students is not so secret. For almost all A-grade pupils, the contribution of their parents was crucial. From infancy, the parents imbued them with a love of learning. They set high standards for their children, and held them to those standards. They encouraged them in their studies, tested them when asked, but did not do the work for them.

In short, the parents impressed the lessons of responsibility on their children, and they delivered.

EDWIN KIESTER
SALLY VALENTINE KIESTER

TASKS

12   There are 11 numbered pieces of advice in the article. Look carefully at each of them and put them in your order of priority. Write one sentence against each heading explaining why you have put it where it is in your priority order.

13   Discuss with your friends your own work methods and compare them with those described in the article. In your discussion you might well offer your friends advice if they seem to be going wrong or making mistakes.

14   Write brief biographies of Amanda Parr and Alex Rodgers, using information from the article.

You will find this article reprinted in your homework book with suggestions for a couple more tasks.

TIME OUT TASK!

The Soliloquy

The soliloquy is an important type of speech in a play. It is when a character is alone and tells the audience the thoughts going through his or her mind.

Here is an example from *Macbeth*.

Macbeth

Act 1 Scene 7

MACBETH:
> If it were done, when 'tis done, then 'twere well
> It were done quickly. If the assassination
> Could trammel up the consequence, and catch,
> With his surcease, success; that but this blow
> Might be the be-all and end-all… here,
> But here, upon this bank and shoal of time,
> We'd jump the life to come. But in these cases
> We still have judgment here, that we but teach
> Bloody instructions, which being taught return
> To plague the inventor. This even-handed justice
> Commends the ingredients of our poisoned chalice
> To our own lips. He's here in double trust:
> First, as I am his kinsman and his subject,
> Strong both against the deed; then, as his host,
> Who should against his murderer shut the door,
> Not bear the knife myself. Besides, this Duncan
> Hath borne his faculties so meek, hath been
> So clear in his great office, that his virtues
> Will plead like angels, trumpet-tongued against
> The deep damnation of his taking-off.
> And pity, like a naked new-born babe,
> Striding the blast, or heaven's cherubin, horsed
> Upon the sightless couriers of the air,
> Shall blow the horried deed in every eye,
> That tears shall drown the wind… I have no spur
> To prick the sides of my intent, but only
> Vaulting ambition, which o'erleaps itself,
> And falls on the other—

WILLIAM SHAKESPEARE

- What are Macbeth's thoughts?
- Write your version of the speech in modern English.
- Write a soliloquy of your own. (Invent a character, a situation and the way your character thinks.)
- What effect could this soliloquy from *Macbeth* have on the audience?
- Find another soliloquy in a Shakespeare play and work out what is going on.

END OF TIME OUT!

Throughout our lives we live in a variety of different worlds. We live in the world of childhood for a time and, eventually, we live in the world of old age: two very different worlds.

We all know old people. But do we know what it is like to be old? Here are two short poems.

Beautiful Old Age

It ought to be lovely to be old
to be full of the peace that comes of experience
and wrinkled ripe fulfilment.

The wrinkled smile of completeness that follows a life
lived undaunted and unsoured with accepted lies.
If people lived without accepting lies
they would ripen like apples, and be scented like pippins
in their old age.

Soothing, old people should be, like apples
when one is tired of love.
Fragrant like yellowing leaves, and dim with the soft
stillness and satisfaction of autumn.

And a girl should say:
It must be wonderful to live and grow old.
Look at my mother, how rich and still she is! –

And a young man should think: By Jove
my father has faced all weathers, but it's been a life!–

D H LAWRENCE

In Oak Terrace

Old and alone, she sits at nights
nodding before the television.
The house is quiet now. She knits,
rises to put the kettle on,

watches a cowboy's killing, reads
the local Births and Deaths, and falls
asleep at 'Growing stock-piles of war-heads'.
A world that threatens worse ills

fades. She dreams of a life spent
in the one house: suffers again
poverty, sickness, abandonment,
a child's death, a brother's brain

melting to madness. Seventy years
of common trouble; the kettle sings.
At midnight she says her silly prayers,
and takes her teeth out, and collects her night-things.

TONY CONNOR

TASKS

15 D H Lawrence says 'It ought to be lovely to be old'. Do you think his poem convinces you of this?

16 Look now at the second poem, *In Oak Terrace*. How do you feel about the old woman here?

17 Compare the two poems. Look at:
  - what they say;
  - their main ideas;
  - how they sound ('tone');
  - the language they use;
  - the feelings they arouse in you.

18 Work with others in a group and decide on the advantages and disadvantages of living in the world of old age.

19 Prepare a presentation on this topic. Think through all the different ways in which you might make a presentation, how you might present your information and ideas, and make your presentation interesting by using as many different methods as you can.

The world of childhood is very special. Small children are special. They have their own ways of thinking and looking at things. In the following short story John Wain enters the world of a six-year-old boy.

A Message from the Pig-man

He was never called Ekky now, because he was getting to be a real boy, nearly six, with grey flannel trousers that had a separate belt and weren't kept up by elastic, and his name was Eric. But this was just one of those changes brought about naturally, by time, not a disturbing alteration; he understood that. His mother hadn't meant that kind of change when she had promised, 'Nothing will be changed.' It was all going to go on as before, except that Dad wouldn't be there, and Donald would be there instead. He knew Donald, of course, and felt all right about his being in the house, though it seemed, when he lay in bed and thought about it, mad and pointless that Donald's coming should mean that Dad had to go. Why should it mean that? The house was quite big.

Dad had bought him a train, just a few weeks ago, and taught him how to fit the lines together. That ought to have meant that he would stay; what sensible person would buy a train, and fit it all up ready to run, even as a present for another person – *and then leave*? Perhaps that meant *he* was going to leave. But that didn't seem likely. Not the way Mum held on to him all the time, even holding him round the middle as if he needed keeping in one piece.

All the same, he was not Ekky now, he was Eric, and he was sensible and grown-up. Probably it was his own fault that everything seemed strange. He was not living up to his grey flannel trousers – perhaps that was it; being afraid of too many things, not asking questions that would probably turn out to have quite simple answers.

The Pig-man, for instance. He had let the Pig-man worry him far too much. None of the grown-ups acted as if the Pig-man was anything to be afraid of. His mother would say, now and then, 'Let me see, it's today the Pig-man comes, isn't it?' or, 'Oh dear, the Pig-man will be coming round soon, and I haven't put anything out.' If she talked like this, Eric's spine would tingle and go cold; he would keep very still and wait, because quite often her next words would be, 'Eric, just take these peelings,' or whatever it was, 'out to the bucket, dear, will you?' The bucket was about 50 yards away from the back door; it as shared by the people in the 2 next-door houses. None of *them* was afraid of the Pig-man, either. What was their attitude, he wondered? Were they sorry for him, having to eat damp old stuff out of a bucket – tea-leaves and eggshells and that sort of thing? Was the Pig-man very poor? Was he sorry for himself, or did he feel all right about being like that? *Like what?* What did the Pig-man look like? He would have little eyes, and a snout with a flat end; but would he have trotters, or hands and feet like a person's? To be called the Pig-man, rather than the Man-pig, surely implied that he was upright, and dressed. Could he talk? Probably, in a kind of grunting way, or else how could he tell the people what kind of food he wanted them to put in his bucket? *Why hadn't he asked Dad about the Pig-man?* That had been his mistake: Dad would have told him exactly all about it. But he had gone. Eric fell asleep, but the next day his questions returned.

A few evenings later, it suddenly came to a crisis. Eric had been allowed, 'just for once', to bring his train into the dining-room after tea, because there was a fire there that made it nicer than the room where he usually played. It was just the part of the day Eric liked best, and bed-time was comfortably far-off. He fitted the sections of rail together, glancing in anticipation at the engine as it stood proudly waiting to haul the carriages round and round, tremendously fast.

Then his mother called 'Eric! Do be a sweet, good boy, and take this stuff out for the Pig-man. My hands are covered with cake mixture. I'll let you scrape out the basin when you come in.'

For a moment he kept quite still, hoping he hadn't really heard her say it, that it was just a voice inside his head. But Donald looked over at him and said, 'Go along, old man. You don't mind, do you?'

Eric said, 'But tonight's when the Pig-man *comes.*'

'All the better,' said Donald, turning back to his paper.

Why was it better? Did they *want* him to meet the Pig-man?

Slowly, wondering why his feet and legs didn't refuse to move, Eric went through into the kitchen. 'There it is,' his mother said, pointing to a brown-paper carrier full of potato peelings and scraps.

He took it up and opened the back door.

He stopped. The bucket wasn't there.

It had gone. Eric peered round, but the light, though faint, was not as faint as *that.* He could see that the bucket had gone. *The Pig-man had already been.*

Back in the house, where it was warm and bright and his train was waiting.

'The Pig-man's gone, Mum. The bucket's not there.'

She frowned, hands deep in the pudding-basin. 'Oh, yes, I do believe I heard him.'

'Yes?' he said politely, putting down the carrier.

'So if you nip along, dear, you can easily catch him up. And I do want that stuff out of the way.'

'Catch him up?' he asked, standing still in the doorway.

'Yes, dear, *catch him up,*' she answered rather sharply.

Before she had finished Eric was outside the door and running. This was a technique he knew. It was the same as getting into icy cold water. If it was the end, if the Pig-man seized him by the hand and dragged him off to his hut, well, so much the worse. Swinging the paper carrier in his hand, he ran fast through the dusk.

The back view of the Pig-man was much as he had expected it to be. A slow, rather lurching gait, hunched shoulders, an old hat crushed down on his head (to hide his ears?) and the pail in his hand. Plod, plod, as if he were tired. Perhaps this was just a ruse, though, probably he could pounce quickly enough.

Eric stopped. His heart was banging like fireworks going off. He could hardly hear anything.

'Mr Pig-man!' he called, and this time the words came out clear and rather high.

The jogging old figure stopped, turned, and looked at him. Eric could not see properly from where he stood. But he had to see. Everything, even his fear, sank and drowned in the raging tide of his curiosity. He moved forward. With each step he saw more clearly. The Pig-man was just an ordinary old man.

'Hello, sonny. Got some stuff there for the old grunters?'

Eric nodded, mutely, and held out his offering. What old grunters? What did he mean?

The Pig-man put down his bucket. He had ordinary hands, ordinary arms. He took the lid off. Eric held out the paper carrier, and the Pig-man's hand actually touched his own for a second. A flood of gratitude rose up inside him. The Pig-man tipped the scraps into the bucket and handed the carrier back.

'Thanks, sonny,' he said.

'Who's it for?' Eric asked. The Pig-man straightened up, puzzled. Then he laughed, in a gurgling sort of way, but not like a pig at all.

'Arh aarh Harh Harh,' the Pig-man went. 'Not for me, if that's whatcher mean, arh, harh.'

He put the lid back on the bucket. 'It's for the old grunters,' he said. 'The old porkers. Just what they like. Only not fruit skins. Never fruit skins. It gives 'em the belly-ache.'

He was called the Pig-man because he had some pigs that he looked after.

'Thank you,' said Eric, 'Good night.' He ran

back towards the house, hearing the Pig-man, the ordinary old man, the ordinary usual normal old man, say in his just ordinary old man's voice, 'Good night, sonny.'

So that was how you did it. You *just* went straight ahead, not worrying about this or that. Like getting into cold water. You *just* did it.

He slowed down as he got to the gate. For instance, if there was a question that you wanted to know the answer to, and you had always just felt you couldn't ask, the thing to do was to ask it. Just straight out, like going up to the Pig-man. Difficult things, troubles, questions, you just treated them like the Pig-man.

So that was it!

The warm light shone through the crack of the door. He opened it and went in. His mother was standing at the table, her hands still working the cake mixture about. She would let him scrape out the basin, and the spoon – he would ask for the spoon, too. But not straight away. There was a more important thing first.

He put the paper carrier down and went up to her. 'Mum,' he said.

'Why can't Dad be with us even if Donald is here? I mean, why can't he live with us as well as Donald?'

His mother turned and went to the sink. She put the tap on and held her hands under it.

'Darling,' she called.

'Yes?' came Donald's voice.

'D'you know what he's just said?'

'What?'

'He's just asked...' She turned the tap off and dried her hands, not looking at Eric. 'He wants to know why we can't have Jack to live with us.'

There was a silence, then Donald said, quietly, so that his voice only just reached Eric's ears, 'That's a hard one.'

'You can scrape out the basin,' his mother said to Eric. She lifted him up and kissed him. Then she rubbed her cheek along his, leaving a wet smear. 'Poor little Ekky,' she said in a funny voice.

She put him down and he began to scrape out the pudding basin, certain at least of one thing, that grown-ups were mad and silly and he hated them all, all, *all.*

JOHN WAIN

TASKS

20 Rewrite the story as a first person narrative, that is re-tell the story in Eric's own words.

21 Write the story of a misunderstanding from your own childhood.

Let us now head off into another world, the world of animals. People have often been fascinated by the behaviour of animals. Many poems have been written describing animals' behaviour. Here are two poems.

Little City

Spider, from his flaming sleep,
staggers out into the window frame;
swings out from the red den where he slept
to nest in the gnarled glass.
Fat hero, burnished cannibal
lets down a frail ladder and ties a knot,
sways down to a landing with furry grace.

By noon this corner is a bullet-coloured city
and the exhausted architect
sleeps in his pale wheel,

waits without pity for a gold visitor
or coppery captive, his aerial enemies
spinning headlong down the window to the trap.

The street of string shakes now and announces
a surprised angel in the tunnel of thread.
Spider dances down his wiry heaven to taste the moth.
A little battle begins and the prison trembles.
The round spider hunches like a judge.
The wheel glistens.
But this transparent town that caves in at a breath
is paved with perfect steel.
The victim hangs by his feet, and the spider
circles invisible avenues, weaving a grave.

By evening the web is heavy with monsters,
bright constellation of wasps and bees,
breathless, surrendered.
Bronze skeletons dangle on the wires
and a thin wing flutters.
The medieval city hangs in its stars.

Spider lumbers down the web
and the city stretches with the weight of his walking.
By night we cannot see the flies' faces
and the spider, rocking.

ROBERT HORAN

The Wasps' Nest

Two aerial tigers,
Striped in ebony and gold
And resonantly, savagely a-hum,
Have lately come
To my mail-box's metal hold
And thought
With paper and with mud
Therein to build
Their insubstantial and their only home.
Neither the sore displeasure
Of the US Mail
Nor all my threats and warnings
Will avail
To turn them from their hummed devotions.
And I think
They know my strength,

Can gauge
The danger of their work:
One blow could crush them
And their nest; and I am not their friend.
And yet they seem
Too deeply and too fiercely occupied
To bother to attend.
Perhaps they sense
I'll never deal the blow,
For, though not in nor of them,
Still I think I know
What it is like to live
In an alien and gigantic universe, a stranger,
Building fragile citadels of love
On the edge of danger.

JAMES L ROSENBERG

TASKS

22 Read the first poem, *Little City*, and write about the way in which the writer builds up a picture of the spider's city.

23 Collect all the terms the writer uses about:
- the spider;
- its web;
- its prey.

Choose five of the terms which you have listed and which you consider to be very effective. Write down each term and, by the side of it, explain why you think it is effective.

24 Does the writer make the spider and its activities attractive or unattractive? Whatever the conclusion you come to, make sure you give reasons for it.

25 The second poem is about the writer as well as the wasps he describes. What does he have to say about himself and the creatures he observes?

26 Once you have studied both poems write a comparison of them. Here are some areas to look at:
- subject matter;
- what happens;
- descriptions;
- use of images (similes and metaphors);
- sounds;
- main ideas or themes;
- your personal response.

Writers have often invited us to explore the animal world by giving the animals a mixture of animal and human characteristics.

Some of these books are popular with children but they also have an appeal to adults. The two extracts which follow are from *Winnie-the-Pooh* by A A Milne and *Watership Down* by Richard Adams.

Winnie-the-Pooh

Winnie-the-Pooh went off to find Eeyore's tail. It was a fine spring morning in the forest as he started out. Little soft clouds played happily in a blue sky, skipping from time to time in front of the sun as if they had come to put it out, and then sliding away suddenly so that the next might have his turn. Through them and between them the sun shone bravely; and a copse which had worn its firs all the year round seemed old and dowdy now beside the new green lace which the beeches had put on so prettily. Through copse and spinney marched Bear; down open slopes of gorse and heather, over rocky beds of streams, up steep banks of sandstone into the heather again; and so at last, tired and hungry, to the Hundred Acre Wood. For it was in the Hundred Acre Wood that Owl lived.

'And if anyone knows anything about anything,' said Bear to himself, 'it's Owl who knows something about something,' he said, 'or my name's not Winnie-the-Pooh,' he said. 'Which it is,' he added. 'So there you are.'

Owl lived at The Chestnuts, an old-world residence of great charm, which was grander than anybody else's, or seemed so to Bear, because it had both a knocker *and a* bell-pull. Underneath the knocker there was a notice which said:

PLES RING IF AN RNSER IS REQIRD.

Underneath the bell-pull there was a notice which said:

PLEZ CNOKE IF AN RNSR IS NOT REQID.

These notices had been written by Christopher Robin, who was the only one in the forest who could spell; for Owl, wise though he was in many ways, able to read and write and spell his own name WOL, yet somehow went all to pieces over delicate words like MEASLES and BUTTEREDTOAST.

Winnie-the-Pooh read the two notices very carefully, first from left to right, and afterwards, in case he had missed some of it, from right to left. Then, to make quite sure, he knocked and pulled the knocker, and he pulled and knocked the bell-rope, and he called out in a very loud voice, 'Owl! I require an answer! It's Bear speaking.' And the door opened, and Owl looked out.

'Hallo, Pooh,' he said. 'How's things?'

'Terrible and Sad,' said Pooh, 'Because Eeyore, who is a friend of mine, has lost his tail. And he's Moping about it. So could you very kindly tell me how to find it for him?'

'Well,' said Owl, 'the customary procedure in such cases is as follows.'

'What does Crustimoney Proseedcake mean?' said Pooh. 'For I am a Bear of Very Little Brain, and long words Bother me.'

'It means the Thing to Do.'

'As long as it means that, I don't mind,' said Pooh humbly.

'The thing to do is as follows. First, Issue a Reward. Then—'

'Just a moment,' said Pooh, holding up his paw. '*What* do we do to this – what you were saying? You sneezed just as you were going to tell me.'

'I *didn't* sneeze.'

'Yes, you did, Owl.'

'Excuse me, Pooh, I didn't. You can't sneeze without knowing it.'

'Well, you can't know it without something having been sneezed.'

'What I *said* was, "First *Issue* a Reward".'

'You're doing it again,' said Pooh sadly.

'A Reward!' said Owl very loudly. 'We write a notice to say that we will give a large something to anybody who finds Eeyore's tail.'

'I see, I see,' said Pooh, nodding his head. 'Talking about large somethings,' he went on dreamily, 'I generally have a small something about now – about this time in the morning,' and he looked wistfully at the cupboard in the corner of Owl's parlour; 'just a mouthful of condensed milk or whatnot, with perhaps a lick of honey—'

'Well, then,' said Owl, 'we write out this notice, and we put it up all over the Forest.'

'A lick of honey,' murmured Bear to himself, 'or – or not, as the case may be.' And he gave a deep sigh, and tried very hard to listen to what Owl was saying.

But Owl went on and on, using longer and longer words, until at last he came back to where he started, and he explained that the person to write out this notice was Christopher Robin.

'It was he who wrote the ones on my front door for me. Did you see them, Pooh?'

For some time now Pooh had been saying 'Yes' and 'No' in turn, with his eyes shut, to all that Owl was saying, and having said, 'Yes, yes,' last time, he said, 'No. Not at all,' now, without really knowing what Owl was talking about.

'Didn't you see them?' said Owl, a little surprised. 'Come and look at them now.'

So they went outside. And Pooh looked at the knocker and the notice below it, and he looked at the bell-rope and the notice below it, and the more he looked at the bell-rope, the more he felt that he had seen something like it, somewhere else, sometime before.

'Handsome bell-rope, isn't it?' said Owl.

Pooh nodded.

'It reminds me of something,' he said, 'but I can't think what. Where did you get it?'

'I just came across it in the forest. It was hanging over a bush, and I thought at first somebody lived there, so I rang it, and nothing happened, and then I rang it again very loudly, and it came off in my hand, and as nobody seemed to want it, I took it home, and—'

'Owl,' said Pooh solemnly, 'you made a mistake. Somebody did want it.'

'Who?'

'Eeyore. My dear friend Eeyore. He was – he was fond of it.'

'Fond of it?'

'Attached to it,' said Winnie-the-Pooh sadly.

A A MILNE

Watership Down

The next day was bright and dry, with a fresh wind that cleared up what remained of the wet. The clouds came racing over the ridge from the south as they had on the May evening when Hazel first climbed the down. But now they were higher and smaller, settling at last into a mackerel sky like a beach at low tide. Hazel took Bigwig and Blackberry to the edge of the escarpment, whence they could look across to Nuthanger on its little hill. He described the approach and went on to explain how the rabbit-hutch was to be found. Bigwig was in high spirits. The wind and the prospect of action excited him and he spent some time with Dandelion, Hawkbit and Speedwell, pretending to be a cat and encouraging them to attack him as realistically as they could. Hazel, whose talk with Fiver had somewhat clouded him, recovered as he watched them tussling over the grass and ended by joining in himself, first as an attacker and then as the cat, staring and quivering for all the world like the Nuthanger tabby.

'I shall be disappointed if we don't meet a cat after all this,' said Dandelion, as he waited for his turn to run at a fallen beech branch from one side, claw it twice and dash out again. 'I feel a really dangerous animal.'

'You vatch heem, Meester Dando,' said Kehaar, who was hunting for snails in the grass near-by. 'Meester Pigvig, 'e vant you t'ink all vun peeg yoke; make you prave. Cat 'e no yoke. You no see 'im, you no 'ear 'im. Den yomp! 'E come.'

'But we're not going there to eat Kehaar,' said Bigwig. 'That makes all the difference. We shan't stop watching for cats the whole time.'

'Why not eat the cat?' said Bluebell. 'Or bring one back here for breeding? That ought to improve the warren stock no end.'

Hazel and Bigwig had decided that the raid should be carried out as soon after dark as the farm was quiet. This meant that they would cover the half mile to the outlying sheds at sunset, instead of risking the confusion of a night journey over ground that only Hazel knew. They could steal a meal among the swedes, halt till darkness and cover the short distance to the farm after a good rest. Then – provided they could cope with the cats – there would be plenty of time to tackle the hutch; whereas if they were to arrive at dawn they would be working against time before men came on the scene. Finally, the hutch rabbits would not be missed until the following morning.

'And remember,' said Hazel, 'it'll probably take these rabbits a long time to get to the down. We shall have to be patient with them. I'd rather do that in darkness, elil or no elil. We don't want to be messing about in broad daylight.'

'If it comes to the worst,' said Bigwig, 'we can leave the hutch rabbits and bolt. Elil take the hindmost, don't they? I know it's tough, but if there's real trouble we ought to save our own rabbits first. Let's hope that doesn't happen, though.'

RICHARD ADAMS

TASKS

27 Explain briefly what you think would be a child's reaction to each of the stories.

28 Describe the link between the animals and the 'human' behaviour that the writer creates for them.

29 If these stories were written about human beings would they be more or less interesting? Give some reasons for your opinion.

30 What effect do you think the writer is trying to have on his readers in each of these extracts?

You will find the 'Watership Down' extract reprinted in your homework book, together with a task inviting you to invent your own animal characters for a story.

TIME OUT TASK!

Different kinds of sentences

Look up a grammar book and you will find references to
- command sentences
- question sentences
- statement sentences
- simple sentences
- compound sentences
- complex sentences

To explain these terms is really quite straightforward.

- A **command sentence** is a group of words which tells you what to do.
- A **question sentence** does just that – it asks a question.
- A **statement sentence** says something clearly and in order.
- A **simple sentence** is generally short because it has only one verb in it and says one thing only.
- A **compound sentence** is really just a series of simple sentences joined together by conjunctions or linking words, the most obvious of which is 'and'. Each part of the sentence is just as important as any other.
- A **complex sentence** is also a series of parts joined together but in this case one part of the sentence is more important than any other and the parts will be joined by words like 'because', 'who', 'when'.

What sorts of sentences should you use?

There isn't a right or wrong answer.

What sort of sentences would you use if you are writing for five-year-old children?

What sort of sentences might you use if you are trying to write an explanation of government policy?

Writing the proper sort of sentences is part of getting your style correct.

Think about the types of sentences you should use while writing the following:
- Clear instructions how to get from your home to your school.
- A paragraph in which you explain the importance of getting a good grade in GCSE English.
- A notice to a group of five-year-olds telling them that an important person is coming to visit their school.

Have a look at your sentences. Have you used different sorts of sentences? Why?

END OF TIME OUT!

The Shakespeare play in this chapter is *Antony and Cleopatra*. The play concerns events in both Egypt and Rome: it is about love and the struggle for power in the ancient Roman Empire. So the strangeness of the play for us is the world of the century BC.

The extract below comes from Act 2 of the play.

Antony and Cleopatra

Act 2 Scene 2

ENOBARBUS:
    The barge she sat in, like a burnish'd throne,
    Burn'd on the water: the poop was beaten gold;
    Purple the sails, and so perfumed that
    The winds were love-sick with them; the oars
        were silver,
    Which to the tune of flutes kept stroke,
        and made
    The water which they beat to follow faster,
    As amorous of their strokes. For her own person,
    It beggar'd all description: she did lie
    In her pavilion — cloth-of-gold of tissue —
    O'er-picturing that Venus where we see
    The fancy outwork nature: on each side her
    Stood pretty dimpled boys, like smiling Cupids,
    With divers-colour'd fans, whose wind did seem
    To glow the delicate cheeks which they did cool,
    And what they undid did.

AGRIPPA:
    O, rare for Antony!

ENOBARBUS:
    Her gentlewomen, like the Nereides,
    So many mermaids, tended her i' the eyes,
    And made their bends adornings: at the helm
    A seeming mermaid steers: the silken tackle
    Swell with the touches of those
        flower-soft hands,
    That yarely frame the office. From the barge
    A strange invisible perfume hits the sense
    Of the adjacent wharfs. The city cast
    Her people out upon her; and Antony,
    Enthroned i' the market-place, did sit alone,
    Whistling to the air; which, but for vacancy,
    Had gone to gaze on Cleopatra too
    And made a gap in nature.

AGRIPPA:
    Rare Egyptian!

ENOBARBUS:
    Upon her landing, Antony sent to her,
    Invited her to supper: she replied,
    It should be better he became her guest;
    Which she entreated: our courteous Antony,
    Whom ne'er the word of 'No' woman heard speak,
    Being barber'd ten times o'er, goes to the feast,
    And for his ordinary pays his heart
    For what his eyes eat only.

AGRIPPA:
    Royal wench!
    She made great Cæsar lay his sword to bed:
    He plough'd her, and she cropp'd.

ENOBARBUS:
    I saw her once
    Hop forty paces through the public street;
    And having lost her breath, she spoke, and panted,
    That she did make defect perfection,
    And, breathless, power breathe forth.

MECÆNAS:
    Now Antony must leave her utterly.

ENOBARBUS:
    Never; he will not:
    Age cannot wither her, nor custom stale
    Her infinite variety: other women cloy
    The appetites they feed; but she makes hungry
    Where most she satisfies: for vilest things
    Become themselves in her; that the holy priests
    Bless her when she is riggish.

MECÆNAS:
    If beauty, wisdom, modesty, can settle
    The heart of Antony, Octavia is
    A blessed lottery to him.

AGRIPPA:
    Let us go.
    Good Enobarbus, make yourself my guest
    Whilst you abide here.

ENOBARBUS:
    Humbly, sir, I thank you.   *Exeunt*.

WILLIAM SHAKESPEARE

TASKS

31 Enobarbus is the main speaker here. Look at his description of Cleopatra and explain it in your own words.

32 Explain how his description of Cleopatra makes her sound attractive.

33 What does Enobarbus say about the meeting between Antony and Cleopatra?

34 Write about the passage, making your own response.
You might like to consider:
- what is said about Antony and Cleopatra;
- the language used;
- the roles of the minor characters.

Having visited Shakespeare in the Middle East, our next piece of stimulus material takes us to the Far East. It is an extract from a book called *Constant Glory* (La Martiniere Saga 1836-1986). La Martiniere is a prestigious school in Calcutta in India, very different from any of your schools.

The extract tells us something of what life was like in the school in the nineteenth century. (R is short for rupee, which is the name for Indian currency. An A is an anna, which is another unit of currency.)

Constant Glory

Stringent rules were laid down for the children as the following account shows:

Regulations About the Distribution of Time, etc.

1   The children shall rise every morning at gun-fire; and after having bathed and dressed, they shall be allowed to play in their respective playgrounds till the bell rings for the morning prayers.

2   From the first of April to the first of October, the bell for morning prayers shall ring at half past six o'clock; and from the first of October to the first of April, at seven o'clock.

3   After prayers, the boys and girls shall return to their respective rooms, and shall remain in them under their Masters and Mistresses till eight o'clock, when the bell shall ring for breakfast.

4   At nine o'clock the bell shall ring for school, where the boys and girls, with the exception of the younger children, whose time of attendance the Head Master and Head Mistress shall have the discretionary power of abridging, are to remain till eleven; and after being allowed to play for half an hour, they are to return to their school rooms, where they shall remain till one o'clock, when the dinner bell shall ring.

5   At three o'clock, the bell shall ring again for school, where the boys and girls shall remain till five o'clock.*

6   In the interval between five o'clock and dusk, the children shall be allowed to play in their respective play grounds.

7   The bell for evening prayers shall ring at dusk, and after prayers, children shall have their supper.

8   The children shall retire to bed at eight o'clock all the year round.

*It is interesting that La Martiniere once held classes in the afternoon. One of the features which sets it apart from most Calcutta schools today is that La Martiniere gives over shortly after 1 pm while classes begin just after 8 am.

Were the early students of La Martiniere to return to school, they would find that very little has changed from the routine they followed – at least for the boarders. But even if the routine has not been altered dramatically, holidays and the rules governing them, have. The Governors had stipulated that Saturdays would be half-holidays, and 'at no other time shall they be allowed to enter the grounds of the school'. Regular holidays totalled only one month: fifteen days for Easter beginning on Good Friday, and fifteen days for Christmas starting that day. But, 'the children shall, neither during Easter and Christmas holidays, nor at any other time, be allowed to leave the school for the purpose of visiting their parents etc, at their own homes', unless, of course, special permission was obtained in extraordinary cases.

In other words, barring some unforeseen events, a child admitted to school was expected never to leave its portals till his education was complete and he was deemed fit to go out into the world.

It is amazing how the Acting Governors of the school examined every conceivable matter in the minutest detail, laying down forms of rewards and punishments, stressing the need to avoid corporal punishment – ruling it out altogether for girls over the age of eleven. They laid down that the children's clothes should be changed every alternate day, girls under eight being given eight suits 'consisting of a frock, petticoat, and shift of calico' annually, and three tuckers of muslin and a cotton shawl handkerchief every two years. Girls above eight were given nine suits 'consisting of nine shirts, nine pairs of pantaloons, nine jackets with a woollen jacket and a pair of pantaloons for the cold season. Both boys and girls received a new pair of shoes every two months. They slept in separate beds with bedding and linen provided by the school.

Such was the Acting Governors' meticulousness that they even laid down the Menu for children which they stipulated was to be 'strictly adhered to the whole year round'.

Mondays
Mutton, roast and boiled, a portion of bread and vegetables to each boy and girl.
Tuesdays
Mutton or kid curry, boiled rice and doll, with a portion of bread and fruit to each.
Wednesdays
Roast beef, potatoes and rice pudding.
Thursdays
The same as Monday.
Fridays
The same as Tuesday.
Saturdays
Roast fowl, pulao and vegetables.
Sundays
The same as Wednesday.
For breakfast: Bread, butter and tea.
For supper: Bread and milk, daily, all the year round.

The Governors also laid down the establishment that would be allowed for the school at commencement, 'to be increased or diminished as may be necessary hereafter'.

	Rs	As
One Sircar for writing daily accounts and monthly bills	16	0
One steward for managing the table	16	0
Three Khidmutgars @ 5/8 each	16	8
One sirdar cook	7	0
Two cooks @ 5/8 each	11	0
Two musalchees @ 4/8 each	9	0
One sirdar bheesty	5	0
Three bheesties @ 4/8 each	13	8
One Ayah	7	0
Two mathranies @ 4/8 each	9	0
Three bearers @ 4/8 each	13	8
Four mathers @ 4/8 each	18	0
Two mallies to keep the grounds clean	8	0
One Lamp man	4	0
Two durwans	10	0
One Tailor	6	8
One hair cutter	4	0
One dhobie, with assistants, to receive 8 annas per month for each boy and girl	25	0
Total	199	0

With the costs of maintaining a hospital establishment whose 'native doctor' was to receive a salary of Rs 16, while Rs 19 was the salary bill of its other staff, the school's total establishment costs came to Rs 234. Not an inconsiderable amount by the standards of the day.

The earliest recollection of life in school comes from a note written by A Stark in 1900 describing his years at La Martiniere between 1841 and 1850. Stark recalls that till 1845, boys and girls shared the same building, but iron railings divided the two 'departments'. Segregation was not complete because they shared the chapel where the service was conducted by the Headmaster. But as was the practice for different 'common' occasions till some years ago, then too, boys and girls trooped in separately. In Stark's time the boys came in first; girls being ushered in only when the boys were seated. They left the chapel separately after the service.

Stark writes that after the girls' school building was completed, the number of students increased quite rapidly. Interestingly, he says that many boarders came from the North-Western Provinces (UP), Burma and the Straits. Paying great compliment to the school's first Principal, AMW Christopher, Stark writes that prior to his arrival, 'the tone of the school was not what it might have been; the large number of boys crowded together without the healthy games and athletics of modern times had its inevitable result, Satan finding mischief for idle hands.'

Stark further recalls: 'The only manly game was cricket, but that was confined to the cold season; there was no football, gymnastics or volunteering. The only other exercise we had was swimming', for which the boys were taken out to the 'Puddapookur tank' (on what is now Sarat Bose Road) by the new junior teacher, Mr Arratoon. But Stark writes that although students were not allowed out of school on any excuse between the Easter and September holidays (clearly a change from the original, for no holidays are stipulated for September in the Acting Governors' Report), boys were allowed to go out on Saturday afternoons and return on Monday mornings during the cold season.

TASKS

35 Use information from all sections of the extract to write about a typical day in the life of a pupil at La Martiniere School in the nineteenth century.

36 Some of the things which are referred to are rather strange to our ears – doll, Sircar, ayah, mallies. You can work out what some of these words mean. Do some research and find out in particular what the words used in the charts mean. (Some of you may be fortunate enough to be able to do your research by asking people you know; others may have to consult books in the library.)

37 Compare the distribution of time at La Martiniere with the distribution of time in your school and say which you think is better. (In your writing you must explain how you have interpreted the word 'better'.)

I t is not necessary to travel to the far side of the globe to find a world which is different from your own.

Printed below is an article from the *Geographical* magazine about a particular type of map which allows you to see at a glance how places are very different from the area in which you live.

Mapping for pleasure

Travellers have always needed maps but it is only recently that tourist maps have become big business. Tony Seaton and Fiona McWilliam report

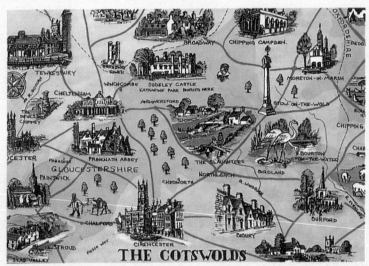

THE COTSWOLDS

Tourist maps are not a recent development. The Romans produced route maps showing hostelries and staging posts, and in medieval times, monks like Matthew Paris of St Albans drew manuscript maps for pilgrims, forerunners of modern tourists, who travelled to Canterbury and the Holy Land. The first published maps, following the invention of printing in the late 15th century, included route maps to Rome and other destinations important to Christian travellers.

Tourist maps only began to appear in significant numbers in Britain and western Europe from the 18th century, in guidebooks, as individual maps and, for the last 70 years, in the diverse promotional material published by tourism marketing agencies.

In Britain, the Grand Tour and the 'opening' of Scotland and the Lake District prompted some of the earlier tourist maps. Later on, motoring organisations, railways, regional and international tourist organisations all used them as a marketing tool to sell their services.

In terms of numbers, the general public is probably more aware of tourist maps than any other type. Yet, with few exceptions, they have been ignored by cartographers, particularly historians of cartography and tourism academics.

Unlike conventional maps, tourist maps are designed to influence travel decisions, not merely to provide spatial pathways. Although usually based on standard maps, they often isolate, elevate and promote particular facets of regions in a bid to attract visitors, and this involves strategic inclusions and omissions. They are also designed to detain the visitor, for example by displaying leisure activities.

A less obvious function of the tourist map is its ability to disguise accessibility problems: being traveller-orientated, they often simplify the logistics of access, minimising perceived distance, cost and travel time. A classic example of this is Harry C Beck's famous topological map of the London Underground.

Tourist maps can also dramatise the social and cultural features of an area: non-tourist maps focus on physical features, whereas tourist maps often include pictures of people or activities that may be pursued by the tourist. They are generally more pictorial than non-tourist maps, whether they are printed on paper, mounted on large boards in parks or museums, or used to adorn promotional material such as mugs and t-shirts. They include a greater variety of 'user-friendly' iconic and natural signs and graphic enhancement such as direction arrows. Iconic signs are pictures of what one actually sees, such as a castle or deer, while natural signs are more symbolic – for example, a cloud indicating bad weather. Nevertheless, both are designed for the eye rather than the intellect, which is just as well, as according to Sue Glyptis, Professor of Recreation Management at Loughborough University, seven out of eight people in Britain are unable to read a map. 'This means the majority of countryside recreation opportunities are effectively hidden from view from many potential visitors,' she says.

In Britain, bird's-eye views (perspective drawings made from an elevated viewpoint) appeared as maps – usually of fortified settlements, for military purposes – from the 16th century. Such maps are pure iconography, and have been used widely since this time to promote tourism, depicting features such as mountains and cities. A notable 19th century example of a bird's-eye panorama is a series of maps of London viewed from St Paul's Cathedral, and published in 1845 to celebrate the opening of the colosseum, a popular Victorian tourist attraction. An interesting modern example is the Reader's Digest Town Tours of Britain, a series of 155 town plans, published in 1990 and produced by a team of artists working from aerial photographs.

Many early tourist maps were based on, and therefore not structurally different from, non-tourist ones. Indeed early guidebooks, such as the 19th century guides of Scotland and the Lake District, used existing maps with lines or colours superimposed across particular roads or paths. Later tourist promoters, however, realised the advantages of eliminating irrelevant detail and drew up more simple maps, such as those published in Reader's Digest atlases. In recent years, many tourism promoters have chosen to produce maps with a single theme. Such maps are particularly useful for promoting special interest tours or trails, such as the vineyards of a particular region, clan maps of Scotland, First World War battlefields, textile history trails or regional food maps. There is even a Billy the Kid trail in the US, and it is now possible to buy maps of Yorkshire that highlight *Emmerdale Farm*, as well as Brontë, country.

Another technique, radical centrification, whereby places are shown in relation to one or a few chosen points, was used for tourist maps from the early 19th century to indicate the places and attractions within visiting distance (usually 30 miles) of major cities such as Edinburgh, London and Manchester. It has been used extensively since then: for example, Bradford can be represented graphically as a 'gateway' to the Yorkshire Dales and Brontë country. Likewise, hotels often provide maps that represent themselves as hubs for surrounding attractions.

Giving equal prominence to a number of 'attractions' of varying interest to the tourist using graphics and lettering style and size, was a technique used widely in the 1930s by oil companies in Europe and the US. Maps displayed an even spread of things to see (many a lot less interesting than others) in a bid to encourage people to drive long distances, and thereby use more petrol. Splendid isolation of a particular feature – showing it as being much larger than the surrounding features – has long been a popular method of drawing attention to commercial ventures, such as shops or hotels, and historical buildings like castles or churches.

With the exception of sea charts, traditional maps rarely took into account the forms of transport that were used to cross the area they covered. This changed, however, with the growth of tourism: the earliest transport-specific maps were the post chaise companions and stagecoach posting maps, published in Britain from the late 18th century and featuring useful information for travellers such as inns and livery stables. These were followed in the 19th century by maps produced specifically for steamboat and rail passengers, walkers and cyclists. From around 1910, maps for motorists began to be published.

Transport-specific maps take account of the opportunities afforded by the type of transport they promote. Railway guides such as the

Great Western Guide of 1854 set out to list features that could be observed from a train carriage, making travel itself a 'touristic experience'. And for activities such as walking, cycling and riding, where the mode of transport, rather than the destination, is the main purpose, maps set out to provide helpful information. For example, walkers' maps often provide the distance of specified walks and cycling maps provide information on road gradients.

So what does the future hold for tourist maps?

'CD-ROM will have an increasingly significant part to play,' says John Miell, manager of Ordnance Survey's co-publications.

'We're very aware that people will browse before they leave home, and CDs can store a lot of information from a variety of sources'. In-car computers, he adds, are becoming increasingly popular for business purposes, and it will not be too long before they too find a role in the leisure environment.

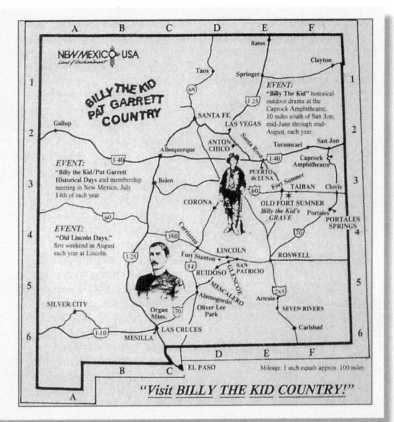

"Visit BILLY THE KID COUNTRY!"

TASKS

38 The maps illustrated here use pictures to give a taste of the different towns. Take the map of the Cotswolds and plan a day out. Write a description of the route you will take, where you will stop and what you will see.

39 You have been put in charge of preparing a similar map of your local area which will be handed out to visitors at your local tourist office. Write brief descriptions of places of interest in the area, which you will be able to give to the artist whom you have engaged to draw the pictures.

40 Read what it says in the article and explain what a 'special interest' map is.

Choose an area and plan a special interest map rather like the 'Billy the Kid Country' map in the article. (An example would be Nottinghamshire and the Robin Hood connection.)

THE WORLD OF WORK

5

For the vast majority of us the world of work is something which will concern us at the end of our education. At that moment in time, the hope is that, somewhere, there will be the right job waiting and it will be a matter of saying 'yes' and getting into the necessary routine.

ENGLISH IN THE NATIONAL CURRICULUM:

Key Skills you will cover in this chapter

☑ You will be given the opportunity to make different types of contribution in discussion.

☑ You will listen to and comment on other people talking. You may also wish to find out more information from other people by asking questions and listening carefully to replies.

☑ You will be asked to read factual and informative passages and will have the chance to make effective use of this material in your written work.

☑ You will practise dialogue and write a script.

☑ You will be encouraged to organise your ideas and information to enable you to persuade the reader to your view.

The world of work proved to be brutal and life-destroying for Iqbal Masih. His working life started at the age of four when, put at its simplest, he was sold by his parents to the owner of a carpet factory.

Read his story, which is printed on the following pages.

Death of a Slave

Suppose British children had no schooling and were sent from the age of 4 to work in factories, where they toiled long hours and were often beaten and tortured. To us it is unthinkable. Yet it is reality for 12m children in Pakistan. One of them was Iqbal Masih: carpet-maker at 4, anti-slavery campaigner at 10, dead at 13.
Report by Jonathan Silvers

At 13, Iqbal Masih was the size of a child half his age. He stood 4ft tall and weighed 60lb. His spine was curved, his gait was slow. His hands were calloused, his fingers contorted by arthritis. His condition was the legacy of six years spent as a child slave making carpets. But Iqbal had an intellectual maturity beyond his years and a strong sense of justice. When he was 10 he escaped from his master and joined the struggle against child labour. By the time he was 13 he had liberated 3,000 of the 12m children in bondage at textile and brick factories, tanneries and steelworks throughout Pakistan. In doing so he drew Western consumers' attention to the plight of the Third World's 200m working children.

On the evening of 16 April this year Iqbal's short, painful but heroic life ended. He was shot while visiting relatives in a village. The killing remains unsolved.

Like millions of children in Pakistan, Iqbal Masih was raised in a two-room hut. His family lived in the village of Muridke, not far from Lahore. He worked from the moment he could walk. At three he planted seeds in the fields. At four he washed clothes and gleaned the fields after harvest. He played cricket when he wasn't minding his infant sister or helping with chores. Fariq Nadeem, a childhood friend, says, 'He was pleased to learn some cricket players are paid handsomely. He decided to become a professional player when he grew up.'

Whatever dreams Iqbal had of becoming the next Imran Khan were dashed when his parents sold him into bondage at the age of four. Children of relatively prosperous parents are bonded at 10 or 11. The poorest families bond their children at five and sometimes at four.

The textile mill and brick kiln in Muridke took in scores of

children every year. So did the landowners, who boasted that children were much cheaper than tractors or oxen. But it was the carpet-makers who pursued them most aggressively. Iqbal's entry into the work-force coincided with a fashion in Europe and America for hand-knotted carpets. Pakistan's carpet-makers trebled production and opened new factories.

A hand-knotted carpet is made by tying short lengths of fine-coloured thread to a lattice of heavier white threads; a pattern is achieved by varying the colours. The process is labour-intensive and tedious: one 8ft x 10ft carpet contains well over 1m knots and takes an experienced weaver, working 10 hours a day, 30 days to complete. Small knots are made most easily by small hands. Small children earn less than adult weavers, learn quickly and make few demands. Thus 500,000 children aged between 4 and 14 work in Pakistan's carpet factories.

In Britain you can buy hand-knotted carpets in many shops. Harrods and Ikea go to lengths to check that child labour has not been involved in the carpets they sell. But an Ikea spokesman points out that it is difficult to be sure that factories don't use child labour when the buyer is not there.

According to Iqbal's mother, Inayat Bibi, she and his father, Saif Masih, received a visit from Sadfar Jodi, factotum to the carpet-master, Arshad. Inayat asked for 800 rupees (a little over £16) for Iqbal. Sadfar agreed. The money, called a *peshgi*, was a loan that Iqbal would repay with five years of labour. The *peshgi* would be paid in instalments, and Arshad would deduct from it any costs associated with Iqbal's 'maintenance and training'.

For the next six years Iqbal

got up six mornings a week at 5.30 and walked two kilometres to Arshad's workshop.

There he and 20 other children knotted carpets from 6am to 7pm, then spent an hour or two cleaning the shop and loading finished carpets onto a lorry. A finished carpet weighed 70lb. Iqbal weighed less than 40lb. Talk was prohibited in case the children made errors. They were allowed one 30-minute break for lunch and were punished if they took longer. They were also punished if they fell asleep, if their workbenches were sloppy, if they misread a pattern, if they complained or talked back.

Children were caned and lashed, hung upside-down by their ankles and had their fingers plunged into boiling water. These torments were doled out in a storage closet. Four children were beaten on a typical day.

Iqbal was often beaten for refusing to work overtime – anything from 4 to 8 hours added to the usual 14 hour workday. On one occasion Arshad pulled the boy out of bed at 3am and dragged him, weeping, to the workshop to repair defective carpets. Iqbal retaliated by running to the district police station and reporting Arshad's abuses to the sergeant. The sergeant forcibly returned Iqbal to the workshop and advised Arshad to 'chain the little traitor' to a loom. However, it was sickness and depression, not chains, that put an end to Iqbal's rebellions. He came down with bronchial infections, muscle and back aches, arthritis and spinal compression. His friend, Nadeem, remembers how Iqbal, on a rare day off, couldn't grip a bat during an improvised cricket game: 'He quit in the middle of the game and ran away in tears.' Most vexing of all, Iqbal stopped growing. Child labourers are, on average, 20% smaller than normal non-working children, but Iqbal was unusually small.

He got little sympathy at home. 'Father had deserted Mother and she was forced to borrow money from Arshad,' says Aslam Masih, Iqbal's elder brother. 'She borrowed more than she could repay and so she couldn't complain. One day Iqbal came home early with bruises and cuts. He begged his mother not to send him back but all she could say was that life in the village was hard and the more he complained the more he would suffer.'

* * *

Speaking officially, Pakistan's leaders deplore child labour. Speaking candidly, they consider the practice a distasteful but unavoidable part of an emerging economy. Only 37% of Pakistan's 25m school-age children attend primary school. The others enter the workforce or become beggars.

Pakistan remains a feudal society. The lords – factory owners, exporters, financiers – tend to oppose reforms. 'Our position is that the government must avoid humanitarian measures that harm our competitive advantages,' says Imran Malik, vice-chairman of the Pakistan Carpet Manufacturers and Exporters Association.

The task of abolishing child labour has fallen on organisations such as the Bonded Labour Liberation Front, founded in 1988 by Essan Ulla Khan with the aim of freeing Pakistan's 20m bonded workers. Since then, the BLLF has freed more than 40,000 adults and children from bondage and has educated 11,000 former child labourers at its own primary schools. As a result of its

campaigning, a law against child labour in hazardous conditions was passed in 1991, and another against bonded labour and the *peshgi* system in 1992. However, business owners routinely disregard the laws and use their economic clout to avoid prosecution.

In September 1992 Khan spoke to a gathering in Shekhupura, a village near Muridke, about the new laws. One of the questions came from a very young child. 'He had pushed his way to the front of the crowd,' recalls Khan. 'He was quite dirty and quite small. He wanted to know how he could leave his master and go to school. He said he was Iqbal Masih and he worked at a carpet factory. He had never been to school. After six years his debt to the master had increased to 13,000 rupees and he feared he would have to work to the end of his days.'

Iqbal struck Khan as unique. 'He was the most determined individual I had met. He spoke with eloquence and intelligence. You couldn't but be moved when he said the carpet-master had robbed him of his childhood.'

Iqbal returned to the carpet factory the next morning and presented Arshad with the Charter of Freedom, a BLLF pamphlet about the rights of child and bonded labourers. He declared that his *peshgi* was void and he would no longer work. Arshad responded by dragging him into a courtyard and beating him severely.

'Arshad came to us a day or two later,' says his mother. 'He demanded the boy or the money we owed him. He threatened us with violence and prison. Saif insisted that Iqbal return to the factory. But Iqbal refused.'

Khan saw that Iqbal was given a writ of release, based on the

new laws to get a child out of a factory, and a place in a BLLF primary school in Lahore. Although Iqbal's family's debt was void because of the 1992 law, they continued to suffer threats and also had to flee to Lahore. 'Before Iqbal left,' says his mother, 'the workers told him he had made an enemy of the most powerful man in the village. He said, "I am not afraid of the carpet-master. He should be afraid of me."'

Iqbal Masih was 10 when he entered school for the first time in November 1992. He learned to read by smuggling a primer into his bed each night at the BLLF hostel. He took the same approach to the study of mathematics, history and science. He drove himself hard 'because I'm afraid they'll send me back (to Muridke) if I don't learn'. Iqbal told his teachers, 'I want to become a lawyer and fight for children's rights.' He charged his conversation with phrases torn from law books, and his classmates nicknamed him Chief Justice.

In late 1993 he began travelling with Khan and other BLLF activists. His first visit was to a carpet factory in Kasur, south-east of Lahore. Iqbal slipped past the guards and questioned workers. Khan included his espionage in an urgent BLLF complaint. In the raid that followed police found 300 children, most aged between 4 and 10, working in hazardous conditions.

Iqbal was fearless in front of crowds, so Khan had him address gatherings at market-places, schools and factories. 'He was authentic in a way that I could never be,' says Khan. 'He spoke as one of them. He inspired 3,000 child labourers to break away from their masters and thousands of adults to demand better working conditions. He was our most effective spokesman.'

In his whitewashed bedroom decorated with Teenage Mutant Ninja Turtle masks, Iqbal wrote speeches. 'I am working for the freedom of the children of Pakistan,' he told classmates. 'I can't waste time playing.'

* * *

In 1992 Pakistan's carpet exports fell for the first time in three decades; only by 2 or 3%, but it showed that Western consumers were beginning to shy away from luxury goods made by Third World children. In 1993 and 1994 exports fell sharply in America, Germany and Britain, the three largest markets for Pakistani goods. An investigation by the Pakistan Carpet Manufacturers and Exporters Association blamed the decline on 'subversive organisations' and singled out Iqbal Masih as 'the child whose testimony is most objectionable and therefore most damaging to our industry'.

In 1994 Reebok, the sportswear giant, awarded Iqbal its Human Rights Youth In Action Award. Iqbal was deluged with invitations to address foreign audiences. In November he travelled to Sweden. While there he was examined by leading paediatricians. The doctors gained some insight into his pulmonary and vascular ailments which included tuberculosis. They estimated his bone age at 11 years and attributed his 'hysterically stunted growth' to malnutrition and chronic abuse. The pharmaceutical company, Pharmacia, gave him a 12-month supply of human growth hormone valued at £10,000.

In December he went to Boston. He played Nintendo and basketball, chewed gum, watched television, dressed in jeans and sneakers. At a large department store the abundance of carpets seemed to intimidate him; he calculated that each cost more than he made in all his years of work. During his visit, NBC and CBS News ran reports on prominent fashion designers whose goods are made by Third World children. The trustees of Brandeis University awarded Iqbal a four-year scholarship, pending completion of his studies. He returned to his schoolwork with his usual aggression, completing a four-year course in two.

But early this year Iqbal and his fellow campaigners began to suffer serious setbacks. At the urging of the carpet manufacturers, the Pakistan Federal Investigation Agency launched an inquiry into the BLLF, detaining and interrogating its workers and teachers. There were also anonymous threats of violence against BLLF workers and property. Iqbal learned from friends in Muridke that the district carpet wallahs were plotting against him.

Nevertheless, in this fearful atmosphere he travelled from the BLLF hostel in Lahore to his mother's home in Muridke on April 16. Iqbal spent the day playing with the local children.

At six that evening he left Muridke with his 20-year-old cousin, Furyad, who promised to put him on a Lahore-bound bus. Furyad suggested they briefly visit their aunt and uncle, who lived on a farm in a nearby village. When they reached the farm, their aunt said their uncle was working in a distant field and had not yet eaten. She asked Furyad and her son, Liquat, to take him a dinner pail. The boys left for the field by bicycle, with Iqbal seated on top.

What happened next has become a matter of international debate. Police investigators claim the three boys encountered a labourer named Muhammad Ashraf, who was violating a she-donkey. Ashraf grabbed a shotgun and fired it in the boy's direction, hoping to scare them off. The shot struck Iqbal Masih in the back and side and Furyad in the arm. Iqbal died instantly. Ashraf confessed to the crime and was charged with second-degree murder. Furyad and Liquat vigorously dispute the police account. Furyad asserts they encountered nobody en route to the field. A shot rang out in the dark, they saw nobody and then Iqbal was dead. 'The police brought Liquat and me to the station that night,' says Furyad. 'The inspector did not question us and he did not take down our statements. Instead, he applied ink to our fingers and made us put thumbprints on blank sheets of paper. Later, they read to us false statements which they said we had signed.'

At Reebok's request, a forensic specialist from Physicians for Human Rights, a Boston organisation, evaluated the postmortem report, the police report, the police report and a diagram of Iqbal's injuries. He concluded: 'The autopsy report and (police report) leave many questions unanswered…. Further investigation is clearly necessary to… provide a complete accounting of the circumstances of Iqbal's murder.' More than 50 governments and human rights groups condemned the police investigation as 'shoddy', 'inept', 'tainted' and 'manifestly corrupt'. Ashraf has now withdrawn his confession.

Eight hundred mourners

crowded into Muridke cemetry for Iqbal's funeral in mid-April. A week later, 3,000 protesters, half of them under 12, marched through Lahore. It became a cause célèbre among such diverse figures as Jimmy Carter, Peter Gabriel and the Tiananmen Square activist, Wang Dan.

Khan called upon the Human Rights Commission of the United Nations to ban the import and sale of all products made by children, especially carpets: 'I appeal to importers and consumers: say no and only no to child-made carpets. This is the last message of Iqbal.' Bowing to public pressure, European importers cancelled contracts valued at £15m.

Months after Iqbal's death, the mound above his grave is flecked with colour: thousands of red, yellow and green petals left in tribute. A few yards away are the bricks that will shelter the grave site. They are from a nearby kiln and were made by children that Iqbal had hoped to free.

TASKS

1 In your own words write about a typical day in the life of a young boy working in the carpet factory in Muridke.

2 We are told that Iqbal wrote speeches. Using information from the article, write one of the speeches which he might have made to a crowd in Lahore.

3 Imagine that you were present at Iqbal's funeral. Describe the scene.

4 You have read the story of Iqbal Masih and feel so strongly that you want to do something to help. You find out that your local carpet store is selling carpets made in Pakistan. Write a letter to the manager of the store. (Remember you don't know for certain that the carpets have been made by child labourers.)

5 We are told that Iqbal won the Reebok Human Rights Youth Action Award. You have been asked to nominate someone for this award. Think of all the children you know or know of. Who would you nominate? Write the name of your nominee at the top of your page and write the citation which you would send to the judges.

D o you look forward to starting work? What do you think it will really be like? Do you know how you will feel?

Here are some poems. The first is by John Betjeman. It is called *Executive*.

Executive

*I am a young executive. No cuffs than mine are cleaner;
I have a Slimline brief-case and I use the firm's Cortina.
In every roadside hostelry from here to Burgess Hill
The maîtres d'hôtel all know me well and let me sign the bill.*

You ask me what it is I do. Well actually, you know,
I'm partly a liaison man and partly PRO
Essentially I integrate the current export drive
And basically I'm viable from ten o'clock till five.

For vital off-the-record work – that's talking transport wise –
I've a scarlet Aston-Martin – and does she go? She flies!
Pedestrians and dogs and cats – we mark them down for slaughter.
I also own a speed-boat which has never touched the water.

She's built of fibre-glass, of course. I call her 'Mandy Jane'
After a bird I used to know – No soda, please, just plain –
And how did I acquire her? Well to tell you about that
And to put you in the picture I must wear my other hat.

I do some mild developing. The sort of place I need
Is a quiet country market town that's rather run to seed.
A luncheon and a drink or two, a little savoir faire –
I fix the Planning Officer, the Town Clerk and the Mayor.

And if some preservationist attempts to interfere
A 'dangerous structure' notice from the Borough engineer
Will settle any buildings that are standing in our way –
The modern style, sir, with respect, has really come to stay.

JOHN BETJEMAN

TASK

6 Explain what picture of a working man this poem creates in your mind.
   You should describe:
    what he says he's good at
    whether he is the sort of man to admire

Vital by Alan Brownjohn is a different sort of poem.

Vital

....

I think my work is important, I am a link
In a long chain.
I had to have the training for it,
And I had to dirty my hands.
They ask my advice when they want to know what would be best.
I might move up even higher, in time.

On Sunday, I woke up shouting. She said,
What on earth's the matter, we're supposed to be
Going out to dinner later; or rather lunch.
I dressed, and played with Lynda, and
Felt a bit better.

I was called into the office from the shop
Floor. 'Mr Fletton, up from London, wants to see you.'
But I was hearing the mutter-mutter,
The kind-of giggling noises inside the machines
Through four thick concrete walls.
I could not read the words in front of my eyes.

She said last Thursday, you haven't said a thing
The whole evening.
I said no. I've been watching:
… I couldn't name a thing I'd seen on the screen.

Today is vital, people are relying on me
To get ten thousand packages out on time.
I am part of a chain, a link, they ask my advice.
I open the front door. After the wind,
It's a lovely cool morning, and sun;
Very bright.
The keys of the Toledo are clenched wet
in my right hand. And I don't move.
I am standing shaking. I am standing, shaking.

ALAN BROWNJOHN

TASKS

7 Answer the following questions:
   a In what ways is the man in this poem thinking about his work?
   b How is he different from the executive?
   c What has made this man behave as he has?

Study the way in which the poem is constructed

Every word in a poem is carefully chosen, and carefully placed on the page.
The lines, the stanzas (verses), the rhythm, the tone, all help to make the poem.
One way of exploring a poem is to read it aloud.

8 Work out with a partner how to read or perform these two poems.
   How does your performance help you to understand the poems?
9 Now carefully explain in writing how the two poets have made their
   poems effective.

Both the previous poems are about men. Now what about women? Here are two poems by women and about women.

Feminine Advice (rap)

Like every other mother, mine
was keen to tell her daughter
to certainly go swimming, but
to not go near the water.
To find myself a Good Career
to Travel and Have Fun
and not to tie myself down at eighteen with
    husband, home
and bloody ungrateful children
like she'd done.
If I cut according to my cloth and didn't
get excited
at around thirty I would find myself miraculously
Mister-Righted.
She said to watch my handbag and keep
    myself nice.

Oh I sure was grateful for the feminine advice.

But I had a lot to learn when I went to school –
like how women weren't
mechanically minded as a rule.
Headmaster, careers mistress, in subtle alliance
to remind us we were rotten at Maths and Science.
Oh, I really shocked her
when I told her, 'Miss,
I want to be a doctor' –
She asked me had I thought it out? A woman
    could do worse
than be a nurse.
And 'in fact, with dedication, any bright girl can
be the driving force behind a really Top Man
(and once you've got him, here's how to please –
    via his stomach and macaroni surprise)

oh, he'll put you on a pedestal,
he'll treat you like a queen
if you just put your trust
in Pristine Clean –
remember in Office Practice the thing that is
    most shocking
is turning up with black-rim nails, or splashes in
    your stocking.
So, when you go for interview,
Knees together in navyblue,
Wear little white collars and be quiet as mice…'

Oh I sure was grateful for the feminine advice.

And those Women's Mags were always telling you
about thrush, the hot flush and what to do
and how to keep your husband true
and what to dip in your fondue.
How to address Royalty (with the minimum
    of slanging)
How to unravel old potscourers and torn tights and
Knit them up into an Attractive Wallhanging.
How New Ways With Eyeshadow turn a
    housewife to a teaser.
How to tan, bake a flan, and plan for your freezer.
How to rescue junkshop finds and strip them
    for Good Use.
And, especially for Christmas,
Sauce for the goose.
Oh, their serving suggestions sounded awfully nice,

So I sure was grateful for the feminine advice.

LIZ LOCHHEAD

Maintenance Engineer

One Friday night it happened, soon after we were wed,
When my old man came in from work as usual I said:
'Your tea is on the table, clean clothes are on the rack,
Your bath will soon be ready, I'll come up and scrub your back.'
He kissed me very tenderly and said, 'I'll tell you flat
The service I give my machine ain't half as good as that.'

I said …
Chorus
I'm not your little woman, your sweetheart or your dear
I'm a wage slave without wages, I'm a maintenance engineer.

Well then we got to talking. I told him how I felt,
How I keep him running just as smooth as some conveyor belt!
Well after all, it's I'm the one provides the power supply
He goes just like the clappers on me steak'n kidney pie.
His fittings are all shining 'cos I keep 'em nice and clean
And he tells me his machine tool is the best I've ever seen.

But …
Chorus

The terms of my employment would make your hair turn grey,
I have to be on call you see for 24 hours a day.
I quite enjoy the perks though while I'm working through the night
For we get job satisfaction. Well he does, and then I might.
If I keep up full production, I should have a kid or two,
So some future boss will have a brand new labour force to screw.

So …
Chorus

The truth began to dawn then, how I keep him fit and trim
So the boss can make a nice fat profit out of me and him.
And, as a solid union man, he got in quite a rage
To think that we're both working hard and getting one man's wage.
I said 'And what about the part-time packing job I do?
That's three men that I work for love, my boss, your boss and you.'

So …
Chorus

He looked a little sheepish and he said, 'As from today
The lads and me will see what we can do on equal pay.
Would you like a housewives' union? Do you think you should get paid?
As a cook and as a cleaner, as a nurse and as a maid?'
I said, 'Don't jump the gun love, if you did your share at home,
Perhaps I'd have some time to fight some battles of my own.'

For …
Chorus

I've often heard you tell me how you'll pull the bosses down.
You'll never do it brother while you're bossing me around.
'Til women join the struggle, married, single, white and black
You're fighting with a blindfold and one arm behind your back.'
The message has got over now for he's realised at last
That power to the sisters must mean power to the class.

And …
Chorus
Repeat: I'm not your little woman, your sweetheart or your dear
       I'm a wage-slave without wages
       I'm a maintenance engineer.

SANDRA KERR

TASKS

10 In groups, discuss these two poems. Here are a few issues to get you started.

- The attitudes of teachers to boys and girls.
- Women's magazines.
- Parents' advice.
- Housewife or househusband?
- The breadwinner.

11 Now consider the opposite point of view. Write (in poetry or prose) your own 'Masculine Advice' or 'The Engineer Talks Back'.

In your homework book you will find another poem about a 'worker', together with a further task for you to do.

M oving into the world of work is an important step in anyone's life. Not many people at 16 can make this step but everyone needs to think about what is involved. Do you know a lot about this subject? Do you have a plan?

Printed on the next two pages is some material from a magazine called '*Appointments* – Britain's brightest recruitment magazine'. You will find a number of advertisements for a variety of jobs.

Have a look at them.

WENDY'S

Opening soon

The leading fast food restaurant in America is arriving in Watford

The restaurant is an integral part of Hollywood Bowl, owned and operated by **Bass Leisure Entertainments**. We have 30 vacancies available and we want you to be part of our success. In return we offer:

- full-time and part-time positions
- free uniform
- performance reviews
- incentive schemes
- £4.00 per hour
- full training/development
- the excitement of being part of an opening team

So if you are enthusiastic, flexible and enjoy working as part of a team, why not apply today – it could be the break you have been waiting for. To obtain an application form, please contact:

The General Manager of Wendy's Watford

Closing date 17 November 1995
We are an equal opportunities employer

hollywood bowl

TASKS

12 Take each advertisement and answer the following questions.
   a What is involved in doing this job?
   b What sort of person is needed?
   c What qualifications are required?

13 These advertisements are targeted not at 16-year-olds but at slightly older people.

When you have answered the questions above, select one of the jobs and draw up a plan of action to prepare yourself for such a job over the next couple of years.

14 Now project yourself forward a couple of years and apply for the job by letter, enclosing a cv. (Remember that you have prepared yourself and your cv will show that you are well qualified for the position.)

You will find another page of advertisements printed in your homework book and a similar exercise.

TIME OUT TASK!

Advertisements

Advertisements are all around us – they are impossible to avoid. You find them:

- in newspapers
- in magazines
- on the television
- at the cinema
- in the streets
- everywhere

Sometimes they influence you and sometimes they don't.

Choose **three** advertisements.

a The most effective advertisement you have seen; one that really makes you want to buy the product.

b The worst advertisement you have seen.

c An advertisement that you just don't understand.

Describe each advertisement and explain carefully why you have chosen it.

Now consider the world of advertising as a whole.

- Do you think that anything goes – subliminal messages – nudity and sex?
- Do you think that some advertisements should not be allowed?

Write a short essay explaining your view with the title:

  'The ethics of advertising'.

END OF TIME OUT!

Work one hundred years ago was very different from nowadays. Labour was cheap and labourers worked long hours. The play, *Hobson's Choice*, is set in the year 1880. The action takes place in Salford in two boot and shoemakers.

Act 1 ends with an employer (Henry Hobson) abusing his employee (Willie Mossop) for wanting to marry his daughter, Maggie Hobson.

Hobson's Choice

Act 1

Hobson drives Alice and Vickey before him. But MAGGIE *stands in Hobson's way as he follows and she closes the door. She looks at her father from the stair.*

MAGGIE:
You and I'ull be straight with one another, father. I'm not a fool and you're not a fool, and things may as well be put in their places as left untidy.

HOBSON:
I tell you my mind's made up. You can't have Willie Mossop. Why, lass, his father was a workhouse brat. A come-by-chance.

MAGGIE:
It's news to me we're snobs in Salford. I'll have Willie Mossop. I've to settle my life's course, and a good course, too, so think on.

HOBSON:
I'd be the laughing-stock of the place if I allowed it. I won't have it, Maggie. It's hardly decent at your time of life.

MAGGIE:
I'm thirty and I'm marrying Willie Mossop. And now I'll tell you my terms.

HOBSON:
You're in a nice position to state terms, my lass.

MAGGIE:
You will pay my man, Will Mossop, the same wages as before. And as for me, I've given you the better part of twenty years of work without wages. I'll work eight hours a day in future and you will pay me fifteen shillings by the week.

HOBSON:
Do you think I'm made of brass?

MAGGIE:
You'll soon be made of less than you are if you let Willie go. And if Willie goes, I go. That's what you've got to face.

HOBSON:
I might face it, Maggie. Shop hands are cheap.

MAGGIE:
Cheap ones are cheap. The sort you'd have to watch all day, and you'd feel happy helping them to tie up parcels and sell laces with Tudsbury and Heeler and Minns supping their ale without you. I'm value to you, so's my man; and you can boast it at the 'Moonraker's' that your daughter Maggie's made the strangest, finest match a woman's made this fifty year. And you can put your hand in your pocket and do what I propose.

HOBSON:
I'll show you what I propose, Maggie. (*He lifts trap and calls.*) Will Mossop! (*He places hat on counter and un-buckles belt.*) I cannot leather you, my lass. You're female, and exempt, but I can leather him. Come up, Will Mossop.

WILL *comes up trap and closes it.*
You've taken up with my Maggie, I hear. (*He conceals strap.*)

WILLIE:
Nay, I've not. she's done the taking up.

HOBSON:
Well, Willie, either way, you've fallen on misfortune. Love's led you astray, and I feel bound to put you right. (*Shows strap.*)

WILLIE:
Maggie, what's this?

MAGGIE:
I'm watching you, my lad.

HOBSON:
Mind, Willie, you can keep your job. I don't bear malice, but we must beat the love from your body, and still sitting in you, you'll get a leathering. (*Getting ready to strike.*)

WILLIE:
You'll not beat love in me. You're making a great mistake, Mr Hobson, and –

HOBSON:
You'll put aside your weakness for my Maggie if you've a liking for a sound skin. You'll waste a gradely lot of brass at chemist's if I am at you

for a week with this. (*He swings the strap.*)

WILLIE:

I'm none wanting thy Maggie, it's her that's after me, but I'll tell you this, Mr Hobson: if you touch me with that belt, I'll take her quick, aye, and stick to her like glue.

HOBSON:

There's nobbut one answer to that kind of talk, my lad. (*He strikes with belt.* MAGGIE *shrinks.*)

WILLIE:

And I've nobbut one answer back. Maggie, I've none kissed you yet. I shirked before. But, by gum, I'll kiss you now – (*he kisses her quickly,*

with temper, not with passion, as quickly leaves her, to face Hobson) – and take you and hold you. And if Mr Hobson raises up that strap again, I'll do more. I'll walk straight out of shop with thee and us two 'ull set up for ourselves.

MAGGIE:

Willie! I knew you had it in you, lad. (*She puts her arm round his neck. He is quite unresponsive. His hands fall limply to his sides.*)

HOBSON *stands in amazed indecision.*

CURTAIN

HAROLD BRIGHOUSE

TASK

15 Here are a number of things for you to do and consider.

a Read the extract through several times, rehearsing how each character would speak.

b How would you sum up each character here?

c What hints are there about the attitude of employers to men and to women?

d This is the climax of Act 1. What makes it dramatically exciting?

e What do you think Will and Maggie will do next? What problems will they face? When you have thought about this write a piece called 'Advice to Will and Maggie'.

Many people work in extremely competitive situations, especially those who are in the retail trade.

Printed below is an article from a magazine called *The Grocer*. In the article, which is entitled 'Talking Dirty', there is some analysis of different soap powders. The article is not particularly difficult to understand. However, there are so many brands of detergent and soap powder that it is very easy to get in a muddle.

Read the article through carefully.

Talking Dirty

As Britons become more concerned with hygiene and cleanliness, the market is expanding at a rapid rate. Jenny Deeprose looks under the UK's sinks.

Two giants are responsible for the nation's clean clothes. Between them they account for an estimated 87% of the £886 million detergents market, according to Mintel's 1995 report. Own label has 10% and other brands 3%.

Procter & Gamble, with Ariel, Daz and Bold, is said to have taken share from Lever Brothers, who market Persil and Radion, over the past five years. But brand share and sales figures are not available – a spokesman for P&G says this is 'for reasons of confidentiality'.

Segmentation of this market has caused 'a high level of confusion'. The choice is bewildering, and includes standard big box powders and liquid alternatives, concentrated liquids and powders, choices of bio-logical and non-biological. Other products are designed for coloureds and some contain fabric softener. Add to this own label alternatives, and it is no surprise research shows confused consumers 'display a high degree of brand loyalty or switch to a simpler own label alternative'.

Concentrated liquids and powders have overtaken standard variants, and sales have increased by about 75% and 19% respectively. Concentrated liquids have grown from £96 million to £177 million since 1992, and concentrated powders are worth an estimated £270 million. Standard powders, despite a decline of 4% in value, still account for 50% of volume sales.

The growing popularity of refills demonstrates concerns about packaging waste and value-for-money, with refillable detergents accounting for 70% in volume and 67% market value in 1994.

Sainsbury, ASDA and Safeway have developed their own sub-brands, and Sainsbury's Novon, introduced in 1993, was said to be about 25% cheaper than other branded alternatives.

The ever-widening range of clothes washing products means only the multiples can carry the full range, which further erodes the ability of independents to offer more than a basic selection.

The multiples have increased their sales to an estimated 81% and £718 million, while other grocery outlets take 9%. There is an additional 5% through convenience stores and forecourts.

Londis trading controller, Fiona Keyzor, says: 'Our plano-grams reflect that micro powders and ultra liquids are growth lines – they generate much higher levels of cash profits than traditional washing powders.' According to Keyzor, standard powders have always been strong in smaller shops, but 'concen-trated liquids have become increasingly successful for independent

retailers, due to a combination of the right pack size – 500ml – and the lower unit cost.' They also take up less valuable shelf space. Auto/ Standard washing powder, a Micro powder and liquid are all available under the Londis brand.

Fabric conditioners have also received the concentrated treat-ment, but with less impact – standard products are not too bulky and only small quantities are used per wash. Refill packs have reached 19%; standard packs 76% and concentrates only 5% of sales volume. The sector was valued at £176 million in 1994.

Lenor Plus, from P&G, has four fragrances, boasting a time release mechanism for 'fresher smelling clothes', lasting up to five days. Lenor Ultra Plus is a concentrated version, offering 'superior softness and cheaper cost per wash'.

The two major brands, Lenor and Comfort (Lever) have healthy competition from own label alternatives. Value is estimated at £64 million for P&G

and £62 million for Lever, with each brand supported by vigorous promotional campaigns.

Handwashing liquids or flakes are still purchased by 15% of consumers, although machine detergents are now designed to wash at lower temperatures. Pre-wash and stain removal products are regularly bought by 13%.

Despite claims that pre-washing is unnecessary, products such as Blumoller's Biotex and specialist stain removers such as Benckiser's Vanish, still formed part of a £26 million sector in 1994, growing at 8% a year.

Vanish, launched in soap bar format, has been joined by Concentrated Stain Gel, Stain Stick and in 1994 by In-Wash stain remover.

Other brands include Dylon International, with three Fabric Care Stain Removers, which benefited from a £300,00 campaign this year; Shout from Johnson's Wax, and Dendron's Beckmann Stain Devils.

TASKS

16 Summarise the passage in your own words, making sure that you cover the following points:

- ▪ Market value.
- ▪ Main brands/own brands/other brands.
- ▪ Powders/liquids/concentrates.
- ▪ Environmental concerns.
- ▪ Alternatives or additives to the standard detergent or powder.

17 Having read this article you now feel yourself to be in a position to advise your mum or a friend's mum about what to buy.

In the form of a dialogue write the conversation you might have.

In your homework book you will find another article from the same magazine which will also require careful reading before completing the tasks.

Shakespeare writes about working men in *A Midsummer Night's Dream*. These workmen are about to rehearse a play which they will perform before the Duke of Athens and his court.

In Act 1 Scene 2 these men meet to assign the parts in the play.

A Midsummer Night's Dream

Act 1 Scene 2

Enter SNUG, BOTTOM, FLUTE, SNOUT, QUINCE *and* STARVELLING.

QUINCE:
  Is all our company here?

BOTTOM:
  You were best to call them generally, man by man, according to the scrip.

QUINCE:
  Here is the scroll of every man's name, which is thought fit, through all Athens, to play in our interlude before the duke and duchess on his wedding-day at night.

BOTTOM:
  First, good Peter Quince, say what the play treats on; then read the names of the actors; and so grow to a point.

QUINCE:
  Marry, our play is – The most lamentable comedy, and most cruel death of Pyramus and Thisby.

BOTTOM:
  A very good piece of work, I assure you, and a merry. – Now, good Peter Quince, call forth your actors by the scroll. – Masters, spread yourselves.

QUINCE:
  Answer, as I call you. – Nick Bottom, the weaver.

BOTTOM:
  Ready. Name what part I am for, and proceed.

QUINCE:
  You, Nick Bottom, are set down for Pyramus.

BOTTOM:
  What is Pyramus? A lover, or a tyrant?

QUINCE:
  A lover, that kills himself most gallantly for love.

BOTTOM:
  That will ask some tears in the true performing of it. If I do it, let the audience look to their eyes; I will move storms; I will condole in some measure. To the rest: – yet my chief humour is for a tyrant: I could play Ercles rarely, or a part to tear a cat in, to make all split.

    The raging rocks,   And Phibbus'car
    With shivering shocks,   Shall shine from far,
    Shall break the locks   And make and mar
     Of prison gates: The foolish Fates.

This was lofty! – Now, name the rest of the players. – This is Ercles' vein, a tyrant's vein; – a lover is more condoling.

QUINCE:

Francis Flute, the bellows-mender.

FLUTE:

Here, Peter Quince.

QUINCE:

You must take Thisby on you.

FLUTE:

What is Thisby? A wondering knight?

QUINCE:

It is the lady that Pyramus must love.

FLUTE:

Nay, faith, let me not play a woman; I have a beard coming.

QUINCE:

That's all one; you shall play it in a mask, and you may speak as small as you will.

BOTTOM:

An I may hide my face, let me play Thisby too: I'll speak in a monstrous little voice; – *Thisne, Thisne. – Ah, Pyramus, my lover dear; thy Thisby dear! and lady dear!*

QUINCE:

No, no, you must play Pyramus; and, Flute, you Thisby.

BOTTOM:

Well, proceed.

QUINCE:

Robin Starvelling, the tailor.

STARVELLING:

Here, Peter Quince.

QUINCE:

Robin Starvelling, you must play Thisby's mother. – Tom Snout, the tinker.

SNOUT:

Here, Peter Quince.

QUINCE:

You, Pyramus's father; myself, Thisby's father; – Snug, the joiner, you, the lion's part; – and, I hope, here is a play fitted.

SNUG:

Have you the lion's part written? Pray you, if it be, give it me, for I am slow of study.

QUINCE:

You may do it extempore, for it is nothing but roaring.

BOTTOM:

Let me play the lion too: I will roar, that I will do any man's heart good to hear me; I will roar, that I will make the duke say, *Let him roar again, let him roar again.*

QUINCE:

An you should do it too terribly you would fright the duchess and the ladies, that they would shriek; and that were enough to hang us all.

ALL:

That would hang us every mother's son.

BOTTOM:

I grant you, friends, if that you should fright the ladies out of their wits, they would have no more discretion but to hand us: but I will aggravate my voice so that I will roar you as gently as any sucking dove; I will roar you an 'twere any nightingale.

QUINCE:

You can play no part but Pyramus, for Pyramus is a sweet-faced man; a proper man, as one shall see on a summer's day; a lovely, gentleman-like man; therefore you must needs play Pyramus.

BOTTOM:

Well, I will undertake it. What beard were I best to play it in?

QUINCE:

Why, what you will.

BOTTOM:

I will discharge it in either your straw coloured beard, your orange-tawny beard, your purple-in-grain beard, or your French-crown-colour beard, your perfect yellow.

QUINCE:

Some of your French crowns have no hair at all, and then you will play barefaced. – But masters, here are your parts; and I am to entreat you, request you, and desire you, to con them by to-morrow night; and meet me in the palace wood, a mile without the town, by moonlight; there will we rehearse; for if we meet in the city, we shall be dogg'd with company, and our devices known. In the meantime I will draw a bill of properties, such as our play wants. I pray you, fail me not.

BOTTOM:

We will meet; and there we may rehearse more obscenely and courageously. Take pains; be perfect; adieu.

QUINCE:

At the duke's oak we meet.

BOTTOM:

Enough; hold, or cut bow-strings.

Exeunt.

WILLIAM SHAKESPEARE

TASKS

18 Answer the following:

   a What sort of men are these?

   b What difficulties does Peter Quince have in organising the other men?

   c Do you think the play will be a success?

19 **Explore…**

   This word is often used in English Literature examinations. It means to:

   ■ read carefully

   ■ think through what is important

   ■ decide how you react to both events and to characters

   Write your own 'exploration' of this scene from Shakespeare. You should pay attention to:

   ■ the characters and their behaviour

   ■ what makes the scene amusing

TIME OUT TASK!

Let's watch television!

These words produce a variety of reactions.

Some people spend an enormous amount of time watching television; some people don't; some people feel the need to pretend that they don't watch television as much as they actually do!

You probably have your favourite television programmes and you probably think other programmes are dreadful.

Put yourself in the position of a television controller

An advertisement has been placed asking people to bid for the franchise for a new television channel. You have decided that you are going to bid for the franchise. You must put together a presentation to support your bid and part of this presentation will be a sample schedule for one week's viewing. You will also have to say why this is a good schedule.

Put your schedule together. You will have to consider the following:

- Between what hours your programmes will be transmitted.
- Who your target audience is – will this change according to the time of the day?
- Whether you want to specialise in a particular sort of programme.
- Your views on violence and sex in programmes.
- Whether you believe you can compete with existing soap operas.
- How important news bulletins might be.
- The place of sport.
- Whether you believe you could improve educational television.
- The balance of comedy and serious programmes.
- Whether you want to involve a big name in the organisation.

The list of considerations could go on and on.

When you have finished your schedule with your justification of it, swap with another member of the class and discuss with them the merits and de-merits of your different ideas.

The whole class may well become involved in the discussion.

END OF TIME OUT!

In your local Job Centre you will find a whole range of leaflets about equal opportunities at work. One set of leaflets is concerned with disabilities.

First of all it is suggested that a firm can show a positive attitude by using the disability symbol. Printed on the next two pages are extracts from two leaflets. The first explains a little about the disability symbol and the second gives some examples.

Do you have a disability?

Have you ever hesitated when you've applied for a job, wondering whether the employer will still be interested if they know you have a disability?

Perhaps you've decided not to mention your disability? Or maybe you've even felt it's not worth applying?

If you're in a job, do you sometimes wonder if your development needs have been forgotten?

And have you wondered whether you'll get a better deal from one employer than another?

But how can you tell?

That's where we may be able to help.

When you see this symbol it will show you at a glance which employers have made a commitment to take a positive look at your *abilities*.

Symbol users are committed to giving you the opportunities and incentive you need to do a good job and to develop and make progress in your career if you want to.

And you can be pretty sure that they will have a more open mind about the sort of things you could do at work.

To be a symbol user, an employer has to make five practical commitments about what they will do to make sure that disabled people can play a positive role in their organisation. These commitments help *you* to know what to expect from the employer. They also help *the employer* to know what they need to do to get the most from your abilities and potential.

So what does the symbol mean?

When you see a job advertised by an organisation displaying the symbol you can be sure that, as long as you meet the minimum requirements set out for the job, you are guaranteed an interview.

And if your employer uses the symbol, at least once a year you will have a chance to put forward your views about how you can best use your abilities at work.

Many disabled people have developed their disability during adult life, so if you're in a job with a symbol user and you become disabled, your employer will do all they can to make sure you can stay in work.

What makes a symbol user?

To use the symbol, an organisation must make five commitments to *action:*

- To interview all applicants with a disability who meet the minimum criteria for a job vacancy and consider them on their abilities.
- To ask disabled employees at least once a year what can be done to make sure they can develop and use their abilities at work.
- To make every effort when employees become disabled to make sure they stay in employment.
- To take action to ensure that key employees develop the awareness of disability needed to make the commitments work.
- Each year, to review these commitments and what has been achieved, plan ways to improve on them and let all employees know about progress and future plans.

Some of the barriers you face in work may be because the people you come across don't know much about people with disabilities. They may even be nervous of meeting you. Symbol using employers have promised to make sure that key employees in the organisation, particularly people involved in recruitment and personnel matters, develop their own awareness of people with disabilities and what they can achieve.

Finally, symbol users will review their commitments each year to see that they are working well, and will keep all their employees in touch with plans and developments.

Does the symbol apply to all people with disabilities?

The symbol is a commitment to all disabled people, whether registered as disabled or not. If your disability affects the kind of work you do, you should consider registering as disabled (ask at the Jobcentre for our leaflet 'Registering as disabled'). But it isn't necessary to register to benefit from the symbol commitments.

A sign you mean business

Vina Limited

Vina is a home-brew and wine-making kit producer in Bootle, Merseyside, employing 60 people.

Four years ago Operations Director Colin Herbert received a job application from Tony Morrisey:

'When I found out Tony was deaf my first reaction was would he hear the forklift trucks! He convinced me that it wouldn't be a problem and I employed Tony because of his ability to do the job.'

Tony progressed quickly and within two weeks was promoted to stock control management:

'We now don't consider Tony as disabled. His disability is only deafness. Nobody else could perform to Tony's standard, he always gives 200% because he wants to prove he can do the job.'

Since employing Tony, Vina have taken on a number of other employees with disabilities, and it's made a real difference to attitudes as Colin explains:

'Our outlook has changed. Now when we recruit people we always look at the ability first, we assess our needs and see whether the person fits.

'All our employees are treated equally and our confidence has built up. David Shephard (an employee with epilepsy) has progressed through the company from doing warehouse duties to quality control work, and Keith Murray (who has cerebral palsy) is constantly striving to achieve to a greater standard and prove his abilities – he will always have a go at any job.'

Colin found out about the disability symbol from his local Disability Employer Adviser. After working with her to make sure Vina could meet all the commitments, he started to use it 12 months ago:

'The symbol has made us more aware of disability. People with disabilities may have the skills and qualifications but are not given enough opportunities. If you have an application from somebody with a disability, put them on the "interview" pile – I think you'll be surprised.'

Burleigh Court Hotel

Burleigh Court is a country hotel near Stroud employing 12 people. In 1993 it was taken over by Ian Hall who retained all the employees including head gardener John Read, who uses a wheelchair. Initially Ian had his doubts:

'I was concerned that what we wanted to achieve in the gardens was within John's capabilities, but it soon became obvious to us that John was more than able to do the job and could turn his hand to work both in the gardens and in the house.

'John's attitude, loyalty and standard of work is very high because he wants to prove his ability and be independent. We don't see him as having any extra special needs. He is very well motivated and just wants to get on and do the job.'

John's motorised tractor has several attachments so that he can do a range of tasks from mowing grass to clearing snow. Ian had some advice and help from Rose King, the Disability Employment Adviser, to make the most of John's gardening abilities. Ian then became interested in using the symbol:

'The symbol is a way to show people with disabilities that we are open for them to apply for the job. Just because somebody has a disability doesn't mean they can't or aren't willing to work, which is one of the misconceptions of most people.

'I've worked in other organisations and employed disabled people purely because they were the best candidates for the job. You have to look past the disability, look at the person and what their abilities are.

'Having worked with John for some time now, I don't see him as having a disability – he's very much part of the team.'

TASKS

20 Imagine that you are one of the disabled people referred to in the leaflets. You are going to speak to a group of local business people and you intend to convince them that, if they don't do so already, they should consider employing disabled people.

Use the information from the leaflets and prepare what you are going to say. Write your speech in the form of a series of notes which will fit neatly onto a few cards about the size of a postcard, which you can carry in your pocket and refer to easily.

21 Imagine that you are a boss and you are interviewing someone who is disabled for a job in your factory. You are unsure but the interviewee is absolutely certain that they will be able to do the job.

Write the interview in the form of a short play scene. You may bring other people into your play scene if you want to.

Work can be fun at times, at other times it can be difficult and painful.

In the next two extracts there is an example of each.

Shooting an Elephant

I had halted on the road. As soon as I saw the elephant I knew with perfect certainty that I ought not to shoot him. It is a serious matter to shoot a working elephant – it is comparable to destroying a huge and costly piece of machinery – and obviously one ought not to do it if it can possibly be avoided. And at that distance, peacefully eating, the elephant looked no more dangerous than a cow. I thought then and I think now that his attack of 'must' was already passing off; in which case he would merely wander harmlessly about until the mahout came back and caught him. Moreover, I did not in the least want to shoot him. I decided that I would watch him for a little to make sure that he did not turn savage again, and then go home.

But at that moment I glanced round at the crowd that had followed me. It was an immense crowd, two thousand at the least and growing every minute. It blocked the road for a long distance on either side. I looked at the sea of yellow faces above the garish clothes – faces all happy and excited over this bit of fun, all certain that the elephant was going to be shot. They were watching me as they would watch a conjurer about to perform a trick. They did not like me, but with the magical rifle in my hands I was momentarily worth watching. And suddenly I realised that I would have to shoot the elephant after all. The people expected it of me and I had got to do it; I could feel their two thousand wills pressing me forward, irresistibly. And it was at this moment, as I stood there with the rifle in my hands, that I first grasped the hollowness, the futility of the white man's dominion in the East. Here was I, the white man with his gun, standing in front of the unarmed native crowd – seemingly the leading actor of the piece; but in reality I was only an absurd puppet pushed to and fro by the will of those yellow faces behind …

But I did not want to shoot the elephant. I watched him beating his bunch of grass against his knees, with that preoccupied grandmotherly air that elephants have. It seemed to me that it would be murder to shoot him. At that age I was not squeamish about killing animals, but I had never shot an elephant and never wanted to. (Somehow it always seems worse to kill a *large* animal.) Besides, there was the beast's owner to be considered. Alive, the elephant was worth at least a hundred pounds: dead, he would only be worth the value of his tusks, five pounds, possibly. But I had got to act quickly. I turned to some experienced-looking Burmans who had been there when we arrived, asked them how the elephant had been behaving. They all said the same thing: he took no notice of you if you left him alone, but he might charge if you went too close to him.

It was perfectly clear to me what I ought to do. I ought to walk up to within, say, 25 yards of the elephant and test his behaviour. If he charged I could shoot, if he took no notice of me it would be safe to leave him until the mahout came back. But also I knew that I was going to do no such thing. I was a poor shot with a rifle and the ground was soft mud into which one would sink at every step. If the elephant charged and I missed him, I should have about as much chance as a toad under a steam-roller. But even then I was not thinking particularly of my own skin, only of the yellow faces behind. For at that moment, with the crowd watching me, I was not afraid in the ordinary sense, as I would have been if I had been alone. A white man mustn't be frightened in front of 'natives'; and so, in general, he isn't frightened. The sole thought in my mind was that if anything went wrong these two thousand

Burmans would see me pursued, caught, trampled on and reduced to a grinning corpse like that Indian up the hill. And if that happened it was quite probable that some of them would laugh. That would never do. There was only one alternative. I shoved the cartridges into the magazine and lay down on the road to get a better aim.

The crowd grew very still, and a deep, low, happy sigh, as of people who see the theatre curtain go up at last, breathed from innumerable throats. They were going to have their bit of fun after all. The rifle was a beautiful German thing with cross-hair sights. I did not then know that in shooting an elephant one should shoot to cut an imaginary bar running from ear-hole to ear-hole. I ought, therefore, as the elephant was sideways on, to have aimed straight at his ear-hole; actually I aimed several inches in front of this, thinking the brain would be further forward.

When I pulled the trigger I did not hear the bang or feel the kick – one never does when a shot goes home – but I heard the devilish roar of glee that went up from the crowd. In that instant, in too short a time, one would have thought even for the bullet to get there, a mysterious, terrible change had come over the elephant. He neither stirred nor fell, but every line of his body had altered. He looked suddenly stricken, shrunken, immensely old, as though the frightful impact of the bullet had paralysed him without knocking him down. At last, after what seemed a long time – it might have been five seconds, I dare say – he sagged flabbily to his knees. His mouth slobbered. An enormous senility seemed to have settled upon him. One could have imagined him thousands of years old. I fired again into the same spot. At the second shot he did not collapse but climbed with desperate slowness to his feet and stood weakly upright, with legs sagging and head drooping. I fired a third time. That was the shot that did for him. You could see the agony of it jolt his whole body and knock the last remnant of strength from his legs. But in falling he seemed for a moment to rise, for as his hind legs collapsed beneath him he seemed to tower upwards like a huge rock toppling, his trunk reaching skywards like a tree. He trumpeted, for the first and only time. And then down he came, his belly towards me, with a crash that seemed to shake the ground even where I lay.

GEORGE ORWELL

Catching Frogs

Two hours later they recalled what they had come for. The frog pool was square – 50 feet wide and 70 feet long and 4 feet deep. Lush soft grass grew about its edge and a little ditch brought the water from the river to it and from it little ditches went out to the orchards. There were frogs there all right, thousands of them. Their voices beat the night, they boomed and barked and croaked and rattled. They sang to the stars, to the waning moon, to the waving grasses. They bellowed love songs and challenges. The men crept through the darkness towards the pool. The captain carried a nearly-filled pitcher of whisky and every man had his own glass. The captain had found them flash-lights that worked. Hughie and Jones carried gunny-sacks. As they drew quietly near, the frogs heard them coming. The night had been roaring with frog song and then suddenly it was silent. Mack and the boys and the captain sat down on the ground to have one last short one and to map their campaign. And the plan was bold.

During the millennia that frogs and men have lived in the same world, it is probable that men have hunted frogs. And during that time a pattern of hunt and parry has developed. The man with net or bow or lance or gun creeps noiselessly, as he thinks, towards the frog. The pattern requires that the frog sit still, sit very still and wait. The rules of the game require the frog to wait until the final flicker of a second, when the net is descending, when the lance is in the air, when the finger squeezes the trigger, then the frog jumps, plops into the water, swims to the bottom and waits until the man goes away. That is the way it is done, the way it has always been done. Frogs have every right to expect it will always be done that way. Now and then the net is too quick, the lance pierces, the gun flicks and that frog is gone, but it is all fair and in the frame-work. Frogs don't resent that. But how could they have anticipated Mack's new method? How could they have foreseen the horror that followed? The sudden flashing of lights, the shouting and squealing of men, the rush of feet. Every frog leaped, plopped into the pool, and swam frantically to the bottom. Then into the pool plunged the line of men, stamping, churning, moving in a crazy line up the pool, flinging their feet about. Hysterically the frogs, displaced from their placid spots, swam ahead of the crazy thrashing feet and the feet came on. Frogs are good swimmers, but they haven't much endurance. Down the pool they went until finally they were bunched and crowded against the ends. And the feet and wildly-plunging bodies followed them. A few frogs lost their heads and floundered among the feet and got through and these were saved. But the majority decided to leave this pool for ever, to find a new home in a new country where this kind of thing didn't happen. A wave of frantic, frustrated frogs, big ones, little ones, brown ones, green ones, men frogs and women frogs, a wave of them broke over the bank, crawled, leaped, scrambled. They clambered up the grass, they clutched at each other, little ones rode on big ones. And then – horror on horror – the flashlights found them. Two men gathered them like berries. The line came out of the water and closed in on their rear and gathered them like potatoes. Tens and fifties of them were flung into the gunny-sacks and the sacks filled with tired, frightened, and disillusioned frogs, with dripping, whimpering frogs. Some got away, of course, and some had been saved in the pool. But never in frog history had such an execution taken place. Frogs by the pound, by the fifty pounds. They weren't counted, but there must have been six or seven hundred. Then happily Mack tied up the necks of the sacks. They were soaking, dripping wet and the air was cool. They had a short one in the grass before they went back to the house, so they wouldn't catch cold.

It is doubtful whether the captain had ever had so much fun. He was indebted to Mack and the boys. Later when the curtains caught fire and were put out with the little towels, the captain told the boys not to mind it. He felt it was an honour to have them burn his house clear down, if they wanted to. 'My wife is a wonderful woman,' he said in a kind of peroration. 'Most wonderful woman. Ought to of been a man.

If she was a man I wouldn' of married her.' He laughed a long time over that and repeated it three or four times and resolved to remember it, so he could tell it to a lot of other people. He filled a jug with whisky and gave it to Mack. He wanted to go to live with them in the Palace Flophouse. He decided that his wife would like Mack and the boys if she only knew them. Finally, he went to sleep on the floor with his head among the puppies. Mack and the boys poured themselves a short one and regarded him seriously.

Mack said: 'He give me that jug of whisky, didn't he? You heard him?'

'Sure he did,' said Eddie. 'I heard him.'

'And he give me a pup?'

'Sure, pick of the litter. We all heard him. Why?'

'I never did roll a drunk and I ain't gonna start now,' said Mack. 'We got to get out of here. He's gonna wake up feelin' lousy and it's goin' to be all our fault. I just don't want to be here.' Mack glanced at the burned curtains, at the floor glistening with whisky and puppy dirt, at the bacon grease that was coagulating on the stove front. He went to the pups, looked them over carefully, felt bone and frame, looked in eyes and regarded jaws, and he picked out a beautifully-spotted bitch with a liver-coloured nose and a fine dark-yellow eye. 'Come on, darling,' he said.

They blew out the lamp because of the danger of fire. It was just turning dawn as they left the house.

'I don't think I ever had such a fine trip,' said Mack. 'But I got to thinkin' about his wife coming back and it gave me the shivers.' The pup whined in his arms and he put it under his coat. 'He's a real nice fella,' said Mack. 'After you get him feelin' easy, that is.' He strode on toward the place where they had parked the Ford. 'We shouldn't go forgettin' we're doin' all this for Doc,' he said. 'From the way things are pannin' out, it looks like Doc is a pretty lucky guy.'

JOHN STEINBECK

TASKS

22 Look at the two stories and discuss what makes shooting the elephant so difficult for Orwell. What makes catching the frogs such good fun?

23 Explain in writing what we learn about Orwell's thoughts as he prepares to shoot. What is it that actually makes him do it?

24 When Steinbeck writes about the frogs he is trying to amuse us. Is he successful? How does he do it?

Working with animals

25 These two pieces of writing raise issues about human beings and animals.

Many aspects of work with animals are controversial:

- zoos
- circuses
- animal testing
- blood sports
- export of live animals
- farming – the meat trade

Choose one topic and do some research to find out the necessary information to enable you to make a presentation to other people. You can make your presentation 'balanced' (giving facts and opinions for and against) or advocating only one point of view.

Stating your own opinion is easy. Persuading others to accept your views is much harder. Prepare a pamphlet, a letter or a speech on one of these topics. Aim at persuading your audience to accept your point of view.

You will find the Steinbeck passage reprinted in your homework book as a reminder and you are invited to choose another of the controversial topics to work on by yourself.

In *A Kestrel for a Knave* Billy Casper is about to leave school. He is told to attend a careers interview in his school. This is what happens.

A Kestrel for a Knave

'Now then, Casper, what kind of job had you in mind?'

He shunted the record cards to one side, and replaced them with a blank form, lined and sectioned for the relevant information. CASPER, WILLIAM, in red on the top line. He copied age, address and other details from the record card, then changed pens and looked up.

'Well?'

'I don't know, I haven't thought about it right.'

'Well you should be thinking about it. You want to start off on the right foot don't you?'

'I suppose so.'

'You haven't looked round for anything yet then?'

'No, not yet.'

'Well what would you like to do? What are you good at?'

He consulted Billy's record card again.

'Offices held ... Aptitudes and Abilities ... right then ... would you like to work in an office? Or would you prefer manual work?'

'What's that, manual work?'

'It means working with your hands, for example, building, farming, engineering. Jobs like that, as opposed to pen pushing jobs.'

'I'd be all right working in an office, wouldn't I? I've a job to read and write.'

The Employment Officer printed MANUAL on the form, then raised his pen hand as though he was going to print it again on the top of his head. He scratched it instead, and the nails left white scratches on the skin. He smoothed his fingers carefully across the plot of hair, then looked up. Billy was staring straight past him out of the window.

'Have you thought about entering a trade as an apprentice? You know, as an electrician, or a bricklayer or something like that. Of course the money isn't too good while you're serving your apprenticeship. You may find that lads of your own age who take dead end jobs will be earning far more than you; but in those jobs there's no satisfaction or security, and if you do stick it out you'll find it well worth your while. And whatever happens, at least you'll always have a trade at your fingertips won't you? ...

'Well, what do you think about it? And as you've already said you feel better working with your hands, perhaps this would be your best bet. Of course this would mean attending Technical College and studying for various examinations, but nowadays most employers encourage their lads to take advantage of these facilities, and allow them time off to attend, usually one day a week. On the other hand, if your firm wouldn't allow you time off in the day, and you were still keen to study, then you'd have to attend classes in your own time. Some lads do it. Some do it for years, two and three nights a week from leaving school, right up to their middle twenties, when some of them take their Higher National, and even degrees.

'But you've got to if you want to get on in life. And they'll all tell you that it's worth it in the end ... Had you considered continuing your education in any form after leaving? ... I say, are you listening, lad?'

'Yes.'

'You don't look as though you are to me. I haven't got all day you know, I've other lads to see before four o'clock.'

He looked down at Billy's form again.

'Now then, where were we? O, yes. Well if nothing I've mentioned already appeals to you, and if you can stand a hard day's graft, and you don't mind getting dirty, then there are good opportunities in mining ...'

'I'm not goin' down t'pit.'

'Conditions have improved tremendously ...'

'I wouldn't be seen dead down t'pit.'

'Well what do you want to do then? There doesn't seem to be a job in England to suit you.'

He scrutinised Billy's record card again as though there might be a hint of one there.

'What about hobbies? What hobbies have you got? Do you like gardening, or constructing Meccano sets, or anything like that?'

Billy shook his head slowly.

'Don't you have any hobbies at all?'

Billy looked at him for a moment, then stood up quickly.

'Can I go now?'

'What's the matter with you, lad? Sit down, I haven't finished yet.'

Billy remained standing. The Youth Employment Officer began to fill in the blanks on the form, quickly and noisily.

'Well I've interviewed some lads in my time, but I've never met one like you. Half the time you're like a cat on hot bricks, the other half you're not even listening.'

He turned the form face down on the blotter and ran the sides of his fist along it, continuing the stroke off the blotter and pinching a blue leaflet off a wad at the front of the desk.

'Here, take this home and read it. It gives you all the relevant information concerned with school leaving and starting work. Things like sickness benefits, National Insurance, etcetera. At the back,' he turned it over and pointed at it, 'there's a detachable form. When you want your cards, fill it in and send it in to the office. The address is given at the top. Have you got that?'

Billy stared at the leaflet and nodded.

'Well take it then ... And if you do have trouble getting fixed up, don't forget, come in and see me. All right?'

The pamphlet was entitled LEAVING SCHOOL. The text on the cover page was built around a sketch which showed a man in square glasses shaking hands across a desk with a strapping youth in blazer and flannels. Their mouths were all teeth. Through the window behind the man was a tree, and a flying V bird. 'Right, Casper, that's all. Tell the next boy to come in.'

BARRY HINES

TASK

26 Answer the following questions.

a What goes wrong in this interview?

b Who is really responsible for things not going well?

c Write your advice to the careers officer, suggesting a better way of dealing with the situation.

d Write the script for a successful interview, one that goes really well. You may base it on your own experience.

TIME OUT TASK!

Writing letters

There is no right or wrong way to set out a letter but there are certain basic guidelines which should be followed.

- The layout should be neat, whatever sort of letter you are writing.
- If the letter is a personal letter then you simply put your own address at the top of the page.
- If the letter is a business letter then you put down the address of the person or firm you are writing to, as well as your own address. This second address will normally be under your own address at the top of the page.
- You should always put the date.
- A business letter will normally finish with either 'Yours faithfully' or 'Yours sincerely'. It is right to use 'Yours faithfully' when you have started the letter with a title like 'Dear Sir' or 'Dear Madam', while you should use 'Yours sincerely' when you have started your letter with a name. A personal letter will normally have a personal ending.

There is never any excuse for setting a letter out badly. Get it right and you won't needlessly lose marks.

What is even more important though is the content. You should consider things like:

- What is the purpose of this letter?
- Who is this letter to? (Who is my audience?)
- How long does it need to be?

and so on.

Practise writing a few letters of different types.

a Write a letter applying for a job. (Choose one of the advertisements in your local paper and apply for the job being advertised.)

b Write a letter to Auntie Nellie thanking her for the hideous red socks or woollen stockings she sent you for your birthday.

c Write a letter to a newspaper complaining about their poor coverage of sports news.

d As a headteacher, write a letter to parents inviting them to a meeting to discuss selling the school playing-field for housing development.

e Write a letter to a friend who has recently gone to live in Australia.

END OF TIME OUT!

Earlier in this chapter you looked at some extracts from leaflets about employing disabled people. We are now going to invite you to consider equality of opportunity from a different angle.

Printed below you will find a brief explanation of some aspects of the Race Relations Act 1976. It is from another leaflet entitled 'Positive Action'. In the extract you will also find a couple of case studies describing what Marks and Spencer and London Weekend Television have done in this area.

The Race Relations Act 1976

'The following notes are not a complete account of the law. Because positive action measures involve singling out members of a particular racial group for special attention, it is very important that you ensure that the action you propose is within the law. It is advisable to consult your legal adviser on proposals for positive action before putting them into effect. The Commission for Racial Equality may also be able to give advice.

The Race Relations Act 1976, which applies in Great Britain, provides the legislative framework for combatting racial discrimination and promoting equality of opportunity for people of different racial groups. The Act makes it generally unlawful to discriminate either directly or indirectly on grounds of colour, race, nationality or ethnic or national origins. So far as employment is concerned, the Act covers recruitment (including advertising), terms and conditions, opportunities for promotion, transfer, training and other benefits and dismissal.

It covers the behaviour of training bodies, qualifying bodies, trade unions and employment agencies as well as employers. There are only limited exceptions to the general principle of non-discrimination.

Training for special needs

Section 35 of the Race Relations act 1976 allows anyone (including employers, training bodies and TECs and LECs) to restrict 'facilities or services' to members of a particular racial group when they meet the special needs of that group in regard to their education, training or welfare. The Employment Department interprets 'special' to mean different rather than greater, and regards 'facilities or services' as including the provision of training courses. For example, an English language course specifically designed for people whose first language is not English might well be covered by the section, but a GCSE English Language course generally would not, because many people from all racial groups would benefit from a GCSE English course.

Positive action by employers to address under-representation in their own workforces

Section 38 of the 1976 Act allows employers to:
- encourage members of a particular racial group to apply for particular work at an establishment where they are under-represented;
- provide training for their existing employees from a particular racial group to help fit them for particular work at an establishment where their group is under-represented in that work.

There is under-representation for these purposes only if, at any time during the previous 12 months, either no people from the racial group were doing the particular work at the establishment in question, or the proportion of those doing the work at that establishment coming from the particular racial group was small in comparison with the proportion of all those employed at the establishment from that group, or with the proportion of the population of the area from which the establishment normally recruits who come from that racial group.

Marks and Spencer

Marks and Spencer is committed to providing equality of opportunity, both as a way of maximising business success and of serving the local community. One of the company's aims is to reflect in each of its stores the racial mix of the local population.

Marks and Spencer took positive action when they opened a new store at the Meadowhall shopping centre in Sheffield. During a major recruitment drive, the company found that Afro-Caribbean, Asian and Somali people were not applying for the jobs available. Although people from these groups formed a significant part of the population of Sheffield, there was evidence that they were under-represented in sales assistant occupations in large stores in the Sheffield area.

The company ran a series of road shows at local community centres in order to attract interest from people in these groups. The road shows included presentations about employment with Marks and Spencer, and advice on the company's recruitment process. Marks and Spencer also teamed up with other retailers at Meadowhall to run a recruitment Fun Day in a local park. The retailers shared costs and staffing for the Fun Day. People from the target groups who came along to these events were encouraged to apply for jobs at the new store, but they were not guaranteed a job.

Marks and Spencer felt that the events attracted people who might not otherwise have thought of the company as a potential employer. The events brought a large number of high calibre job applicants from the target racial groups. Some of those individuals are now working in the store and are progressing well. Marks and Spencer believe that the racial mix of employees on the sales floor makes the store attractive to customers from a wider range of racial groups.

London Weekend Television

London Weekend Television (LWT) serves a regional population of which 14% is made up of people from ethnic minorities. The company is committed at the highest level to equal opportunities, seeing it as a real business issue. A key aim is to attract creative and talented people from all parts of the community. This will give the company a competitive edge in programme making, reflecting the interests of all its viewers. LWT decided to take positive action after identifying that a very low proportion of journalists and programme researchers in the current affairs department were Asian or Afro-Caribbean. This reflected the under-representation of these groups in television journalism generally. LWT could not attract job applicants from these groups who had the right professional training and experience. LWT found that in fact people from these groups often could not secure funding for their first professional training.

LWT has responded by offering journalism scholarships to graduates who have an Asian or Afro-Caribbean background. Students are not invited to apply for jobs with LWT straight after the course; they are expected to go out and test their skills through a range of work experience.

Students completing the course have moved into a range of fields which otherwise might not have been open to them. Some have jobs in print journalism, and others are working with local independent and BBC radio stations.

LWT sees long-term benefits coming from the scheme. By widening the pool of journalists from a range of racial backgrounds, the company will be able to draw on a broad range of talent in years to come.

TASKS

27 Answer the following questions in your own words.
   a What is the purpose of the Race Relations Act 1976?
   b Why is it important that firms proposing to take 'positive action' know the law?
   c Why did Marks and Spencer act in the way they did in Sheffield?
   d Why did London Weekend Television decide to fund courses?
   e Design a leaflet for London Weekend Television encouraging people to apply for the scholarships which they are funding.

28 Either in groups or as a whole class discuss the issue of equality of opportunity in work.
   Use as a starting point the leaflets you have studied in this chapter and bring in ideas from your own experience.
   You might research the topic by talking to people and by reading relevant material before the discussion.

TASK

Your own writing

29 Choose a topic and write your own story.

- First day at the factory or office.
- Boss at last!
- Finished at forty!

- The day I wanted a rise.
- 'All work and no play…'

The ambition of a lot of working people is for something to happen which will mean that they do not have to work any more.

There a has been a lot of argument about the National Lottery since it was introduced. Here are some of the points which have been made:

- Suddenly winning millions of pounds could spoil people's lives.
- The Lottery is turning us into a country of people who want something for nothing.
- We no longer believe in achieving an ambition by working hard.
- The money raised by the Lottery goes to the wrong causes.

Printed below is the story of a family who won the National Lottery.

The National Lottery

Gary and Tracey Hipkiss were living on £30 a week when they won £265,637 in December. Gary, 31, is a security guard and Tracey, 30, is a housewife. They live in Dudley Port on the outskirts of Birmingham with their two children, Clair, 10 and Robbie, 8. This is Gary's story.

'A few weeks after the lottery began, I had a dream in which we picked numbers on my son's toy bingo machine and won. The dream seemed so real that when I awoke we fetched the machine and took turns to draw six numbers. We took our last £5 of the week and put it on the lottery, and then I told everybody I knew that we were going to win. That night, while I was at work guarding a bus depot, I watched it

on the telly and the very first numbers that we drew were the ones that won. I went mental. I locked up the site, dashed home, phoned Tracey, phoned our families, phoned Camelot. We were all screaming, especially the kids.

We didn't know how much we'd won. We had five numbers plus the bonus number, so we knew it wasn't millions. All we hoped for was £30,000, enough to pay off our debts and take the edge off our stress. My job is 12 hours a night, seven nights a week, for £2.60 an hour. After basic bills, we had £30 a week to buy food and live off. Those hours and that kind of financial stress take its toll on a marriage. Tracey and I separated for nine months.

Winning £265,637 was incredibly exciting. We drew £12,000 and put it in envelopes for our parents, brothers and sisters. Everyone got the same. It was a wonderful feeling to be able to give.

The next we knew the press were on to us. We think that one of Tracey's brothers phoned the *Sun*, which, at the time, was offering a £10,000 reward if a tip led to an interview. Camelot advised us that the only way to stop them bothering us was to hold a press conference. We did, but the pestering didn't stop. At the same time, some of our extended family were finding our win difficult to handle. They kept phoning us up and bursting into tears. One of them even took briefly to the bottle.

Then things started to spiral. We lived in a council house on an estate and although most of our neighbours were wonderful, a few bad eggs started making our lives a misery. They tried to break in, then threw broken bottles at our new 4-wheel drive Vauxhall. To cap it all, we started getting dozens of cranky phone calls. We had to have the phone disconnected.

The pressure caused a lot of tension between Tracey and myself and we started to argue. We liked our council house (we were going to buy it for £25,000) and our community and we didn't want to move, but the aggro drove us out and in the end, we couldn't wait to leave. We found a new home a few miles away and bought a caravan to live in while we did it up. But the tabloid press tailed us to our new address.

We went for a holiday to Switzerland. One night while we were there, I had pains in my chest and I couldn't breathe. I thought I was having a heart attack. The doctor said it was a mild stroke caused by a build-up of stress. He told me to stay in bed and advised me to change my job and see a counsellor.

I still haven't left my job. The same week that I won the lottery I was made deputy shop steward in the union, something I'd always aimed for. My dad works at the same firm and I'm committed to fighting for a decent wage for all of the lads. We get paid less than cleaners. I know I should leave and I desperately want to leave. But I don't want the lads to feel that I've let then down or to be able to say that the money's changed Gary Hipkiss.

The kids have had a difficult time. Robbie loved the attention of being a winner and apparently kept bragging about it. One day his teacher grabbed him and shouted at him to stop going on about the lottery. I went to see the headmaster and threatened to lay his teacher out. After that we moved schools, but Clair has been a bit miserable, missing her old friends.

Despite everything, I'm still mega-pleased we've won. The feeling of never having to worry about bills outweighs all the short-term trouble we've had. I love going into smart shops dressed as my usual scruffy self and surprising shopkeepers who think I can't afford anything. We've had loads of fun with the money.

Apart from the house, the car and the caravan, we've bought a new 680-watt, compact disc stereo system complete with pro-logic Dolby 'surround sound' (the effect is like sitting in a cinema); a television for every room; an 80cc off-road scrambler for Robbie; three porcelain dolls for Tracey (she's a collector), two Penny Blacks for my stamp album; a dinghy; a multi-gym (the doctor said I need exercise); five train sets, the complete set of Disney videos; a tank of tropical fish, some finches and two chipmunks. And for next year we've booked a cruise. We've spent £140,000 which is £40,000 more than our bank manager advised. The rest we've invested for our children's future.

The most extraordinary thing is that we're not the only ones in our family to have won. A few weeks after we won, my uncle's brother-in-law scooped £2.8 million. He gave some money to his family and then with all the hounding from the press, he disappeared. Nobody's seen or heard from him since. Then Tracy's cousin was in a syndicate that won £2.4 million and his share was £170,000. He bought a new house and between us moving and him moving, we don't know where he lives now either.'

TASKS

30 In groups, discuss the story which you have read and the ways in which the people reacted to their win.

31 Organise a class debate on this topic. The motion could be 'The Lottery is a big mistake'.

32 Write a story of your own called 'Sudden Wealth' or 'The Day I Won the Lottery'.

MISFITS

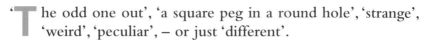

6

'The odd one out', 'a square peg in a round hole', 'strange', 'weird', 'peculiar', – or just 'different'.

These are just some of the words or phrases we use to describe people who are different from others – who are 'misfits'.

In this chapter we shall be looking at examples of this. Perhaps our studies will make us ask ourselves what we feel about not fitting in and perhaps we will apply our thoughts to ourselves as well as to other people.

ENGLISH IN THE NATIONAL CURRICULUM:

Key Skills you will cover in this chapter

- ☑ You will be looking at the way in which language is used for different purposes.
- ☑ You will be asked to examine and to analyse the techniques which writers use to produce their effects. You will be asked to look at how characters are created and how settings are important.
- ☑ You will be asked to make good use of the information to be found in the passages you study.
- ☑ You will have the chance to write in a narrative way, imitating what you have read, exploring how you might improve your technique, using what you have been reading yourself to help you develop characters of your own.
- ☑ You will be given the chance to study non–fiction as well as fiction.

A Drink in the Passage is a story by Alan Paton set in South Africa in 1960 when it was still a very oppressed country.

A Drink in the Passage

In the year 1960 the Union of South Africa celebrated its Golden Jubilee, and there was a nation-wide sensation when the one-thousand-pound prize for the finest piece of sculpture was won by a black man, Edward Simelane. His work, 'African Mother and Child', not only excited the admiration, but touched the conscience or heart or whatever it is, of white South Africa, and was likely to make him famous in other countries.

It was by an oversight that his work was accepted, for it was the policy of the Government that all the celebrations and competitions should be strictly segregated. The committee of the sculpture section received a private reprimand for having been so careless as to omit the words 'for whites only' from the conditions, but was told, by a very high personage it is said, that if Simelane's work was indisputably the best, it should receive the award. The committee then decided that this prize must be given along with the others, at the public ceremony which would bring this particular part of the celebrations to a close.

For this decision it received a surprising amount of support from the white public, but in certain powerful quarters there was an outcry against any departure from the 'traditional policies' of the country, and a threat that many white prize-winners would renounce their prizes. However, a crisis was averted, because the sculptor was 'unfortunately unable to attend the ceremony'.

'I wasn't feeling up to it,' Simelane said mischievously to me. 'My parents, and my wife's parents, and our priest, decided that I wasn't feeling up to it. And finally I decided so too. Of course Majosi and Sola and the others wanted me to go and get my prize personally, but I said, "Boys, I'm a sculptor, not a demonstrator."'

'This cognac is wonderful,' he said, 'especially in these big glasses. It's the first time I've had such a glass. It's also the first time I've drunk a brandy so slowly. In Orlando you develop a throat of iron, and you just put back your head and pour it down, in case the police should arrive.'

He said to me, 'This is the second cognac I've had in my life. Would you like to hear the story of how I had my first?'

*   *   *

'You know the Alabaster Bookshop in Von Brandis Street? Well, after the competition they asked me if they could exhibit my 'African Mother and Child'. They gave a whole window to it, with a white velvet backdrop, if there is anything called white velvet, and some complimentary words, '*Black man conquers white world*.'

Well somehow I could never go and look in that window. On my way from the station to the Herald office, I sometimes went past there, and I felt good when I saw all the people standing there, but I would only squint at it out of the corner of my eye.

Then one night I was working late at the Herald, and when I came out there was hardly anyone in the streets, so I thought I'd go and see the window, and indulge certain pleasurable human feelings. I must have got a little lost in the contemplation of my own genius, because suddenly there was a young white man standing next to me.

He said to me, 'What do you think of that, mate?' And you know, one doesn't get called 'mate' every day.

'I'm looking at it,' I said.

'I live near here,' he said, 'and I come and look at it nearly every night. You know it's by one of your own boys, don't you? See, Edward Simelane.'

'Yes, I know.'

'It's beautiful,' he said. 'Look at that mother's head. She's loving that child, but she's somehow watching too. Do you see that? Like someone guarding. She knows it won't be an easy life.'

He cocked his head on one side, to see the thing better.

'He got a thousand pounds for it,' he said.

'That's a lot of money for one of your boys. But good luck to him. You don't get much luck, do you?'

Then he said confidentially, 'Mate, would you like a drink?'

Well honestly I didn't feel like a drink at that time of night, with a white stranger and all, and me still with a train to catch to Orlando.

'You know we black people must be out of the city by eleven,' I said.

'It won't take long. My flat's just round the corner. Do you speak Afrikaans?'

'Since I was a child,' I said in Afrikaans.

'We'll speak Afrikaans then. My English isn't too wonderful. I'm van Rensburg. And you?'

I couldn't have told him my name. I said I was Vakalisa, living in Orlando.

'Vakalisa, eh? I haven't hard that name before.'

By this time he had started off, and I was following, but not willingly. That's my trouble, as you'll soon see. I can't break off an encounter. We didn't exactly walk abreast, but he didn't exactly walk in front of me. He didn't look constrained. He wasn't looking round to see if anyone might be watching.

He said to me, 'Do you know what I wanted to do?'

'No,' I said.

'I wanted a bookshop, like that one there. I always wanted that, ever since I can remember. When I was small, I had a little shop of my own.' He laughed at himself. 'Some were real books, of course, but some of them I wrote myself. But I had bad luck. My parents died before I could finish school.'

Then he said to me, 'Are you educated?'

I said unwillingly, 'Yes.' Then I thought to myself, how stupid, for leaving the question open.

And sure enough he asked, 'Far?'

And again unwillingly, I said, 'Far.'

He took a big leap and said, 'Degree?'

'Yes.'

'Literature?'

'Yes.'

He expelled his breath, and gave a long 'Ah'. We had reached his building, Majorca Mansins, not one of those luxurious places. I was glad to see that the entrance lobby was deserted. I wasn't at my ease. I don't feel at my ease in such places, not unless I am protected by friends, and this man was a stranger. The lift was at ground level, marked 'Whites only. Slegs vir Blankes.' Van Rensburg opened the door and waved me in. Was he constrained? To this day I don't know. While I was waiting for him to press the button, so that we could get moving and away from that ground floor, he stood with his finger suspended over it, and looked at me with a kind of honest, unselfish envy.

'You were lucky,' he said. 'Literature, that's what I wanted to do.'

He shook his head and pressed the button, and he didn't speak again until we stopped high up. But before we got out he said suddenly, 'If I had had a bookshop, I'd have given that boy a window too.'

We got out and walked along one of those polished concrete passageways, I suppose you could call it a stoep if it weren't so high up; let's call it a passage. On the one side was a wall, and plenty of fresh air, and far down below, Von Brandis Street. On the other side were the doors, impersonal doors; you could hear radios and people talking, but there wasn't a soul in sight. I wouldn't like living so high; we Africans like being close to the earth. Van Rensburg stopped at one of the doors, and said to me, 'I won't be a minute.' Then he went in, leaving the door open, and inside I could hear voices. I thought to myself, he's telling them who's here. Then after a minute or so, he came back to the door, holding two glasses of red wine. He was warm and smiling.

'Sorry there's no brandy,' he said. 'Only wine. Here's happiness.'

Now I certainly had not expected that I would have my drink in the passage. I wasn't only feeling what you may be thinking. I was thinking that one of the impersonal doors might open at any moment and someone might see me in a 'White' building, and see me and van Rensburg breaking the liquor laws of the country. Anger could have saved me from the whole embarrassing situation, but you know I can't easily be angry. Even if I could have been, I might have found it hard to be angry with this particular man. But I wanted to get away from there, and I couldn't. My mother used to say to me, when I had said something anti-white, 'Son, don't talk like that, talk as you are.' She would have understood at once why I took a drink from a man who gave it to me in the passage.

Van Rensburg said to me, 'Don't you know this fellow Simelane?'

'I've heard of him,' I said.

'I'd like to meet him,' he said. 'I'd like to talk to him.' He added in explanation, 'You know, talk out my heart to him.'

A woman of about 50 years of age came from the room beyond, bringing a plate of biscuits. She smiled and bowed to me. I took one of the biscuits, but not for all the money in the world could I have

said to her 'Dankie, my nooi,' or that disgusting 'Dankie, missus,' nor did I want to speak to her in English because her language was Afrikaans, so I took the risk of it and used the word '*mevrou*' for the politeness of which some Afrikaners would knock a black man down, and I said, in high Afrikaans, with a smile and a bow too, 'Ek is u dankbaar, mevrou.'

But nobody knocked me down. The woman smiled and bowed, and van Rensburg, in a strained voice that suddenly came out of nowhere, said, 'Our land is beautiful. But it breaks my heart.'

The woman put her hand on his arm, and said, 'Jannie, Jannie.'

Then another woman and a man, all about the same age, came up and stood behind van Rensburg.

'He's a B A,' van Rensburg told them. 'What do you think of that?

The first woman smiled and bowed to me again, and van Rensburg said, as though it were a matter for grief, 'I wanted to give him brandy, but there's only wine.'

The second woman said, 'I remember, Jannie. Come with me.'

She went back into the room, and he followed her. The first woman said to me, 'Jannie's a good man. Strange, but good.'

And I thought the whole thing was mad, and getting beyond me, with me a black stranger being shown a testimonial for the son of the house, with these white strangers standing and looking at me in the passage, as though they wanted for God's sake to touch me somewhere and didn't know how, but I saw the earnestness of the woman who had smiled and bowed to me, and I said to her, 'I can see that, mevrou.'

'He goes down every night to look at the statue,' she said. 'He says only God could make something so beautiful, therefore God must be in the man who made it, and he wants to meet him and talk out his heart to him.'

She looked back at the room, and then she dropped her voice a little, and said to me, 'Can't you see, it's somehow because it's a black woman and a black child?'

And I said to her, 'I can see that, mevrou.'

She turned to the man and said of me, 'He's a good boy.'

Then the other woman returned with van Rensburg, and van Rensburg had a bottle of brandy. He was smiling and pleased, and he said to me, 'This isn't ordinary brandy, it's French.'

He showed me the bottle, and I, wanting to get

the hell out of that place, looked at it and saw it was cognac. He turned to the man and said, 'Uncle, you remember? When you were ill? The doctor said you must have good brandy. And the man at the bottle-store said this was the best brandy in the world.'

'I must go,' I said. 'I must catch that train.'

'I'll take you to the station,' he said. 'Don't you worry about that.'

He poured me a drink and one for himself.

'Uncle,' he said, 'what about one for yourself?'

The older man said, 'I don't mind if I do,' and he went inside to get himself a glass.

Van Rensburg said, 'Happiness,' and lifted his glass to me. It was good brandy, the best I've ever tasted. But I wanted to get the hell out of there. I stood in the passage and drank van Rensburg's brandy. Then Uncle came back with his glass, and van Rensburg poured him a brandy, and Uncle raised his glass to me too. All of us were full of goodwill, but I was waiting for the opening of one of the impersonal doors. Perhaps they were too, I don't know. Perhaps when you want so badly to touch someone you don't care. I was drinking my brandy almost as fast as I would have drunk it in Orlando.

'I must go,' I said.

Van Rensburg said, 'I'll take you to the station.' He finished his brandy, and I finished mine too. We handed the glasses to Uncle, who said to me, 'Good night, my boy.' The first woman said, 'May God bless you,' and the other woman bowed and smiled. Then van Rensburg and I went down in the lift to the basement, and got into his car.

'I told you I'd take you to the station,' he said. 'I'd take you home, but I'm frightened of Orlando at night.'

We drove up Eloff Street, and he said, 'Did you know what I meant?' I knew that he wanted an answer to something, and I wanted to answer him, but I couldn't be talking about being frightened of Orlando at night, because what more could one mean than just that?

'By what?' I asked.

'You know,' he said, 'about our land being beautiful?'

Yes, I knew what he meant, and I knew that for God's sake he wanted to touch me too and he couldn't; for his eyes had been blinded by years in the dark. And I thought it was a pity, for if men never touch each other, they'll hurt each other one day. And it was a pity he was blind, and couldn't touch me, for black men don't touch white men any more; only by accident, when they make something like 'Mother and Child'.

He said to me, 'What are you thinking?'

I said, 'Many things,' and my inarticulateness distressed me, for I knew he wanted something from me. I felt him fall back, angry, hurt, despairing, I didn't know. He stopped at the main entrance to the station, but I didn't tell him I couldn't go in there. I got out and said to him, 'Thank you for the sociable evening.'

'They liked having you,' he said. 'Did you see that they did?'

I said, 'Yes, I saw that they did.'

He sat slumped in his seat, like a man with a burden of incomprehensible, insoluble grief. I wanted to touch him, but I was thinking about the train. He said good night, and I said it too. We each saluted the other. What he was thinking, God knows, but I was thinking he was like a man trying to run a race in iron shoes, and not understanding why he cannot move.

When I got back to Orlando, I told my wife the story, and she wept.

ALAN PATON

TASKS

1 Talk about the situation as it was in South Africa, which forms the background to this story.
   If you don't know about 'apartheid' you could find out about it in the library. However, if you read the story carefully you will be able to work out the system for yourself.

2 List all the experiences Edward Simelane has which are unusual.
   What are his feelings about these experiences?

3 At the end of the story we are told that Edward's wife 'wept' when she was told about what had happened.
   Writing as Edward's wife, explain why she reacted in this way.

E dward Simelane was considered a misfit because of his race and colour. Many writers have used this subject as the background to their writing.

Mildred Taylor has set three books about the Logan family in the American deep south in the 1930s. In order, the books are *Roll of Thunder, Hear My Cry*; *Let the Circle be Unbroken* and *The Road to Memphis*.

Here is an extract from the first of these books.

Roll of Thunder, Hear My Cry

We stood patiently waiting behind the people in front of us and when our turn came, T J handed his list to the man. 'Mr Barnett, sir,' he said, 'I got me this here list of things my mama want.'

The storekeeper studied the list and without looking up asked 'You one of Mr Granger's people?'

'Yessir,' answered T J.

Mr Barnett walked to another counter and began filling the order, but before he finished a white woman called, 'Mr Barnett, you waiting on anybody just now?'

Mr Barnett turned around. 'Just them,' he said, indicating us with a wave of his hand. 'What can I do for you, Miz Emmaline?' The woman handed him a list twice as long as T J's and the storekeeper, without a word of apology to us, proceeded to fill it.

'What's he doing?' I objected.

'Hush, Cassie,' said Stacey, looking very embarrassed and uncomfortable. T J's face was totally bland, as if nothing at all had happened.

When the woman's order was finally filled, Mr Barnett again picked up T J's list, but before he had gotten the next item his wife called, 'Jim Lee, these folks needing help over here and I got my hands full.' And as if we were not even there, he walked away.

'Where's he going?' I cried.

'He'll be back,' said T J, wandering away.

After waiting several minutes for his return, Stacey said, 'Come on Cassie, let's get out of here.' He started toward the door and I followed. But as we passed one of the counters, I spied Mr Barnett wrapping an order of pork chops for a white girl. Adults were one thing; I could almost understand that. They ruled things and there was nothing that could be done about them. But some kid who was no bigger than me was something else again. Certainly Mr Barnett had simply forgotten about T J's order. I decided to remind him and, without saying anything to Stacey, I turned around and marched over to Mr Barnett.

'Uh…'scuse me, Mr Barnett,' I said as politely as I could, waiting a moment for him to look up from his wrapping. 'I think you forgot, but you was waiting on us 'fore you was waiting on this girl here, and we been waiting a good while now for you to get back.'

The girl gazed at me strangely, but Mr Barnett did not look up. I assumed that he had not heard me. I was near the end of the counter so I merely went to the other side of it and tugged on his shirt sleeve to get his attention.

He recoiled as if I had struck him.

'Y-you was helping us,' I said, backing to the front of the counter again.

'Well, you just get your little black self back over there and wait some more,' he said in a low, tight voice.

I was hot. I had been as nice as I could be to him and here he was talking like this. 'We been waiting on you for near an hour,' I hissed, 'while you 'round here waiting on everybody else. And it ain't fair. You got no right –'

'Whose little nigger is this!' bellowed Mr Barnett.

Everyone in the store turned and stared at me. 'I ain't nobody's little nigger!' I screamed, angry and humiliated. 'And you ought not be waiting on everybody 'fore you wait on us.'

'Hush up, child, hush up,' someone whispered behind me. I looked around. A woman who had occupied the wagon next to ours at the market looked down upon me. Mr Barnett, his face red and eyes bulging, immediately pounded on her.

'This gal yourn, Hazel?'

'No, suh,' answered the woman meekly, stepping hastily away to show she had nothing to do with me. As I watched her turn her back on me, Stacey emerged and took my hand.

'Come on, Cassie, let's get out of here.'

'Stacey!' I exclaimed, relieved to see him by my

side. 'Tell him! You know he ain't fair making us wait –'

'She your sister, boy?' Mr Barnett spat across the counter.

Stacey bit his lower lip and gazed into Mr Barnett's eyes. 'Yessir.'

'Then you get her out of here,' he said with hateful force. 'And make sure she don't come back till yo' mammy teach her what she is.'

'I already know what I am!' I retaliated. 'But I betcha you don't know what you are! And I could sure tell you, too, you ole –'

Stacey jerked me forward, crushing my hand in the effort, and whispered angrily, 'Shut up, Cassie!' His dark eyes flashed malevolently as he pushed me in front of him through the crowd.

MILDRED TAYLOR

TASKS

4 Think about what is happening to Cassie here. Explain how people expect her to behave.

5 Cassie is telling the story. How do her feelings come across to you as you read the story?

6 Describe your own reactions and feelings as you read the story.

You will find this extract reprinted in your homework book together with a further task for you to do.

GCSE examinations, in both English and English Literature, often supply candidates with 'pre-released' material. This means that you will be given some passages to read for yourself and prepare them for examinations. Of course you can discuss them with others to help you make sense of your reading.

Here are three poems about people of different types, but you will see that they are linked.

Ninetieth Birthday

*You go up the long track
That will take a car, but is best walked
On slow foot, noting the lichen
That writes history on the page
Of the grey rock. Trees are abut you
At first, but yield to the green bracken,
The nightjar's house: you can hear it spin
On warm evenings; it is still now
In the noonday heat, only the lesser
Voices sound, blue-fly and gnat
And the stream's whisper. As the road climbs,
You will pause for breath and the far sea's
Signal will flash, till you turn again
To the steep track, buttressed with cloud.*

And there at the top that old woman,
Born almost a century back
In that stone farm, awaits your coming;
Waits for the news of the lost village
She thinks she knows, a place that exists
In her memory only.

You bring her greeting
And praise for having lasted so long
With time's knife shaving the bone.
Yet no bridge joins her own
World with yours, all you can do
Is lean kindly across the abyss
To hear words that were once wise.

R S THOMAS

Aunt Julia

Aunt Julia spoke Gaelic
very loud and very fast.
I could not answer her –
I could not understand her.

She wore men's boots
when she wore any.
– I can see her strong foot.
stained with peat.
paddling the treadle of the spinningwheel
while her right hand drew yarn
marvellously out of the air.

Hers was the only house
where I've lain at night
in the absolute darkness
of a box bed, listening to
crickets being friendly.

She was buckets
and water flouncing into them.
She was winds pouring wetly
round house-ends.
She was brown eggs, black skirts
and a keeper of threepenny bits
in a teapot.

Aunt Julia spoke Gaelic
very loud and very fast
By the time I had learned
a little, she lay
silenced in the absolute black
of a sandy grave
at Luskentyre.
But I hear her still, welcoming me
with a seagull's voice
across a hundred yards
of peatscrapes and lazybeds
and getting angry, getting angry
with so many questions
unanswered.

NORMAN MACCAIG

The Hunchback in the Park

The hunchback in the park
A solitary mister
Propped between trees and water
From the opening of the garden lock

That lets the trees and water enter
Until the Sunday sombre bell at dark

Eating bread from a newspaper
Drinking water from the chained cup
That the children filled with gravel
In the fountain basin where I sailed my ship
Slept at night in a dog kennel
But nobody chained him up.

Like the park birds he came early
Like the water he sat down
And Mister they called Hey mister
The truant boys from the town
Running when he had heard them clearly
On out of sound

Past lake and rockery
Laughing when he shook his paper
Hunchbacked in mockery
Through the loud zoo of the willow groves
Dodging the park keeper
With his stick that picked up leaves.

And the old dog sleeper
Alone between nurses and swans
While the boys among willows
Made the tigers jump out of their eyes
To roar on the rockery stones
And the groves were blue with sailors

Made all day until bell time
A woman figure without fault
Straight as a young elm
Straight and tall from his crooked bones
That she might stand in the night
After the locks and chains

All night in the unmade park
After the railings and shrubberies
The birds the grass the tree the lake
And the wild boys innocent as strawberries
Had followed the hunchback
To his kennel in the dark.

DYLAN THOMAS

TASKS

7 Read the poems, think about them and write down points of interest.
8 Now, for a change, instead of writing answers, write some questions
  about the poems.
  Your questions should be designed to bring out the following:
  - what a reader understands;
  - what a reader feels as she or he reads the poem;
  - how the poems are constructed;
  - the language and vocabulary that is used;
  - the similarities or differences between two or more of the poems.

Now take this further. Exchange your questions with a colleague and write the answers. Then hand your answers to your colleague for marking.

Before you mark someone else's work you should:

- remind yourself of the poems again;
- look back at your question and jot down what points you expected to be made in the answer;
- be prepared to give credit for good ideas which you didn't think of.

When you have finished award a grade or a mark and write a comment. Remember the comment should:

- explain why you gave a particular mark or grade;
- give some advice for the next piece of work.

TIME OUT TASK!

A look at language

COURAGE – COWARDICE

We can group many words into pairs of opposites. In small groups 'brainstorm' all the words you can think of to do with courage. Find for each one a word opposite in meaning.

Figurative language

Many phrases have been invented to show courage or cowardice. A brave person is 'red-blooded' (or 'full-blooded'); a coward is 'lily-livered'.

Collect as many phrases as you can of this type. When you have your list, comment on the meaning of each and try to find out and note their origins.

END OF TIME OUT!

We are now going on to study an extract from Robert Swindell's novel *Stone Cold*. It tells the story of Link, who runs away from home to live on the streets of London.

Before you read the extract write lists of different points of view about teenagers who live rough. One list should show sympathy and understanding, the other be critical and hostile.

Stone Cold

If you think sleeping rough's just a matter of finding a dry spot where the fuzz won't move you on and getting your head down, you're wrong. Not your fault of course – if you've never tried it you've no way of knowing what it's like, so what I thought I'd do was sort of talk you through a typical night. That night in the Vaudeville alcove won't do, because there were two of us and it's worse if you're by yourself.

So you pick your spot. Wherever it is (unless you're in a squat or a derelict house or something) it's going to have a floor of stone, tile, concrete or brick. In other words it's going to be hard and cold. It might be a bit cramped, too – shop doorways often are. And remember, if it's winter you're going to be half frozen before you even start. Anyway you've got your place, and if you're lucky enough to have a sleeping-bag you unroll it and get in.

Settled for the night? Well maybe, maybe not. Remember my first night? The Scouser? 'Course you do. He kicked me out of my bedroom and pinched my watch. Well, that sort of thing can happen any night, and there are worse things. You could be peed on by a drunk or a dog. Happens all the time – one man's bedroom is another man's lavatory. You might be spotted by a gang of lager louts on the lookout for someone to maim. That happens all the time too, and if they get carried away you can end up dead. There are the guys who like young boys, who think because you're a dosser you'll do anything for dosh, and there's the psycho who'll knife you for your pack.

So, you lie listening. You bet you do. Footsteps. Voices. Breathing, even. Doesn't help you sleep.

Then there's your bruises. What bruises? Try lying on a stone floor for half an hour. Just half an hour. You can choose any position you fancy, and you can change position as often as you like. You won't find it comfy, I can tell you. You won't sleep unless you're dead drunk or zonked on downers. And if you are, and do, you're going to wake up with bruises on hips, shoulders, elbows,

ankles and knees – especially if you're a bit thin from not eating properly. And if you do that six hours a night for six nights you'll feel like you fell out of a train. Try sleeping on concrete then.

And don't forget the cold. If you've ever tried dropping off to sleep with cold feet, even in bed, you'll know it's impossible. You've got to warm up those feet, or lie awake. And in January, in a doorway, in wet trainers, it can be quite a struggle. And if you manage it, chances are you'll need to get up for a pee, and then it starts all over again.

And those are only some of the hassles. I haven't mentioned stomach cramps from hunger, headaches from the flu, toothache, fleas and lice. I haven't talked about homesickness, depression or despair. I haven't gone into how it feels to want a girl-friend when your circumstances make it virtually impossible for you to get one – how it feels to know you're a social outcast in fact, a non-person to whom every ordinary everyday activity is closed.

So. You lie on your bruises, listening. Trying to warm your feet. You curl up on your side and your hip hurts, so you can stretch out on your back so your feet stay cold an the concrete hurts your heels. You force yourself to lie still for a bit, thinking that'll help you drop off, but it doesn't. Your pack feels like a rock under your head and your nose is cold. You wonder what time it is. Can you stop listening now, or could someone still come? Distant chimes. You strain your ears, counting. One o'clock? It can't be only one o'clock, surely? I've been here hours. Did I miss a chime?

What's that? Sounds like breathing. Heavy breathing, as in maniac. Lie still. Quiet. Maybe he won't see you. Listen. Is he still there? Silence now. Creeping up, perhaps. No. Relax. Jeez, my feet are cold.

A thought out of nowhere – my old room at home. My little bed. What I wouldn't give for – no, mustn't. Mustn't think about that. No sleep that way. Somebody could be asleep in that room right now. Warm and dry. Safe. Lucky sod.

Food. God, don't start on about food! (Remember that time in Whitby – fish and chip caff? Long, sizzling haddock, heap of chips like a mountain. So many, you had to leave some.) Wish I had them now.

Mum. Wonder what Mum's doing? Wonder if she wonders where I am? How would she feel if she knew? I miss you, Mum. Do you miss me? Does anybody?

Chimes again. Quarter past. Quarter past one? I don't believe it.

DSS. Are they considering any claim? (Not now they're not – they're sleeping. Snug as a bug in a rug.) Do they know what it feels like, kipping in a doorway? No.

And so it goes on, hour after hour. Now and then you doze a bit, but only a bit. You're so cold, so frightened and it hurts so much that you end up praying for morning even though you're dog-tired – even though tomorrow is certain to be every bit as grim as yesterday.

And the worst part is knowing you haven't deserved any of it.

ROBERT SWINDELL

TASKS

9   How has Link's account affected you? Did it change any of your own attitudes?

10   Write about the sorts of things which, in your opinion, cause young people to leave home.

11   Write a story of your own about being down and out.

Wole Soyinka is a Nigerian writer. In his poem *Telephone Conversation* he too explores people's reactions to and feelings about race.

Telephone Conversation

The price seemed reasonable, location
Indifferent. The landlady swore she lived
Off premises. Nothing remained
But self-confession. 'Madam,' I warned,
'I hate a wasted journey – I am African.'
Silence. Silenced transmission of
Pressurised good-breeding. Voice, when it came,
Lipstick coated, long gold-rolled
Cigarette-holder piped. Caught I was, foully.
'HOW DARK?'... I had not misheard... 'ARE YOU LIGHT
OR VERY DARK?' Button B. Button A. Stench
Of rancid breath of public hide-and-speak.
Red booth. Red pillar-box. Red double-tiered
Omnibus squelching tar. It **was** real! Shamed
By ill-mannered silence, surrender
Pushed dumbfoundment to beg simplification.
Considerate she was, varying the emphasis –
'ARE YOU DARK? OR VERY LIGHT?' Revelation came.
'You mean – like plain or milk chocolate?'
Her assent was clinical, crushing in its light
Impersonality. Rapidly, wave-length adjusted,
I chose. 'West African sepia' – and as afterthought,
'Down in my passport.' Silence for spectroscopic
Flight of fancy, till truthfulness clanged her accent
Hard on the mouthpiece. 'WHAT'S THAT?' conceding
'DON'T KNOW WHAT THAT IS.' 'Like brunette.'
'THAT'S DARK, ISN'T IT?' 'Not altogether.
Facially, I am brunette, but madam, you should see
The rest of me. Palm of my hand, soles of my feet
Are a peroxide blond. Friction, caused –
Foolishly, madam – by sitting down, has turned
My bottom raven black – One moment, madam!' – sensing
Her receiver rearing on the thunderclap
About my ears – 'Madam,' I pleaded, 'wouldn't you rather
See for yourself?'

WOLE SOYINKA

TASKS

12 With a partner work out a reading of this poem and present it to
    your class.

13 This poem moves through several stages. Devise ways in which the
    poem may be divided into sections. Give a heading to each.
    Take each of your sections and write about the feelings of each of the
    two people involved.

14 Colours are very important in this poem. Look at all the words associated
    with colour. List them and explain how they have been used in the poem.

15 At the end of the poem the landlady puts down the telephone. How do
    you think she will explain the situation to a friend?
    Write a conversation between the lady and her friend.

Consider the following three photographs – how are they connected with the theme of misfits? Here are some thoughts to get you started:

■ Are people behaving 'normally' here?
■ What are the characteristics of the three different groups of people?
■ How important is it to 'belong' to something?

Mods

Football fans

ANC supporters

TASKS

16 In groups discuss the pictures and what the people in them are doing.
17 How do the pictures make you feel (sad, angry, excited, happy)?
Explain your feelings to someone else.
18 Choose one of the pictures as a basis for a story of your own. You might
like to imagine what happened next, after the photograph was taken.

Martin Amis visited China in 1991. He wrote about some of the things which happened to him. Here is an extract from an article which appeared in *The Independent* newspaper.

THE room in the Public Security Bureau was familiar. I had sat in scores like it, a musty parlour with overstuffed armchairs, a ragged red carpet and soiled white curtains. No office in China is without one. Even the stains and cigarette burns seemed the same, emblems of a dreary uniformity enforced down to the last squalid detail.

Only one thing was missing: there were no cups of tea, a lapse in official protocol with a message as blunt as the words I had been summoned to hear. 'We have received orders from relevant higher organs that you must leave China by 15 September,' said the official, his face frozen in a professional scowl, his eyes fixed on a notebook scribbled with his script.

He wore a baggy green uniform and bullying manner to match. Naïvely, I asked who these 'higher organs' might be. He frowned, looked down at his notebook and repeated the one sentence he had been empowered to utter. 'We have received orders from relevant higher organs…' Could he perhaps tell me his own name and title? 'We have received orders…' But what if there are no flights? 'We have received orders.'

The encounter lasted no more than 15 minutes. It was to be my last rendezvous with the dictatorship of the proletariat. Two days later, I obeyed the 'relevant higher organs', packed what I could of my belongings and left, flying out of Peking on a rainy Sunday evening.

Through windows streaked with drizzle I looked down at a city I never imagined I would leave with such sadness. Grey and disfigured by layers of concrete, Peking had often been a place to endure rather than enjoy, its pleasures – ice skating on the moat of the Forbidden City in winter, cycling through tree-shaded lanes in spring and many happy friendships – crimped by police surveillance, tapped phones and other reminders of the ugliness behind the city's resilient ancient charm.

It was in Peking that I shared a trajectory of hope and despair whose joys and horrors neither I nor anyone else who lived through them will ever forget. The cold, monotonous voice that ordered me to leave within 48 hours belonged to the same higher organs that, 2 years earlier, had issued a similar command to students camped in Tiananmen Square. There, too, the voice had no name, no rank, and invited no questions. It was a disembodied drone, intoning the same message like a broken record from loudspeakers hanging from scores of lamp posts around the square. 'You must leave. You must leave. You must leave.'

But, unlike me, the students did not obey. They stood their ground. They ignored the higher organs. They paid a high price for their defiance: a military assault of a ferocity calculated not merely to bludgeon recalcitrant youth into submission but to ensure that neither they nor their elders would challenge the higher organs again. I spent much of

that night crouched in the bushes along the Avenue of Eternal Peace, my ears ringing from the constant crackle of gunfire and the thundering din of that awful, droning voice. Behind me hung a giant portrait of Mao Tse-tung, his face eerily illuminated by flaming debris.

The terror of 4 June 1989 took China's revolution back to its roots. The peasants who carried Mao to power in 1949 had again encircled the city. The brutish certainties of the countryside had swamped the dithering debate of the urban élite. Unlike the soldiers who would later be called into Moscow in a similar spasm of desperate revolutionary nostalgia, the men summoned to Peking had no qualms about silencing their noisy compatriots. The People's Liberation Army was founded as a peasant army and remained one.

My most vivid memory of that night, however, is not of the killing but the look on the killers' faces. They were blank. Rumour had it that the soldiers were drunk or drugged. They weren't. They didn't need to be. 'The People's Army loves the people,' they chanted as they sprayed bullets into the crowd. 'Serve the people. Long live the people.'

That the people, or at least several hundred of them, lay dead or dying did not seem to matter. In China, power in its purest form is the power over language, the power to impose a bogus order of words on the uncomfortable chaos of fact. The soldiers, in their own minds, were not killing unarmed people but defending the people from their enemies. Through a manipulation of words, their messy, murderous work had become righteous duty.

As the Communist Party's propaganda apparatus spewed out its vision of events in the weeks and months that followed, as officials, scholars and generals came forward to parrot the official line, I was reminded of how China's first dynasty, the Qin, tested the loyalty of its own servants more than 2,000 years earlier. They were summoned to the palace to see what their eyes told them was a deer but which the most powerful official in the land insisted was a horse. One by one they were asked to name the animal. Those who said what they saw were executed, those who said what they had been told to see were rewarded.

The message of this ancient ritual is embedded in a popular saying still used today: 'Point at a deer and call it a horse.' In its Marxist-Leninist form it is known as *biaotai* – to declare one's stand. All must come forward and declare that the deer is in fact a horse, that the students' peaceful protest movement was in fact a 'counter-revolutionary rebellion', that the massacre was not a massacre but 'correct, necessary and timely'. The only criticism allowed is self-criticism.

* * *

Of course, this hectoring insistence on 'unity of thinking' does not always work. China has its brave men and women who dare to think for themselves. I met perhaps the bravest, and certainly the most persistent, in Shanghai earlier this year. His name is Wang Ruowang, a 73-year-old writer whose refusal to call a deer a horse has landed him jail for much of the past 50 years. Chiang Kai-shek locked him up as a Communist, Mao as a rightist, Red Guards as a counter-revolutionary and, most recently, Mr Deng as a bourgeois liberal. Yet he still talks and writes.

And it is not just dissidents such as Mr Wang who fluff the party's carefully scripted lines. Several months after the Peking massacre, I visited China's most sacred revolutionary Mecca, the birthplace of Mao Tse-tung, deep in the lush hills and valleys of Hunan. A colleague and I arranged a meeting there with Wen Huikang, the head of the local Mao Tse-tung Thought Society.

We asked Mr Wen to name his favourite work in the Maoist canon. A look of pure terror crossed his face. His mind had gone blank. Seconds ticked by. We waited. He fidgeted nervously in his seat. Finally, we freed him from his misery, suggesting that he might like one of Mao's best-known pamphlets, *On Contradictions*. Mr Wen beamed. 'Yes, yes, that's it. *On Contradictions*. That's my favourite.' He kept muttering the title as if to implement it firmly in his memory so as to avoid future embarrassment. It was a revealing commentary on just how hollow official ideology had become. Here was a creed whose fundamental texts even the salaried priesthood had forgotten.

MARTIN AMIS

In 1945 George Orwell published a story called *Animal Farm*. It is about a revolution carried out by animals, expelling their human masters. Once the animals are in charge for themselves, things begin to go wrong.

At one point in the book Boxer, a strong, hard-working and dedicated farm horse, is seriously injured. The pigs, led by Napoleon, are in charge of the farm.

Animal Farm

The animals were all at work weeding turnips under the supervision of a pig, when they were astonished to see Benjamin come galloping from the direction of the farm buildings, braying at the top of his voice. It was the first time that they had ever seen Benjamin excited – indeed, it was the first time that anyone had ever seen him gallop. 'Quick, quick!' he shouted. 'Come at once! They're taking Boxer away!' Without waiting for orders from the pig, the animals broke off work and raced back to the farm buildings. Sure enough, there in the yard was a large closed van, drawn by two horses, with lettering on its side and a sly-looking man in a low-crowned bowler hat sitting on the driver's seat. And Boxer's stall was empty.

The animals crowded round the van. 'Good-bye, Boxer!' they chorused, 'good-bye!'

'Fools! Fools!' shouted Benjamin, prancing round them and stamping the earth with his small hoofs. 'Fools! Do you not see what is written on the side of that van?'

That gave the animals pause, and there was a hush. Muriel began to spell out the words. But Benjamin pushed her aside and in the midst of a deadly silence he read:

' "Alfred Simmonds, Horse Slaughterer and Glue Boiler, Willingdon. Dealer in Hides and Bone-Meal. Kennels Supplied." Do you not understand what that means? They are taking Boxer to the knacker's!'

A cry of horror burst from all the animals. At this moment the man on the box whipped up his horses and the van moved out of the yard at a smart trot. All the animals followed, crying out at the tops of their voices. Clover forced her way to the front. The van began to gather speed. Clover tried to stir her stout limbs to a gallop, and achieved a canter. 'Boxer!' she cried. 'Boxer! Boxer! Boxer!' And just at this moment, as though he had heard the uproar outside, Boxer's face, with the white stripe down his nose, appeared at the small window at the back of the van.

'Boxer!' cried Clover in a terrible voice. 'Boxer! Get out! Get out quickly! They are taking you to your death!'

All the animals took up the cry of 'Get out, Boxer, get out!' But the van was already gathering speed and drawing away from them. It was uncertain whether Boxer had understood what Clover had said. But a moment later his face disappeared from the window and there was the sound of a tremendous drumming of hoofs inside the van. He was trying to kick his way out. The time had been when a few kicks from Boxer's hoofs would have smashed the van to matchwood. But alas! his strength had left him; and in a few moments the sound of drumming hoofs grew fainter and died away. In desperation the animals began appealing to the two horses which drew the van to stop. 'Comrades, comrades!' they shouted. 'Don't take your own brother to his death!' But the stupid brutes, too ignorant to realise what was happening, merely set back their ears and quickened their pace. Boxer's face did not reappear at the window. Too late, someone thought of racing ahead and shutting the five-barred gate; but in another moment the van was through it and rapidly disappearing down the road. Boxer was never seen again.

Three days later it was announced that he had died in the hospital at Willingdon, in spite of receiving every attention a horse could have. Squealer came to announce the news to the others. He had, he said, been present during Boxer's last hours.

'It was the most affecting sight I have ever seen!' said Squealer, lifting his trotter and wiping away a tear. 'I was at his bedside at the very last. And at the end, almost too weak to speak, he whispered in my ear that his sole sorrow was to have passed on before the windmill was finished. "Forward, comrades!" he whispered. "Forward in the name of the Rebellion. Long live Animal Farm! Long live Comrade Napoleon! Napoleon is always right." Those were his very last words, comrades.'

Here Squealer's demeanour suddenly changed. He fell silent for a moment, and his little eyes darted suspicious glances from side to side before he proceeded.

It had come to his knowledge, he said, that a foolish and wicked rumour had been circulated at the time of Boxer's removal. Some of the animals had noticed that the van which took Boxer away was marked 'Horse Slaughterer', and had actually jumped to the conclusion that Boxer was being sent to the knacker's. It was almost unbelievable, said Squealer, that any animal could be so stupid. Surely, he cried indignantly, whisking his tail and skipping from side to side, surely they knew their beloved Leader, Comrade Napoleon, better than that? But the explanation was really very simple. The van had previously been the property of the knacker, and had been bought by the veterinary surgeon, who had not yet painted the old name out. That was how the mistake had arisen.

The animals were enormously relieved to hear this. And when Squealer went on to give further graphic details of Boxer's death bed, the admirable care he had received, and the expensive medicines for which Napoleon had paid without a thought as to the cost, their last doubts disappeared and the sorrow that they felt for their comrade's death was tempered by the thought that at least he had died happy.

Napoleon himself appeared at the meeting on the following Sunday morning and pronounced a short oration in Boxer's honour. It had not been possible, he said, to bring back their lamented comrade's remains for interment on the farm, but he had ordered a large wreath to be made from the laurels in the farmhouse garden and sent down to be placed on Boxer's grave. And in a few days' time the pigs intended to hold a memorial banquet in Boxer's honour. Napoleon ended his speech with a reminder of Boxer's two favourite maxims, 'I will work harder' and 'Comrade Napoleon is always right' – maxims, he said, which every animal would do well to adopt as his own.

On the day appointed for the banquet, a grocer's van drove up from Willingdon and delivered a large wooden crate at the farmhouse. That night there was the sound of uproarious singing, which was followed by what sounded like a violent quarrel and ended at about eleven o'clock with a tremendous crash of glass. No one stirred in the farmhouse before noon on the following day, and the word went round that from somewhere or other the pigs had acquired the money to buy themselves another case of whisky.

GEORGE ORWELL

TASKS

19 Look at the Martin Amis article and explain what is so strange about his visit to China.

20 Now consider how the ordinary animals on the farm feel about the way Boxer is treated and write down your thoughts.

21 In the real world of China and the fictional world of *Animal Farm* strange things are happening.
    What part does the use of language play in accounting for what is happening? You should pay special attention to ideas such as:
    ▪ orders;
    ▪ repetition;
    ▪ military chants;
    ▪ the story of the deer and the horse;
    ▪ Squealer's speech to the other animals.

TIME OUT TASK!

Slogans

Whenever people have a cause to promote (or a product to sell!) they invent slogans. Here are a few:

> Votes for Women!
> Your Country Needs You!
> Ban the Bomb!
> Education Cuts Don't Heal!
> Back to Basics!
> How do You eat Yours…?
> One to Remember!
> A Mars A Day…!

- Collect a range of these slogans. Don't just use advertisements for things to buy and sell. Look also for slogans to promote political and social causes.
- When you have made a collection write about them, showing why they are effective. Look at the choice and arrangement of words; consider how there might be several meanings or a clearer use of words.
- Invent slogans of your own
  - for a cause of your own
  - for a group of people or an idea that you support
  - to advertise a product.

Discuss your slogans in groups and try to decide objectively whose are best and why.

END OF TIME OUT!

Some people seem to be misfits through no fault of their own and struggle against their problems until, magnificently, they prove that they belong just as much as anyone else.

One such person was Stephen Hawking. He was a brilliant student who was struck down by a crippling illness called motor neurone disease. Although it had a dreadful effect on his body it did not affect his brain, and he continued to be a brilliant mathematician and scientist.

A Brief History of Stephen Hawking

In an upmarket restaurant near Cambridge city centre one lunchtime during December 1988, 12 graduates are sitting around a large table. To one side, slumped in a wheelchair and being spoon-fed by a nurse, is a man in his mid-forties.

His neat open-necked shirt and plain jacket contrast favourably with the general scruffiness of the young men and women, and behind steel-rimmed spectacles his clear blue eyes are alert. But he looks terribly frail, almost withered away to nothing.

He cannot talk because of a tracheotomy; set into the centre of his sinewy throat is a plastic breathing device about two inches in diameter. So when the young people make a flippant remark in his direction, he painstakingly moves two fingers of one hand – almost his last vestige of bodily freedom – to spell out his reply with the computer control on his lap, and a voice-synthesiser, connected to the computer, turns the words into speech. His metallic reply brings peals of mirth from the whole table.

Then, excitement: the arrival in the restaurant of the guest of honour, a glamorous redhead in a fake-fur coat. 'Sorry I'm late,' she says. 'My car was wheel-clamped in London.'

She adds, laughing, 'There must be some cosmic significance in that!'

The man's eyes light up. What has been called 'the greatest smile in the world' envelopes his boyish face. The redhead crouches in front of him.

'Professor Hawking, I'm delighted to meet you. I'm Shirley MacLaine.'

For the rest of the meal the Oscar-winning Hollywood actress, who is deeply interested in metaphysics and spiritual matters, and has strong beliefs about the meaning of life, plies Hawking with questions, wanting his views. When she asks: 'Do you believe there is a God who created the Universe and guides His creation?' Hawking smiles momentarily. The Star Wars voice says, 'No.'

It is not what Shirley MacLaine wants to hear and she doesn't agree; she has already spoken to holy men and teachers in many countries. But she can only listen and take note, for if nothing else, Stephen Hawking's views have to be respected. His field is theoretical cosmology: the study of the Universe at large – in terms of ideas the biggest of big science.

His fundamental breakthroughs, pushing forward our understanding of the origin of the Universe, the laws which govern its existence and the eventual fate of everybody and everything, have made Hawking arguably the greatest physicist of our time.

He has been proclaimed 'the finest mind alive' and 'the greatest genius of the late twentieth century'; even 'Einstein's heir'.

Moreover, he is known to millions, far and wide, for his science book *A Brief History of Time*. Aimed at the lay reader, it is a publishing phenomenon. An instant bestseller in Britain and America, it has earned a place in the *Guinness Book of Records* for spending 184 weeks in *The Sunday Times* 'top-ten' lists, and has sold more than five million copies worldwide.

How did all this happen? How has a man who is almost completely paralysed and weighs less than six and a half stone overcome every obstacle and achieved far more than most able-bodied people ever dream of accomplishing?

Stephen William Hawking was a healthy baby, born to intellectual, eccentric parents. His father Frank, a doctor specialising in tropical diseases, and his mother Isobel, a Glasgow doctor's daughter, had a large rambling house in St Albans, Hertfordshire, cluttered with books. Carpets and furniture stayed in use until they fell apart; wallpaper was allowed to dangle where it had peeled through old age. The family car was a London taxi, bought for £50.

Hawking, who has two younger sisters and a younger adopted brother, is fascinated by his birthdate: January 8, 1942. It was the three hundredth anniversary of the death of Galileo, the Italian mathematician and astronomer who revolutionised astronomy and was persecuted by the Inquisition for maintaining that the Sun is the centre of our planetary system – not the Earth, as ancient astronomers believed.

'Galileo', says Hawking, 'was the first scientist to start using his eyes, both figuratively and physically. In a sense, he was responsible for the age of science we now enjoy.'

Hawking went to St Albans School, a private school noted for academic excellence. By the end of his third year, when he won the school divinity prize, he was part of a small group, the brightest of the bright students, who hung around together. They listened to classical music (pop was *infra dig*) and read only the 'smart' authors: Kingsley Amis, Aldous Huxley and Hawking's hero, Bertrand Russell, at once intellectual giant and liberal activist.

Hawking spent very little time on maths homework, yet got full marks. A friend recalls: 'While I would be worrying away at a complicated problem, he just knew the answer. He didn't have to think about it.'

This instinctive insight also impressed his teachers. In 1958, during a science lesson in the sixth form (where Hawking and his friends built a rudimentary computer, at a time when only a few large companies and universities had computers), the teacher posed the question: 'Does a cup of hot tea reach a drinkable temperature more quickly if you put the milk in first, or add the milk after pouring?' While the rest of the class struggled with a muddle of concepts, Hawking almost instantly announced the correct answer: 'Add the milk after pouring, of course,' (the hotter the tea, initially, the faster it will cool).

Hawking the schoolboy was a typical swot, awkward, skinny and puny. His grey uniform always looked a mess and he jabbered rather than talked clearly, having inherited a slight lisp from his father. His friends dubbed his speech 'Hawkingese'.

It had nothing to do with early signs of illness; he was just that sort of kid – a figure of classroom fun, respected by his friends, avoided by most.

All this changed when Hawking went up to Oxford, winning a scholarship to read Natural Science, a course which combined mathematics and physics, at University College. He found much of the work easy and averaged only one hour's work a day.

Once, when his tutor set some physics problems from a textbook, Hawking did not even bother to do them. Asked why, he spent 20 minutes pointing out errors in the book.

Hawking was feeling bored, and in danger of sliding into apathy, when luckily he found an interest: the Boat Club. His wraithlike physique was perfectly suited to coxing. He had a loud voice with which he enjoyed barking instructions, and he cultivated a daredevil image when navigating on the river. Many times he returned to shore with bits of the boat knocked off and oar blades damaged, having tried to guide his crew through an impossible narrow gap. Norman Dix, his rowing trainer, suspects, 'Half the time, he was sitting in the stern with his head in the stars, working out mathematical formulae.'

Hawking has never been interested in observational astronomy. While at Oxford he did a vacation course at the Royal Greenwich Observatory, helping the then Astronomer Royal, Sir Richard Woolley, with research into binary stars. However, upon looking through the telescope and seeing merely a couple of hazy dots, he was convinced that theoretical cosmology would be much more interesting.

MICHAEL WHITE
JOHN GRIBBIN

TASKS

22 Imagine that you were in the same class as Stephen Hawking at school. Write about him, saying what you thought of him.

23 Now try to imagine you are Stephen Hawking. Write about your frustrations and depressions as you fight your way through life. Remember Shirley MacLaine calls him 'professor' – he is a professor at Cambridge University.

You will find the article reprinted in your homework book together with an imaginative task for you to tackle.

Charles Dickens wrote about many characters who were odd or misfits. The word 'Dickensian' has come to mean a person who is quaint or strange in some way.

In *Great Expectations* Dickens includes the description of two houses and their occupants. Pip, the main character in the story, first visits Satis House as a boy. He meets Estella and then the very odd Miss Havisham.

Great Expectations

My young conductress locked the gate, and we went across the courtyard. It was paved and clean, but grass was growing in every crevice. The brewery buildings had a little lane of communication with it; and the wooden gates of that lane stood open, and all the brewery beyond stood open, away to the high enclosing wall; and all was empty and disused. The cold wind seemed to blow colder there, than outside the gate; and it made a shrill noise in howling in and out at the open sides of the brewery, like the noise of wind in the rigging of a ship at sea.

She saw me looking at it, and she said, 'You could drink without hurt all the strong beer that's brewed there now, boy.'

'I should think I could, miss,' said I, in a shy way.

'Better not try to brew beer there now, or it would turn out sour, boy; don't you think so?'

'It looks like it, miss.'

'Not that anybody means to try,' she added, 'for that's all done with, and the place will stand as idle as it is, till it falls. As to strong beer, there's enough of it in the cellars already, to drown the Manor House.'

'Is that the name of this house, miss?'

'One of its names, boy.'

'It has more than one, then, miss?'

'One more. Its other name was Satis; which is Greek, or Latin, or Hebrew, or all three – or all one to me – for enough.'

'Enough House!' said I: 'that's a curious name, miss.'

'Yes,' she replied; 'but it meant more than it said. It meant, when it was given, that whoever had this house, could want nothing else. They must have been easily satisfied in those days, I should think. But don't loiter, boy.'

Though she called me 'boy' so often, and with a carelessness that was far from complimentary, she was of about my own age. She seemed much older than I, of course, being a girl, and beautiful and self-possessed; and she was as scornful of me as if she had been one-and-twenty, and a queen.

We went into the house by a side door – the great front entrance had two chains across it outside – and the first thing I noticed was, that the passages were all dark, and that she had left a candle burning there. She took it up, and we went through more passages and up a staircase, and still it was all dark, and only the candle lighted us.

At last we came to the door of a room, and she said, 'Go in.'

I answered, more in shyness than politeness, 'After you, miss.'

To this she returned: 'Don't be ridiculous, boy; I am not going in.' And scornfully walked away, and – what was worse – took the candle with her.

This was very uncomfortable, and I was half afraid. However, the only thing to be done being to knock at the door, I knocked, and was told from within to enter. I entered, therefore, and found myself in a pretty large room, well lighted with wax candles. No glimpse of daylight was to be seen in it. It was a dressing-room, as I supposed from the furniture, though much of it was of forms and uses then quite unknown to me. But prominent in it was a draped table with a glided looking-glass, and that I made out at first sight to be a fine lady's dressing-table.

Whether I should have made out this object so soon, if there had been no fine lady sitting at it, I cannot say. In an armchair, with an elbow resting on the table and her head leaning on that hand, sat the strangest lady I have ever seen, or shall ever see.

She was dressed in rich materials – satins, and lace, and silks – all of white. Her shoes were white. And she had a long white veil dependent from her hair, and she had bridal flowers in her hair, but her hair was white. Some bright jewels sparkled on her neck and on her hands, and some other jewels lay sparkling on the table. Dresses, less splendid than the dress she wore, and half-packed trunks, were scattered about. She had not quite finished dressing, for she had but one shoe on – the other was on the table near her hand – her veil was but half arranged, her watch and chain were not put on, and some lace for her bosom lay with those trinkets, and with her handkerchief, and gloves, and some flowers, and a Prayer-book, all confusedly heaped about the looking-glass.

It was not in the first few moments that I saw all these things, though I saw more of them in the first moments than might be supposed. But, I saw that everything within my view which ought to be white, had been white long ago, and had lost its lustre, and was faded and yellow. I saw that the bride within the bridal dress had withered like the dress, and like the flowers, and had no brightness left but the brightness of her sunken eyes. I saw that the dress had been put upon the rounded figure of a young woman, and that the figure upon which it now hung loose, had shrunk to skin and bone. Once, I had been taken to see some ghastly waxwork at the Fair, representing I know not what impossible personage lying in state. Once, I had been taken to one of our old marsh churches to see a skeleton in the ashes of a rich dress, that had been dug out of a vault under the church pavement. Now, waxwork and skeleton seemed to have dark eyes that moved and looked at me. I should have cried out, if I could.

Who is it?' said the lady at the table.

'Pip, ma'am.'

'Pip?'

'Mr Pumblechook's boy, ma'am. Come – to play.'

'Come nearer; let me look at you. Come close.'

It was when I stood before her, avoiding her eyes, that I took note of the surrounding objects in detail, and saw that her watch had stopped at twenty minutes to nine, and that a clock in the room had stopped at twenty minutes to nine.

CHARLES DICKENS

Later in his life Pip goes to live in London, in order to learn how to become a young gentleman. One day he visits the house of John Wemmick, a solicitor's clerk.

Great Expectations

He conducted me to a bower about a dozen yards off, but which was approached by such ingenious twists of path that it took quite a long time to get at; and in this retreat our glasses were already set forth. Our punch was cooling in an ornamental lake, on whose margin the bower was raised. This piece of water (with an island in the middle which might have been the salad for supper) was of a circular form, and he had constructed a fountain in it, which, when you set a little mill going and took a cork out of a pipe, played to that powerful extent that it made the back of your hand quite wet.

'I am my own engineer, and my own carpenter, and my own plumber, and my own gardener, and my own Jack of all Trades,' said Wemmick, in acknowledging my compliments. 'Well, it's a good thing, you know. It brushes the Newgate cobwebs away, and pleases the Aged. You wouldn't mind being at once introduced to the Aged, would you? It wouldn't put you out?'

I expressed the readiness I felt, and we went into the castle. Then, we found, sitting by a fire, a very old man in a flannel coat: clean, cheerful, comfortable, and well cared for, but intensely deaf.

'Well, aged parent,' said Wemmick, shaking hands with him in a cordial and jocose way, 'how am you?'

'All right, John; all right!' replied the old man.

'Here's Mr Pip, aged parent,' said Wemmick, 'and I wish you could hear his name. Nod away at him, Mr Pip; that's what he likes. Nod away at him, if you please, like winking!'

'This is a fine place of my son's, sir,' cried the old man, while I nodded as hard as I possibly could. 'This is a pretty pleasure-ground, sir. This

spot and these beautiful works upon it ought to be kept together by the Nation, after my son's time, for the people's enjoyment.'

'You're as proud of it as Punch; ain't you, Aged?' said Wemmick, contemplating the old man, with his hard face really softened; 'there's a nod for you;' giving him a tremendous one; 'there's another for you;' giving him a still more tremendous one; 'you like that, don't you? If you're not tired, Mr Pip – though I know it's tiring to strangers – will you tip him one more? You can't think how it pleases him.'

I tipped him several more, and he was in great spirits. We left him bestirring himself to feed the fowls, and we sat down to our punch in the arbour; where Wemmick told me as he smoked a pipe, that it had taken him a good many years to bring the property up to its present pitch of perfection.

'Is it your own, Mr Wemmick?'

'O yes,' said Wemmick. 'I have got hold of it, a bit at a time. It's a freehold, by George!'

'Is it, indeed? I hope Mr Jaggers admires it?'

'Never seen it,' said Wemmick. 'Never heard of it. Never seen the Aged. Never heard of him. No; the office is one thing, and private life is another. While I go into the office, I leave the Castle behind me, and when I come into the Castle, I leave the office behind me. If it's not in any way disagreeable to you, you'll oblige me by doing the same. I don't wish it professionally spoken about.'

Of course I felt my good faith involved in the observance of his request. The punch being very nice, we sat there drinking it and talking, until it was almost nine o'clock.

'Getting near gun-fire,' said Wemmick then, as he laid down his pipe; 'it's the Aged's treat.'

Proceeding into the Castle again, we found the Aged heating the poker, with expectant eyes, as a preliminary to the performance of this great nightly ceremony. Wemmick stood with his watch in his hand until the moment was come for him to take the red-hot poker from the Aged, and repair to the battery. He took it, and went out, and presently the Stinger went off with a bang that shook the crazy little box of a cottage as if it must fall to pieces, and made every glass and teacup in it ring. Upon this the Aged – who I believe would have been blown out of his armchair but for holding on by the elbows – cried out exultingly, 'He's fired! I heerd him!' and I nodded at the old gentleman until it is no figure of speech to declare that I absolutely could not see him.

The interval between that time and supper, Wemmick devoted to showing me his collection of curiosities. They were mostly of a felonious character; comprising the pen with which a celebrated forgery had been committed, a distinguished razor or two, some locks of hair, and several manuscript confessions written under condemnation – upon which Mr Wemmick set particular value as being, to use his own words, 'every one of 'em Lies, sir.' These were agreeably dispersed among small specimens of china and glass, various neat trifles made by the proprietor of the museum, and some tobacco-stoppers carved by the Aged. They were all displayed in that chamber of the Castle into which I had been first inducted, and which served, not only as the general sitting-room, but as the kitchen too, if I might judge from a saucepan on the hob, and a brazen bijou over the fireplace designed for the suspension of a roasting-jack.

There was a neat little girl in attendance, who looked after the Aged in the day. When she had laid the supper-cloth, the bridge was lowered to give her the means of egress, and she withdrew for the night. The supper was excellent; and though the Castle was rather subject to dry-rot, insomuch that it tasted like a bad nut, and though the pig might have been farther off, I was heartily pleased with my whole entertainment. Nor was there any drawback on my little turret bedroom, beyond there being such a very thin ceiling between me and the flagstaff, that when I lay down on my back in bed, it seemed as if I had to balance that pole on my forehead all night.

Wemmick was up early in the morning, and I am afraid I heard him cleaning my boots. After that, he fell to gardening, and I saw him from my gothic window pretending to employ the Aged, and nodding at him in a most devoted manner. Our breakfast was as good as the supper, and at half-past eight precisely we started for Little Britain. By degrees, Wemmick got dryer and harder as we went along, and his mouth tightened into a post-office again. At last, when we got to his place of business and he pulled out his key from his coat-collar, he looked as unconscious of his Walworth property as if the Castle and the drawbridge and the arbour and the lake and the fountain and the Aged, had all been blown into space together by the last discharge of the Stinger.

CHARLES DICKENS

TASKS

24 Describe in your own words what each house is like.

25 Explain carefully the ways in which the people Pip meets are strange.

26 Look carefully at the passages and explain how Dickens has created a strange atmosphere in each description.

The second extract which introduced Wemmick and the Aged Parent is reprinted in your homework book together with a 'Dickensian' task.

TIME OUT TASK!

Concentrate on pre-twentieth century literature

In this book we can only deal closely with extracts from novels and plays. The National Curriculum suggests that you should be reading some whole major works of literature written before the twentieth century.

Choose a novel that fits well with this chapter's theme of misfits and read it. Why not read *Pride and Prejudice* by Jane Austen and see Mrs Bennett struggling to marry off her daughters.
Or *Oliver Twist* by Charles Dickens and discover how Oliver, who doesn't seem to fit in anywhere, copes with the trials and tribulations of his early life.
Or *The Mayor of Casterbridge* by Thomas Hardy to see how a character like Michael Henchard tries to fit in and mature as time goes by and how people learn, or fail to learn, from a tangle of relationships.

END OF TIME OUT!

TASK

27   Your own writing
Here are some titles for writing of your own. Remember to use description and dialogue in your own stories.
- A strange meeting
- The weirdest place I've ever been to
- Old, strange and alone
- Why did they treat me like that?
- Out on a limb
- The need to belong
- The gang

Shakespeare, like Dickens, created characters who were misfits. Sometimes they are objects of fun; sometimes they are frightening.

In *Twelfth Night* Malvolio is Olivia's steward. He has a reputation for being pompous and giving himself airs. Maria, Sir Toby and Sir Andrew decide to play a trick on him. They plant a letter and hide from Malvolio's view as he reads it.

Twelfth Night

Act 2 Scene 5

MALVOLIO:

What employment have we here?

[Taking up the letter]

FABIANO:

Now is the woodcock near the gin.

SIR TOBY:

O, peace! and the spirit of humours intimate reading aloud to him!

MALVOLIO:

By my life, this is my lady's hand: these be her very *C*'s, her *U*'s, and her *T*'s; and thus makes she her great *P*'s. It is in contempt of question, her hand.

SIR ANDREW:

Her *C*'s, her *U*'s, and her *T*'s.
Why that?

MALVOLIO:

[reads.] To the unknown beloved, this, and my good wishes: her very phrases! – By your leave, wax. – Soft ! – and the impressure her Lucrece, with which she uses to seal: 'tis my lady. To whom should this be?

FABIANO:

This wins him, liver and all.

MALVOLIO:

[reads.] Jove knows I love:
> *But who?*
> *Lips do not move,*
> *No man must know.*
> *No man must know. –*

What follows? the numbers altered! – *No man must know:* – If this should be there, Malvolio?

SIR TOBY:

Marry, hang thee, brock!

MALVOLIO:

I may command where I adore:
But silence, like a Lucrece knight,
With bloodless stroke my heart doth gore;
M, O, A, I, doth sway my life.

FABIANO:

A fustian riddle!

SIR TOBY:

Excellent wench, say I.

MALVOLIO:

M, O, A, I, doth sway my life. – Nay, but first let me see, – let me see, – let me see.

FABIANO:

What a dish of poison hath she dressed him!

SIR TOBY:

And with what wing the stannyel checks at it!

MALVOLIO:

I may command where I adore. Why, she may command me: I serve her, she is my lady. Why, this is evident to any formal capacity. There is no obstruction in this; – And the end, – What should that alphabetical position portend? If I could make that resemble something in me, – Softly! – *M, O, A, I.* –

SIR TOBY:

O, ay! make up that: – he is now at a cold scent.

FABIANO:

Sowter will cry upon 't for all this, though it be as rank as a fox.

MALVOLIO:

M, – Malvolio; – *M,* – why, that begins my name.

FABIANO:

Did not I say he would work it out? the cur is excellent at faults.

MALVOLIO:

M, – But then there is no consonancy in the sequel; that suffers under probation: *A* should follow, but *O* does.

FABIANO:

and *O* shall end, I hope.

SIR TOBY:

Ay, or I'll cudgel him, and make him cry *O*.

MALVOLIO:

And then *I* comes behind.

FABIANO:

Ay, an you had any eye behind you, you might see more detraction at your heels than fortunes before you.

MALVOLIO:

M, O, A, I; – this simulation is not as the former: – and yet, to crush this a little, it would bow to me, for every one of these letters are in my name. Soft; here follows prose. –

If this fall into thy hand, revolve. In my stars I am above thee; but be not afraid of greatness. Some are born great, some achieve greatness, and some have greatness thrust upon them. Thy fates open their hands; let they blood and spirit embrace them. And, to inure thyself to what thou art like to be, cast thy humble slough and appear fresh. Be opposite with a kinsman, surly with servants: let thy tongue tang arguments of state; put thyself into the trick of singularity: She thus advises thee that sighs for thee. Remember who commended they yellow stockings, and wished to see thee ever cross-gartered. I say, remember. Go to; thou art made, if thou desirest to be so; if not, let me see thee a steward still, the fellow of servants, and not worthy to touch fortune's fingers. Farewell. She that would alter services with thee, The fortunate unhappy.

Daylight and champian discovers not more: this is open. I will be proud, I will read polite authors, I will baffle Sir Toby, I will wash off gross acquaintance, I will be point-de-vice, the very man. I do not now fool myself to let imagination jade me; for every reason excites to this, that my lady loves me. She did commend my yellow stockings of late, she did praise my leg being cross-gartered; and in this she manifests herself to my love, and, with a kind of injunction, drives me to these habits of her liking. I thank my stars I am happy. I will be strange, stout, in yellow stockings, and cross-gartered, even with the swiftness of putting on. Jove and my stars be praised! – Here is yet a postscript. *Thou canst not choose but know who I am. If thou entertainest my love, let it appear in thy smiling; thy smiles becothe thee well: therefore in my presence still smile, dear my sweet, I pr'ythee.* Jove, I thank thee. – I will smile: I will do everything that thou wilt have me.

[Exit.]

FABIANO:
   I will not give my part of this sport for a pension of thousands to be paid from the Sophy.
SIR TOBY:
   I could marry this wench for this device:
SIR ANDREW:
   So could I too.
SIR TOBY:
   And ask no other dowry with her but such another jest.

WILLIAM SHAKESPEARE

TASKS

28 Explain the trick which is being played upon Malvolio.

29 Explain how we know that Maria, Sir Toby and Sir Andrew are enjoying themselves.

30 Describe the ways in which the audience would find this scene amusing.

King Richard III is one of Shakespeare's most notorious villains. Here are two extracts from the play *Richard III*. In the first Richard, the Duke of Gloucester, speaks of himself, his plans and intentions.

Richard III

Act 1 Scene 1

Enter Richard, Duke of Gloucester, alone.
RICHARD:
   Now is the winter of our discontent
   Made glorious summer by this sun of York,
   And all the clouds that loured upon our house
   In the deep bosom of the ocean buried.
   Now are our brows bound with victorious wreaths,
   Our bruisèd arms hung up for monuments,
   Our stern alarums changed to merry meetings,
   Our dreadful marches to delightful measures.
   Grim-visaged war hath smoothed his wrinkled front,
   And now, instead of mounting barbèd steeds
   To fright the souls of fearful adversaries,
   He capers nimbly in a lady's chamber
   To the lascivious pleasing of a lute.

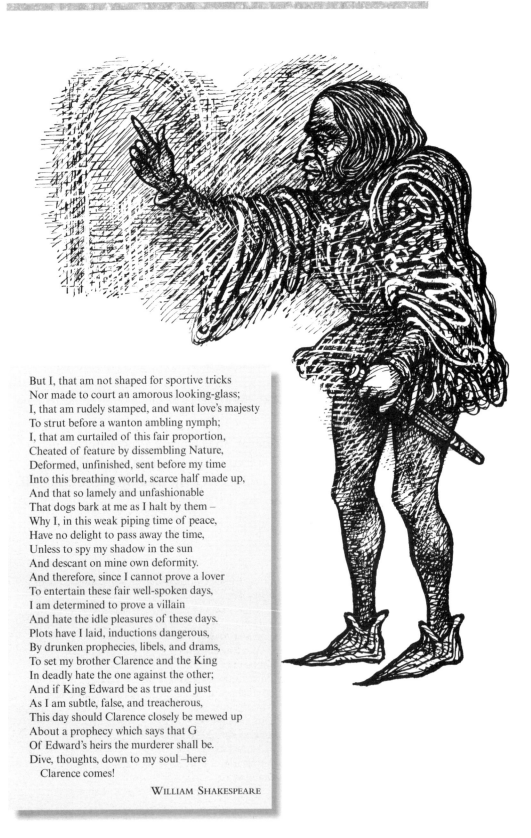

But I, that am not shaped for sportive tricks
Nor made to court an amorous looking-glass;
I, that am rudely stamped, and want love's majesty
To strut before a wanton ambling nymph;
I, that am curtailed of this fair proportion,
Cheated of feature by dissembling Nature,
Deformed, unfinished, sent before my time
Into this breathing world, scarce half made up,
And that so lamely and unfashionable
That dogs bark at me as I halt by them –
Why I, in this weak piping time of peace,
Have no delight to pass away the time,
Unless to spy my shadow in the sun
And descant on mine own deformity.
And therefore, since I cannot prove a lover
To entertain these fair well-spoken days,
I am determined to prove a villain
And hate the idle pleasures of these days.
Plots have I laid, inductions dangerous,
By drunken prophecies, libels, and drams,
To set my brother Clarence and the King
In deadly hate the one against the other;
And if King Edward be as true and just
As I am subtle, false, and treacherous,
This day should Clarence closely be mewed up
About a prophecy which says that G
Of Edward's heirs the murderer shall be.
Dive, thoughts, down to my soul –here
    Clarence comes!

WILLIAM SHAKESPEARE

R ichard is responsible for the murders of both King
Henry VI and his son Edward. At the time of Henry's
burial Richard woos Anne, the wife of the murdered Edward.
So Richard has killed both her husband and her father-in-law.

Richard III

Act 1 Scene 2

RICHARD:
I did not kill your husband.

ANNE
Why, then, he is alive.

RICHARD:
Nay, he is dead; and slain by Edward's hand.

ANNE:
In thy foul throat thou liest: Queen Margaret saw
Thy murderous falchion smoking in his blood;
The which thou once didst bend against her breast,
But that thy brothers beat aside the point.

RICHARD:
I was provoked by her slanderous tongue,
That laid their guilt upon my guiltless shoulders.

ANNE:
Thou wast provoked by thy bloody mind,
That never dreamt on aught but butcheries:
Didst thou not kill this king?

RICHARD:
I grant ye.

ANNE:
Dost grant me, hedgehog? then, God grant me too
Thou mayst be damned for that wicked deed! O,
he was gentle, mild, and virtuous.

RICHARD:
The fitter for the King of Heaven, that hath him.

ANNE:
He is in heaven, where thou shalt never come.

RICHARD:
Let him thank me, that holp to send him thither;
for he was fitter for that place than earth.

ANNE:
And thou unfit for any place but hell.

RICHARD:
Yes, one place else, if you will hear me name it.

ANNE:
Some dungeon.

RICHARD:
Your bed-chamber.

ANNE:
Ill rest betide the chamber where thou liest!

RICHARD:
So will it, madam, till I lie with you.

ANNE:
I hope so.

RICHARD:
I know so. – But, gentle Lady
To leave this keen encounter of our wits,
And fall somewhat into a slower method, –
Is not the causer of the timeless deaths
Of these Plantagenets, Henry and Edward,
As blameful as the executioner?

ANNE:
Thou wast the cause and most accurs'd effect.

RICHARD:
Your beauty was the cause of that effect;
Your beauty, that did haunt me in my sleep.
To undertake the death of all the world,
So I might live one hour in your sweet bosom.

ANNE:
If I thought that, I tell thee, homicide,
These nails should rend that beauty from my
cheeks.

RICHARD:
These eyes could not endure that beauty's wreck.
You should not blemish if it I stood by:
As all the world is cheered by the sun,
So I by that; it is my day, my life.

ANNE:
Black night o'ershade thy day, and death
thy life!

RICHARD:
Curse not thyself, fair creature; thou art both.

ANNE:
I would I were, to be reveng'd on thee.

RICHARD:
It is a quarrel most unnatural,
To be reveng'd on him that loveth thee.

ANNE:
It is a quarrel just and reasonable,
To be reveng'd on him that kill'd my husband.

RICHARD:
He that bereft thee, lady, of thy husband,
Did it to help thee to a better husband.

ANNE:
His better doth not breath upon the earth.

RICHARD:
He lives that loves the better than he could.

ANNE:

Name him.

RICHARD:

Plantagenet.

ANNE:

Why, that was he.

RICHARD:

The self-same name, but one of better nature.

ANNE:

Where is he?

RICHARD:

Here. [*She spits at him.*] Why dost thou spit at me?

ANNE:

Would it were mortal poison, for thy sake!

RICHARD:

Never came poison from so sweet a place.

ANNE:

Never hung poison on a fouler toad. Out of my sight! Thou dost infect mine eyes.

RICHARD:

Thine eyes, sweet lady, have infected mine.

ANNE:

Would they were basilisks, to strike thee dead!

RICHARD:

I would they were, that I might die at once;
For now they kill me with a living death.
Those eyes of thine from mine have drawn salt tears,
Sham'd their aspécts with store of childish drops:
These eyes, which never shed remorseful tear,
No, when my father York and Edward wept,
To bear the piteous moan that Rutland made
When black-fac'd Clifford shook his sword at him;
Nor when thy warlike father, like a child,
Told the sad story of my father's death,
And twenty times made pause, to sob and weep,
That all the standers-by had wet their cheeks,
Like trees bedash'd with rain; in that sad time
My manly eyes did scorn an humble tear;
And what these sorrows could not thence exhale,
Thy beauty hath, and made them blind with weeping.
I never su'd to friend nor enemy;
My tongue could never learn sweet smoothing word;
But, now thy beauty is propos'd my fee,
My proud heart sues, and prompts my tongue to speak. [*She looks scornfully at him.*]
Teach not thy lip such scorn; for it was made
For kissing, lady, not for such contempt.
If thy revengeful heart cannot forgive,
Lo, here I lend thee this sharp-pointed sword;
Which if thou please to hide in this true breast,
And let the soul forth that adoreth thee,
I lay it naked to the deadly stroke,
And humbly beg the death upon my knee.
Nay, do not pause; for I did kill King Henry, –
                    [*He lays his breast open;
                    she offers at it with his sword.*]
But 'twas thy beauty that provoked me.
Nay, now despatch: 'twas I that stabb'd young Edward, –
                    [*She again offers at his breast.*]
But 'twas thy heavenly face that set me on.
                    [*She lets fall the sword.*]
Take up the sword again, or take up me.

ANNE:

Arise, dissembler: though I wish thy death,
I will not be thy executioner.

RICHARD:

Then bid me kill myself, and I will do it.

ANNE:

I have already.

RICHARD:

That was in thy rage:
Speak it again, and, even with the word,
This hand, which for they love did kill they love,
Shall, for thy love, kill a far truer love;
To both their deaths shalt thou be accessary.

ANNE:

I would I knew thy heart.

RICHARD:

'Tis figured in my tongue.

ANNE:

I fear me both are false.

RICHARD:

Then never man was true.

ANNE:

Well, well, put up your sword.

RICHARD:

Say, then, my peace is made.

ANNE:

That shalt thou know hereafter.

RICHARD:

But shall I live in hope?

ANNE:

All men, I hope, live so.

RICHARD:

Vouchsafe to wear this ring.

ANNE:

To take is not to give.   [*She puts on the ring.*]

RICHARD:

Look, how this ring encompasseth thy finger,
Even so thy breast encloseth my poor heart;
Wear both of them, for both of them are thine.

WILLIAM SHAKESPEARE

TASKS

31 Look at Richard's first speech. What does he tell us about himself as a person?

32 What does Richard tell us about his plans?

33 Describe your reactions to Richard's words and thoughts.

34 In the second extract Richard is trying to persuade Anne to become his wife. Against all the odds, he succeeds. What signs are there that he is going to succeed? What persuasion does he use?

To finish this chapter we are going to look at a whole group of misfits. They are referred to in the story *Don't Waste Your Time With Those Kids* which is printed below.

Don't Waste Your Time With Those Kids

On my first day of teaching, all my classes were going well. Being a teacher would be a doddle, I decided. Then came Period Seven, the last class of the day.

As I walked towards the room, I heard furniture crash. Rounding the corner, I saw one boy pinning another to the floor. 'Listen, you retard!' yelled the one on the bottom. 'I don't give a damn about your sister!'

'You keep your hands off her, you hear me?' the boy on top threatened.

I drew up my short frame and asked them to stop fighting. Suddenly 14 pairs of eyes were riveted on my face. I knew I did not look convincing. Glaring at each other and me, the two boys slowly took their seats. At that moment, the teacher from across the corridor stuck his head in the door and shouted at my pupils to sit down, shut up and do what I said. I was left feeling powerless.

I tried to teach the lesson I had prepared, but was met with a sea of guarded faces. As the class was leaving, I detained the boy who had instigated the fight. I'll call him Mark. 'Don't waste your time,' he told me. 'We're the retards.' Then Mark strolled out of the room.

Dumbstruck, I slumped into my chair and wondered if I should have become a teacher. Was the only cure for problems like this to get out? I told myself I'd suffer for one year, and after my marriage that next summer I'd do something more rewarding.

'They upset you, didn't they?' It was the colleague who had come into my classroom earlier. I nodded.

'Don't worry,' he said. 'I taught many of them in summer school. There are only 14 of them, and most will drop out anyway. Don't waste your time on them.'

'What do you mean?'

'They live in shacks in the fields. They're migrant workers, pickers' kids. They come to school only when they feel like it. The boy on the floor had pestered Mark's sister while they were picking beans together. I had to tell them to shut up at lunch today. Just keep them busy and quiet. If they cause trouble, send them to me.'

As I gathered my things to go home, I couldn't forget the look on Mark's face as he said, 'We're the retards.' *Retards.* That word clattered in my brain. I knew I had to do something drastic.

The next afternoon I asked my colleague not to come into my class again. I needed to handle the kids my own way. I returned to my room and made eye contact with each student. Then I went to the board and wrote ECINAJ.

'That's my first name,' I said.

'Can you tell me what it is?'

They told me my name was 'weird' and that they had never seen it before. I went to the board again and this time wrote JANICE. Several of them blurted the word, then gave me a funny look.

'You're right, my name is Janice,' I said. 'I'm learning-impaired, something called dyslexia. When I started school I couldn't write my own name correctly. I couldn't spell words, and numbers swam in my head. I was labelled "retarded." That's right – I was a "retard". I can still hear those awful voices and feel the shame.'

'So how'd you become a teacher?' someone asked.

'Because I hate labels and I'm not stupid and I love to learn. That's what this class is going to be about. If you like the label 'retard', then you don't belong here. Change classes. There are no retarded people in this room.

'I'm not going to be easy on you,' I continued. 'We're going to work and work until you catch up. You *will* graduate, and I hope some of you will go to university. That's not a joke –it's a promise. I don't *ever* want to hear the word "retard" in this room again. Do you understand?'

They seemed to sit up a little straighter.

We did work hard, and I soon caught glimpses of promise. Mark, especially, was very bright. I heard him tell a boy in the corridor, 'This book's real good. We don't read baby books in there.' He was holding a copy of *To Kill a Mockingbird*.

Months flew by, and the improvement was wonderful. Then one day Mark said, 'But people still think we're stupid 'cause we don't talk right.' It was the moment I had been waiting for. Now we could begin an intensive study of grammar, because they wanted it.

I was sorry to see the month of June approach; they wanted to learn so much. All my pupils knew I was getting married and moving. The pupils in my last-period class were visibly agitated whenever I mentioned it. I was glad they had become fond of me, but what was wrong? Were they angry I was leaving the school?

On my final day there, the headmaster greeted me as I entered the building. 'Will you come with me, please?' he said sternly. 'There's a problem in your room.' He looked straight ahead as he led me down the hall. *What now?* I wondered.

There, standing outside my classroom, was my Period Seven class, all smiles. 'Miss Anderson,' Mark said proudly, 'Period Two got you roses and Period Three got you a corsage, but we love you more.' He motioned to my door, and I looked inside.

It was amazing! There were sprays of flowers in each corner, bouquets on the kids' desks and filing cabinets, and a huge blanket of flowers lying on my desk. *How could they have done this?* I thought. Most of them came from families so poor that they relied on the school assistance programme for warm clothing and decent meals.

I started to cry, and they all joined me.

Later I learned how they had pulled it off. Mark, who worked in the local flower shop at weekends, had seen orders from several of my other classes. He mentioned them to his classmates.

Too proud ever to again wear an insulting label like 'poor', Mark had asked the florist for all the 'tired' flowers in the shop. Then he phoned all the undertakers and explained that his class needed flowers for a teacher who was leaving. They agreed to give him bouquets saved after each funeral.

That was not the only tribute they paid me, though. Two years later, all 14 of them graduated, and 6 earned university scholarships.

* * *

Twenty-eight years later, I'm teaching in an academically strong school not too far from where I began my career. I learned that Mark married his university sweetheart and is a successful businessman. And, coincidentally, three years ago Mark's son was one of my top English students.

Sometimes I laugh when I recall the end of my first day as a teacher. To think I considered giving up to do something *rewarding!*

JANICE ANDERSON CONNOLLY

TASKS

35 Imagine that you are Mark in the story and write about your experiences in class from the moment that the new English teacher walked in.

36 How would you describe the English teacher's methods? Explain why you think they succeeded.

37 Think of someone you regard as a misfit. **Don't name them**. Write their story sympathetically from their point of view.

If you have ever flown in an aeroplane and been able to watch as you take off, the difference between town and country will have been clear to you. Leaving a busy town airport you climb steeply over houses and buildings; if you fly over a great city you may spot famous landmarks. Then there is traffic, busily passing along roads and motorways but once all this is passed, there are wide open spaces, a patchwork of fields, of forests, of rivers and lakes.

ENGLISH IN THE NATIONAL CURRICULUM:

Key Skills you will cover in this chapter

☑ You will be encouraged to take different views in discussion and in more formal debates and to construct persuasive arguments.

☑ There will be situations where you will need to be an effective listener so that, in formal debate, you can both ask pertinent questions and refute arguments with which you do not agree.

☑ You will be given opportunities to read a wide range of texts including significant pre-twentieth century literature.

☑ You will be asked to consider the language of the stimulus material which you are reading, including the main characteristics of literary language.

☑ You will be asked to organise your writing in a variety of different ways: such as in the form of play script, summary, argument and narrative.

When we read about 'town and country' the differences between them are made very clear.

et us start with a 'poet of nature'. Much of what William Wordsworth (1770–1850) wrote was in praise of nature. Here is part of a longer poem entitled *Lines composed, a few miles above Tintern Abbey, on revisiting the banks of the Wye during a tour, 13 July, 1798.*

Lines

••

Composed a few miles above Tintern Abbey, on revisiting the banks of the Wye during a tour. 13 July, 1798

(Composed 13 July, 1798. – Published 1798.)

Five years have past; five summers, with the length
Of five long winters! and again I hear
These waters, rolling from their mountain-springs
With a soft inland murmur. – Once again
Do I behold these steep and lofty cliffs,
That on a wild secluded scene impress
Thoughts of more deep seclusion; and connect
The landscape with the quiet of the sky.
The day is come when I again repose
Here, under this dark sycamore, and view
These plots of cottage-ground, these orchard-tufts,
Which at this season, with their unripe fruits,
Are clad in one green hue, and lose themselves
'Mid groves and copses. Once again I see
These hedge-rows, hardly hedge-rows, little lines
Of sportive wood run wild: these pastoral farms,
Green to the very door; and wreaths of smoke
Sent up, in silence, from among the trees!
With some uncertain notice, as might seem
Of vagrant dwellers in the houseless woods,
Or of some Hermit's cave, where by his fire
The Hermit sits alone.

These beauteous forms,
Through a long absence, have not been to me
As is a landscape to a blind man's eye:

But oft, in lonely rooms, and 'mid the din
Of towns and cities, I have owed to them,
In hours of weariness, sensations sweet,
Felt in the blood, and felt along the heart;
And passing even into my purer mind,
With tranquil restoration: – feelings too
Of unremembered pleasure: such, perhaps,
As have no slight or trivial influence
On that best portion of a good man's life,
His little, nameless, unremembered, acts
Of kindness and of love. Nor less, I trust,
To them I may have owed another gift,
Of aspect more sublime; that blessed mood,
In which the burthen of the mystery,
In which the heavy and the weary weight
Of all this unintelligible world,
Is lightened: – that serene and blessed mood
In which the affections gently lead us on, –
Until, the breath of this corporeal frame
And even the motion of our human blood
Almost suspended, we are laid asleep
In body, and become a living soul:
While with an eye made quiet by the power
Of harmony, and the deep power of joy,
We see into the life of things.

WILLIAM WORDSWORTH

TASKS

1 Discuss the picture of the river valley which Wordsworth creates in our minds. Is it pleasant and attractive?

2 Wordsworth tells us he has visited this spot before. What has happened in his thoughts during the time between his two visits? Explain how the language helps us to share the poet's feelings about this scene.

Wordsworth didn't write only about the countryside. Here is a sonnet he wrote in 1802, in which he describes the view from Westminster Bridge in London.

Sonnet

Composed upon Westminster Bridge, 3 September, 1802

(Composed 31 July, 1802. – Published 1807.)

Earth has not anything to show more fair:
Dull would he be of soul who could pass by
A sight so touching in its majesty:
This City now doth, like a garment, wear
The beauty of the morning; silent, bare,
Ships, towers, domes, theatres, and temples lie
Open unto the fields, and to the sky;
All bright and glittering in the smokeless air.
Never did sun more beautifully steep
In his first splendour, valley, rock, or hill;
Ne'er saw I, never felt, a calm so deep!
The river glideth at his own sweet will:
Dear God! the very houses seem asleep;
And all that mighty heart is lying still!

WILLIAM WORDSWORTH

TASKS

3 Discuss what made Wordsworth want to write about London.

4 How do the setting, the time of day, the weather all contribute to Wordsworth's view?

5 Do you share his opinion that 'Earth has not anything to show more fair'?

Your own writing

6 Describe a scene that you remember. Try to make the reader share your feelings.
Write in prose or poetry.

7 Write two short, contrasting descriptions, either of the same place at different times or of different places.

8 Everybody likes to reminisce about places they have been to. Write about a place you recall.
Try to use words effectively to create a vivid picture.

Charles Dickens often wrote about London. City life is important in many of his novels. The following extract is the opening of *Bleak House*.

Bleak House

LONDON. Michaelmas Term lately over, and the Lord Chancellor sitting in Lincoln's Inn Hall. Implacable November weather. As much mud in the streets as if the waters had but newly retired from the face of the earth, and it would not be wonderful to meet a Megalosaurus, 40 feet long or so, waddling like an elephantine lizard up Holborn Hill. Smoke lowering down from chimney-pots, making a soft black drizzle, with flakes of soot in it as big as full-grown snowflakes – gone into mourning, one might imagine, for the death of the sun. Dogs, undistinguishable in mire. Horses, scarcely better – splashed to their very blinkers. Foot passengers, jostling one another's umbrellas, in a general infection of ill-temper, and losing their foothold at street corners, where tens of thousands of other foot passengers have been slipping and sliding since the day broke (if this day ever broke), adding new deposits to the crust upon crust of mud, sticking at those points tenaciously to the pavement, and accumulating at compound interest.

Fog everywhere. Fog up the river, where it flows among green aits and meadows; fog down the river, where it rolls defiled among the tiers of shipping and the waterside pollutions of a great (and dirty) city. Fog on the Essex marshes, fog on the Kentish heights. Fog creeping into the cabooses of collier-brigs; fog lying out on the yards and hovering in the rigging of great ships; fog drooping on the gunwales of barges and small boats. Fog in the eyes and throats of ancient Greenwich pensioners, wheezing by the firesides of their wards; fog in the stem and bowl of the afternoon pipe of the wrathful skipper, down in his close cabin; fog cruelly pinching the toes and fingers of his shivering little 'prentice boy on deck. Chance people on the bridges peeping over the parapets into a nether sky of fog, with fog all round them, as if they were up in a balloon, and hanging in the misty clouds.

Gas looming through the fog in divers places in the streets, much as the sun may, from the spongy fields, be seen to loom by husbandman and ploughboy. Most of the shops lighted two hours before their time – as the gas seems to know, for it has a haggard and unwilling look.

The raw afternoon is rawest, and the dense fog is densest, and the muddy streets are muddiest, near that leaden-headed old obstruction, appropriate ornament for the threshold of a leaden-headed old corporation – Temple Bar. And hard by Temple Bar, in Lincoln's Inn Hall, at the very heart of the fog, sits the Lord High Chancellor in his High Court of Chancery.

Never can there come fog too thick, never can there come mud and mire too deep, to assort with the groping and floundering condition which this High Court of Chancery, most pestilent of hoary sinners, holds, this day, in the sight of heaven and earth.

On such an afternoon, if ever, the Lord High Chancellor ought to be sitting here – as here he is – with a foggy glory round his head, softly fenced in with crimson cloth and curtains, addressed by a large advocate with great whiskers, a little voice, and an interminable brief, and outwardly directing his contemplation to the lantern in the roof, where he can see nothing but fog. On such an afternoon, some score of members of the High Court of Chancery bar ought to be – as here they are – mistily engaged in one of the ten thousand stages of an endless cause, tripping one another up on slippery precedents, groping knee-deep in technicalities, running their goat-hair and horse-hair warded heads against walls of words, and making a pretence of equity with serious faces, as players might. On such an afternoon, the various solicitors in the cause, some two or three of whom have inherited it from their fathers, who made a fortune by it, ought to be – as are they not? – ranged in a line, in a long, matted well (but you might look in vain for Truth at the bottom of it), between the registrar's red table and the silk gowns, with bills, cross-bills, answers, rejoinders, injunctions, affidavits, issues, references to masters, masters' reports, mountains of costly nonsense, piled before them. Well may the court be dim, with wasting candles here and there; well may the fog hang heavy in it, as if it would never get out; well may the stained-glass windows lose their colour, and admit no light of day into the place; well may the uninitiated from the streets, who peep in through the glass panes in the door, be deterred from entrance by its owlish aspect, and by the drawl languidly echoing to the roof from the padded dais where the Lord High Chancellor looks into the lantern that has no light in it, and where the attendant wigs are all stuck in a fog bank! This is the Court of Chancery, which has its decaying houses and its blighted lands in every shire; which has its worn-out lunatic in every madhouse, and its dead in every churchyard; which has its ruined suitor, with his slipshod heels and threadbare dress, borrowing and begging through the round of every man's acquaintance; which gives to moneyed might the means abundantly of wearying out the right; which so exhausts finances, patience, courage, hope, so overthrows the brain and breaks the heart, that there is not an honourable man among its practitioners who would not give – who does not often give – the warning, 'Suffer any wrong that can be done you, rather than come here!'

CHARLES DICKENS

TASKS

9 Look closely at the first three paragraphs. What picture of London does Dickens create? Is it attractive? How successful is Dickens in creating his picture of London?

10 After the third paragraph Dickens introduces a new idea. Discuss what he is describing. Who are the people involved? What are they doing?

11 Explain how Dickens feels about the people he describes.

12 Considering the passage as a whole, what is the link between the fog and the Court of Chancery?

You will find this extract from 'Bleak House' reprinted in your homework book with a task for you to do arising from it.

TIME OUT TASK!

Some more thoughts about verbs

Verbs change according to time or 'tense'. Take the list of verbs below and write each one in its 'past', 'present' and 'future' forms.

- bring
- go
- have
- write
- eat

In addition to the above classification the tense may be continuous or finished ('perfect'). Revise your list to include continuous and 'perfect' forms.

END OF TIME OUT!

Sometimes writers invent marvellous places as the settings for their stories. One such person was JRR Tolkien who invented amazing town and country settings in his books *The Hobbit* and *The Lord of the Rings*.

Bag End was the home of a group of strange beings called 'hobbits' and was generally peaceful. The rolling countryside of Bag End is represented below.

The white stone city of Gondolin was the home of the Noldor Elves of Eldamar and the picture below shows it secure and peaceful, even when surrounded by dragons and armies.

TASKS

13 Take the two pictures and weave the two places into a story of your own. For your story to be effective you should:
- decide on your audience
- concentrate hard on the vocabulary you choose to use
- decide what 'people' are going to inhabit your world

14 Take one of the places illustrated and imagine that you live there. Write about a day in your life.

15 Invent a town of your own in a similar way to Tolkien and write your own story with it as the setting.

In *The Importance of being Earnest* Oscar Wilde uses the difference between 'town' and 'country' very effectively. 'Town' is London and 'country' a part of Shropshire.

In Act 1 (set in London) Algernon Moncrieff is talking to his friend 'Ernest' Worthing. (Although Algernon knows his friend as 'Ernest' his real name is 'Jack'.) The conversation is about a gentleman's cigarette case.

The Importance of being Earnest

Act 1

ALGERNON:
  Bring me that cigarette case Mr Worthing left in the smoking-room the last time he dined here.
JACK:
  Do you mean to say you have had my cigarette case all this time? I wish to goodness you had let me know. I have been writing frantic letters to Scotland Yard about it. I was very nearly offering a large reward.
ALGERNON:
  Well, I wish you would offer one. I happen to be more than usually hard up.
JACK:
  There is no good offering a large reward now that the thing is found.
Enter LANE *with the cigarette case on a salver.*
ALGERNON *takes it at once.* LANE *goes out.*
ALGERNON:
  I think that is rather mean of you, Ernest, I must say. (*Opens case and examines it.*) However, it makes no matter, for, now that I look at the inscription inside, I find that the thing isn't yours after all.
JACK:
  Of course it's mine. (*Moving to him.*) You have seen me with it a hundred times, and you have no right whatsoever to read what is written inside. It is a very ungentlemanly thing to read a private cigarette case.
ALGERNON:
  Oh! it is absurd to have a hard and fast rule about what one should read and what one shouldn't. More than half of modern culture depends on what one shouldn't read.
JACK:
  I am quite aware of the fact, and I don't propose to discuss modern culture. It isn't the sort of thing one should talk of in private. I simply want my cigarette case back.

ALGERNON:
  Yes; but this isn't your cigarette case. This cigarette case is a present from someone of the name of Cecily, and you said you didn't know any one of that name.
JACK:
  Well, if you want to know, Cecily happens to be my aunt.
ALGERNON:
  Your aunt!
JACK:
  Yes. Charming old lady she is, too. Lives at Tunbridge Wells. Just give it back to me, Algy.
ALGERNON (*retreating to back of sofa*):
  But why does she call herself little Cecily if she is your aunt and lives at Tunbridge Wells? (*Reading.*) 'From little Cecily with her fondest love.'
JACK (*moving to sofa and kneeling upon it*):
  My dear fellow, what on earth is there in that? Some aunts are tall, some aunts are not tall. That is a matter that surely an aunt may be allowed to decide for herself. You seem to think that every aunt should be exactly like your aunt! That is absurd! For Heaven's sake give me back my cigarette case. (*Follows* ALGERNON *round the room.*)
ALGERNON:
  Yes. But why does your aunt call you her uncle? 'From little Cecily, with her fondest love to her dear Uncle Jack.' There is no objection, I admit, to an aunt being a small aunt, but why an aunt, no matter what her size may be, should call her own nephew her uncle, I can't quite make out. Besides, your name isn't Jack at all; it is Ernest.
JACK:
  It isn't Ernest; it's Jack.
ALGERNON:
  You have always told me it was Ernest. I have introduced you to every one as Ernest. You answer to the name of Ernest. You look as if your name was Ernest. You are the most earnest-looking person I ever saw in my life. It is

perfectly absurd your saying that your name isn't Ernest. It's on your cards. Here is one of them. (*Taking it from case.*) 'Mr Ernest Worthing, B. 4, The Albany.' I'll keep this as a proof that your name is Ernest if ever you attempt to deny it to me, or to Gwendolen, or to anyone else. (*Puts the card in his pocket.*)

JACK:

Well, my name is Ernest in town and Jack in the country, and the cigarette case was given to me in the country.

ALGERNON:

Yes, but that does not account for the fact that your small Aunt Cecily, who lives at Tunbridge Wells, calls you her dear uncle. Come, old boy, you had much better have the thing out at once.

JACK:

My dear Algy, you talk exactly as if you were a dentist. It is very vulgar to talk like a dentist when one isn't a dentist. It produces a false impression.

ALGERNON:

Well, that is exactly what dentists always do. Now, go on! Tell me the whole thing. I may mention that I have always suspected you of being a confirmed and secret Bunburyist; and I am quite sure of it now.

JACK:

Bunburyist? What on earth do you mean by a Bunburyist?

ALGERNON:

I'll reveal to you the meaning of that incomparable expression as soon as you are kind enough to inform me why you are Ernest in town and Jack in the country.

JACK:

Well, produce my cigarette case first.

ALGERNON:

Here it is. (*Hands cigarette case.*) Now produce your explanation, and pray make it improbable. (*Sits on sofa.*)

JACK:

My dear fellow, there is nothing improbable about my explanation at all. In fact it's perfectly ordinary. Old Mr Thomas Cardew, who adopted me when I was a little boy, made me in his will guardian to his grand-daughter, Miss Cecily Cardew. Cecily, who addresses me as her uncle from motives of respect that you could not possibly appreciate, lives at my place in the country under the charge of her admirable governess, Miss Prism.

ALGERNON:

Where is that place in the country, by the way?

JACK:

That is nothing to you, dear boy. You are not going to be invited .... I may tell you candidly that the place is not in Shropshire.

ALGERNON:

I suspected that, my dear fellow! I have Bunburyed all over Shropshire on two separate occasions. Now, go on. Why are you Ernest in town and Jack in the country?

JACK:

My dear Algy, I don't know whether you will be able to understand my real motives. You are hardly serious enough. When one is placed in the position of guardian, one has to adopt a very high moral tone on all subjects. It's one's duty to do so. And as a high moral tone can hardly be said to conduce very much to either one's health or one's happiness, in order to get up to town I have always pretended to have a younger brother of the name of Ernest, who lives in the Albany, and gets into the most dreadful scrapes. That, my dear Algy, is the whole truth pure and simple.

ALGERNON:

The truth is rarely pure and never simple. Modern life would be very tedious if it were either, and modern literature a complete impossibility!

JACK:

That wouldn't be at all a bad thing.

ALGERNON:

Literary criticism is not your forte, my dear fellow. Don't try it. You should leave that to people who haven't been at a university. They do it so well in the daily papers. What you really are is a Bunburyist. I was quite right in saying you were a Bunburyist. You are one of the most advanced Bunburyists I know.

JACK:

What on earth do you mean?

ALGERNON:

You have invented a very useful younger brother called Ernest, in order that you may be able to come up to town as often as you like. I have invented an invaluable permanent invalid called Bunbury, in order that I may be able to go down into the country whenever I choose. Bunbury is perfectly invaluable. If it wasn't for Bunbury's extraordinary bad health, for instance, I wouldn't be able to dine with you at Willis's to-night, for I have been really engaged to Aunt Augusta for more than a week.

JACK:

I haven't asked you to dine with me anywhere tonight.

ALGERNON:

I know. You are absurdly careless about sending out invitations. It is very foolish of you. Nothing annoys people so much as not receiving invitations.

JACK:

You had much better dine with your Aunt Augusta.

ALGERNON:

I haven't the smallest intention of doing anything of the kind. To begin with, I dined there on Monday, and once a week is quite enough to dine with one's own relations. In the second place, whenever I do dine there I am always treated as a member of the family, and sent down with either no woman at all, or two. In the third place, I know perfectly well whom she will place me next to, tonight. She will place me next to Mary Farquhar, who always flirts with her own husband across the dinner-table. That is not very pleasant. Indeed, it is not even decent… and that sort of thing is enormously on the increase. The amount of women in London who flirt with their own husbands is perfectly scandalous. It looks so bad. It is simply washing one's clean linen in public. Besides, now that I know you to be a confirmed Bunburyist I naturally want to talk to you about Bunburying. I want to tell you the rules.

JACK:

I'm not a Bunburyist at all. If Gwendolen accepts me, I am going to kill my brother, indeed I think I'll kill him in any case. Cecily is a little too much interested in him. It is rather a bore. So I am going to get rid of Ernest. And I strongly advise you to do the same with Mr … with your invalid friend who has the absurd name.

ALGERNON:

Nothing will induce me to part with Bunbury, and if you ever get married, which seems to me extremely problematic, you will be very glad to know Bunbury. A man who marries without knowing Bunbury has a very tedious time of it.

OSCAR WILDE

TASK

16 Again your reading will be tested through a series of questions.

a Explain exactly what is going on here.

b Who is enjoying this conversation more, Jack or Algernon? Give reasons for your opinion.

c In what ways is going to the country useful to Jack and Algernon?

d What impression do you have of the lives these young men lead in London?

e 'Ernest in town, Jack in the country.' Would you like two identities? How would they be useful to you?

f Imagine Jack writes a letter to Cecily later the same day. Once you have studied the scene carefully, write the letter for him.

In *She Stoops to Conquer* (first performed in 1773) there is another clash of town and country. The play opens in a room in 'an old-fashioned house'.

She Stoops to Conquer: Or, The Mistakes of a Night

Act 1

Scene – A chamber in an old-fashioned house.

Enter MRS HARDCASTLE *and* MR HARDCASTLE.

MRS HARDCASTLE:

I vow, Mr Hardcastle, you're very particular. Is there a creature in the whole country, but ourselves, that does not take a trip to town now and then, to rub off the rust a little? There's the two Miss Hoggs, and our neighbour, Mrs Grigsby, go to take a month's polishing every winter.

HARDCASTLE:

Ay, and bring back vanity and affectation to last them the whole year. I wonder why London cannot keep its own fools at home. In my time, the follies of the town crept slowly among us, but now they travel faster than a stage-coach. Its fopperies come down, not only as inside passengers, but in the very basket.

MRS HARDCASTLE:

Ay, *your* times were fine times, indeed; you have been telling us of *them* for many a long year. Here we live in an old rumbling mansion, that looks for all the world like an inn, but that we never see company. Our best visitors are old Mrs Oddfish, the curate's wife, and little Cripplegate, the lame dancing-master. And all our entertainment your old stories of Prince Eugene and the Duke of Marlborough. I hate such old-fashioned trumpery.

HARDCASTLE:

And I love it. I love everything that's old: old friends, old times, old manners, old books, old wine, and, I believe, Dorothy (*taking her hand*), you'll own I have been pretty fond of an old wife.

MRS HARDCASTLE:

Lord, Mr Hardcastle, you're for ever at your Dorothys and your old wifes. You may be a Darby, but I'll be no Joan, I promise you. I'm not so old as you'd make me, by more than one good year. Add twenty to twenty, and make money of that.

HARDCASTLE:

Let me see; twenty added to twenty, makes just fifty and seven!

MRS HARDCASTLE:

It's false, Mr Hardcastle: I was but twenty when I was brought to bed of Tony, that I had by Mr Lumpkin, my first husband; and he's not come to years of discretion yet.

HARDCASTLE:

Nor ever will, I dare answer for him. Ay, you have taught *him* finely!

MRS HARDCASTLE:

No matter, Tony Lumpkin has a good fortune. My son is not to live by his learning. I don't think a boy wants much learning to spend fifteen hundred a year.

HARDCASTLE:

Learning, quotha! A mere composition of tricks and mischief!

MRS HARDCASTLE:

Humour, my dear: nothing but humour. Come, Mr Hardcastle, you must allow the boy a little humour.

HARDCASTLE:

I'd sooner allow him a horse-pond! If burning the footmen's shoes, frightening the maids, and worrying the kittens, be humour, he has it. It was but yesterday he fastened my wig to the back of my chair, and when I went to make a bow, I popped my bald head in Mrs Frizzle's face!

MRS HARDCASTLE:

And am I to blame? The poor boy was always too sickly to do any good. A school would be his death. When he comes to be a little stronger, who knows what a year or two's Latin may do for him?

HARDCASTLE:

Latin for him! A cat and fiddle! No, no, the alehouse and the stable are the only schools he'll ever go to!

MRS HARDCASTLE:

Well, we must not snub the poor boy now, for I believe we shan't have him long among us. Anybody that looks in his face may see he's consumptive.

HARDCASTLE:

Ay, if growing too fat be one of the symptoms.

MRS HARDCASTLE:

He coughs sometimes.

HARDCASTLE:

Yes, when his liquor goes the wrong way.

MRS HARDCASTLE:

I'm actually afraid of his lungs.

HARDCASTLE:

And truly, so am I; for he sometimes whoops like a speaking-trumpet – (TONY *hallooing behind the scenes.*) – O, there he goes. – A very consumptive figure, truly!

Enter TONY, *crossing the stage.*

MRS HARDCASTLE:

Tony, where are you going, my charmer? Won't you give papa and I a little of your company, lovey?

TONY:

I'm in haste, mother, I cannot stay.

MRS HARDCASTLE:

You shan't venture out this raw evening, my dear. You look most shockingly.

TONY:

I can't stay, I tell you. The Three Pigeons expects me down every moment. There's some fun going forward.

HARDCASTLE:

Ay; the alehouse, the old place: I thought so.

MRS HARDCASTLE:

A low, paltry set of fellows.

TONY:

Not so low, neither. There's Dick Muggins the exciseman, Jack Slang the horse doctor, Little Aminadab that grinds the music-box, and Tom Twist that spins the pewter platter.

MRS HARDCASTLE:

Pray, my dear, disappoint them for one night, at least.

TONY:

As for disappointing *them*, I should not much mind; but I can't abide to disappoint *myself*!

MRS HARDCASTLE (*Detaining him*):

You shan't go.

TONY:

I will, I tell you.

MRS HARDCASTLE:

I say you shan't.

TONY:

We'll see which is strongest, you or I.

Exit hauling her out.

HARDCASTLE *solus.*

HARDCASTLE:

Ay, there goes a pair that only spoil each other. But is not the whole age in a combination to drive sense and discretion out of doors? There's my pretty darling Kate; the fashions of the times have almost infected her too. By living a year or two in town, she is fond of gauze, and French frippery, as the best of them.

Enter MISS HARDCASTLE.

HARDCASTLE:

Blessings on my pretty innocence! Dressed out as usual, my Kate! Goodness! What a quantity of superfluous silk has thou got about thee, girl! I could never teach the fools of this age that the indigent world could be clothed out of the trimmings of the vain.

MISS HARDCASTLE:

You know our agreement, sir. You allow me the morning to receive and pay visits, and to dress in my own manner; and in the evening, I put on my housewife's dress, to please you.

HARDCASTLE:

Well, remember, I insist on the terms of our agreement; and, by-the-bye, I believe I shall have occasion to try your obedience this very evening.

MISS HARDCASTLE:

I protest, sir, I don't comprehend your meaning.

HARDCASTLE:

Then to be plain with you, Kate, I expect the young gentleman I have chosen to be your husband from town this very day. I have his father's letter, in which he informs me his son is set out, and that he intends to follow himself shortly after.

MISS HARDCASTLE:

Indeed! I wish I had known something of this before. Bless me, how shall I behave? It's a thousand to one I shan't like him; our meeting will be so formal, and so like a thing of business, that I shall find no room for friendship or esteem.

OLIVER GOLDSMITH

TASKS

17 Answer this series of questions.

   a Discuss why Mrs Hardcastle wants to go to London and why Mr Hardcastle doesn't.

   b What do we learn about Tony Lumpkin's way of life?

   c What does Kate Hardcastle like doing with her time?

   d How might a modern version of this scene be portrayed? Set your own modern-day version in the country.

18 **Your own writing**

Write a comparsion between the two scenes you have just studied. You might like to consider:

- ▨ the behaviour of the characters;
- ▨ their opinions and attitudes;
- ▨ the use of humour.

Enjoying the countryside

Many people who live in towns enjoy visiting the countryside for weekends or longer holidays.

TASK

19 In groups or as a class discuss:

- ▨ what attracts people to the countryside
- ▨ what problems this might lead to
- ▨ how those living in the countryside might feel about this

Here is part of a leaflet produced by The National Trust about the Lake District.

Land under National Trust protection within The National Park

Protecting traditional buildings

Of course with so many working hill farms along with the 250 Lake District cottages owned by the Trust there is an awful lot of building work to be done.

Rebuilding, renovation and repair of these important properties has to be carried our regularly with the added complication of maintaining traditional appearances. This means specially skilled professionals to do the work and expensive traditional materials to complete the appearance.

Lime mortar is used as a weather coating to walls as opposed to unsuitable sand and cement render. The dressing of slate, the use of wooden pegs in

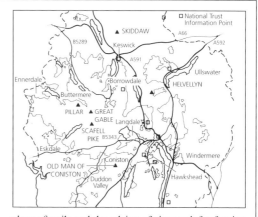

place of nails and the adzing of riven oak for fencing or rafters are all more costly and time consuming methods, but are longer lasting and necessary in retaining the character of Lakeland property.

Fells, valleys & lakes

The National Trust now protects and cares for over a quarter of the Lake District National Park. In all 12 valleys the Trust protects large areas and there is access for everyone along both public and National Trust footpaths.

Borrowdale – 15,000 acres including 9 farms, half of Derwent-water including the main islands, the hamlets of Watendlath and Seathwaite, woodlands and popular sites such as the Bowder Stone, Friars's Crag and Ashness Bridge.

Buttermere – the lakes of Buttermere, Crummock and Loweswater, farms in Buttermere village and land around the lakes themselves.

Coniston – 4 miles of lakeshore, 865 acres of woodland, 8 farms, 50 cottages, campsites and even the gracious Steam Yacht Gondola.

Duddon – 8 working farms covering nearly 6,000 acres, including Cockley Beck, the Trust's first fell farm, given in 1929.

Ennerdale – in this remote valley the Trust protects 7,700 acres, including the 5,000 acres of the wild and solitary Kinniside Common.

Eskdale – the 3,300 acres of Brotherilkeld Farm bought to prevent afforestation of the valley head, and another 5 working farms in upper Eskdale and the 7,900 acres of Eskdale Common.

Grasmere – the bed of the lake itself, 3 fell farms with a total of 800 acres of enclosed land plus several thousand acres of fell common and half of Rydal Water.

Hawkshead – extensive woodland along the west side of Windermere with public access to the shore and 5 farms. The Beatrix Potter Gallery, Hill Top and Hawkshead Courthouse are important buildings protected by the Trust.

Langdale – a favourite valley for visitors; the Trust has 9 farms, 22 cottages, a major campsite, the Old Dungeon Ghyll Hotel and a Youth Hostel.

Ullswater – Gowbarrow Park was acquired in 1906. Trust ownership now extends to 12,500 acres including 6 farms and Brotherswater.

Wastwater – the Trust protects virtually all the valley, 16,000 acres with 5 farms, the lake itself and the magnificent mountains that overlook it on all sides. Also, the Nether Wasdale estate comprising 1,000 acres with 7 farms and 420 acres of important woodland.

Windermere (Crosthwaite), Troutbeck and Ambleside – shore fields on Windermere, Townend in Troutbeck, and in total 12 farms, 12 cottages and 320 acres of woodland.

Lakeshores

Lakeshores always appear so unchanging but they too need constant care. Wave action can often undercut vegetation making bank reinforcements necessary, but of course these must be visually unobtrusive; in other places alders may be planted to help stabilise a shoreline.

At Yew Tree Tarn a geological fault led to the periodic draining of the Tarn. Thanks to the contributions of the Lake District Appeal a team of workers has rebuilt the dam to solve the problem and re-landscaped the area to preserve its beauty for generations to come.

Footpaths

One of the great pleasures of the Lake District, shared by local people and visitors alike, is to escape the pressures of life by walking the fells. In many places, however, paths have been turned into rivers of scree up to 100 feet (30 metres) wide in places, by the constant pounding of thousands of feet combined with the ravages of Lakeland weather. The Lake District Appeal has enabled the National Trust to take on people to form 4 footpath repair gangs in Borrowdale, Langdale, Grasmere and Wasdale. These dedicated individuals have fought doggedly against time and the elements over recent years to restore over 50 miles (80 kilometres) of the most eroded footpaths by the ancient method known as 'pitching'. This is slow, labour-intensive work, using only local materials – often averaging a mere 18 yards (15 metres) a day – but with continued maintenance this work will ensure that these paths last for hundreds of years to come.

TASKS

20 Continue your discussion.
- What sounds attractive as you read this?
- What is the National Trust trying to do?
- What problems is it facing?

21 Using the information given, write a 200-word appeal on behalf of The National Trust to appear in a local newspaper in your own area.

22 Design an A5 size leaflet to accompany your appeal.

The Lake District is now one of the National Parks in the United Kingdom. The aims of the park are set out below.

The National Park aims

British National Parks wrestle with three competing aims:

a To maintain the natural beauty;
b To promote enjoyment;
c To have concern for the social and economic welfare of the National Park.

Keeping a balance between the three aims is always difficult: it is the essential dilemma of British National Parks. There must be a balance between, on the one hand, people's freedom to enjoy the National Park and to live in it and, on the other hand, reasonable controls to ensure that the Park's essential qualities are not harmed and life is not made intolerable for its inhabitants. Yet another balance has to be between the tourism industry, which provides jobs and which has to modernise and advertise to survive, and the effect of tourism on the natural environment, which is the base on which tourism survives.

Many problems arise from access to the National Park. Here are just two aspects:

- ■ Footpath erosion
- ■ Traffic

Main factors affecting erosion of footpaths in the Lake District

1 Recreational pressure
Many independent surveys have been conducted to assess the intensity of footpath use. Although methods of measurement are crude, they have usually shown that the state of a certain path is related to intensity of use.

2 Slope angle
Research has indicated (Coleman 1981, and others) that paths on slopes with angles greater than 18° to the horizontal are more likely to suffer erosion, with gravity playing a greater part in transporting detached soil and rock particles down the slope.

3 Volume of water run-off
Heavy rain can have a strong erosive power, particularly on steeper slopes.

4 Soil type
Factors such as particle size, stoniness and resistance to shearing forces have been shown to be of greatest importance.

5 Vegetation type
There are marked variations in the resistance of plants to trampling. Grasses such as Mat grass (*Nardus stricta*), Bents (*Agrostis* spp) and Fescues (*Festuca* spp) are relatively resistant to trampling. In contrast, bracken and most heath species are susceptible, and cannot survive when trampled.

Regrowth of vegetation is limited owing to climatic and soil conditions.

6 Frost heave

During freezing conditions, water which is trapped between exposed soil particles expands, causing the soil surface to be pushed upwards. The ice so formed is often called 'needle ice' because of its appearance. On thawing, the soil is loosened and is easily eroded by the action of walkers, water or wind. On gulley sides this process leads to undercutting and the eventual collapse of overhanging soil and vegetation.

7 Exposure of the site to wind

Soil particles which have been disturbed and loosened by the various means mentioned above are more readily blown or washed away from exposed sites.

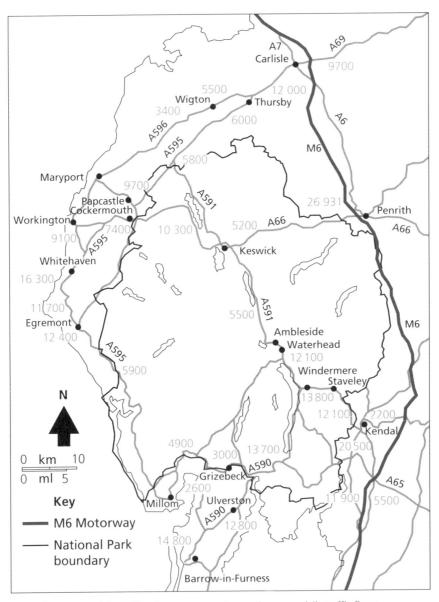

Traffic flows in Cumbria 1987 – figures represent annual average daily traffic flows.

	16 hrs (6 am–10 pm)	24 hrs
Jan	6,942	7,229
Feb	8,332	8,694
March	8,603	8,967
April	13,023	13,518
May	12,542	13,056
June	12,216	12,728
July	15,749	16,388
Aug	17,189	17,827
Sept	15,033	15,540
Oct	12,852	13,329
Nov	8,910	9,304
Dec	7,750	8,122

Average daily north and southbound traffic flows at Waterhead, Ambleside (A591) 1987

	February	August
1974	5,000	16,000
1975	5,650	16,611
1976	5,544	16,053
1977	6,375	16,045
1978	5,581	16,190
1979	5,684	15,424
1980	6,028	14,306
1981	6,387	14,217
1982	6,479	14,186
1983	6,559	16,271
1984	7,113	16,432
1985	n/a	16,413
1986	8,218	17,421
1987	8,694	17,827

Average daily north and southbound traffic flows at Waterhead (A591) Feb–Aug 1974–87 (24 hours)

TASK

Look at the information given.

23 Write a guide to visitors who come to walk the fells, informing them of the problems.
Tell them what they need to know so that they can help to preserve the countryside as well as enjoying themselves.

You will find the extract from The National Trust leaflet reprinted in your homework book with another task for you to do arising from it.

Shakespeare's plays tend to move between the sophistication of town society and the simplicity of country life. We can nearly always find characters who belong to both worlds.

In many of his plays Shakespeare writes about the exercise of power by both wise and unjust rulers. He writes too of wars and battles between different countries. These ideas are to be found in *Hamlet*. The play is set in Denmark. There is a new king, Claudius, who has succeeded his brother who died suddenly. The new king has married his dead brother's wife. As the play starts the mourning is over, there is celebration in the air. But not for young Hamlet. The events have left him shocked and disillusioned.

Hamlet

Act 3 Scene 1

HAMLET:
To be, or not to be, that is the question,
Whether 'tis nobler in the mind to suffer
The slings and arrows of outrageous fortune,
Or to take arms against a sea of troubles,
And by opposing, end them. To die, to sleep –
No more, and by a sleep to say we end
The heart-ache, and the thousand natural shocks
That flesh is heir to; 'tis a consummation
Devoutly to be wished to die to sleep!
To sleep, perchance to dream, ay there's the rub,
For in that sleep of death what dreams may come
When we have shuffled off this mortal coil,
Must give us pause – there's the respect
That makes calamity of so long life:
For who would bear the whips and scorns of time,
Th'oppressor's wrong, the proud man's contumely,
The pangs of disprized love, the law's delay,
The insolence of office, and the spurns
That patient merit of th'unworthy takes,
When he himself might his quietus make
With a bare bodkin; who would fardels bear,
To grunt and sweat under a weary life,
But that the dread of something after death,
The undiscovered country, from whose bourn
No traveller returns, puzzles the will,
And makes us rather bear those ills we have,
Than fly to others that we know not of?
Thus conscience does make cowards of us all,
And thus the native hue of resolution
Is sicklied o'er with the pale cast of thought,
And enterprises of great pitch and moment
With this regard their currents turn awry,
And lose the name of action....

WILLIAM SHAKESPEARE

TASKS

24 Discuss with others the way Hamlet's thoughts develop here. Make a list of the main points and compare them with the lists of other groups.

25 Using your first discussion, work out the reasons Hamlet can give for and against suicide.

26 'Counselling' is a word used a lot these days. 'Counsellors' have to be good listeners as well as people who can make sensible suggestions. Write a script in which a counsellor talks to Hamlet.

One of the things the imagined 'counsellor' might tell Hamlet is to 'get away from it all'. A quiet and peaceful time in the country might be just what he needs. In an article in *The Independent* (October 1995) Ken Warpole argued for a new approach to town and country.

Here is an extract from the article.

We must end this war of town v country

The complexity of the increasing overlap between town and country patterns and lifestyles is, daunting, and in urgent need of new thinking and greater public debate. A sustainable future depends on it. We have to start by asking whether the British actually like cities or, even after 200 years of intense urbanisation, have yet come to terms with urban life. There are still major contradictions in attitudes and aspirations, for while more than 80 per cent of British people live in cities, more than two-thirds would choose to live in a small town or country village if they could, according to recent research.

Some manage to escape. In 11 cities or urban boroughs – Bristol, Bromley, Cardiff, Greenwich, Hounslow, Leicester, Merton, Middlesbrough, Sheffield, Southwark and Sutton – studied recently for the Comedia/Demos *Park Life* report on urban parks and open spaces, all suffered depopulation between 1981 and 1991. In just one decade, Bristol dropped from 438,038 to 370,300 and Southwark from 313,413 to 196,500, although both now claim to have halted the exodus.

The flight from the cities in post-war Britain had been uneven but pronounced, and would be more noticeable but for the numbers of ethnic minority immigrants who replaced those who left. Britain's black and Asian communities overwhelmingly live in cities (and within them in quite specific concentrations or districts), and are likely to be the last groups to venture into the rural hinterland – even for a day, let alone to live. It is still the case that the countryside remains 'white'. Racism is, of course, one of the unspoken factors that informs some people's decisions to seek the rural idyll.

However, the usual reasons are the softer 'quality of life' issues rather than housing or job prospects. People fear street crime, they worry about pollution and the health of their children, and

view with increasing dismay the ageing infrastructure of services around them – pre-war schools, 19th-century hospitals, Carnegie libraries, Victorian parks fraying at the edges, privatised buses churning out diesel smoke, boarded up department stores and shuttered high streets.

What they want are out-of-town shopping malls easily accessible by car, multi-facility 'leisure boxes' built on green-field sites, country parks with car parks and interpretation centres, and modern schools to which their children can walk in safety.

The *Park Life* study showed that city dwellers with cars preferred to visit a country park or out-of-town garden centre at the weekend than to walk to their local park; and the Council for the Protection of Rural England's report *Leisure Landscapes*, published last year, detailed the scale of the urban invasion into the countryside as a place for sport and recreation, noting that 45 per cent of all car journeys are now made for leisure purposes.

The CPRE report showed

how great the pressures on the countryside are in terms of active sports and recreation, as leisure and tourism-based jobs replace agricultural jobs and leisure woodlands and golf courses take up set-aside arable land. In 1950 there were 700,000 agricultural workers; today there are 200,000. Only 6 per cent of rural workers are now employed in agriculture. The very notion of a working landscape, or rural life as a productive agricultural life, is now under siege as the Common Agricultural Policy and discretionary leisure spending combine to turn the countryside into a playground, heritage trail or site for new kinds of expensive housing estates, confirming that urban and rural problems are becoming increasingly interlocked.

As was obvious at last month's National Trust centenary conference (a watershed of public heart-searching and self-criticism), an increasing part of the Trust's work in managing its rural sites and properties is in reducing rather than increasing visitors.

As a body the National Trust is quietly powerful, not just in terms of its 2 million membership but also in its extensive ownership of land and organisational strength. It could park a lot of metaphorical tanks on other people's lawns, if it so wished, including the government's.

It was obvious at the Manchester conference that the National Trust now has its eye on the urban heritage and a keen interest in urban issues, organising workshops in association with the Black Environmental Network and on a number of other city initiatives.

It is significant that the Countryside Commission, too, is beginning to make inroads into urban planning policy. Its offshoot, the Groundwork Trust,

now largely works in urban areas on derelict land reclamation, and the commission has recently published a report on *Urban Trees*. Even more provocative, perhaps, was the recent launch by the CPRE of its 'Urban Footprints' campaign, in favour of increased urban consolidation under the slogan: 'The future of our countryside depends on our towns and cities treading more lightly on the environment.'

The sub-text of this campaign could be thought to suggest, be it ever so gently, that city-dwellers should stay where they belong. Suddenly in Britain it seems that we are getting to a ridiculous situation where urban policy is being developed, by default, by rural pressure groups, some of which are keen to ensure that the urban masses stay put in their city enclaves.

Cynics might also detect a degree of opportunism in the way in which rural and landed interests are wrapping themselves in the green flag and claiming environmental reasons for keeping the countryside free of outside intruders. However, there is little that can prevent the urban rich from buying into rural life, rather than simply visiting it. The modern village or market town, certainly in the South-east, is becoming a dormitory settlement, as people work in the city but go home at night to their version of the rural idyll.

It was ever thus according to the historian Martin Weiner, whose book *English Culture and the Decline of the Industrial Spirit* noted how frequently the industrial masters moved to join the rural aristocracy once they had made their pile.

But the urge to leave Albert Square or Coronation Street to live in Ambridge still seems a pervasive ingredient of the

English dream.

The only people who claim to love cities are the families and children of immigrants who have settled here. When I recently interviewed the Guyana-born novelist Mike Phillips for a Radio 4 programme, he was effusive about the magnetism of the city: 'You must understand,' he told me, 'we never had the myth of a rural paradise. We embraced the city because it meant progress – material progress, intellectual progress and educational progress.'

The positive contribution that ethnic minority communities have made to British urban life remains largely unacknowledged.

The problem is, as Raymond Williams put it in *The Country and the City*, that if the countryside represents the past and the city the future, where does this leave the present? The challenge which Jonathon Porritt threw out at the National Trust conference was precisely on this issue: that the countryside has to be developed to suit modern needs. He raised the spectre of wind farms, currently a powerful symbol of rural opposition to modern life – almost wholly on aesthetic grounds. Porritt is in favour of wind farms and went on to unnerve some of the audience by arguing that in the move to develop environmentally sustainable ways of life, 'landscape is not high on the list of factors which should be taken into account'.

This was always Williams' argument – landscape was the enemy of a working rural economy – and that aesthetic arguments about rural landscapes were invariably invoked to prevent any new thinking about new ways of working and living.

But new ways of working and living are precisely what Britain needs, as more and more demographic and social pressures and conflicts come to a head both in urban and rural areas. As the boundaries are breached between men's work and women's roles, between education and livelihood, between work and home, it is time to reconfigure the relations between town and country. We need planning and social policies which can provide both liveable cities and a productive, working countryside – and all the settlements and ways of life that might emerge in the spaces in between.

TASKS

27 Use this article to prepare a talk under the title 'The way things are changing'.

Contrast what your audience probably thinks is true with what is revealed here.

28 People often have views about others based on 'stereotyping'.

a What is the typical stereotype of a country dweller?

b What do phrases such as 'man about town', 'businessman', 'financial and business world', 'city centre', 'inter-city' suggest?

TIME OUT TASK!

A language test – testing vocabulary

(the technical name for this type of test is a 'cloze test')

What you will find printed below is a passage from a short story which has a number of words missed out. The gaps are numbered 1 to 43. What you have to do is fill the gaps in logically and sensibly with the most suitable words. You will find clues in the passage which will steer you towards the correct answers.

The Kite

It had become a passion with Herbert, and as he grew older and bigger his mother bought him larger and larger kites. He grew very clever at gauging the winds and could do things with his kite you wouldn't have thought possible. There were other kite flyers on the common, not ___(1)___ children, but men, and since nothing ___(2)___ people together so naturally as ___(3)___ hobby they share it was not ___(4)___ before Mrs Sunbury, not withstanding her exclusiveness, ___(5)___ that she, her Samuel and her ___(6)___ were on speaking terms with all ___(7)___ sundry. They would compare their respective ___(8)___ and boast of their accomplishments. Sometimes ___(9)___, a big boy of sixteen now, ___(10)___ challenge another kite-flyer. Then he ___(11)___ manoeuvre his kite to windward of ___(12)___ other fellow's, allow his cord to ___(13)___ against his, and by a sudden ___(14)___ bring the enemy kite down. But ___(15)___ before this Mr Sunbury had succumbed ___(16)___ his son's enthusiasm and he would ___(17)___ ask to have a go himself. ___(18)___ must have been a funny sight ___(19)___ see him running down the hill ___(20)___ his striped trousers, black coat and ___(21)___ hat. Mrs Sunbury would trot sedately ___(22)___ him and when the kite was ___(23)___ free would take the cord from ___(24)___ and watch it as it soared. ___(25)___ afternoon became the great day of ___(26)___ week for them, and when Mr ___(27)___ and Herbert left the house ___(28)___ the morning to catch their train ___(29)___ the city the first thing they ___(30)___ was to look up at the ___(31)___ to see if it was flying ___(32)___ . They liked best of all a ___(33)___ day, with uncertain winds, for that ___(34)___ them the chance to exercise ___(35)___ skill. All through the week, in ___(36)___ evenings, they talked about it. They ___(37)___ contemptuous of smaller kites than theirs ___(38)___ envious of bigger ones. They discussed ___(39)___ performances of other flyers as hotly, and ___(40)___ scornfully, as boxers or footballers discuss ___(41)___ rivals. Their ambition was to ___(42)___ a bigger kite than anyone else ___(43)___ a kite that would go higher.

W SOMERSET MAUGHAM.

END OF TIME OUT!

R ead two extracts from two novels, one written in 1860 and the other in 1995. In *The Mill on the Floss* Mr Tulliver is talking to his wife about their son, Tom.

The Mill on the Floss

'What I want, you know,' said Mr Tulliver – 'what I want is to give Tom a good eddication; and eddication as'll be a bread to him. That was what I was thinking of when I gave notice for him to leave th' academy at Ladyday. I mean to put him to a downright good school at Midsummer. The two years at th' academy 'ud ha' done well enough, if I'd meant to make a miller and farmer of him; for he's had a fine sight more schoolin' nor I ever got: all the learnin' *my* father ever paid for was a bit o'birch at one end and the alphabet at th' other. But I should like Tom to be a bit of a scholard, so as he might be up to the tricks o' these fellows as talk fine and write with a flourish. It 'ud be a help to me wi' these law-suits, and arbitrations, and things. I wouldn't make a downright lawyer o' the lad – I should be sorry for him to be a raskill – but a sort o' engineer, or a surveyor, or an auctioneer and vallyer, like Riley, or one o' them smartish businesses as are all profits and no outlay, only for a big watch-chain and a high stool. They're pretty nigh all one, and they're not far off being even wi' the law, *I* believe; for Riley looks Lawyer Wakem i' the face as hard as one cat looks another. *He's* none frightened at him.'

Mr Tulliver was speaking to his wife, a blond comely woman, in a fan-shaped cap (I am afraid to think how long it is since fan-shaped caps were worn – they must be so near coming in again. At that time, when Mrs Tulliver was nearly forty, they were new at St. Ogg's, and considered sweet things).

'Well, Mr. Tulliver, you know best; *I've* no objections. But hadn't I better kill a couple o' fowl and have th' aunts and uncles to dinner next week, so as you may hear what sister Glegg and sister Pullet have got to say about it? There's a couple o' fowl *wants* killing!'

'You may kill every fowl i' the yard, if you like, Bessy; but I shall ask neither aunt nor uncle what I'm to do wi' my own lad,' said Mr Tulliver, defiantly.

'Dear heart!' said Mrs Tulliver, shocked at this sanguinary rhetoric, 'how can you talk so, Mr Tulliver? But it's your way to speak disrespectful o' my family; and sister Glegg throws all the blame upo' me, though I'm sure I'm as innocent as the babe unborn. For nobody's ever heard *me* say as it wasn't lucky for my children to have aunts and uncles as can live independent. Howiver, if Tom's to go to a new school, I should like him to go where I can wash him and mend him; else he might as well have calico as linen, for they'd be one as yellow as th'other before they'd been washed half-a-dozen times. And then when the box is goin' backards and forrards, I could send the lad a cake, or a pork-pie, or an apple; for he can do with any extry bit, bless him, whether they stint him at his meals or no. My children can eat as much victuals as most, thank God.'

'Well, well, we won't send him out o' reach o' the carrier's cart, if other things fit in,' said Mr Tulliver. 'But you mustn't put a spoke i' the wheel about the washin', if we can't get a school near enough. That's the fault I have to find wi' you, Bessy: if you see a stick in the road, you're allays thinkin' you can't step over it. You'd want me not to hire a good waggoner, 'cause he'd got a mole on his face.'

'Dear heart!' said Mrs Tulliver, in mild surprise, 'when did I iver make objections to a man because he'd got a mole on his face? I'm sure I'm rether fond o' the moles; for my brother, as is dead an' gone, had a mole on his brow. But I can't remember your iver offering to hire a waggoner with a mole, Mr Tulliver. There was John Gibbs hadn't a mole on his face no more nor you have, an' I was all for having you hire *him*; an' so you did hire him, an' if he hadn't died o' the inflammation, as we paid Dr Turnbull for attending him, he'd very like ha' been driving the waggon now. He might have a mole somewhere out o' sight, but how was I to know that, Mr Tulliver?'

'No, no, Bessy; I didn't mean justly the mole; I meant it to stand for summat else; but niver mind – it's puzzling work, talking is. What I'm thinking on, is how to find the right sort o' school to send Tom to, for I might be ta'en in again, as I've been wi' the academy. I'll have nothing to do wi' a 'cademy again; whativer school I send Tom to, it shan't be a 'cademy; it shall be a place where the lads spend their time i' summat else besides blacking the family's shoes, and getting up the potatoes. It's an uncommon puzzling thing to know what school to pick.'

Mr Tulliver paused a minute or two, and dived with both hands into his breeches pockets as if he hoped to find some suggestion there. Apparently he was not disappointed, for he presently said, 'I know what I'll do – I'll talk it over wi' Riley: he's coming to-morrow, t'arbitrate about the dam.'

'Well, Mr Tulliver, I've put the sheets out for the best bed, and Kezia's got 'em hanging at the fire. They aren't the best sheets, but they're good enough for anybody to sleep in, be he who he will; for as for them best Holland sheets, I should repent buying 'em, only they'll do to lay us out in. An' if you was to die to-morrow, Mr Tulliver, they're mangled beautiful, an'all ready, an' smell o' lavender as it 'ud be a pleasure to lay 'em out; an' they lie at the left-hand corner o' the big oak linen-chest, at the back; not as I should trust anybody to look 'em out but myself.'

As Mrs Tulliver uttered the last sentence, she drew a bright bunch of keys from her pocket, and singled out one, rubbing her thumb and finger up and down it with a placid smile while she looked at the clear fire. If Mr Tulliver had been a susceptible man in his conjugal relation, he might have supposed that she drew out the key to aid her imagination in anticipating the moment when he would be in a state to justify the production of the best Holland sheets. happily he was not so; he was only susceptible in respect of his right to water-power; moreover, he had the marital habit of not listening very closely, and, since his mention of Mr Riley, had been apparently occupied in a tactile examination of his woollen stockings.

'I think I've hit it, Bessy,' was his first remark after a short silence. 'Riley's as likely a man as any to know o' some school; he's had schooling himself, an' goes about to all sorts o' places – arbitratin' and vallyin' and that. And we shall have time to talk it over tomorrow night when the business is done. I want Tom to be such a sort o' man as Riley, you know – as can talk pretty nigh as well as if it was all wrote out for him, and knows a good lot o' words as don't mean much, so as you can't lay hold of 'em i' law; and a good solid knowledge o' business too.'

GEORGE ELIOT

The second extract, printed overleaf, is from the novel *Touch and Go*, by Elizabeth Berridge. Emma Rowlands has recently moved into a house in Wales, situated in a village where she lived as a child. She has given up her flat in London. In this extract she has accepted an invitation to a rat hunt: Ivor has issued the invitation.

Touch and Go

'Right then, let's get started. Where's Harry?'

There was now a restless mass of dogs in front of the barn. A brown-and-white surge of Jack Russells with a scattering of sharp lean terriers. Whimpering and barking in anticipation, they strained at their leashes, tails going, paws scrabbling with excitement.

Ivor had told her that a pack of twenty could kill as many as a hundred rats on a good day.

It was a big storage barn with a tiled roof and openings on either side, room for haycarts to be driven in back in the old days. Three hundred years old, at a guess. Nowadays it was used for grain storage, in bins.

Emma shivered at the thought of the carnage to come, wandered inside, leaned against the wall and looked around her. It had a gloom and quietness that cut off the confused din from outside. A sturdy geometric symmetry of huge oak beams supported the length and breadth of the walls and the soaring inverted Vs that braced the shadowy roof. Daylight shafted in through cubes and rectangles left by a few shattered tiles. Long rods of dusty light pierced that upper darkness and diffused into daylight halfway down.

Harry passed her, an executioner's figure in his red rubber gloves and black knitted cap pulled well down over his ears. his black sweater had one scarlet word knitted into it. HOSANNA. He carried a chainsaw without the blade; instead a pipe had been fixed.

'This'll smoke 'em out, see?' he flung over his shoulder as he made for the further wall.

A group of youths ran in and started beating the huge grain containers with staves. It seemed as if a heavy-metal band filled the barn. Emma slipped out before she was ordered to do so. She was nearly tripped up by the dogs, now released. And all hell broke out. Rats were suddenly everywhere, swarming over the tops of the containers, running across the floor, leaping up at the walls, dashing for exit holes.

The dogs were on them, urged by the shouts; they pounced, shook, left the dead and went on joyfully to despatch the living. The floor heaved with a black, white, brown tide, splashed with red. A shout from above as Glyn, astride a beam, flailing an iron bar, beat down rats on to the men and dogs below. Yelping, squealing, savage laughter, fear and a hot excited rage and exhilaration filled the barn from floor to roof as the sun rose higher and the frost melted on the ground outside.

Emma's hand trembled as she slashed swiftly at her pad with a stick of charcoal. It was a hopeless task, but it kept her from being sick. She retreated further from the opening and watched a line of four youngsters with their dogs, who had been set to stop that escape route. As a squealing tide of terrified rats poured out they beat about them with pitchforks and heavy sticks while their dogs finished off the crawling wounded. One boy had an airgun and pot-shotted dangerously at escapees.

'Daft bugger, leave it to Scorcher or you'll hit him!' yelled an undersized lad with huge kicking boots. The boy with the gun had RATS painted on his motor-cycle helmet and out of bravado fired up into the air.

'Scares 'em, though, dunnit?' he yelled back, hate blazing in his eyes.

Then a huge rat, as big as a size 12 wellington boot, ran across Emma's foot. From its pointed muzzle came blood and a keening sound. Up dashed a small Jack Russell and seized it behind the ears. He got it down on the ground, but it gave a convulsive jerk, and twisting upwards bit hard into the dog's throat, hanging on as it was thrown from side to side.

'Come on, Scorcher, shake 'im, boy! Kill 'im!'

But the rat was nearly as big as the dog and Emma watched, terrified, unable to move. This was a nightmare. At that moment Ivor ran past her and she grasped his arm.

'That dog will be killed, oh –'

Ivor snatched the pitchfork from the yelling boy and neatly skewered the rat as it clung, not touching the dog. The jaws relaxed, the rat twitched in its last agony on the prongs and the dog sank on to the ground, shaking its head groggily.

'It's a monster and Scorcher got it. It's a monster an'–' The lad was pulling the rat off the prongs of the pitchfork by its tail, when Ivor, his face mottled with anger, hit him hard. The lad toppled over sideways, rat in hand, landing by his coughing dog.

'What's that for then?' he asked. 'Scorcher got it. It's Scorcher's.'

'It damn nearly got Scorcher, you young fool! That dog's too young for the hunt. I told you not to bring him. Glyn'd say the same. Now he's bitten. He might die. Stupid little git. Now get him to the vet.'

The boy's mouth drew down at the corners. He couldn't be more than twelve. He stretched out a hand to the shivering dog, looked up at Ivor, but Ivor flung off back into the barn.

'I'll miss the rest of it –' he said, torn. Emma saw that the little dog was only half grown.

'I'll take you,' she said, helping the boy up. 'What's your name? You carry Scorcher.'

'Scorcher would've finished 'im off. We get prize money for the biggest rat. I'd better hide it else someone'll pinch it off me. I'm Dewi.'

He shoved the rat under the stone wall and piled stones on it. Then he picked up his dog and followed Emma to the car. It didn't cross his mind to thank her, but as he sank on the seat, the dog in his lap, he caressed its head and gave a long sigh. There was blood on his boots.

'You won't peg out, will you, Scorcher? Not you. You're a champion you are. In't he, missis?'

They were driving at a fair pace across the field. Emma could have kissed Dewi. She had been able to retreat with dignity, with a purpose. They negotiated the overgrown lane, and the chained-up dog gave its mournful greeting as they passed the farmhouse. The day was clear and blue now, warm for November. Across the fields the sound of church bells blew towards them. Sunday, a day of prayer.

She followed Dewi's directions, hoping the vet was in, his midday Sabbath dinner finished. The time had fled.

'Ivor probably saved his life,' said Emma, and Dewi grunted.

Morgan Griffiths was in, playing a small harmonium in the front room for his mother and sisters. One of those born to bachelorhood, was Emma's first impression as he led the way to the surgery. He looked well-fleshed and docile, but his manner changed as he closed the door between his work and the rest of the house. He looked keenly through his spectacles, his hands touched the little dog with professional firmness.

'Put him up on here, Dewi,' he said. 'Ratting, were you? This fellow's got a bit to go to his full strength. He's like you, bach, got to fill out, get some muscles.' He reached over and squeezed Dewi's upper arm. 'Get some biceps, man. Duw, plenty of porridge.'

He cleaned the torn throat. 'Nasty bite that –'

'He near killed a monster, big as your boot –'

'I'll have to give him an injection. Hold him still now.'

While he swabbed a place on the dog's backside, then deftly slid in the needle, pushing the plunger down, Emma asked whether a rat's bite was poisonous.

Mr Griffiths withdrew the syringe, swabbed again and looked at her directly for the first time.

'Ever heard of Weil's disease?' She shook her head.

'Carried in rat's saliva, and its urine. A rat urinates every thirty seconds. Contaminates everything it touches.' He turned again to Dewi. 'Come you now, boy, and wash your hands while I wash – what's this fellow's name?'

'Scorcher,' said Dewi.

'Scorcher's neck and head and belly. See what I'm doing? You do the same, soap around the nails, now, then use a paper towel. Particular you have to be. How about you, missis?'

'I'm Emma Rowlands. I've moved back to Bryntanat.'

'Good of you to bring the lad here. Better wash your hands, just in case. And you, my lad, should be wearing rubber gloves.'

As she and Dewi did as they were told, Mr Griffiths dried his patient with paper towels and went on talking.

'Rats. Need a Pied Piper to get rid of them. Warfarin's meat and drink to them, especially now some farmers are growing maize. Love maize, those creatures, makes 'em immune to Warfarin.'

'It's good fun, ratting,' said Dewi. 'We'll get near a hundred today, counting the old pigsties after the barn. You should have seen Glyn, Tregaron, up on the beam. Grand he was.' He looked at his dog lying obediently on the table. 'Scorcher'll be a champion, won't he, Mr Griffiths, when he gets better?'

'*If* he gets better, Dewi. If luck and the Lord agree. Then he won't get poisoned again. Once bitten, no more trouble. Have to watch, mind. Keep him quiet, warm bread and milk.' Abruptly he turned to Emma, adjusting his spectacles with a large, soft, very clean hand. 'Know why the men carry pheasants home from a shoot by the necks, Mrs Rowlands?' So he had spotted her wedding ring. Should she after all keep it on? Looking down at it now, as she dried her fingers, it seemed like a forged passport. 'Dewi knows, ask him. His father beats for Talycoed.'

As they left, Mr Griffiths said again, 'Straight home with him now, and let me know how he goes on. Quiet and comfy he needs to be for a day or two.'

ELIZABETH BERRIDGE

TASKS

29   Look at the two extracts and in groups discuss the following points.

    a   Discuss what is typical of town and country people in the extracts.

    b   Explain what we learn of the two women here, Mrs Tulliver and Emma Rowlands.

    c   Look at the ways in which these novels are written. What differences do you notice?

30   Write a study of the two extracts in which you consider:

    ■   the main events in each

    ■   the behaviour of the characters

    ■   the ways in which they are written

You will find the extract from 'Touch and Go' reprinted in your homework book, together with another task.

Towns and the countryside have been the subject of many poems.

Here are three different poems written to express three different attitudes.

Town and Country

People who live in towns
Often talk to themselves.
They have little sunlight,
Less quiet, and nothing very fresh to eat.
Loving is quite a problem.

Their pleasures are not all that pleasant,
Though they pay dearly for them.
In a dry summer,
Towns smell of money going bad.

Country people have skins like fruit, and vote like grandad.
They treat cattle like cows,
And speak kindly to strangers –
Though they use too many poisons
Which they buy from towns.

Suburban people are different from either,
Bringing up their gardens.
They are kind by committee,
And smile behind gates.
They are not seen talking to themselves.

Town people try very hard
Not to be taken in.
Sometimes they die of not being taken in
Anywhere by anyone.

The sky grows closer,
The landlords more so.
Chimneys get cleaner,
Green belts blacker.

GORDON SYMES

Wind

This house has been far out at sea all night,
The woods crashing through darkness, the booming hills,
Winds stampeding the fields under the window
Floundering black astride and blinding wet

Till day rose; then under an orange sky
The hills had new places, and wind wielded
Blade-light, luminous black and emerald,
Flexing like the lens of a mad eye.

At noon I scaled along the house-side as far as
The coal-house door. I dared once to look up –
Through the brunt wind that dented the balls of my eyes
The tent of the hills drummed and strained its guyrope,

The fields quivering, the skyline a grimace,
At any second to bang and vanish with a flap:
The wind flung a magpie away and a black-
Back gull bent like an iron bar slowly. The house

Rang like some fine green goblet in the note
That any second would shatter it. Now deep
In chairs, in front of the great fire, we grip
Our hearts and cannot entertain book, thought,

Or each other. We watch the fire blazing,
And feel the roots of the house move, but sit on,
Seeing the window tremble to come in,
Hearing the stones cry out under the horizons.

TED HUGHES

God's Grandeur

The world is charged with the grandeur of God.
It will flame out, like shining from shook foil;
It gathers to a greatness, like the ooze of oil
Crushed. Why do men then now not reck his rod?
Generations have trod, have trod, have trod;
And all is seared with trade; bleared, smeared with toil;
And wears man's smudge and shares man's smell: the soil
Is bare now, nor can foot feel, being shod.

And for all this, nature is never spent;
There lives the dearest freshness deep down things;
And though the last lights off the black West went
Oh, morning, at the brown brink eastward, springs –
Because the Holy Ghost over the bent
World broods with warm breast and with ah! bright wings.

GERARD MANLEY HOPKINS

TASK

31 Read the poems and then choose one for a presentation to others.
You should consider the following points when deciding how best to
read the poem aloud:

- speed
- stress
- pauses
- tone of voice

After reading the poem aloud, talk for two minutes on why you chose
this poem.

You will find another poem printed in your homework book as a basis
for a further task.

TIME OUT TASK!

Think about poetry

Poetry may seem difficult to understand. Often this difficulty lies in the fact that ideas and thoughts can be expressed in very few words.

Here are just three of the many 'tools' a poet uses to convey meaning in relatively few words.

Sound – a poet uses certain words because of the sound they make when read aloud.

Tone – a poet will ensure that the tone or mood of a poem is linked to its meaning.

Association – a poet will choose a word knowing that it will conjure up specific associations in the reader's mind.

Read the following poem aloud and consider how Ted Hughes has used sound, tone and association in the writing of this poem.

The Horses

I climbed through woods in the hour-before-dawn dark.
Evil air, a frost-making stillness,

Not a leaf, not a bird, –
A world cast in frost. I came out above the wood

Where my breath left tortuous statues in the iron light.
But the valleys were draining the darkness

Till the moorline – blackening dregs of the brightening grey –
Halved the sky ahead. And I saw the horses:

Huge in the dense grey – ten together –
Megalith-still. They breathed, making no move,

With draped manes and tilted hind-hooves,
Making no sound.

I passed: not one snorted or jerked its head.
Grey silent fragments

Of a grey silent world.

I listened in emptiness on the moor-ridge.
The curlew's tear turned its edge on the silence.

Slowly detail leafed from the darkness. Then the sun
Orange, red, red erupted.

Silently, and splitting to its core tore and flung the cloud,
Shook the gulf open, showed blue,

And the big planets hanging –
I turned

Stumbling in the fever of a dream, down towards
The dark woods, from the kindling tops,

And came to the horses,
There, still they stood,
But now steaming and glistening under the flow of light,

Their draped stone manes, their tilted hind-hooves
Stirring under a thaw while all around them

The frost showed its fires. But still they made no sound.
Not one snorted or stamped,

Their hung heads patient as the horizons,
High over valleys, in the red levelling rays –

In the din of the crowded streets, going among the years, the faces,
May I still meet my memory in so lonely a place

Between the streams and the red clouds, hearing curlews,
Hearing the horizons endure.

TED HUGHES

END OF TIME OUT!

Printed below is an extract from the AA *Book of the British Countryside* entitled 'Where wildlife hides in the heart of a town'.

Where wildlife hides in the heart of a town

For the town dweller, the world of nature begins before he reaches his front door. Up to 50 species of plants and animals may live in and around his house, and beyond the door there is an even greater wealth of wildlife.

Over the centuries roads, buildings and industry have gradually submerged large areas of Britain's natural landscape. Nevertheless, wildlife has not been exterminated in towns – it exists even in the heart of great conurbations; and while it can be argued that London's starling flocks and the Trafalgar Square pigeons, not to mention the pelicans of St James' Park, are merely grace-and-favour residents fed by man, many species of insects, invertebrates, mammals, birds and plants have displayed nature's ability to overcome even the most unpromising of man-made habitats.

Most towns have parks, commons or other open spaces which provide 'mini-countrysides' especially attractive to birds: more than 100 different species have been recorded in London's Regent's Park in one year. But even if migrant birds settle and are able to breed in such areas, they do not become part of the town's natural history in the strict sense for, without the artificial habitat created by man, they would not survive.

True town wildlife exists because of its ability to adapt and live in close proximity to man. Wild flowers in towns have to overcome the following handicaps: reduced light caused by the screening effect of smoke, dust and fog; choked pores from oily deposits; sour soil and reduced soil bacteria; the corrosive effects of sulphates absorbed through the leaves; and limited water. In spite of all this, some thrive.

Within a space of seven years a bombed site in the City of London turned from barren rubble to a teeming haven of wildlife. A study carried out between 1946 and 1953 showed that the first plants to arrive were those which reproduce by airborne spores: algae, mosses and ferns. The came the plants with light seeds borne by 'parachutes' – dandelion and sycamores, fruiting thistles, rosebays and Oxford ragwort.

Grasses followed: seaside species came from the contents of sandbags and fodder plants from food for horses stabled in London. Apple, tomato, plum, date and cherry plants developed from food remnants. Plants with hooked fruits were carried in by man. Pellitory-of-the-wall and ivy grew in the dry cracks of walls, and Canadian fleabane, brambles and buddleia also appeared. Before the blitz, only pellitory-of-the-wall was firmly established in the City, but by 1952 there were 269 species of wild flowers, grasses and ferns on record.

Where previously few wild animals were seen in the City, apart from pigeons, starlings and rats, by the end of the 7-year study, 4 mammals, 31 birds, 56 insects and 30 other invertebrates had been noted. They included snails, slugs, woodlice, centipedes, aphids, spiders, caterpillars, moths and butterflies. The cat, mouse and rat population was augmented by hedgehogs, lizards, snakes and tortoises, and other lost pets.

Ornithological history was made when the black redstart, formerly a rare summer migrant, bred in the ruins. It now nests regularly in factory yards, sidings and power stations.

Railways and canal embankments reach into the centres of most cities bringing wildlife with them. Embankments, covered with grass, flowers, shrubs and a variety of trees, harbour insects, birds, mice, voles, shrews and rabbits and provide foraging ground for hedgehogs, foxes, badgers and squirrels.

The fish in canals attract a variety of birds, including herons, and many aquatic plants thrive in disused waterways.

Sewage farms and rubbish tips are an important source of food for birds and animals on the fringe of towns. It had been estimated that 40 million flies feed on each acre of filter beds. This attracts wagtails, flycatchers, warblers and starlings.

Reservoirs contain bacteria, algae, small crustaceans and insect larvae. Pike, perch, roach and trout are often introduced for sport, and herons, grebes and cormorants appear, together with visiting waders, ducks, geese and swans. Common, herring and blackheaded gulls roost on the water after spending the winter days scavenging on rubbish tips.

Open rubbish dumps also provide a ready supply of food for insects, invertebrates, birds and even rats, foxes, hedgehogs, rabbits and badgers.

Away from town centres, suburban gardens

form an ideal habitat for birds, particularly where man stocks bird tables and provides nest boxes. In addition to the ubiquitous house sparrow and starling, robins, blue and great tits, greenfinches, chaffinches, dunnocks, wood pigeons, blackbirds, song and mistle thrushes are common suburbanites. Swifts and house martins are numerous, feeding on flying insects.

While squirrels and hedgehogs have long been known as visitors to the garden, in recent years, possibly because of the decline in rabbits since 1953, foxes have become a nuisance in some areas, tearing open modern paper-bag type dustbins. Most gardens contain a large number of insects and, if neglected, soon display a variety of weeds. In return, many attractive 'wild' flowers, such as the michaelmas daisy and lupin, have spread from gardens to grow wild.

In many places, old churchyards survive and are often neglected. Colonies of lichen grow on tombstones, the older ones carrying more species since aerial pollution, particularly sulphur dioxide, has killed off less hardy forms. Owls and weasels may sometimes be found, preying on rats and mice.

Dockland is an area where wildlife can flourish, with foreign plants growing among the native wild flowers. The food produced by spillage attracts insects, rats, mice, hedgehogs, weasels and rabbits, which are preyed on by owls, kestrels and even foxes. In addition, linnets, goldfinches, wrens, blackbirds, song thrushes and gulls live and breed in the area.

The average householder would be surprised if it were possible for him to count the number of wild creatures which shelter under his roof; there are at least 50 species which are often found indoors. Rats, mice or bats are usually eradicated as soon as discovered, and common toads hibernating in basements and cellars are usually removed promptly. But a whole range of insects, including houseflies, silverfish, and scavenging beetles are not so conspicuous. Minute spores can produce mould on neglected food, clothing or walls, and dry rot fungi can germinate in suitable places. Open windows let in moths and other night-flying insects, and garden insects are often brought into the house on clothes or flowers.

Some animals show a remarkable ability to adapt to specialised urban environments: brown rats and mice living and breeding in sub-zero temperatures at a refrigerated store developed thicker fur and a protective layer of fat. Moths have developed darker colours to merge with sooty backgrounds – a process known as industrial melanism.

As man changes the environment, some species of plants and animals are driven out, while others thrive. In this process man's waste products have come to form an important link or supplement to the natural food chain in urban areas.

In watching for changes in urban wildlife, it is important not to be misled by oddities mentioned from time to time in the Press, such as peregrines hunting over Big Ben, a stone curlew resting in a child's sandpit or field mice appearing in an uncompleted office block. While no doubt interesting additions to town wildlife, they are merely freak occurrences.

TASKS

32 Summarise in your own words how wildlife not only exists but increases in the town environment.

33 Some of you are probably excited by the natural life around you whether you live in the town or country, while others among you probably couldn't care less.

Prepare a speech either for or against the motion 'People must take more care of wildlife, which has just as much of a right to live as they do.'

Have a formal debate in class on the motion.

You will find the AA extract reprinted in your homework book, together with another task.

YOUNG AND OLD

I n this chapter we are going to explore the relationships between young and old. Sometimes there is a conflict between generations; perhaps more often there is understanding and mutual caring.

When a situation is looked at from a child's point of view, we sometimes see fascinating, even baffling attitudes shown – baffling for adults that is!

ENGLISH IN THE NATIONAL CURRICULUM:

Key Skills you will cover in this chapter

- ☑ In the speaking and listening tasks you will be trying out role play and performance in your role.
- ☑ You will be looking at different types of writing and you will be invited to use your imagination and perhaps to create something particularly pleasing and attractive.
- ☑ In developing your writing skills further you will be asked to explain and to describe and you will also have opportunities to tell stories.
- ☑ When looking at individuals it is inevitable that the society and community in which they live will have an impact on their lives. You will be looking at the impact of society on some of the individuals you will meet.
- ☑ You will also gain practice at selecting the right information for particular purposes.

I n the short story *The Man by the Fountain* the different ways in which an old man and a little boy think are very important.

The Man by the Fountain

As always, John Deweck sat by the fountain.

The spring sun loomed up out of the seething foam. The children honoured the memories of heroic admirals. Their galleons and cutters backed to and fro across the wide pond. Nursemaids and grandmothers glanced anxiously at frocks and trousers. Over the wide world the fountain sang, thrusting a quivering plume of water at the scudding clouds. Liquid pattered noisily into bowls of marble.

John Deweck sat on his usual bench, speaking to no one. There were a few rules he stubbornly clung to. People spoke so much ill of each other. He no longer listened to their chatter. He had eyes now only for students and soldiers, for young girls and children. Young people fascinated his old

carcass. He knew a great deal and had forgotten even more. He craved for youth and approached death's kingdom with reluctant steps.

One by one the frequenters of the fountain left the park. It was time for lunch. John smiled without quite knowing why. Now that he was alone it seemed to him that he was the head park keeper. It was Thursday. The day on which his wife always used to serve his veal-steak with a delicious sour sauce and potatoes as round as marbles. She had been able to work miracles with a potato. Since her death he had fallen into irregular eating habits. Three slices of bread and jam in the morning. At midday, often not even a bite. Round about five, some lumpy porridge with rusks and

225

some fruit. Usually a sour apple. Sour apples, he believed, kept the mental juices clean and preserved the understanding.

He sat now alone with the violence of the fountain.

Perhaps some little boy would turn up? He longed for a serious conversation. Eyes that were still keen swept the avenue that led to the outskirts of the town. Far off in the distance, as in a dream, the little boy came into view. The youngster came tearing up to him, flopped down on the bench and gazed spellbound at the rippling surface of the pond and at the dragons letting the water flow over their green breasts.

'Hello, young man,' said John Deweck solemnly.

The child stared at him but said nothing.

'Isn't it your dinner time?'

'I'm not hungry,' said the boy. 'I eat once a day. Raw buffalo-meat, as I roam the prairie on my bronco.'

'Well, now,' said John Deweck, 'Well now… who might you be then?'

The boy looked up at him full of pride.

'I am the last of the Mohicans. I lost my friend – the paleface. He was caught in an ambush. But I scented danger. Now I wander alone through the wood and valley…'

'Where are your feathers?' asked old John sternly.

The child gazed at him with lively interest. Tiny flames flickered in the golden eyes. He flushed with excitement.

'I don't wear feathers in enemy country,' he said in a whisper. 'But still, I'm on the warpath. I've no warpaint on but I've dug up the hatchet. I am the last of my tribe. Are you my friend or foe?'

'What a thing to ask! My name is John. I have always been the foe of the buffaloes and the friend of the Indians. I made a block-pact with Winnetou. Now I am too old for the hunt. Against whom have you dug up the hatchet?'

'Against the tribe of grown-ups,' answered the boy. 'They threaten my hunting-grounds and my freedom. They don't understand a thing. How can an Indian live in stuffy school-buildings?'

'Of course he can't,' said John. 'Though a paleface myself, I'm all for freedom, too. But still, I think school is necessary….'

The youngster threw him a piercing look.

'Perhaps you're a spy,' he said thoughtfully. 'The enemy is cunning.'

John Deweck gave a high-pitched laugh.

'Nonsense. Take a look around. We're quite alone here. No, I'm not a member of the tribe of grown-ups.'

'How strange. So old, yet still a good Indian.'

The old man gave a loud sniff. He held his hand out to the young brave.

'Peace,' he said, 'and many scalps.'

'I'll tell you my adventure,' said the boy, 'provided you can keep a secret.'

'Even if I was bound to the torture-post I wouldn't breathe a word.'

'This morning I had to hunt for buffalo. As you know, the time has come. Besides, I'm looking for a squaw for my new wigwam. I was creeping out of the kitchen when Dad caught me by the hair. He walloped me for not being ready for school. I didn't make a sound. Only cunning could save me. Meekly I let myself be led to Hook Nose.'

'Who is Hook Nose?'

'The school chief,' replied the boy. 'He's not strong but he's terribly cunning. He laughed like a wild horse and spoke of giving me lines. At ten o'clock, during break, I sneaked out at the gate. I ran as fast as I could…. I don't want to go home again. My homeland is the prairie. Tonight I'm looking for a boat and tomorrow I'll be sailing across the seas.'

John Deweck looked at the fountain. Impetuously as life itself it leapt up towards the light of the boundless sky. Cherubs spattered with water, blew on their conches as if to warn of impending danger.

A wrinkle creased the aged forehead.

'It's not going to be an easy plan,' sighed John Deweck.

'I *must* get a boat,' said the boy stubbornly. 'You've got to help me.'

Heavy clouds drifted towards the spring sun. The birds were silent in the pruned trees.

'First come and eat in my wigwam,' faltered John Deweck.

'I'm not hungry.'

'You can't refuse bread and salt….'

The boy thought this over.

'Your mouth speaks the truth,' he said. 'I must set out on my long journey free from hunger. But I shan't eat meat.'

'Bread and salt, O Warrior….'

The boy trotted at the old man's side, looking neither left nor right. He thought of the wild scents of the prairie. He had met an old buffalo hunter who gave him invaluable tips.

They stepped into the police station. The door closed behind them with a bang. The boy looked about him and understood.

He sat down on a bench and freely volunteered information to a fat man with a ruddy complexion. His head sank on his chest. He did not even glance at John Deweck.

The car arrived shortly afterwards. The father

stepped out and thanked the old man. The boy took his place in the car. Suddenly, he turned to the buffalo hunter.

'You belong to the tribe of grown-ups,' he said. 'You have betrayed my confidence. I will pay for it at the torture-post. I despise you.'

He spat on the ground.

'What did he say?' asked the father.

'That you ought to make him happy,' said John Deweck.

Father and son vanished in a cloud of dust.

'The youth of today,' grunted the inspector.

Slowly the old man paced through the streets of the little town.

He was never seen again at the fountain.

GEORGE HEBBELINCK

TASKS

1 In groups, discuss whether the old man behaved in the right way. What else could he have done? What effect would it have on the boy's life? Consider the little boy. What do you think of his attitude? How did he affect the life of the old man?

2 Concentrate on the old man for a moment – in discussion work out how he would have told his wife if she were still alive. You could then go on to write a playscript of their conversation.

3 In a piece of your own writing place yourself in the old man's position. Imagine he keeps a diary in which he writes about events and his personal feelings. Write his diary entry for the day of the story. Remember his mood and feelings at the end of the story. This will affect your choice of words in trying to capture the way in which the old man expresses himself.

4 In a 'Time Out' (p221–2) we have invited you to think about poetry. Alan Bennett is a writer who published his diaries in 1994. He has written many plays. He says in his diaries that he fears he has just added to the number of words in the world. 'That is why poetry is supreme. It makes less mess'.

Taking a hint from Alan Bennett, write a poem about the old man's or the young boy's feelings.

Alternatively you could write about your own feelings when you made a difficult decision or you had been badly let down.

You will find this story reprinted in your homework book where you are invited to consider the feelings of the boy at the end of the story.

You are now invited to spend some time concentrating on advancing age through three poems.

Follower by Seamus Heaney is written from the standpoint of a young man watching his father with a consciousness that his father is changing as he gets older.

My Grandmother by Elizabeth Jennings shows an uncertainty about the behaviour expected of the young towards the very old.

Funeral Blues by W H Auden addresses what is the inevitability of death and the poet considers his reaction to it.

Follower

My father worked with a horse-plough,
His shoulders globed like a full sail strung
Between the shafts and the furrow.
The horses strained at his clicking tongue.

An expert. He would set the wing
And fit the bright steel-pointed sock.
The sod rolled over without breaking.
At the headrig, with a single pluck

Of reins, the sweating team turned round
And back into the land. His eye
Narrowed and angled at the ground,
Mapping the furrow exactly.

I stumbled in his hob-nailed wake,
Fell sometimes on the polished sod;
Sometimes he rode me on his back
Dipping and rising to his plod.

I wanted to grow up and plough,
To close one eye, stiffen my arm.
All I ever did was follow
In his broad shadow round the farm.

I was a nuisance, tripping, falling,
Yapping always. But today
It is my father who keeps stumbling
Behind me, and will not go away.

SEAMUS HEANEY

My Grandmother

She kept an antique shop – or it kept her.
Among Apostle spoons and Bristol glass,
The faded silks, the heavy furniture,
She watched her own reflection in the brass
Salvers and silver bowls, as if to prove
Polish was all, there was no need of love.

And I remember how I once refused
To go out with her, since I was afraid.
It was perhaps a wish not to be used
Like antique objects. Though she never said
That she was hurt, I still could feel the guilt
Of that refusal, guessing how she felt.

Later, too frail to keep a shop, she put
All her best things in one long narrow room.
The place smelt old, of things too long kept shut,
The smell of absences where shadows come
That can't be polished. There was nothing then
To give her own reflection back again.

And when she died I felt no grief at all,
Only the guilt of what I once refused.
I walked into her room among the tall
Sideboards and cupboards – things she never used
But needed: and no finger-marks were there.
Only the new dust falling through the air.

ELIZABETH JENNINGS

Funeral Blues

Stop all the clocks, cut off the telephone,
Prevent the dog from barking with a juicy bone,
Silence the pianos and with muffled drum
Bring out the coffin, let the mourners come.

Let aeroplanes circle moaning overhead
Scribbling on the sky the message He Is Dead,
Put crepe bows round the white necks of the public doves,
Let the traffic policemen wear black cotton gloves.

He was my North, my South, my East and West,
My working week and my Sunday rest,
My noon, my midnight, my talk, my song;
I thought that love would last for ever: I was wrong.

The stars are not wanted now; put out every one:
Pack up the moon and dismantle the sun:
Pour away the ocean and sweep up the wood:
For nothing now can ever come to any good.

W H AUDEN

TASKS

5 Take any of the poems and consider your reactions to it.
   a Consider what the poet has said.
   b What do you think of the way in which the poet has treated
      the subject?
   c Write your opinion of the poem with an explanation of the reasons for
      your view.

6 Choose one of the topics and consider how you would have treated the
   subject. What would you say about your father? Your grandmother?
   How would you express your feelings about the death of a close friend?

   Now write either a poem of your own or a short piece of writing which
   you control carefully.

   In a 'Time Out' on p39–40 we considered drafting and re-drafting. This is
   the sort of writing where it is essential.

With the passing of time we all have changing expectations of ourselves and of other people. Spend some time with this amusing article by Jonathan Miller in which he writes about his children, in particular his teenage daughter. You will notice that at times he writes with heavy irony, using, you might think, rather pompous language, for instance 'or take upon herself the exhausting imposition of transporting an empty crisp packet to a bin'. Probably a large number of you will find yourselves identifying with this teenager.

Heaven preserve the family from teenage girls

DID anyone notice that last year was, courtesy of the United Nations, the Year of the Family? One clue might have been that every newspaper writer to have had a baby promptly regaled the rest of us with a string of articles about baby's first nappy change, the difficulty of reconciling the interior decorating scheme with baby's first high chair and the angst of hiring baby's first nanny.

Babies are, in fact, fundamentally uninteresting except to their swooning parents. Today's teenagers, on the other hand, turn out to be extremely interesting, as there is no precedent for them.

I am at present the keeper of one fully fledged teenager, a 1981 model, who celebrates her 14th birthday later this month. In September I shall add a male teenager to my collection. He is only 12 but already showing many symptoms.

As my teenager is abroad on the school ski trip today and has in any case pronounced this column 'boring', it is safe to share a few observations, which, having consulted other parents of similarly aged daughters, I believe to be not untypical.

The modern female teenager is a vegetarian. This diet does not actually encompass the consumption of many vegetables, merely the refusal to eat meat. Neither, in any conventional sense, are meals taken. Feeding behaviour is instead akin to that of a ruminant, with more or less continual grazing on sweets, Coca-Cola and chips, with an occasional McDonald's filet-o-fish.

She is extremely clean. Baths and showers are taken at least twice daily. These are not quick dunk-and-scrub affairs, but prolonged aquatic manoeuvres, involving the employment of vast quantities of hot water spiced with overpriced unguents, lotions and potions. It does not matter how many of these are held in stock in the bathroom – more are always required.

Despite this obsession with bodily hygiene, her bedroom is a nesting ground for vermin of all types, as clothes, shoes, sheet music, incomplete homework, empty bottles of Body Shop preparations and copies of *Just Seventeen* magazine are piled into tumuli on the floor.

Susceptibility to squalor is perhaps not unique to this generation of adolescents; what is novel is the sheer quantity of material possessions with which they are capable of demonstrating their indifference to conventional standards of domestic order.

Notwithstanding her technical facility with satellite receiver, video recorder and computer equipment of all types, she has yet to work out the basic operation of the washing machine or vacuum cleaner.

She has achieved a sophisticated understanding of finance, knowing that money does not grow on trees, but comes through a hole in the wall, accessed by means of her father's cash card. Although she has hundreds and hundreds of pounds a year passing through her bank account, receiving a lavish monthly allowance, with cash top-ups from grandparents at birthdays and at Christmas, she expects that all significant costs will be met by her parents.

She is fit for postgraduate employment in the civil service, having maintained an obsessional secrecy over all information concerning her social life.

She is embarrassed to be seen in public with her parents, who are, variously, 'sad' and 'tragic'. Although not so sad and tragic as to be above delivering, on her 17th birthday, a white

Volkswagen Beetle convertible (she hopes).

Despite the vast sums that are expended and the bulging closet of garments available, her clothing is always inappropriate to the season; she will happily go out in the middle of winter wearing only a T-shirt.

When she is not being completely charming – a transient condition invariably related to her need to be driven to a distant shopping precinct to resupply herself with unguents or compact discs – she employs to her parents and sibling manner of address interspersed with frequent contemptuous groans and grunts. These sound effects are triggered whenever a suggestion is made that she might tidy her bedroom, or take upon herself the exhausting imposition of transporting an empty crisp packet to the bin.

You might ask why I continue to finance this creature, and the answer, of course, is that in approximately 10 or 15 years, she will, I trust, provide me with the material to write a column on the joys of 21st century grandparenting, allowing me in my dotage to coo at children who go home after tea.

JONATHAN MILLER

TASK

7 Write a reply to Jonathan Miller's article.

In your writing consider:

- if you are going to write as yourself or perhaps as Jonathan Miller's daughter;
- the form your reply might take – you might choose to write a letter or an article.

Here is an example from pre-twentieth century literature. In *Agnes Grey* Anne Brontë writes about a very difficult early life.

Agnes Grey

The useful pony phaeton was sold, together with the stout well-fed pony – the old favourite that we had fully determined should end its days in peace, and never pass from our hands; the little coach-house and stable were let; the servant boy and the more efficient (being the more expensive) of the two maid-servants were dismissed. Our clothes were mended, turned, and darned to the utmost verge of decency; our food, always plain, was not simplified to an unprecedented degree – except my father's favourite dishes; our coals and candles were painfully economised – the pair of candles reduced to one, and that most sparingly used; the coals carefully husbanded in the half-empty grate: especially when my father was out on his parish duties, or confined to bed through illness – then we sat with our feet on the fender, scraping the perishing embers together from time to time, and occasionally adding a slight scattering of the dust and fragments of coal, just to keep them alive. As for our carpets, they in time were worn threadbare, and patched and darned even to a greater extent than our garments. To save the expense of a gardener, Mary and I undertook to keep the garden in order; and all the cooking and household work that could not easily be managed by one servant girl was done by my mother and sister, with a little occasional help from me: only a little, because, though a woman in my own estimation, I was still a child in theirs; and my mother, like most active, managing women, was not gifted with very active daughters: for this reason – that being so clever and diligent herself, she was never tempted to trust her affairs to a deputy, but on the contrary, was willing to act and think for others as well as for number one; and whatever was the business in hand, she was apt to think that no one could do it so well as herself: so that whenever I offered to assist her, I received such an answer as – 'No, love, you cannot indeed –

there's nothing here you can do. Go and help your sister, or get her to take a walk with you – tell her she must not sit so much, and stay so constantly in the house as she does – she may well look thin and dejected.'

'Mary, mamma says I'm to help you; or get you to take a walk with me: she says you may well look thin and dejected, if you sit so constantly in the house.'

'Help me you cannot, Agnes; and I cannot go out with *you* – I have far too much to do.'

'Then let me help you.'

'You cannot, indeed, dear child. Go and practise your music, or play with the kitten.'

There was always plenty of sewing on hand; but I had not been taught to cut out a single garment, and, except plain hemming and seaming, there was little I could do even in that line; for they both asserted that it was far easier to do the work themselves than to prepare it for me: and, besides, they liked better to see me prosecuting my studies, or amusing myself – it was time enough for me to sit bending over my work, like a grave matron, when my favourite little pussy was become a steady old cat. Under such circumstances, although I was not many degrees more useful than the kitten, my idleness was not entirely without excuse.

Through all our troubles, I never but once heard my mother complain of our want of money. As summer was coming on, she observed to Mary and me, 'What a desirable thing it would be for your papa to spend a few weeks at a watering-place. I am convinced the sea-air and the change of scene would be of incalculable service to him. But then, you see, there's no money,' she added, with a sigh. We both wished exceedingly that the thing might be done, and lamented greatly that it could not. 'Well, well!' said she, 'it's no use complaining. Possibly something might be done to further the project after all. Mary, you are a beautiful drawer. What do you say to doing a few more pictures in your best style, and getting them framed, with the water-coloured drawings you have already done, and trying to dispose of them to some liberal picture-dealer, who has the sense to discern their merits?'

'Mamma, I should be delighted if you think they *could* be sold; and for anything worth while.'

'It's worth while trying, however, my dear: do you procure the drawings, and I'll endeavour to find a purchaser.'

'I wish *I* could do something,' said I.

'You, Agnes! well, who knows? You draw pretty well, too: if you choose some simple piece for your subject, I dare say you will be able to produce something we shall all be proud to exhibit.'

'But I have another scheme in my head, mamma, and have had long, only I did not like to mention it.'

'Indeed! pray tell us what it is.'

'I should like to be a governess.'

My mother uttered an exclamation of surprise, and laughed. My sister dropped her work in astonishment, explaining, '*You* a governess, Agnes! What *can* you be dreaming of!'

'Well! I don't see anything so *very* extraordinary in it. I do not pretend to be able to instruct great girls; but surely I could teach little ones: and I should like it *so* much: I am fond of children. Do let me, mamma!'

'But, my love, you have not learned to take care of *yourself* yet: and young children require more judgement and experience to manage than elder ones.'

'But, mamma, I am above eighteen, and quite able to take care of myself, and others too. You do not know half the wisdom and prudence I possess, because I have never been tried.'

ANNE BRONTË

TASK

8   Discuss and then write briefly about the frustrations of Agnes Grey during this period of her life.

You will find that we have printed this extract again in your homework book together with a task which will require you to do some additional research.

TIME OUT TASK!

Reading

In this classbook we have used a number of extracts from novels.

Pick one of the extracts which you have enjoyed and visit either your school or local library and borrow the book so that you can read it in its entirety.

END OF TIME OUT!

It is always interesting to look outside your own experience and your own culture.

The next three pieces of stimulus material come from different editions of a Malaysian newspaper, *The New Straits Times*. You will find the language a little different at times, perhaps a little quaint and amusing, but that will not prevent understanding.

Perhaps in the Far East family values are a little different from those in England. The first two articles look at the situation of elderly parents and their expectations of younger relatives.

Ray of hope for destitute parents

SINGAPORE, Wed. – A Singapore courtroom could soon witness the unusual scene of an elderly parent too poor to support herself using the law to extract money from her children.

The measure seems desperate but she may well have no other course in a State that frowns on the idea of welfare and insists its younger generation shoulder its filial duties.

Under a recently tabled private member's Bill, destitute parents could approach the courts to compel one or more of their children to pay maintenance. The money could be a monthly allowance or a lump sum.

The Government has yet to take a formal position on the Bill, but is thought to support it. Similar laws already exist in India, Israel and some American states.

Ignoring a court maintenance order could, under Singapore's version, mean a fine of up to S$1,000 (RM1,650) or a jail term of up to a year or both.

The move has stirred a debate which goes to the heart of Singaporeans' family values.

Opponents say the Bill is unwarranted and un-Asian. But others cite cases of aged and poor parents abandoned by their children.

Walter Woon, an academic and a nominated member of parliament, said his Bill did not seek to replace or undermine family ties but was aimed at the small number of children who can afford to take care of their parents but refuse to.

Bruce Gale, regional manager for Political and Economic Risk Consultancy in Singapore, said the Bill appeared to enjoy the Government's blessing and to be part of a wider attempt to institutionalise Asian values in Singapore society.

'But Singaporeans, who genuinely hold such values, might consider it shameful that the Government finds it necessary to enforce them through the law,' he said.

The Government has not yet formally committed itself in the debate, although analysts say the government is unlikely to oppose the Bill because it fits in with its anti-handout philosophy.

Singapore leaders, including former premier Lee Kuan Yew, have frequently opposed State welfare.

In 1982, Lee, now a senior Minister, told the nation he had been dismayed to discover on a visit to a new housing development that it had two homes for the elderly.

'It is not something to be proud of. It must not be encouraged…. It is unsound for a government to take over family responsibilities, for we shall damage the basic unit of society, the family, the building bricks of our society.'

Official figures show that by 2030 the portion of the population over 60 is likely to rise to 26 per cent, from 9.1 per cent in the 1990 census.

'The proposed law will place another barrier in the way of any possible movement towards social welfare, by ensuring that the child, and not the State, is responsible for his parents,' columnist Koh Buck Song wrote in the *Straits Times*.

Reader S K Chakrayarti wrote to the *Times*: 'Perhaps Mr Woon is right. Our materialistic ambition and purpose of life have blinded us to such an extent that rules and laws are the only way to govern our society.

'If that is true, then it is a sad day for Singapore.'

Analysts said the issue is largely economic.

However, several of them warned that the high costs of court battles may discourage poor parents from trying to extract cash from their family.

A Singapore-based policy analyst said the problem of financing aged and retired Singaporeans is much more complex than the question of their children not supporting them in the tiny republic, whose per capita income is about S$27,680 (RM45,670) a year.

'It would be more useful to explore ways in which the present national provident fund system and the public assistance programme are modified to ensure that a minimum amount is available to every elderly person,' the analyst said.

'This is not difficult. The government's coffers are flush with funds,' he said.

Singapore's overall Budget surplus for 1993–94 to March was S$11.3 billion (RM18.64 billion), equivalent to 13.6 per cent of the country's gross domestic product.

'True, cases of abandoned aged parents are rare but the problem is with those who are poorly educated and have low or no pension fund balances,' a university lawyer said.

'They are hopelessly dependent on their children,' he said.

REUTER

Lament of a 65-year-old man

Is it justified for an old man to burst into tantrums over the cheeky uncaring attitude of some of his kith and kin? There is every reason for it when the young upstarts (when very young, they came seeking favours) do not appear cooperative, let alone obliging.

When he asks them for a special favour, they are quick to say that they are too busy, heavily committed and unable to render any help.

Once in a while, it is reasonable for an old man to ask to be driven to the nearest barber shop for an overdue hair crop, or to be dropped at the post office to draw his pension, or to be driven to the nearest mosque for the Friday prayers.

A smart Alec among them had the temerity to blurt out: 'To solve the matter, it's best for you *Pakcik*, to take during lessons and buy yourself a car.'

At 65 plus, he asked himself, would he venture to take a driving licence? After weighing the pros and cons on the issue, the answer is still a straightforward 'no' for the simple reason that our traffic system is chaotic.

At his age, he would consider himself a security risk on the road.

With poor eyesight and being hard of hearing, it is wise that he should not take risks.

Being unduly clumsy he might make himself a laughing stock.

One of his recent experiences was when his car stalled in a labyrinth of frenzied traffic, with inconsiderate motorists honking all the way as if he was some kind of freak.

How is he to react if someone calls him *bodoh, lembab or lesen kopi 'O'* and people stare at him as if they are ready to eat him up?

Besides, the driving sense of some of our local road users is a disgrace.

They are still lacking in civic-mindedness.

They seem to regard the highway as a Grand Prix track. When the coast is clear, they are the kings of the road.

In the event of accident they are quick to make scapegoats of others.

For those who have attained the age of 65, it is best they do not drive a car. If they need a ride, they should be chauffeur-driven.

AHMAD ARI ECKHARDT

TASKS

9 In small groups, discuss the two articles and the attitudes and values they express.

10 In your groups honestly discuss your opinions on these attitudes and values.

11 Then discuss what **you** believe are the responsibilities of children towards their parents in later life.

12 Independently plan and make notes for the speech you are going to make in a formal debate on the motion:

'This house believes that, once they have left home, children have no responsibility towards their parents.'

You can choose to prepare your speech for or against the motion.

The third article is written by a young man looking back on his own school life. In it he explains how he has mixed feelings about friends, classes and teachers.

You will find that some of the vocabulary which he uses is probably different from your own natural vocabulary but remember that he is someone who learnt English as a second language. I wonder if your French or German is as good!

Memorable moments of school life

Just like the hapless man who watched his in-law drive over a cliff in his brand new car, I was tormented by ambivalent feelings on my last day in school.

While I was happy to find myself on the threshold of a new life, with countless opportunities waiting on the horizon (so I then thought), I was at the same time rather sad to part company with friends and foes of so many years.

It does not require an elephant's memory for a person to remember the highlights in his school life. So, disregarding chronology, I shall describe some memorable moments in my 13 years of school life.

I was in Form One when I first heard the term 'free period'. This meant that there was a cessation of knowledge acquisition and we were required to indulge in an ostensible self-recapitulation. For instance, we were asked to go through what we were taught about parallelograms, rhombuses and triangles the previous week. Some of us smarter ones figured that the teacher was not in a proper frame of mind to teach.

I can remember those exciting football matches which we played when the term exams were over. There was one match that was particularly exciting for me: it ended in a 1-1 draw – and I scored both the goals.

And there was the usual exam fever which made its presence felt, both in school and at home. My nervous disposition on one occasion caused me to break a few dishes in our dining room. It didn't take a sledgehammer blow over the head for my mother to realise that I wasn't sufficiently prepared for the big test.

A classmate once confessed to me: 'I like to look cool to impress the invigilators, although my feelings belie my outward expression.' And one kind teacher told the class: 'Stay calm, or you'd have fear written on your face, and rubbish on your answer sheets.'

Whenever I did badly in a subject paper and my friends asked me the reason for my poor performance, I always told them that I was an animal lover: I did not put up my hand to request for more blank answer sheets because I couldn't find it in my heart to give an unnecessary fright to those poor lizards on the ceiling of the exam hall. This extraordinary explanation never failed to put the matter at rest.

One of my favourite subjects was chemistry. I especially liked studying about gases such as hydrogen and helium. These may be light gases, but I did not treat the study of them lightly.

Where biology was concerned, my favourite topics were those that dealt with organisms like the amoeba. I enjoyed drawing an amoeba: I would first darken a spot to represent the nucleus and then make innumerable dots around it so that the whole thing resembled some measly mass. The interesting thing about an amoeba is that it multiples by dividing.

I was a failure at physics. It had never been my forte. Come to think of it, I did not even know where the strongest point of such and such a thing was.

My attitude towards most of the other subjects was perfunctory, but I did have a special liking for English Literature.

One of our literature texts for Form Five was *Great Expectations*. I enjoyed seeing the movie version of this Dickens work more than reading the book, and was enormously impressed by the performance of John Mills in the black-and-white film.

My father had great expectation where I was concerned, and took a great interest in my academic progress. Without fail, he would ask for my report card every fortnight. He was not impressed by my performance, and sometimes just couldn't believe what he saw. I didn't have the heart to tell him: 'I don't get the highest marks in my class. Do you get the highest salary at your office?'

Still, I was not such a bad student. There was one pint-sized boy – with the potential to make Dennis the Menace look like a Cub Scout – who wanted to drop out of school: the only thing he ever took up in school was space.

A story went around the school for some three weeks that the headmaster said to him: 'It's very generous of you, but I don't think your leaving would solve the population crisis in the school.'

I didn't believe the headmaster said that: there were many rumour-mongers in my school.

One of the most memorable events was the revenge I inflicted on a teacher. When I was in Standard Six, I fought with the teacher's blue-eyed boy and made him cry. The vindictive teacher made me write, 'I am a naughty boy' 500 times.

After I had executed the Herculean task, she screwed the papers up into a furious ball and – with a gleam of satisfaction in her eyes – tossed it into the wastebasket.

But, ha ha ha, I got even with her when I reached home. In the quiet of my room I said 'Teacher is a naughty woman' 500 times.

This cathartic chore left me in a curious state of euphoria and thirst.

OH TEIK THEAM

TASK

13 Put yourself in the same position as Oh Teik Theam and, as a recent former student at your own school, write an article for the school newspaper.

I n the article you have just been working from the writer remembers reading *Great Expectations* when he was in Form Five.

Printed on the following pages is an extract from *Great Expectations*. Pip, the young hero of the story, is an orphan who has been brought up by his much older sister. The two features of his upbringing have been that he has been punished by being smacked and any ills have been 'cured' by an awful concoction called 'tar water'.

In this extract Pip is sitting with a crowd of family and acquaintances at Christmas dinner. He is terrified because he has stolen some brandy and has filled up the bottle with his hated tar water, so that no one will notice that the level has gone down.

Great Expectations

It began the moment we sat down to dinner. Mr Wopsle said grace with theatrical declamation – as it now appears to me, something like a religious cross of the Ghost in Hamlet with Richard the Third – and ended with the very proper aspiration that we might be truly grateful. Upon which my sister fixed me with her eye, and said, in a low reproachful voice, 'Do you hear that? Be grateful.'

'Especially,' said Mr Pumblechook, 'be grateful, boy, to them which brought you up by hand.'

Mrs Hubble shook her head, and contemplating me with a mournful presentiment that I should come to no good, asked, 'Why is it that the young are never grateful?' This moral system seemed too much for the company until Mr Hubble tersely solved it by saying, 'Naterally wicious.' Everybody then murmured 'True!' and looked at me in a particularly unpleasant and personal manner.

Joe's station and influence were something feebler (if possible) when there was company, than when there was none. But he always aided and comforted me when he could, in some way of his own, and he always did so at dinner-time by giving me gravy, if there were any. There being plenty of gravy today, Joe spooned into my plate, at this point, about half a pint.

A little later on in the dinner, Mr Wopsle reviewed the sermon with some severity, and intimated – in the usual hypothetical case of the Church being 'thrown open' – what kind of sermon *he* would have given them. After favouring them with some heads of that discourse, he remarked that he considered the subject of the day's homily, ill-chosen; which was the less excusable, he added, when there were so many subjects 'going about.'

'True again,' said Uncle Pumblechook. 'You've hit it, sir! Plenty of subjects going about, for them that know how to put salt upon their tails. That's what's wanted. A man needn't go far to find a subject, if he's ready with his salt-box.' Mr Pumblechook added, after a short interval of reflection, 'Look at Pork alone. There's a subject! If you want a subject, look at Pork!'

'True, sir. Many a moral for the young,' returned Mr Wopsle; and I knew he was going to lug me in, before he said it; 'might be deduced from that text.'

('You listen to this,' said my sister to me, in a severe parenthesis.)

Joe gave me some more gravy.

'Swine,' pursued Mr Wopsle, in his deepest voice, and pointing his fork at my blushes, as if he were mentioning my Christian name; 'Swine were the companions of the prodigal. The gluttony of Swine is put before us, as an example to the young.' (I thought this pretty well in him who had been praising up the pork for being so plump and juicy.) 'What is detestable in a pig, is more detestable in a boy.'

'Or girl,' suggested Mr Hubble.

'Of course, or girl, Mr Hubble,' assented Mr Wopsle, rather irritably, 'but there is no girl present.'

'Besides,' said Mr Pumblechook, turning sharp on me, 'think what you've got to be grateful for. If you'd been born a Squeaker—'

'He *was*, if ever a child was,' said my sister, most emphatically.

Joe gave me some more gravy.

'Well, but I mean a four-footed Squeaker,' said Mr Pumblechook. 'If you had been born such, would you have been here now? Not you—'

'Unless in that form,' said Mr Wopsle, nodding towards the dish.

'But I don't mean in that form sir,' returned Mr Pumblechook, who had an objection to being interrupted; 'I mean, enjoying himself with his elders and betters, and improving himself with their conversation, and rolling in the lap of luxury. Would he have been doing that? No, he wouldn't. And what would have been your destination?' turning on me again. 'You would have been disposed of for so many shillings according to the market price of the article, and Dunstable the butcher would have come up to you as you lay in your straw, and he would have whipped you under his left arm, and with his right he would have tucked up his frock to get a penknife from out of his waistcoat-pocket, and he would have shed your blood and had your life. No bringing up by hand then. Not a bit of it!'

Joe offered me more gravy, which I was afraid to take.

'He was a world of trouble to you, ma'am,' said Mrs Hubble, commiserating my sister.

'Trouble?' Echoed my sister, 'trouble?' And then entered on a fearful catalogue of all the illnesses I had been guilty of, and all the acts of sleeplessness I had committed, and all the high places I had tumbled from, and all the low places I had tumbled into, and all the injuries I had done myself, and all the times she had wished me in my grave, and I had contumaciously refused to go there.

I think the Romans must have aggravated one

another very much, with their noses. Perhaps, they became the restless people they were, in consequence. Anyhow Mr Wopsle's Roman nose so aggravated me, during the recital of my misdemeanours, that I should have liked to pull it until he howled. But, all I had endured up to this time, was nothing in comparison with the awful feelings that took possession of me when the pause was broken which ensued upon my sister's recital, and in which pause everybody had looked at me (as I felt painfully conscious) with indignation and abhorrence.

'Yet,' said Mr Pumblechook, leading the company gently back to the theme from which they had strayed, 'Pork – regarded as biled – is rich, too; ain't it?'

'Have a little brandy, uncle,' said my sister.

O Heavens, it had come at last! He would find it was weak, he would say it was weak, and I was lost! I held tight to the leg of the table, under the cloth, with both hands, and awaited my fate.

My sister wanted for the stone bottle, came back with the stone bottle, and poured his brandy out: no one else taking any. The wretched man trifled with his glass – took it up, looked at it through the light, put it down – prolonged my misery. All this time Mrs Joe and Joe were briskly clearing the table for the pie and pudding.

I couldn't keep my eyes off him. Always holding tight by the leg of the table with my hands and feet, I saw the miserable creature finger his glass playfully, take it up, smile, throw his head back, and drink the brandy off. Instantly afterwards, the company were seized with unspeakable consternation, owing to his springing to his feet, turning round several times in an appalling spasmodic whooping-cough dance, and rushing out at the door; he then became visible through the window, violently plunging and expectorating, making the most hideous faces, and apparently out of his mind.

I held on tight, while Mrs Joe and Joe ran to him. I didn't know how I had done it, but I had no doubt I had murdered him somehow. In my dreadful situation, it was a relief when he was brought back, and, surveying the company all round as if *they* had disagreed with him, sank down into his chair with the one significant gasp, 'Tar!'

I had filled up the bottle from the tar-water jug. I knew he would be worse by-and-by. I moved the table, like a Medium of the present day, by the vigour of my unseen hold upon it.

'Tar!' cried my sister, in amazement. 'Why, how ever could Tar come there?'

But, Uncle Pumblechook, who was omnipotent

in that kitchen, wouldn't hear the word, wouldn't hear of the subject, imperiously waved it all away with his hand, and asked for hot gin-and-water. My sister, who had begun to be alarmingly meditative, had to employ herself actively in getting the gin, the hot water, the sugar, and the lemon peel, and mixing them. For the time at least, I was saved. I still held on to the leg of the table, but clutched it now with the fervour of gratitude.

By degrees, I became calm enough to release my grasp, and partake of pudding. Mr Pumblechook partook of pudding. All partook of pudding. The course terminated, and Mr Pumblechook had begun to beam under the genial influence of a gin-and-water. I began to think I should get over the day, when my sister said to Joe, 'Clean plates – cold.'

I clutched the leg of the table again immediately, and pressed it to my bosom and if it had been the companion of my youth and friend of my soul. I foresaw what was coming, and I felt that this time I really was gone.

'You must taste,' said my sister, addressing the guests with her best grace, 'you must taste, to finish with, such a delightful and delicious present of Uncle Pumblechook's!'

Must they! Let them not hope to taste it!

'You must know,' said my sister, rising, 'it's a pie: a savoury pork pie.'

The company murmured their compliments. Uncle Pumblechook, sensible of having deserved well of his fellow-creatures, said – quite vivaciously, all things considered – 'Well, Mrs Joe, we'll do our best endeavours; let us have a cut at this same pie.'

My sister went out to get it. I heard her steps proceed to the pantry. I saw Mr Pumblechook balance his knife. I saw re-awakening appetite in the Roman nostrils of Mr Wopsle. I heard Mr Hubble remark that 'a bit of savoury pork pie would lay atop of anything you could mention, and do no harm,' and I heard Joe say, 'You shall have some, Pip.' I have never been absolutely certain whether I uttered a shrill yell of terror, merely in spirit, or in the bodily hearing of the company. I felt that I could bear no more, and that I must run away. I released the leg of the table, and ran for my life.

But I ran no further than the house door, for there I ran head foremost into a party of soldiers with their muskets: one of whom held out a pair of handcuffs to me, saying, 'Here you are, look sharp, come on!'

CHARLES DICKENS

TASKS

14 As well as saying he remembers reading *Great Expectations*, the writer in *The New Straits Times* says that he enjoyed the movie version more. You may have had the opportunity to see a film or television version of the novel yourself. There may be one in school. If you have access to a film or television version, watch part or all of it.

15 Take the extract you have just read and turn it into a scene from a film. You will need to write the script and you might think about the set, costuming and characters, camera angles and effects which you would want to create.

16 In groups, compare your scenes (or even compare your version with the same scene in a film or television version). You might even choose the best and work on it to produce either a performance or a video.

Printed below is a poem by Norman Nicholson. Read it through carefully and then discuss the task in class before writing the answers.

Rising Five

'I'm rising five,' he said.
'Not four,' and little coils of hair
Unclicked themselves upon his head.
His spectacles, brimful of eyes to stare
at me and the meadow, reflected cones of light
Above his toffee-buckled cheeks. He'd been alive
Fifty-six months or perhaps a week more:

                           not four,

But rising five.

Around him in the field the cells of spring
Bubbled and doubled; buds unbuttoned; shoot
And stem shook out the creases from their frills,
And every tree was swilled with green.
It was the season after blossoming,
Before the forming of the fruit:

                           not May,

But rising June.

               And in the sky
The dust dissected in the tangential light:

                           not day,

But rising night;

               not now,

But rising soon.

The new buds pushed the old leaves from the bough.
We drop our youth behind us like a boy
Throwing away his toffee wrappers. We never see the flower,
But only the fruit in the flower; never the fruit,
But only the rot in the fruit. We look for the marriage bed
In the baby's cradle, we look for the grave in the bed:

not living,

But rising dead.

NORMAN NICHOLSON

TASK

17 This task takes you through the poem and asks you to think of different aspects of it.

   a How does the title relate to the thought of the poem?

   b What impression of the boy is suggested by the description in lines two to six?

   c How does the passage about spring relate to what is said about the boy?

   d How does the last section (from 'The new buds...') fit into the pattern of thought and imagery in the poem?

   e What effect do the final words of the poem have?

You will find this poem printed again in your homework book with an additional task.

Inevitably getting older means that old relationships end and new ones begin. It's a question of increasing maturity. Printed on the following pages is an article in which a mother explains how her relationship with her daughter altered as her daughter grew up. Part of their relationship was, rather unusually perhaps, based on letter writing.

My Daughter, My Friend

At the age of six my daughter Julie wrote a letter to the tooth fairy and put it under her pillow with her tooth. I wrote back, telling her to be a good girl and always brush her teeth carefully. I didn't know we were starting a tradition.

By the time Julie was nine years old, she had discovered that handwritten notes could do more than welcome the tooth fairy. Once, after a heated discussion we'd had about why she couldn't buy a pair of clogs, Julie wrote the following:

Dear Mum,

Here are the reasons I want clogs:

1 You wanted boots for a long time and you finally got them.

2 If clogs hurt my feet that's my problem.

3 When Granny gave us money for Christmas she said we could get whatever we wanted with it.

Love, Julie

I gave in – and Julie learned the power of the written word.

Over the next few years, Julie and I exchanged notes about boys, homework, phone calls and housework. Some notes were apologies after shouting matches. Others were just happy thoughts spilling on to paper. When Julie was 13, she responded to a love-note of mine:

Dear Mum,

Your letters make me feel great no matter what kind of mood I'm in. Sometimes they even make me cry because they touch me so deeply. I'm really glad we have the kind of relationship that we do, even though we have our arguments. I suppose that's life with a teenager – or with a 39-year-old!

I love you. Julie

PS Writing my feelings down to you is much easier for me than trying to express them verbally.

Julie's postscript explained why the note system worked so well for us. She was going through the traumas of adolescence, and I was having some problems of my own. Writing was the most effective way for us to communicate our feelings.

One summer Julie left her razor by the bath where her five-year-old brother might have cut himself. After I pointed out her carelessness, I asked Julie what she thought her punishment should be. She stomped off in a huff, but an hour later left a note on the kitchen counter.

Dear Mum,

I'm sorry for being so thoughtless. For my punishment I will not:

1 Go to the shopping centre after school.

2 Watch television in the afternoon.

3 Snack before dinner.

She never left her razor by the bath again.

Two months later, on Julie's first day at a new school, we had a fight about whether it was appropriate for her to wear make-up.

That evening, I received a six-page, hand-written letter from her.

Dear Mum,

I'm sorry if I acted up this morning, but I really got angry. You didn't even give me a chance to say anything! If you would at least discuss things with me maybe it would be a little easier for us.

Instead of telling me how awful my eyes look, you could help to make them look better.

Page three contained all the logic my tormented teen could muster.

1 I think I'm very responsible and can learn to put make-up on in ways that both you and I would like.

2 I don't 'cake it on' like some of my friends do – I read the directions on the package and advice in magazine articles on how to apply it.

3 I'm growing up; I want to add to my looks and bring out my eyes.

4 How about a three-week trial period to test my ability to wear it?

Needless to say, my daughter wore make-up – discreetly – from then on. Her whole face seemed to light up, not only from the touch of blusher, but from the sense of freedom she had prised out of her mother.

Not long after that my husband and I separated. The next few months were chaotic. Besides trying to provide stability for my four children, I had to budget our funds and work longer hours. As my raw emotions caused my mothering skills to dwindle, Julie came to the rescue with this note.

Dear Mum,

I know you're going through a hard time and I wish I could make all your problems disappear. Unfortunately, I can only tell you how much I love you. We're all upset about the divorce, but you're still a great, helpful and loving mum.

Love, Jules

There were quite a few times that year when I took my frustrations out on the children. After one particularly nasty tirade, Julie dropped this message in my handbag for me to read at work:

Dear Mum,

I know things are difficult for you just now, and we all understand. I think you should go out more often to distract yourself. We are all growing up and have our own interests and friends. We'll

always be your kids and you won't lose us.
I love you! Jules

Just before her eighteenth birthday I asked Julie what she wanted. 'I'm working on it,' she said.

I should have known that Julie was writing me the letter of her life. Here's what some of it said:

Soon I will be living on my own at university.
I feel I have matured by following your rules with very few exceptions.
For my eighteenth birthday I would like to be treated and respected as a mature and responsible person. I'd like:
1 A later curfew or none at all.
2 Permission to make and receive telephone calls after 10pm.
3 The freedom to make my own decisions.
4 To be thought of as a close friend.

Now it was my turn to respond. I sat writing late into the night.

Dearest Julie,
Adulthood isn't a sudden jolt of freedom to do whatever you want. It is simply being responsible. If you believe you can behave like an adult, I will treat you as one.

I then answered her birthday proposition list, asking her to be considerate about curfews and phone calls. I agreed that she should make decisions and said I would offer advice only when requested. I ended with this:

Julie, I wish you a happy life filled with love and solid decisions based on solid values. I hope you continue to develop the many talents God has given you.
Happy birthday, my friend! Mum

My daughter left home for university a few years ago. I've missed her tremendously, but our tradition has pulled us through again – her letters have been wonderful!

PATRICIA LORENZ

TASK

18 We probably all have arguments, differences of opinion, perhaps even blazing rows with our parents occasionally.

Think of a time when you were having great difficulty persuading your parents of something; perhaps you wanted to go to a party which would not finish until very late; perhaps you wanted to buy some clothes of which they disapproved. Write a letter to your parents carefully explaining your point of view, as Julie would have done in the circumstances.

You will find that we have reprinted this article in your homework book and have set you the task of writing your parents' reply to your letter.

On the next few pages you will find some pictures of people of various ages.

TASK

19 Use one or more of the characters in the photographs as the focus of some personal imaginative writing.

You may write about a day in the life of your character, or a story, or you might see the face of someone with immense problems …

In your homework book we invite you to search out a photo of your own and to use it for your writing.

These next two extracts are from Shakespeare's plays, *The Merchant of Venice* and *King Lear*. We see here fathers with their sons. Old Gobbo is a blind man, the Duke of Gloucester is a man who has been brutally blinded. Launcelot Gobbo knows his father well and wants his help. Edgar hasn't seen his father for some time and is shocked by what he sees.

The Merchant of Venice

Act 2 Scene 2

Enter old GOBBO *with a basket.*

GOBBO:
Master young man, you I pray you, which is the way to Master Jew's?

LAUNCELOT (*Aside*):
O heavens! this is my true-begotten father, who, being more than sand-blind, high gravel-blind, knows me not. I will try confusions with him.

GOBBO:
Master young gentleman, I pray you, which is the way to Master Jew's?

LAUNCELOT:
Turn up on your right hand at the next turning, but at the next turning of all on your left; marry, at the very next turning turn of no hand, but turn down indirectly to the Jew's house.

GOBBO:
By God's sonties, 't will be a hard way to hit. Can you tell me whether one Launcelot that dwells with him, dwell with him or no?

LAUNCELOT:
Talk you of young *Master* Launcelot? (*Aside*) Mark me now, now will I raise the waters. (*To* GOBBO) Talk you of young *Master* Launcelot?

GOBBO:
No 'master', sir, but a poor man's son. His father, though I say 't, is an honest, exceeding poor man, and, God be thanked, well to live.

LAUNCELOT:
Well, let his father be what a will, we talk of young Master Launcelot.

GOBBO:
Your worship's friend and Launcelot, sir.

LAUNCELOT:
But I pray you, ergo old man, ergo I beseech you, talk you of young Master Launcelot?

GOBBO:
Of Launcelot, ain't please your mastership.

LAUNCELOT:
Ergo Master Launcelot. Talk not of Master Launcelot, father, for the young gentleman, according to fates and destinies, and such odd sayings, the Sisters Three, and such branches of learning, is indeed decreased, or, as you would say in plain terms, gone to heaven.

GOBBO:
Marry, God forbid! The boy was the very staff of my age, my very prop.

LAUNCELOT (*Aside*):
Do I look like a cudgel or a hovel-post, a staff, or a prop? – Do you know me, father?

GOBBO:
Alack the day! I know you not, young gentleman, but I pray you tell me, is my boy, God rest his soul, alive or dead?

LAUNCELOT:
Do you not know me, father?

GOBBO:
Alack, sir, I am sand-blind; I know you not.

LAUNCELOT:

Nay indeed, if you had your eyes you might fail of the knowing me; it is a wise father that knows his own child. Well, old man, I will tell you news of your son. (*Kneels with his back to* GOBBO) Give me your blessing; truth will come to light, murder cannot be hid long – a man's son may, but in the end truth will out.

GOBBO (*placing his hands on* LAUNCELOT's *head*):

Pray you, sir, stand up; I am sure you are not Launcelot my boy.

LAUNCELOT:

Pray you, let's have no more fooling about it, but give me your blessing; I am Launcelot your boy that was, your son that is, your child that shall be.

GOBBO:

I cannot think you are my son.

LAUNCELOT:

I know not what I shall think of that; but I am Launcelot, the Jew's man, and I am sure Margery your wife is my mother.

GOBBO:

Her name is Margery indeed; I'll be sworn, if thou be Launcelot, thou art mine own flesh and blood. (*He feels the back of* LAUNCELOT's *head*) Lord! (worshipped might He be), what a beard hast thou got! Though hast got more hair on thy chin than Dobbin my fill-horse has on his tail.

LAUNCELOT:

It should seem, then, that Dobbin's tail grows backward. I am sure he had more hair of his tail than I have of my face, when I last saw him.

GOBBO:

Lord, how art thou changed! How dost thou and thy master agree? I have brought him a present; how 'gree you now?

LAUNCELOT:

Well, well; but for mine own part, as I have set up my rest to run away, so I will not rest till I have run some ground; my master's a very Jew. Give him a present? Give him a halter! I am famished in his service. (*He makes* GOBBO *feel the fingers of his left hand, which he stretches out on his chest like ribs*) You may tell every finger I have with my ribs. Father, I am glad you are come; give me your present to one Master Bassanio, who indeed gives rare new liveries; if I serve not him, I will run as far as God has any ground. O rare fortune! Here comes the man; to him father, for I am a Jew if I serve the Jew any longer.

WILLIAM SHAKESPEARE

King Lear

Act 4 Scene 1

Enter EDGAR.
EDGAR:
    Yet better thus, and known to be contemn'd,
    Than, still contemn'd and flatter'd, to be worst.
    The lowest and most dejected thing of Fortune
    Stands still in esperance, lives not in fear:
    The lamentable change is from the best;
    The worst returns to laughter. Welcome, then,
    Thou unsubstantial air that I embrace:
    The wretch that thou has blown unto the worst
    Owes nothing to thy blasts. But who comes here?

Enter GLOUCESTER, *led by an old man.*

    My father, poorly led? World, world, O world!
    But that thy strange mutations make us hate thee,
    Life would not yield to age.
OLD MAN:
    O my good Lord!
    I have been your tenant, and your father's tenant,
    These fourscore years.
GLOUCESTER:
    Away, get thee away; good friend, be gone:
    Thy comforts can do me no good at all;
    Thee they may hurt.
OLD MAN:
    You cannot see your way.
GLOUCESTER:
    I have no way, and therefore want no eyes;
    I stumbled when I saw. Full oft 'tis seen,
    Our means secure us, and our mere defects
    Prove our commodities. Oh! dear son Edgar,
    The food of they abused father's wrath;
    Might I but live to see thee in my touch,
    I'd say I had eyes again.
OLD MAN:
    How now! Who's there?
EDGAR [*Aside*]:
    O Gods! Who is't can say 'I am at the worst'?
    I am worse than e'er I was.
OLD MAN:
    'Tis poor mad Tom.
EDGAR [*Aside*]:
    And worse I may be yet; the worst is not
    So long as we can say 'This is the worst.'
OLD MAN:
    Fellow, where goest?
GLOUCESTER:
    Is it a beggar-man?
OLD MAN:
    Madman and beggar too.

GLOUCESTER:
    He has some reason, else he could not beg.
    I'th'last night's storm I such a fellow saw,
    Which made me think a man a worm. My son
    Came then into my mind; and yet my mind
    Was then scarce friends with him. I have heard
    more since:
    As flies to wanton boys, are we to th'Gods;
    They kill us for their sport.
EDGAR [*Aside*]:
    How should this be?
    Bad is the trade that must play fool to sorrow,
    Ang'ring itself and others. [*Aloud*] Bless
      thee, master!
GLOUCESTER:
    Is that the naked fellow?
OLD MAN:
    Ay, my Lord.
GLOUCESTER:
    Then, prithee, get thee away. If, for my sake,
    Thou wilt o'ertake us, hence a mile or twain,
    I'th'way toward Dover, do it for ancient love;
    And bring some covering for this naked soul,
    Which I'll entreat to lead me.
OLD MAN:
    Alack, sir! he is mad.
GLOUCESTER:
    'Tis the times' plague, when madmen lead
    the blind.
    Do as I bid thee, or rather do thy pleasure;
    Above the rest, be gone.
OLD MAN:
    I'll bring him the best 'parel that I have,
    Come on't what will. [*Exit*]
GLOUCESTER:
    Sirrah, naked fellow, –
EDGAR:
    Poor Tom's a-cold. [*Aside*] I cannot daub
      it further.
GLOUCESTER:
    Come hither, fellow.
EDGAR [*Aside*]:
    And yet I must. Bless thy sweet eyes, they bleed.
GLOUCESTER:
    Know'st thou the way to Dover?
EDGAR:
    Both stile and gate, horse-way and foot-path.
    Poor Tom hath been scar'd out of his good wits:
    bless thee, good man's son, from the foul fiend!
    Five fiends have been in poor Tom at once; as
    Obidicut, of lust; Hoberdidance, prince of
    dumbness; Mahu, of stealing; Modo, of

murder; Flibbertigibbet, of mopping and
mowing; who since possesses chambermaids
and waiting-women. So, bless thee, master!
GLOUCESTER:
  Here, take this purse, thou whom the heav'ns'
    plagues
  Have humbled to all strokes: that I am wretched
  Makes thee the happier: Heavens, deal so still!
  Let the superfluous and lust-dieted man,
  That slaves your ordinance, that will not see
  Because he does not feel, feel your power quickly;
  So distribution should undo excess,
  And each man have enough. Dost thou
    know Dover?

EDGAR:
  Ay, master.
GLOUCESTER:
  There is a cliff, whose high and bending head
  Looks fearfully in the confined deep;
  Bring me but to the very brim of it,
  And I'll repair the misery thou dost bear
  With something rich about me; from that place
  I shall no leading need.
EDGAR:
  Give me thy arm:
  Poor Tom shall lead thee. [*Exeunt*]

WILLIAM SHAKESPEARE

TASKS

20 In groups of three or four talk about the following topics:
- what is happening in the extracts;
- how the old men are presented;
- how the young men behave;
- how you would feel if you were Old Gobbo or if you were Edgar.

21 One scene is humorous, the other tragic.
In your groups discuss how, for you, the humour and the tragedy are created effectively.

22 Following on from your discussions, in writing, compare these two scenes, taking note of what happens, of the characters and of the mood in each scene.

23 Write briefly explaining how you react to the way these sons treat their fathers.
Sometimes old people are respected and thought of as wise: at other times they are looked upon as foolish and out of date. Write about an old person you know and your feelings about him or her.

TIME OUT TASK!

Annotating your texts

More and more, perhaps all over the world, examinations are becoming 'open book', which means quite simply that you can have your books in the examination with you.

This is certainly the case in the majority of GCSE English Literature examinations.

You are also allowed to annotate your texts. The phrase which is generally used is 'within the body of the text'. What this means is that you are not allowed to write pages of notes on the spare pages which may be at the front and back of the book; you are certainly not allowed to stick pages of notes in your books.

So what can you do?

- You can write in the margins of the pages, perhaps notes like 'good description', 'this is a key point in the plot', 'very good example of the writer's style of characterisation', you may also put explanations of rather difficult bits.
- You may choose to use highlighter pens. For instance in a play you might choose to use one colour for a particular character and pick out a few quotations which you would use if you were writing a study of that character.

Don't believe that having the text in the room means that you don't have to know it.

Don't believe that annotating text is a substitute for knowing the text.

Don't annotate too much – because you'll waste too much time in the examination trying to read the text and your notes.

Printed below is an extract from an article which appeared in a Malaysian newspaper.

Textbooks at Exams

JITRA, Sat. – Primary and secondary school students will be allowed to refer to books when sitting in examinations by the year 2000, Education Ministry director-general Tan Sri Dr Wan Mohd Zahid Mohd Noordin said today.

Examination questions will be aimed at testing the students' intellectual skills and gauging their mental ability to process information rather than the memorising of facts.

At present, students sitting for the Sijil Pelajaran Malaysia and Sijil Tinggi Pelajaran Malaysia mathematics paper are allowed to refer to their logarithm book.

The students are also allowed to use calculators with basic arithemetic functions during the examination.

'In future, they will be allowed to refer to books. But if they have not done their revision, they will not know where or what book to look for to answer the questions.

'This is similar to law students who are also allowed to take their books into the examination halls,' he told reporters after presenting excellent service awards to teachers at the Institute Perguruan Darul Aman here today.

Wan Mohd Zahid said the Ministry realised that many students just memorised important facts and figures without actually understanding or being inquisitive on the subject matter.

'Once the new ruling comes into effect, students would have to be more analytical and their capability to process facts will be enhanced.

'The ruling will also promote reading habits as students will be required to understand thoroughly the subject for which they are studying if they are to pass,' he said.

SHARANJIT SINGH

Probably the most important things that are said in the article are:

- 'Examination questions will test a student's ability to process information rather than the memorising of facts.'
- 'if they have not done their revision they will not know where to look …'

END OF TIME OUT!

The extract overleaf is a scene from *David and Broccoli* by John Mortimer. David, a young boy, is afraid of Broccoli, who is the boxing instructor at David's school. David has made a mistake earlier and has taken his model glider into school. Broccoli has broken the glider. David goes to see his friend, the old man who looks after the boiler.

David and Broccoli

The school boiler-room

This small, warm shed is where David comes as a refuge to see his friend, the old gnome-like man who looks after the boiler and does odd jobs abut the school.

BOILERMAN:
(*looking at the broken glider*) I'll give it a touch of glue when I've got a moment.

DAVID:
He did it on purpose.

BOILERMAN:
Broccoli? (*He puts the glider on a shelf.*) Scares you, doesn't he? (*David nods.*) When's the next lesson?

DAVID:
Thursday… I wish there wasn't a next Thursday.

BOILERMAN:
Then it's… over the top? Like in the nineteen-fourteen. Over the top tomorrow, they said… and I thought, tomorrow is a day that won't ever be missed. Let's go to sleep and wake up next summer. Of course they offered you comforts, tots of rum, nice hymn, new pair of khaki mittens knitted by her old ladyship in some nice, safe dugout in Wimbledon. There was I, like you, boy, staring straight in the face of danger…

DAVID:
What did you do?

BOILERMAN:
Well, you had three alternatives. Go through with it, shoot yourself in the foot, or run away. Personally, I took my courage in both hands, and I runned away.

DAVID:
That was brave…

BOILERMAN:
Damned stupid. I runned in the wrong direction. Slap into the Jerry trenches. Saw a young chap there and I said, 'For God's sake give me a whiff of gas, just to put me under for the duration'. Of course, not being educated, he couldn't understand what I was saying. He shot me in the hand, just lovely. They put me on cook-house duties after that. They got some terrible meals. There was one Christmas dinner… Not fit for human consumption. We gave it to the officers….

DAVID:
Does it hurt much? Being shot in the hand?

BOILERMAN:
No… irritates a bit, that's all. Here. Don't you go and get ideas, now. Don't you go to the length of self-inflicted wounds… He's not so bad, old Broccoli. Well, just a bit horrible, perhaps. He can't help that. It's his living. He comes in here, with those magazines what he reads… and talks about the end of the world….

DAVID:
The what?

BOILERMAN:
He's got it fixed for the year three thousand. Says it's a mathematical certainty. Well, it's got to end some time, hasn't it? I mean, it just can't go on and on, stands to reason.

DAVID:
No.

BOILERMAN:
But he gives us till the year three thousand….

DAVID:
That's a long time….

BOILERMAN:
It'll see him out, anyway.

DAVID:
I wish it was next Thursday!

BOILERMAN:
What?

DAVID:
The end of the world.

BOILERMAN:
Why… Oh, I see. To stop the lesson. (*David nods.*) You'd carry it to those lengths?

DAVID:
If I could put a stop to it….

BOILERMAN:
You've got a very brilliant brain, I don't doubt.

DAVID:
Quite clever….

BOILERMAN:
Which is where you'll finally be one up on Mr Smith.

DAVID:
(*incredulous*) I will?

BOILERMAN:
I don't doubt that, boy. But leave the rest of the universe alone, Will you? Do me a great favour? Leave the world turning until next Saturday week. I haven't got my peas planted, not yet….

JOHN MORTIMER

TASK

24 David has been told by the boilerman, 'you've got a very brilliant brain' and that this will ultimately allow him to outsmart Mr Smith (Broccoli). David goes off home and begins thinking. What is he thinking? Continue the story for a few pages. You may write in play form if you wish.

You will find this scene reprinted in your homework book with a further invitation to take the story on.

As we grow older we perhaps make mistakes which we live to regret. This article, which is about a play, also shows that the idea for the play came from one such mistake. Perhaps the people in the article are lucky as, now older, they are able to recover some of the time they lost when they were apart.

Mother in half a million

Dramatist Sue Schilperoort and the daughter she gave up for adoption at eight days old were recently reunited. They talk to **Reva Klein** about the emotional legacy of their lives apart.

The first time Helen Nicholls heard her mother's voice was on a telephone answering machine. It was on her 21st birthday last June. The last time the two had been together, Helen was eight days old and her mother, Sue Schilperoort, was a 15-year-old schoolgirl who unwillingly handed her baby over to a social worker for adoption.

For months after the birth, Sue cried herself to sleep. For years after that, she would think of her daughter every day, trying to imagine what she looked like, celebrating her birthdays with symbolic gestures such as planting a tree. But Helen was unaware of the tears and torment that her birth mother had experienced since the day she gave up her new-born baby. Until last June.

If you've ever doubted that saying about truth being stranger than fiction, read on. Sue and Helen finally met an hour before the premiere of *Half a Million Women*, a play written and directed by Sue. This isn't just any play. It is the autobiographical story of a schoolgirl who gives her baby up for adoption and the legacy of that action on the mother as an adult. The reunion would have been dramatic enough in itself. Watching the play side by side an hour after being reunited was almost unbearably emotional for mother and daughter.

Half a Million Women, which is touring schools, colleges and theatres, is performed by Sue's theatre company, Women's Issues. It is a powerful exploration of teenage pregnancy and adoption from myriad angles. The teenage Sue – called Sarah in the play – is presented as a young and naïve character who believes her boyfriend when he says that if you 'do it' standing up it's safe. She also believes that if she doesn't think about her pregnancy, it will go away.

Much of what she is going through is articulated through an older Sarah, reading her journal out loud. The other main character is Sarah's mother, hidebound by convention, fearful of her daughter's life being ruined by an accidental pregnancy. She sees the baby as a problem that needs to be dealt with quickly and firmly.

Young Sarah has no say in what happens. She is not asked what she thinks would be best. Her mother bludgeons her into signing the adoption papers. She spends most of her long, frightening labour alone. When the baby is delivered, there are no congratulations, no comfort, no reflected joy in the faces of those around her. She is stitched up 'like a piece of leather'.

It is through the older Sarah that we discover the extent to which the adoption was against her will, how great was her love for her baby and how searing the pain of being wrenched apart from her. 'Hoping that you'll find me on your 18th birthday,' she reads from her journal as the younger, recently bereft Sarah promises: 'I'll follow women with prams, in case it's you inside. I'll turn white when I hear that a school bus has crashed, in case it's you involved.'

The impact of the piece is immense, even without the two real-life central players in the audience. Despite its second act, which has been developed as a workshop for schools (in which scenes are reworked and each of the characters are questioned by the audience), it's not your typical pedagogic health education theatre project, nor does it belong to the yawningly familiar kitchen-sink-drama genre. While there are intentional stereotypes – the heavy-handed mother; the even-handed GP – the issues depicted in the play are far from black and white.

Instead, Sue Schilperoort has created a piece of theatre that presents the subject of teenage pregnancy and adoption and then examines the many grey areas, looking at implications without moralising about the 'should haves' and the 'shouldn't haves'. The central conflict, of course, is between Sarah's desire to keep the baby and her mother's insistence that it should be given up for adoption. The young and adult Sarah and the mother tell the audience – not each other – how they feel.

In the workshop session, a 15-year-old girl in the audience asks the adult Sarah character is she has any regrets. She answers: 'I still feel I should have kept the baby, even now in my 30s. I spent a long time blaming my parents for what happened. Now, I think they're victims. I understand the enormous social pressures my mother was under. But my daughter is a big part of me that's missing.'

For her part, the mother remains resolute under questioning. 'I did what was best for my daughter. She hadn't even done her O'levels yet. I worked and I wouldn't have

been able to look after the baby. She would have had no future if she'd kept it. She was a child herself.' The audience, as a result, sees both sides: it is Sarah's baby and it is her life, but what kind of life would she have had if she had kept the baby?

The object of the play is not to provide answers, but to air issues in a way that has rarely been done before. The title refers to the number of women who have had children whom they gave up for adoption. Three-quarters of a million people in this country are adopted but, say Sue and Helen, there is little in the way of support or reference points for the mothers or children. Sue hopes that her play will give both the strength to come out, address their pent-up unease and pain and try to resolve it through counselling, as both Sue and Helen have done.

What happened in real life where the play leaves off could be a dramatised sequel for the play: for Sue, how a miscarriage 18 months ago hurtled her back to the loss of her daughter to the point of temporarily 'falling apart', how mother and daughter came together and effortlessly found a familial closeness, how Helen has integrated Sue into her life and vice versa; the impact of their new relationship on Helen's adoptive parents. The process of writing about such gruelling intimate material was in itself an intense experience.

The reunion changed the lives of both women. For Sue, a former teacher who is now an economics lecturer and dramatist living in Cambridge, it has been liberating as well as exhilarating.

'Before I met Helen, I felt that I'd been looking backwards for the whole of my life, but there was something back there that I

couldn't reach.

'It's what's called an adoption complex – you never want the wound to heal because to do so would mean denying the experience altogether. But now, for the first time in my life, I feel I can stop looking behind me.' Sue's baby son Ben, born two months after she was reunited with her daughter, is helping that process.

For Helen, a student in art and design at Wolverhampton, meeting her birth mother has been an ecstatic experience, but also a difficult one. Where Sue has had 21 years to work through, in her words, 'the emotional stuff', Helen is only just confronting the anger, the insecurity and the fear of being left, all of which have erupted since meeting Sue. Her life had been normal and happy. Her adoptive parents had told her early on that she had been adopted but it had not been talked about. 'Maybe I never brought it up because I didn't want to upset them, make them feel that they weren't good enough parents. But at the same time, I had always known that someday I would meet my birth mother.'

There was yet more drama as Helen attempted to track Sue down. Two years before they met, she had asked for and received social services reports, which gave her parents' names and their address at the time of her birth, in a small village near Aberdare in South Wales. She did nothing with that information until three weeks before her 21st birthday when her boyfriend Martin egged her on to investigate.

They went to the village and advertised in the local paper. In response, Helen was directed to an address where her father was said to live. 'I wasn't sure if I wanted to go ahead with it or not. I felt like stopping the car and getting out. But I didn't. I knocked on the door and a young-looking man answered. I knew instantly that he was my father. I couldn't speak to him. Martin made small talk and then we left.

'After that, we went to the *Cynon Valley News* and suggested they write a feature about me looking for my parents. I felt I had nothing to lose. My great-aunt responded to the article, writing to me that my father had pieced together that it was me who had come to the door after seeing the article in the paper. He had known that Sue had been pregnant, although Sue hadn't known that he'd known, and hadn't been 'interested.''

The newspaper article helped Helen to make the final links. Two days before her birthday, she received a card. It said 'Happy 21st. I'm your mum's sister.' The next day she received a letter from Sue saying that she had been trying to call for three days.

When the two finally spoke on the telephone, it was strange. Sue says to Helen, 'I never pictured you till we spoke on the phone. The only image I had of you was a photograph that I requested from social services after the birth. It was a three-month-old baby. Since then, I would look at girls of different ages and think 'oh, that's what 12-year-old girls look like', wondering if you looked like them.'

For Helen, 'it was like we'd rediscovered best friends. When I put the phone down, I felt that I had found something that had been missing all my life. I felt whole.' Their first meeting lasted 10 days. Helen stayed with Sue, who was seven months pregnant, and her Dutch husband, Bert. From the first moment, they felt a closeness that neither had anticipated. 'We've found that we're very alike, sometimes uncannily so,' smiles Helen. 'We both sit on our hands, we crack the same jokes – at times we seem to mirror each other.' There was also, they found, a huge expanse of emotional landscape to cover, which continues to this day. 'One of the first things I asked Sue was whether she could have done all she did in her life if she had kept me.'

For the first few months, they saw each other every weekend. Helen was there when Sue brought Ben home from hospital and began to help look after him. Ben clearly symbolises a bridge with the past for both of them. Watching Ben getting all the cuddles, kisses and love that she never received from Sue must affect Helen in ways she is not yet able to express outwardly. But Sue can. She remembers her precious few days with her baby daughter. 'I had her with me in the hospital for eight days. I went form being exhilarated and proud, playing mummies and babies with her, to preparing myself for her being taken away. I remember I wept all night when the nurses took her away because they were afraid I'd roll over her.'

Helen, listening and no doubt picturing these scenes, bounds across the room to hug and kiss her mum, as she does frequently. It must be an odd thing to hear how much your mother grieved over losing you, to know how much pain she felt and to have been oblivious all those years, secure in the love of adoptive parents.

Now, Helen is having to handle all the latest emotions that have been stirred up as a result of this reunion as well as deal with the upset that this has caused her adoptive parents, let alone tell them when she had met Sue.

They found out the day before the story of the reunion was told in a national newspaper. Helen and Martin tore down the motorway from Wolverhampton to Cornwall, where her parents were caravanning, to warn them. Not, perhaps, the best way to have broached the subject. There are clearly still bruised feelings all round. A meeting has yet to take place between Sue and the Nicholls but Helen believes that it is inevitable.

Sue understands the sensitivities and shares them. 'I'd like us to be an extended part of Helen's family, but I can understand how it can be threatening to Helen's mum. I don't want to take her away from her family – I just want to add to it.'

She turns and asks Helen, believing she knows the answer: 'You don't want me to play a mother role to you, do you?' To which Helen replies, emphatically, 'Yes!'

TASKS

25 In class, discuss the passage.
- Was the mother right to let her daughter go?
- In the daughter's place would you have been so understanding?
- What about the feelings of the adoptive parents?

There are other discussion points you might want to raise yourselves.

26 Describe and explain the attitude of the mother in the play.

27 The reunion of Helen and Sue was clearly very traumatic and emotional. In your own words describe:
- how the reunion came about;
- the initial reactions of the two women;
- how their relationship has developed.

Say what you think of the event.

28 Some of you will have watched the television programme 'Surprise, Surprise'. You will know that sometimes events similar to the reunion in this article happen in front of you on the programme.

Imagine you are on your way to meet a long-lost relative whom you haven't seen for at least ten years. Describe your feelings as you are on your journey and what happens when you finally meet.

TIME OUT TASK!

Be aware of your audience

If you look through this classbook you will find that very frequently, when there is a writing task, you will be told who you are writing for, who your audience is.

In the National Curriculum Orders it says very clearly that you should have the opportunity 'to write for an extended range of readers, eg the teacher, the class, other children, adults in the school or community, imagined audiences'.

The whole point is that you are going to write differently, depending on who you are writing for. You will write different styles of letters depending on whether you are writing to your headteacher or Auntie Nellie. (It would probably be inadvisable to end the letter to your headteacher – 'Love and kisses'!)

Think of your audience as you try one or two of the following:
- You have just done something absolutely dreadful and are being excluded from school. As your headteacher, write a letter to your parents explaining the action which has been taken and requesting an interview.
- Write a thank you letter to an elderly relative of whom you are very fond.
- You are the sports reporter for your local newspaper. Your local football team has just lost a very controversial match. Write your report but remember that the majority of your readers will support the local team.
- You want to encourage young children to visit the library and to read more. Compose a handout which will be distributed in primary schools.

■ You are writing an examination answer. Choose a character from one of the books you are studying for GCSE English Literature and write a study of her or him.

It's a mixed bag of things to do. It is a mixed bag of audiences and, therefore, should produce a variety of writing styles.

END OF TIME OUT!

Some of you may well have read *Animal Farm* by George Orwell. It is a story where animals take over the running of a farm from a brutal, inefficient farmer. One of the hardest-working animals on the farm is Boxer, a carthorse. He has been promised a comfortable retirement by the pigs who are running the farm. However, it becomes clear that their real attitude to old animals is that they might as well be got rid of as they are no use.

Read the extract from *Animal Farm* which is printed on the following pages.

Animal Farm

After his hoof had healed up, Boxer worked harder than ever. Indeed, all the animals worked like slaves that year. Apart from the regular work of the farm, and the rebuilding of the windmill, there was the schoolhouse for the young pigs, which was started in March. Sometimes the long hours on insufficient food were hard to bear, but Boxer never faltered. In nothing that he said or did was there any sign that his strength was not what it had been. It was only his appearance that was a little altered; his hide was less shiny than it had used to be, and his great haunches seemed to have shrunken. The others said, 'Boxer will pick up when the spring grass comes on'; but the spring came and Boxer grew no fatter. Sometimes on the slope leading to the top of the quarry, when he braced his muscles against the weight of some vast boulder, it seemed that nothing kept him on his feet except the will to continue. At such times his lips were seen to form the words, 'I will work harder'; he had no voice left. Once again Clover and Benjamin warned him to take care of his health, but Boxer did not care what happened so long as a good store of stone was accumulated before he went on pension.

Late one evening in the summer, a sudden rumour ran round the farm that something had happened to Boxer. He had gone out alone to drag a load of stone down to the windmill. And sure enough, the rumour was true. A few minutes later

two pigeons came racing in with the news: 'Boxer has fallen! He is lying on his side and can't get up!'

About half the animals on the farm rushed out to the knoll where the windmill stood. There lay Boxer, between the shafts of the cart, his neck stretched out, unable even to raise his head. His eyes were glazed, his sides matted with sweat. A thin stream of blood had trickled out of his mouth. Clover dropped to her knees at his side.

'Boxer!' she cried, 'how are you?'

'It is my lung,' said Boxer in a weak voice. 'It does not matter. I think you will be able to finish the windmill without me. There is a pretty good store of stone accumulated. I had only another month to go in any case. To tell you the truth, I had been looking forward to my retirement. And perhaps, as Benjamin is growing old too, they will let him retire at the same time and be a companion to me.'

'We must get help at once,' said Clover. 'Run, somebody, and tell Squealer what has happened.'

All the other animals immediately raced back to the farmhouse to give Squealer the news. Only Clover remained, and Benjamin, who lay down at Boxer's side, and, without speaking, kept the flies off him with his long tail. After about a quarter of an hour Squealer appeared, full of sympathy and concern. He said that Comrade Napoleon had learned with the very deepest distress of this misfortune to one of the most loyal workers on the farm, and was already making arrangements to send Boxer to be treated in the hospital at Willingdon. The animals felt a little uneasy at this. Except for Mollie and Snowball, no other animal had ever left the farm, and they did not like to think of their sick comrade in the hands of human beings. However, Squealer easily convinced them that the veterinary surgeon in Willingdon could treat Boxer's case more satisfactorily than could be done on the farm. And about half an hour later, when Boxer had somewhat recovered, he was with difficulty got on to his feet, and managed to limp back to his stall, where Clover and Benjamin had prepared a good bed of straw for him.

For the next two days Boxer remained in his stall. The pigs had sent out a large bottle of pink medicine which they had found in the medicine chest in the bathroom, and Clover administered it to Boxer twice a day after meals. In the evenings she lay in his stall and talked to him, while Benjamin kept the flies off him. Boxer professed not to be sorry for what had happened. If he made a good recovery, he might expect to live another three years, and he looked forward to the peaceful days that he would spend in the corner of the big pasture. It would be the first time that he had had leisure to study and improve his mind. He intended, he said, to devote the rest of his life to learning the remaining twenty-two letters of the alphabet.

However, Benjamin and Clover could only be with Boxer after working hours, and it was in the middle of the day when the van came to take him away. The animals were all at work weeding turnips under the supervision of a pig, when they were astonished to see Benjamin come galloping from the direction of the farm buildings, braying at the top of his voice. It was the first time that they had ever seen Benjamin excited – indeed, it was the first time that anyone had ever seen him gallop. 'Quick, quick!' he shouted. 'Come at once! They're taking Boxer away!' Without waiting for orders from the pig, the animals broke off work and raced back to the farm buildings. Sure enough, there in the yard was a large closed van, drawn by two horses, with lettering on its site and a sly-looking man in a low-crowned bowler hat sitting on the driver's seat. And Boxer's stall was empty.

The animals crowded round the van. 'Good-bye Boxer!' they chorused, 'good-bye!'

'Fools! Fools!' shouted Benjamin, prancing round them and stamping the earth with his small hoofs. 'Fools! Do you not see what is written on the side of that van?'

That gave the animals pause, and there was a hush. Muriel began to spell out the words. But Benjamin pushed her aside and in the midst of a deadly silence he read:

' "Alfred Simonds, Horse Slaughterer and Glue-Boiler, Willingdon. Dealer in Hides and Bone-Meal. Kennels Supplied." Do you not understand what that means? They are taking Boxer to the knacker's!'

A cry of horror burst from all the animals. At this moment the man on the box whipped up his horses and the van moved out of the yard at a smart trot. All the animals followed, crying out at the tops of their voices. Clover forced her way to the front. The van began to gather speed. Clover tried to stir her stout limbs to a gallop, and achieved a canter. 'Boxer!' she cried. 'Boxer! Boxer! Boxer!' and just at this moment, as though he had heard the uproar outside, Boxer's face, with the white stripe down his nose, appeared at the small window at the back of the van.

'Boxer!' cried Clover in a terrible voice. 'Boxer! Get out! Get out quickly! They are taking you to your death!'

GEORGE ORWELL

TASKS

29   We learn of the genuine concern of friends for a colleague who is getting old and of the phoney dishonesty of others from this passage. Explain in your own words what we learn.

30   How, from the information which we can take from this extract, would you sum up the character of Boxer?

31   Imagine that you have a pet dog which is getting very old and ill and the vet advises that it should be put to sleep. Write about your thoughts as you try to make up your mind what to do.

DEATH AND DESTRUCTION

This may not sound like a very cheerful subject for study or title for a chapter. It isn't really! However, death is inevitable for everyone; it concerns everyone; everyone thinks about death; everyone is fascinated by death. And sometimes death and dying test human beings and lead others to admire them. What about destruction? If you watch the television news you know that there only has to be a disaster, natural or man-made, and the cameras will be there immediately filming the destruction because, again, everyone will be fascinated by it, and the television producers know it!

ENGLISH IN THE NATIONAL CURRICULUM:

Key Skills you will cover in this chapter

☑ You will be asked to select information from the texts and other stimulus material you have studied.

☑ The National Curriculum talks of implicit and explicit meaning. You will read passages and will not only be asked to explain the straightforward facts, you will be asked to interpret those facts as well.

☑ You will be looking at good quality literature and, through studying it, will be able to understand and explain why it is good literature.

☑ You will be asked to write clear and concise explanations of what you have read.

☑ You will be asked to summarise the content of what you have read.

DH Lawrence, who was born in 1885, grew up in the coalmining area of Nottinghamshire. In the short story *Odour of Chrysanthemums* he wrote about the death of a miner. In part one of the story he writes of the miner's wife, waiting for her husband at the end of the day.

Odour of Chrysanthemums

The small locomotive engine, Number 4, came clanking, stumbling down from Selston with seven full wagons. It appeared round the corner with loud threats of speed, but the colt that it startled from among the gorse, which still flickered indistinctly in the raw afternoon, out-distanced it at a canter. A woman, walking up the railway line to Underwood, drew back into the hedge, held her basket aside, and watched the footplate of the engine advancing. The trucks thumped heavily past, one by one, with slow inevitable movement, as she stood insignificantly trapped between the jolting black wagons and the hedge; then they curved away towards the coppice where the withered oak leaves dropped noiselessly, while the birds, pulling at the scarlet hips beside the track, made off into the dusk that had already crept into the spinney. In the open, the smoke from the engine sank and cleaved to the rough grass. The fields were dreary and forsaken, and in the marshy strip that led to the whimsey, a reedy pit-pond, the fowls had already abandoned their run among the alders, to roost in the tarred fowl-house. The pit-bank loomed up beyond the pond, flames like red sores licking its ashy sides, in the afternoon's stagnant light. Just beyond rose the tapering chimneys and the clumsy black headstocks of Brinsley Colliery. The two wheels were spinning fast up against the sky, and the winding engine rapped out its little spasms. The miners were being turned up.

The engine whistled as it came into the wide bay of railway lines beside the colliery, where rows of trucks stood in harbour.

Miners, single, trailing and in groups, passed like shadows diverging home. At the edge of the ribbed level of sidings squat a low cottage, three steps down from the cinder track. A large bony vine clutched at the house, as if to claw down the tiled roof. Round the bricked yard grew a few wintry primroses. Beyond, the long garden sloped down to a bush-covered brook course. There were some twiggy apple trees, winter-crack trees, and ragged cabbages. Beside the path hung dishevelled pink chrysanthemums, like pink clothes hung on bushes. A woman came stooping out of the felt-covered fowl-house, half-way down the garden. She closed and padlocked the door, then drew herself erect, having brushed some bits from her white apron.

She was a tall woman of imperious mien, handsome, with definite black eyebrows. Her smooth black hair was parted exactly. For a few moments she stood watching the miners as they passed along the railway: then she turned towards the brook course. Her face was calm and set, her mouth was closed with disillusionment. After a moment she called:

'John!' There was no answer. She waited, and then said distinctly:

'Where are you?'

'Here!' replied a child's sulky voice from among the bushes. The woman looked piercingly through the dusk.

'Are you at that brook?' she asked sternly.

For answer the child showed himself before the raspberry-canes that rose like whips. He was a small, sturdy boy of five. He stood quite still, defiantly.

'Oh!' said the mother, conciliated. 'I thought you were down at that wet brook – and you remember what I told you—'

The boy did not move or answer.

'Come, come on in,' she said more gently, 'it's getting dark. There's your grandfather's engine coming down the line!'

The lad advanced slowly, with resentful, taciturn movement. He was dressed in trousers and waistcoat of cloth that was too thick and hard for the size of the garments. They were evidently cut down from a man's clothes.

As they went slowly towards the house he tore at the ragged wisps of chrysanthemums and dropped the petals in handfuls along the path.

'Don't do that – it does look nasty,' said his mother. He refrained, and she, suddenly pitiful, broke off a twig with three or four wan flowers and held them against her face. When mother and son reached the yard her hand hesitated, and instead of laying the flower aside, she pushed it in her apron-band. The mother and son stood at the foot of the three steps looking across the bay of lines at the passing home of the miners. The trundle of the small train was imminent. Suddenly the engine loomed past the house and came to a stop opposite the gate.

The engine-driver, a short man with round grey beard, leaned out of the cap high above the woman.

'Have you got a cup of tea?' he said in a cheery, hearty fashion.

It was her father. She went in, saying she would mash. Directly, she returned.

'I didn't come to see you on Sunday,' began the little grey-bearded man.

'I didn't expect you,' said his daughter.

The engine-driver winced; then, reassuming his cheery, airy manner, he said:

'Oh, have you heard then? Well, and what do you think—?'

'I think it is soon enough,' she replied.

At her brief censure the little man made an impatient gesture, and said coaxingly, yet with dangerous coldness:

'Well, what's a man to do? It's no sort of life for a man of my years, to sit at my own hearth like a stranger. And if I'm going to marry again it may as well be soon as late – what does it matter to anybody?'

The woman did not reply, but turned and went into the house. The man in the engine-cab stood assertive, till she returned with a cup of tea and a piece of bread and butter on a plate. She went up the steps and stood near the footplate of the hissing engine.

'You needn't 'a' brought me bread an' butter,' said her father. 'But a cup of tea' – he sipped appreciatively – 'it's very nice.' He sipped for a moment or two, then: 'I hear as Walter's got another bout on,' he said.

'When hasn't he?' said the woman bitterly.

'I heerd tell of him in the "Lord Nelson" braggin' as he was going to spend that b—— afore he went: half a sovereign that was.'

'When?' asked the woman.

'A' Sat'day night – I know that's true.'

'Very likely,' she laughed bitterly. 'He gives me twenty-three shillings.'

'Aye, it's a nice thing, when a man can do nothing with his money but make a beast of himself!' said the grey-whiskered man. The woman turned her head away. Her father swallowed the last of his tea and handed her the cup.

'Aye,' he sighed, wiping his mouth. 'It's a settler, it is—'

He put his hand on the lever. The little engine strained and groaned, and the train rumbled towards the crossing. The woman again looked across the metals. Darkness was settling over the spaces of the railway and trucks: the miners, in grey sombre groups, were still passing home. The winding engine pulsed hurriedly, with brief pauses. Elizabeth Bates looked at the dreary flow of men, then she went indoors. Her husband did not come.

The kitchen was small and full of firelight; red coals piled glowing up the chimney mouth. All the life of the room seemed in the white, warm hearth and the steel fender reflecting the red fire. The cloth was laid for tea; cups glinted in the shadows. At the back, where the lowest stairs protruded into the room, the boy sat struggling with a knife and a piece of whitewood. He was almost hidden in the shadow. It was half-past four. They had but to await the father's coming to begin tea. As the mother watched her son's sullen little struggle with the wood, she saw herself in his silence and pertinacity; she saw the father in her child's indifference to all but himself. She seemed to be occupied by her husband. He had probably gone past his home, slung past his own door, to drink before he came in, while his dinner spoiled and wasted in waiting. She glanced at the clock, then took the potatoes to strain them in the yard. The garden and fields beyond the brook were closed in uncertain darkness. When she rose with the saucepan, leaving the drain steaming into the night behind her, she saw the yellow lamps were lit along the high road that went up the hill away beyond the space of the railway lines and the field.

Then again she watched the men trooping home, fewer now and fewer.

Indoors the fire was sinking and the room was dark red. The woman put her saucepan on the hob, and set a batter-pudding near the mouth of the oven. Then she stood unmoving. Directly, gratefully, came quick young steps to the door. Someone hung on the latch of a moment, then a little girl entered and began pulling off her outdoor things, dragging a mass of curls, just ripening from gold to brown, over her eyes with her hat.

Her mother chid her for coming late from school, and said she would have to keep her at home the dark winter days.

'Why, mother, it's hardly a bit dark yet. The lamp's not lighted, and my father's not home.'

'No, he isn't. But it's a quarter to five! Did you see anything of him?'

The child became serious. She looked at her mother with large, wistful blue eyes.

'No, mother, I've never seen him. Why? has he come up an' gone past, to Old Brinsley? He hasn't, mother, 'cos I never saw him.'

'He'd watch that,' said the mother bitterly, 'he'd take care as you didn't see him. But you may depend upon it, he's seated in the "Prince o' Wales". He wouldn't be this late.'

The girl looked at her mother piteously.

'Let's have our teas, mother, should we?' said she.

The mother called John to table. She opened the door once more and looked out across the darkness of the lines. All was deserted: she could not hear the winding-engines.

'Perhaps,' she said to herself, 'he's stopped to get some ripping done.'

They sat down to tea. John, at the end of the table near the door, was almost lost in the darkness. Their faces were hidden from each other. The girl crouched against the fender slowly moving a thick piece of bread before the fire. The lad, his face a dusky mark on the shadow, sat watching her who was transfigured in the red glow.

'I do think it's beautiful to look in the fire,' said the child.

'Do you?' said her mother. 'Why?'

'It's so red, and full of little caves – and it feels so nice, and you can fair smell it.'

'It'll want mending directly,' replied her mother, 'and then if your father comes he'll carry on and say there never is a fire when a man comes home sweating from the pit. A public-house is always warm enough.'

There was silence till the boy said complainingly: 'Make haste, our Annie.'

'Well, I am doing! I can't make the fire do it no faster, can I?'

'She keeps wafflin' it about so's to make 'er slow,' grumbled the boy.

'Don't have such an evil imagination, child,' replied the mother.

Soon the room was busy in the darkness with the crisp sound of crunching. The mother ate very little. She drank her tea determinedly, and sat thinking. When she rose her anger was evident in the stern unbending of her head. She looked at the pudding in the fender, and broke out:

'It is a scandalous thing as a man can't even come home to his dinner! If it's crozzled up to a cinder I don't see why I should care. Past his very door he goes to get to a public-house, and here I sit with his dinner waiting for him—'

She went out. As she dropped piece after piece of coal on the red fire, the shadows fell on the walls, till the room was almost in total darkness.

'I canna see,' grumbled the invisible John. In spite of herself, the mother laughed.

'You know the way to your mouth,' she said. She set the dustpan outside the door. When she came again like a shadow on the hearth, the lad repeated, complainingly sulkily:

'I canna see.'

'Good gracious!' cried the mother irritably, 'you're as bad as your father if it's a bit dusk!'

Nevertheless, she took a paper spill from a sheaf on the mantelpiece and proceeded to light the lamp that hung from the ceiling in the middle of the room. As she reached up, her figure displayed itself just rounding with maternity.

'Oh, mother—!' exclaimed the girl.

'What?' said the woman, suspended in the act of putting the lamp-glass over the flame. The copper reflector shone handsomely on her, as she stood with uplifted arm, turning to face her daughter.

'You've got a flower in your apron!' said the child, in a little rapture at this unusual event.

'Goodness me!' exclaimed the woman, relieved. 'One would think the house was afire.' She replaced the glass and waited a moment before turning up the wick. A pale shadow was seen floating vaguely on the floor.

'Let me smell!' said the child, still rapturously, coming forward and putting her face to her mother's waist.

'Go along, silly!' said the mother, turning up the lamp. The light revealed their suspense so that the woman felt it almost unbearable. Annie was still bending at her waist. Irritably, the mother took the flowers out from her apron-band.

'Oh, mother – don't take them out!' Annie cried, catching her hand and trying to replace the spring.

'Such nonsense!' said the mother, turning away. The child put the pale chrysanthemums to her lips, murmuring:

'Don't they smell beautiful!'

Her mother gave a short laugh.

'No,' she said, 'not to me. It was chrysanthemums when I married him, and chrysanthemums when you were born, and the first time they ever brought him home drink, he'd got brown chrysanthemums in his button-hole.'

She looked at the children. Their eyes and their parted lips were wondering. The mother sat rocking in silence for some time. Then she looked at the clock.

'Twenty minutes to six!' In a tone of fine bitter carelessness she continued: 'Eh, he'll not come now till they bring him. There he'll stick! But he needn't come rolling in here in his pit-dirt, for I won't wash him. He can lie on the floor— Eh, what a fool I've been, what a fool! And this is what I came here for, to this dirty hole, rats and all, for him to slink past his very door. Twice last week – he's begun now—'

She silenced herself, and rose to clear the table.

While for an hour or more the children played, subduedly intent, fertile of imagination, united in fear of the mother's wrath, and in dread of their father's home-coming. Mrs Bates sat in her rocking-chair making a 'singlet' of thick cream-coloured flannel, which gave a dull wounded sound as she tore off the grey edge. She worked at her sewing with energy, listening to the children, and her anger wearied itself, lay down to rest, opening its eyes from time to time and steadily watching, its ears raised to listen. Sometimes even her anger quailed and shrank, and the mother suspended her sewing, tracing the footsteps that thudded along the sleepers outside; she would lift her head sharply to bid the children 'hush', but she recovered herself in time, and the footsteps went past the gate, and the children were not flung out of their play-world.

But at last Annie sighed, and gave in. She glanced at her wagon of slippers, and loathed the game. She turned plaintively to her mother.

'Mother!' – but she was inarticulate.

John crept out like a frog under the sofa. His mother glanced up.

'Yes,' she said, 'just look at those shirt-sleeves!'

The boy held them out to survey them, saying nothing. Then somebody called in a hoarse voice away down the line, and suspense bristled in the room, till two people had gone by outside, talking.

'It is time for bed,' said the mother.

'My father hasn't come,' wailed Annie plaintively. But her mother was primed with courage.

'Never mind. They'll bring him when he does come – like a log.' She meant there would be no scene. 'And he may sleep on the floor till he wakes himself. I know he'll not go to work tomorrow after this!'

The children had their hands and faces wiped with a flannel. They were very quiet. When they had put on their night-dresses, they said their prayers, the boy mumbling. The mother looked down at them, at the brown silken bush of intertwining curls in the nape of the girl's neck, at the little black head of the lad, and her heart burst with anger at their father, who caused all three such distress. The children hid their faces in her skirts for comfort.

When Mrs Bates came down, the room was strangely empty, with a tension of expectancy. She took up her sewing and stitched for some time without raising her head. Meantime her anger was tinged with fear.

D H LAWRENCE

TASKS

1 Write about how the story tells you a great deal about this mining area in Nottinghamshire.

2 What picture do you gradually build up of the wife and her family?

3 Look back at what you have written for the first two tasks. D H Lawrence combines the setting, the characterisation and the theme of the story. How does he do this? Try to explain Lawrence's style of writing.

For instance, to give you a start, in the first paragraph he describes the fields as 'dreary and foresaken' but he could just as well use these words to describe the people.

4 Explain how you know, without being told, that the miner is dead.

In the story we have just read children are important. Children can be fascinated by growing old and dying. Laurie Lee's book *Cider with Rosie* is about his own childhood in Stroud in Gloucestershire. In the extracts which follow he writes about two old women ('grannies') and the death of one of them.

Cider with Rosie

Granny Trill and Granny Wallon were traditional ancients of a kind we won't see today, the last of that dignity of grandmothers to whom age was its own embellishment. The grandmothers of those days dressed for the part in that curious but endearing uniform which is now known to us only through music-hall. And our two old neighbours, when setting forth on errands, always prepared themselves scrupulously so. They wore high laced boots and long muslin dresses, beaded chokers and candlewick shawls, crowned by tall poke bonnets tied with trailing ribbons and smothered with inky sequins. They looked like starlings, flecked with jet, and they walked in a tinkle of darkness.

Those severe and similar old bodies enthralled me when they dressed that way. When I finally became King (I used to think) I would command a parade of grandmas, and drill them, and march them up and down – rank upon rank of hobbling boots, nodding bonnets, flying shawls, and furious chewing faces. They would be gathered from all the towns and villages and brought to my palace in wagon-loads. No more than a monarch's whim, of course, like eating cocoa or drinking jellies; but far more spectacular any day than those usual trudging guardsmen.

In spite of their formal dressing-up, the two old ladies never went very far – now and again to church for the sermon, and to the village shop once a week. Granny Wallon went for her sugar and yeast; Granny Trill for her tuppence of snuff.

Snuff was Granny T's one horrible vice, and she indulged it with no moderation. A fine brown dust coated all her clothes and she had nostrils like badger-holes. She kept her snuff in a small round box, made of tin and worn smooth as a pebble. She was continually tapping and snapping it open, pinching a nailful, gasping *Ah!*, flicking her fingers and wiping her eyes, and leaving on the air a faint dry cloud like an explosion of fungoid dust.

The snuff-fox repelled and excited us boys and we opened its lid with awe. Reeking substance of the underworld, clay-brown dust of decay, of powdered flesh and crushed old bones, rust-scrapings, and the rubbish of graves. How sharp and stinging was this fearful spice, eddying up from its box, animating the air with tingling fumes like a secret breath of witchery. Though we clawed and sniffed it we could not enjoy it, but neither could we leave it alone.

'You at me snuff agen, you boys? I'll skin yer bottoms, I will!'

We looked up guiltily, saw her cackling face, so took a big pinch between us. With choking tears and head-rocking convulsions we rolled across the floor. The old lady regarded us with pleasure; our paroxysms shook the house.

'That'll learn you, I reckon; you thieving mites. Here, give it to me, I'll show 'ee.'

She took up the box and tapped the lid, then elegantly fed her nose. A shudder of ecstasy closed her eyes. She was borne very far away.

LAURIE LEE

Cider with Rosie

For several more years the lives of the two old ladies continued to revolve in intimate enmity around each other. Like cold twin stars, linked but divided, they survived by a mutual balance. Both of them reached back similarly in time, shared the same models and habits, the same sense of feudal order, the same rampaging terrible God. They were far more alike than unalike, and could not abide each other.

They arranged things therefore so that they never met. They used separate paths when they climbed the bank, they shopped on different days, they relieved themselves in different areas, and staggered their church-going hours. But each one knew always what the other was up to, and passionately disapproved. Granny Wallon worked at her flowering vats, boiling and blending her wines; or crawled through her cabbages; or tapped on our windows, gossiped, complained, or sang. Granny Trill continued to rise in the dark, comb her waxen hair, sit out in the wood chew, sniff, and suck up porridge, and study her almanac. Yet between them they sustained a mutual awareness based solely on ear and nostril. When Granny Wallon's wines boiled, Granny Trill had convulsions; when Granny Trill took snuff,

Granny Wallon had strictures – and neither let the other forget it. So all day they listened, sniffed, and pried, rapping on floors and ceilings, and prowled their rooms with hawking coughs, chivvying each other long-range. It was a tranquil, bitter-pleasant life, perfected by years of custom; and to me they both seemed everlasting, deathless crones of an eternal mythology; they had always been somewhere there in the wainscot and I could imagine no world without them.

Then one day, as Granny Trill was clambering out of her wood, she stumbled and broke her hip. She went to bed then for ever. She lay patient and yellow in a calico coat, her combed hair fine as a girl's. She accepted her doom without complaint, as though some giant authority – Squire, father, or God – had ordered her there to receive it.

'I knowed it was coming,' she told our Mother, 'after that visitation. I saw it last week sitting at the foot of my bed. Some person in white, I dunno ...'

There was a sharp early rap on our window next morning. Granny Wallon was bobbing outside.

'Did you hear him, missus?' she asked knowingly. 'He been a-screeching around since midnight.' The death-bird was Granny Wallon's private pet and messenger, and she gave a skip as she told us about him. 'He called three-a-four times. Up in them yews. Her's going, you mark my words.'

And that day indeed Granny Trill died, whose bones were too old to mend. Like a delicate pale bubble, blown a little higher and further than the other girls of her generation, she had floated just long enough for us to catch sight of her, had hovered for an instant before our eyes; and then popped suddenly, and disappeared for ever, leaving nothing on the air but a faint-drying image and the tiniest cloud of snuff.

The little church was packed for her funeral, for the old lady had been a landmark. They carried her coffin along the edge of the wood and then drew it on a cart through the village. Granny Wallon, dressed in a shower of jets, followed some distance behind; and during the service she kept to the back of the church and everybody admired her.

All went well till the lowering of the coffin, when there was a sudden and distressing commotion. Granny Wallon, ribbons flying, her bonnet awry, fought her way to the side of the grave.

'It's a lie!' she screeched, pointing down at the coffin.

'That baggage were younger'n me! Ninety-five she says! – ain't more'n ninety, an' I gone on ninety-two! It's a crime you letting 'er go to 'er Maker got up in such brazen lies! Dig up the old devil! Get 'er brass plate off! It's insulting the living church!...'

They carried her away, struggling and crying, kicking out with her steel-sprung boots. Her cries grew fainter and were soon obliterated by the sounds of the grave-diggers' spades. The clump of clay falling on Granny Trill's coffin sealed her with her inscription for ever; for no one knew the truth of her age, there was no one old enough to know.

Granny Wallon had triumphed, she had buried her rival; and now there was no more to do. From then on she faded and diminished daily, kept to her house and would not be seen. Sometimes we heard mysterious knocks in the night, rousing and summoning sounds. But the days were silent, no one walked in the garden, or came skipping to claw at our window. The wine fires sank and died in the kitchen, as did the sweet fires of obsession.

About two weeks later, of no special disease, Granny Wallon gave up in her sleep. She was found on her bed, dressed in bonnet and shawl, and her signalling broom in her hand. Her open eyes were fixed on the ceiling in a listening stare of death. There was nothing in fact to keep her alive; no cause, no bite, no fury. 'Er-Down-Under had joined 'Er-Up-Atop, having lived closer than anyone knew.

LAURIE LEE

TASKS

5   What do you think of the relationship between the two old grannies? Did they hate each other?

6   The stories of the two old grannies may remind you of some old people you knew when you were younger. Tell your story about your old people to a colleague in the class. Then work together to see how you can make your story interesting for the whole class.

When you have helped each other in this way then, individually, write the stories you have prepared.

Finally, look at your story again and make it suitable for telling to a group of five- or six-year olds.

In your homework book you will find another extract from 'Cider with Rosie' together with another task for you to do.

You are now invited to read two extracts which describe different types of death in the natural world.

A supernova is a star which is dying. This article describes the time when Ian Shelton saw a supernova in February 1987.

Supernova! A Star Explodes

'Behold, directly overhead, a strange star was suddenly seen, flashing its light with a radiant gleam. I was struck by such astonishment that I could not help doubting my own eyes.'

It was 1572 when the sight of a supernova, an expiring star, startled Tycho Brahe, the great Danish astronomer, who wrote about it in his *De Nova Stella*. In 1604 Brahe's famous assistant, Johann Kepler, saw another supernova explode. That was it for the next 383 years. No one spotted another supernova that could be seen by the naked eye until February 1987 when Ian Shelton – during a night on which he nearly wrecked his telescope – discovered one while listening to Pink Floyd on his Walkman.

Shelton wasn't quite in Brahe and Kepler's league. He was a 30-year-old starstruck Canadian who had already dropped out of two graduate courses. At the time of his find, he was earning only a modest salary as a resident astronomer in northern Chile for the University of Toronto. It was a fluke that he saw the supernova first. On that all agree, Shelton as well as the hundreds of astronomers who rushed to swivel their telescopes towards the astronomical event of the century. Yet the annals of supernova, which include the finds of Brahe and Kepler, will henceforth recognise Shelton's discovery.

But that's one of astronomy's charms. It's a field in which a novice can still make a difference. And among the lonely souls who spend their nights in mountaintop domes, there was a feeling that nobody deserved the supernova more than Ian Shelton.

Shelton grew up in Winnipeg, where his parents were both doctors, in a typical suburban home – except for the ten-foot-high observatory he built in the garden. In 1981, at the age of 23, he moved to a 7,400-foot peak in Chile.

To reach this mountain, Las Campanas, you drive two hours north from the coastal town of La Serena, up into the foothills of the Andes, through vast valleys of cactus and scrub grass in the Atacama Desert. You might encounter a miner or a herd of goats, but mostly you see empty, dusty expanse, uninhabited valleys, inaccessible peaks and no rainfall. It is one of the best places on earth to look at the sky, which is why North Americans and Europeans have spent the past two decades covering three peaks in northern Chile with their biggest telescopes.

The hundreds of people who work at the Chilean observatories go up for a week or two and then return to civilisation for at least a few days.

Shelton was the only one whose home was on the mountain, and his zeal was such that he stayed there even when he had time off. He just kept watching the sky at night and maintaining the telescope by day.

On the evening of 23 February 1987, Shelton was, as usual, making work for himself at the Las Campanas Observatory complex. He had finished his official job, making sure the University of Toronto's 24-inch telescope was ready for a visiting professor. He was sometimes allowed to use it himself, though not as often as he'd have liked.

So that night Shelton was shivering in a nearby one-storey breeze-block building which housed a small telescope, an astrograph, abandoned years earlier. At ten inches in diameter, it was useful only for taking pictures of large areas of the sky. (Most astronomers prefer using powerful telescopes to magnify one spot.) By the time Shelton got to Las Campanas, the astrograph hadn't been used for some time, its manual was lost, and no one knew how to work it. Shelton overhauled it, and in 1986 had used it to photograph Halley's Comet.

The roof, however, remained a problem. The winch that slid it out of the way was jammed. Shelton had to climb up and push the corrugated sheet open. He pointed the telescope south towards the Milky Way's closest companion, a satellite galaxy called the Large Magellanic Cloud (LMC). There was no particular reason to photograph it. Shelton just wanted to see how the equipment would work during a three-hour exposure.

He stood alone on a ladder in the dark, squinting into a viewfinder and delicately moving the telescope to keep pace with the earth's rotation. The work became especially onerous when the winds across the peak picked up to 40 mph and roared against the building.

When the exposure was finished, he began taking another picture. At about three in the morning, the sky suddenly went black. 'All the stars started disappearing,' Shelton says. 'Then the telescope was knocked horizontal. I didn't know what was happening – the wind was so loud I couldn't hear anything else.'

When he realised that the roof was being blown shut, it was too late to stop it. Stumbling about in the dark – torchlight would have ruined the photograph – he found that the telescope had survived the roof's blow. Tired and disgusted, Shelton was ready for bed.

First, though, he had to develop the exposed plate. In his darkroom he was confused by a large round blotch in the photo. He first thought that it was a flaw in the plate – there weren't any stars that bright n that part of the sky. 'My next reaction was – that's one hell of a flaw,' he recalls.

He could not immediately run outside to check the sky as he had to complete processing the plate, but as soon as he had finished he went to look. The bright spot was clearly visible.

It was a glittering point due south about magnitude 5, comparable to the faint stars in the Little Bear (*Ursa Minor*), and some 170,000 light-years away. It was next to a bright fuzzy patch of gas and dust called 30 Doradus, or the Tarantula nebula. Shelton had taken a picture of this area the night before, and there was no bright blotch then.

Shelton walked up the road to the observatory's building where a 40-inch telescope was housed. Inside the dome were Barry Madore, a professor from the University of Toronto, and Oscar Duhalde, a Chilean technician. Shelton tried to sound casual as he asked, 'What do you think of a fifth-magnitude object in the LMC?'

'It has to be a supernova,' Madore replied.

Duhalde was nodding his head. 'Yes, I saw it around two,' he said, 'Near 30 Doradus.' Now Duhalde realised why the Tarantula nebula had looked oddly luminous when he had gone outside for a coffee two hours earlier. He had meant to mention it, but the work had become hectic and he now had the frustrating distinction of probably being the first person to see the supernova but definitely the second to report it.

The International Astronomical Union flashed the news around the world. Madore entered the sighting, 'an astronomer's dream come true', in the observatory log.

Within a few hours, life at observatories from Chile to South Africa to Australia was as close to pandemonium as it ever gets. There was a rare moment of communion: all the domes in the Southern hemisphere pointing in the same direction, all the star-gazers looking at the same thing. For the first time modern astronomers had the opportunity to study, at fairly close range, a phenomenon believed essential to the origin and evolution of life on earth.

The building blocks of our bodies and our planet – from carbon and oxygen to silicon, iron, silver and gold – are thought to have been created in ancient supernovae. Theorists devised an elaborate scenario to explain how these elements were formed in dying stars and then spewed into space, but the theory was a lot better than the data. It was based on observations of old debris, on radio signals from pulsars – the tiny neutron stars that remain spinning after the outer layers of their parent stars have been blown away – and on the faint light from the dozen or so supernovae sighted each year in distant galaxies.

But now that astronomers could see a supernova at close range, it wasn't behaving the way it should. It was expected to brighten dramatically within a couple of weeks; instead, its brightness remained constant for a week and a half, then grew steadily over the next two months to reach magnitude 2.88 (as intensity increases, the number on the scale decreases). By the end of May it began declining, dropping to around 5 by mid-July.

There was also a question as to what had blown up. The conventional wisdom was that an explosion would occur in a red supergiant star. But pictures taken of the region before the explosion didn't show any red supergiants there. 'This is a very, very strange supernova – or perhaps it seems strange only because we're able to study it in such detail,' said Nicholas Suntzeff, a staff astronomer at the Cerro Tololo Observatory, about 80 miles south of Las Campanas. Pre-explosion photographs did show a star named Sanduleak. But it was a blue supergiant believed to be too young and too small to explode. Was some other nearby star the one? Was Sanduleak still there? By the beginning of April, Sanduleak was established as the supernova.

Shelton, promoted from his small astrograph by the supernova, spent every night for five months observing it with the 24-inch telescope and reporting his results. He was studying the light to see what was going on inside the supernova as its cloud of debris expanded at 11,000 miles per second. But, like other astronomers, he couldn't clearly envision what was happening in that point of light.

'I think of it as a monstrous shell moving outwards – like our sun getting larger,' he said. 'But you can't really comprehend the speed or the violence. This is trillions of times more luminous than the sun – and a trillion means nothing to your mind.'

Theorists expected the supernova should be visible to the naked eye for at least a few months, and through telescopes for a couple of years. One part of Shelton wanted to stay to watch, but another said it was time to leave the mountain. He applied to study astronomy at the University of Toronto and was welcome despite his unimpressive academic record. 'He's shown other evidence of creative professional achievement,' an official said. In 1990 he was awarded an MA and went on to take his PhD, to be completed this spring.

Leaving Las Campanas – where he had spent four of the past six years – meant leaving a very special place for Shelton, who liked to go outside on a clear winter's night and reflect.

'You lie on your back and look straight up,' he explains. 'You feel that the planets are closer, that the Large Magellanic Cloud is just outside the galaxy. All you see filling your view from one horizon to the other is the Milky Way. From the Northern hemisphere you don't see the centre of the Milky Way, but in Las Campanas you look up and there's the dust lane around the centre of the galaxy, and everything suddenly connects – you *know* that we're part of the galaxy.'

JOHN TIERNEY

TASKS

7   Carry out the following tasks.

a   Using information from the passage, write a brief biography of Ian Shelton.

b   Explain why Shelton was in Chile.

c   Describe the supernova which Shelton saw.

d   Explain what is thought to happen to a supernova as it declines.

8   In the last paragraph of the article Ian Shelton tries to explain what fascinates him about the sky.

'You lie on your back and look straight up ...'

Go outside on a clear night and look up at the sky (whether you lie on your back or not is entirely up to you).

Write about what you can see and what you feel as you gaze up at the sky.

You can write either a side of prose or a short poem.

The next article puts forward a theory about why dinosaurs suddenly vanished from the face of the earth. Whether it is true or not, the fact remains that dinosaurs were wiped out or destroyed for some reason.

Read the article and, while you are reading it, make notes about the theory which is being discussed.

Did Comets Kill the Dinosaurs?

Sixty-five million years ago, dinosaurs abruptly vanished. Why? One theory says that a giant extraterrestrial object collided with the earth. Another, even more intriguing, that a 'Death Star' orbiting our sun triggers mass extinctions at regular intervals. A scientist explains how he and his fellows arrived at their sensational theories.

As a child, I loved dinosaurs. I drew them nearly every day. I learned that the great creatures had all disappeared 65 million years ago. Nobody knew why. It was the first unsolved problem I ever heard about in science. I wanted to be a palaeontologist.

Then I started reading books about the history of the earth and its formation. They had reproductions of dinosaur paintings, as well as pictures of the moon and planets. They were full of excitement: discussions of infinity, photographs of molecules, theories about the beginning of time. But it was physicists who did most of the work, and a physicist was what I had by then decided I wanted to be.

As a postgraduate at the University of California at Berkeley, I studied elementary particles – the tiny pieces that make up the atom's nucleus. This seemed as far from the study of dinosaurs as one could imagine. Certainly I could never have guessed that my thesis adviser, Nobel prize-winner Luis Alvarez, would head the team that proposed a solution to the riddle of the dinosaurs' destruction, and that I would be led to a search for what may be the ultimate cause: a Death Star that orbits the sun.

Working with Alvarez was constantly exciting. He seemed to be one of the few physicists developing methods to investigate new areas of science. After six years of formal physics training, my education was finally beginning. I found myself studying Alvarez, trying to understand his approach to problems.

Alvarez has made more discoveries than any living physicist I know, and I could sense he did it for the excitement. He was not a scholar; I was amazed at the facts of physics he did not know. He didn't clutter his mind needlessly. But when he needed to know something to solve a problem, he learned it with amazing speed.

Alvarez did his 'experimental physics' from a desk, thinking the problem through before assembling equipment. When others expressed an interest in his work he welcomed their help. This procedure of organisation was his greatest lesson to me.

One day in 1978, Alvarez showed me a present from his son Walter, a geologist. It was a piece of 65-million-year-old sedimentary rock from Italy. Trapped in it were many small fossils of sea creatures. But they were almost all in the bottom half; something had killed virtually all microscopic life before the top half was formed. Walter told his father that the catastrophe had struck *at the same time* the dinosaurs vanished.

Luis Alvarez was fascinated, and thought that a new technique of radioactive dating I had developed could help untangle the mystery. But the experiment failed. This seemed only to sharpen Alvarez's interest. He searched for weeks until he found an approach he was certain would work. The key was iridium (a rare metal in the platinum group), which rains on the earth in minute quantities when micrometeorites vapourise on entering our atmosphere.

In analysing the rock from Italy, Alvarez and his colleagues found to their surprise that the concentration of iridium rose abruptly at the time of the dinosaur disaster – far more than could be accounted for by vapourising micrometeorites alone. Most likely, this was a mistake. But it had to be investigated. Alvarez had missed discovering how to split the atom because he failed to follow up on a seemingly unimportant observation.

The high iridium content of the rock proved difficult to explain. Perhaps it had come from volcanoes. There is iridium in the earth's core, and volcanoes, Alvarez postulated, could have brought it to the surface. Subsequently, that was ruled out. Perhaps it came from chemical precipitation in the oceans. Alvarez also found that implausible.

He seemed to come up with one new explanation per week, which he patiently explained to me and my colleagues. But by the time we understood the details (usually a week or so later), he had disproved his own hypothesis and come up with an alternative.

After months of concentration, Alvarez finally found an explanation that held. An extraterrestrial object has struck the earth, creating a rain of iridium-enriched dust. He could estimate the object's diameter in two independent ways, and they both agreed: about six miles. (An object that size striking the earth would have released energy equivalent to 10,000 times the combined nuclear arsenals of the US and USSR.)

Dust thrown up by the impact could account for the loss of life, since sunlight would have been blocked for months, causing photosynthesis to cease and temperatures to drop. The dinosaurs would have died by starvation and freezing.

None of us could find anything wrong with Alvarez's reasoning, and his theory was published in 1979. It was first met with scepticism, but by the mid-1980s few experts disputed that an extraterrestrial object had hit earth at the same time as the mass extinctions.

I had watched all this work, but had made no useful contribution of my own. Then an unexpected opening came along. Palaeontologists at the University of Chicago found evidence suggesting that mass extinctions occurred regularly every 26 million years. (On the basis of their calculations, the next one is due 13 million years from now.)

Alvarez didn't believe their findings, and composed a letter outlining his objections. However, I found their work difficult to dismiss. I didn't convince Alvarez, but I convinced myself.

It's strangely uncomfortable to believe something true when most of your colleagues don't. I was tempted by all the pressures of normal academic life to abandon the search. All the pressures except one: Alvarez. Every day he asked how my work was going. Did I have a theory that could explain the periodic extinctions (that *he* didn't believe in)?

Within two months, I developed six theories, but proved each wrong. Then, with help from an astronomer and an expert in orbital dynamics, I came up with a model that seemed to explain the periodic extinctions.

The theory is simple. The sun has a companion star orbiting it. Every 26 million to 30 million years, the star passes relatively close to a reservoir of some million million comets inhabiting the solar system's outer reaches (far beyond Pluto). The comets are perturbed by the Death Star's gravitational pull, and a storm of perhaps a thousand million of them is sent into our inner solar system. One or more hit the earth.

Nearly two years have passed since we published our theory as the 'Nemesis hypothesis' (after the Greek goddess who punished the excessively proud and powerful – the dinosaurs for instance). Despite vigorous examination, no one has yet proved the theory wrong. If we are right – or if Alvarez's impact theory is right – the consequences for evolution are staggering.

Classical Darwinian evolution has species competing against species, but now we hypothesise that this is the case only during the relatively benign periods between catastrophic impacts of extraterrestrial objects. According to the Nemesis theory, every 26 million to 30 million years, the earth suffers a catastrophe that otherwise successful species can't prepare for. New ecological niches are opened, allowing previously suppressed species to gain footholds.

Had it not been for the comet or comets that hit 65 million years ago, mammals might never have wrested the earth from the dinosaurs. At the time they vanished, the dinosaurs possibly were more intelligent than the mammals, and they might have stayed ahead. Highly intelligent creatures could still have evolved, but with reptilian features.

It is strange and wonderful suddenly to be thinking seriously about dinosaurs for the first time since primary school. I recently drew a picture for my six-year-old daughter of a *Tyrannosaurus rex* fighting a *Triceratops*. As the picture flowed from my hand, I realised that my skill had not diminished one bit.

Of course, the Nemesis hypothesis has not yet been proved or positively disproved. But if the sun does have a companion star, we should be able to find it and confirm its orbit in the near future. It is probably a red star about 20 million million miles away, barely bright enough to be seen with powerful binoculars. A team of physicists and astronomers at Berkeley is examining 5,000 candidates. If they find the real Death Star, there will be little room for controversy. This latest adventure is just under way.

RICHARD MULLER

TASKS

9 The article you have been reading is quite complicated. Check through your notes.

In groups, discuss the ideas in the passage. It is possible that some of you will think the ideas are feasible and others may think them highly unlikely. Put forward your views but listen carefully to the views of others.

10 In your own words write a clear explanation of the Nemesis theory.

11 Now use your imagination and write your own story –
'When dinosaurs roamed the earth.'

TIME OUT TASK!

A sonnet

A sonnet is a poem written in a particular way.

- It has 14 lines.
- These lines rhyme (the rhyming pattern is not always the same).
- Each line has ten syllables in a pattern of stressed and unstressed: these lines are called 'iambic pentameters'.
- The lines are grouped in one of two ways – eight lines (the octave) followed by six lines (the sestet) – three groups of four lines (quatraines) followed by a final two lines (couplet).

Below you will find examples of three different types of sonnet. We are more interested at the moment in the form of the poem than in the content.

Anthem for Doomed Youth

What passing bells for those who die as cattle?
   Only the monstrous anger of the guns.
   Only the stuttering rifles' rapid rattle
Can patter out their hasty orisons.
No mockeries for them from prayers or bells,
Nor any voice of mourning save the choirs, –
The shrill, demented choirs of wailing shells;
   And bugles calling for them from sad shires.

What candles may be held to speed them all?
   Not in the hands of boys, but in their eyes
Shall shine the holy glimmers of good-byes.
   The pallor of girls' brows shall be their pall;
Their flowers the tenderness of patient minds,
And each slow dusk a drawing-down of blinds.

WILFRED OWEN

Design

I found a dimpled spider, fat and white,
On a white heal-all, holding up a moth
Like a white piece of rigid satin cloth –
Assorted characters of death and blight
Mixed ready to begin the morning right,
Like the ingredients of a witches' broth –
A snow-drop spider, a flower like a froth,
And dead wings carried like a paper kite.

What had that flower to do with being white,
The wayside blue and innocent heal-all?
What brought the kindred spider to that height,
Then steered the white moth thither in the night?
What but design of darkness to appal? –
If design govern in a thing so small.

ROBERT FROST

269

- Work out the rhyming scheme for these two sonnets.
- What do you notice about the arrangement of the lines?
- What is the connection between the arrangement you notice and the ideas in the poem?

Now look at a sonnet by Shakespeare.

Sonnet CXVI

Let me not to the marriage of true minds
Admit impediments: love is not love
Which alters when it alteration finds,
Or bends with the remover to remove.
Oh no! It is an ever fixed mark
That looks on tempests and is never shaken;
It is the star to every wandering bark,
Whose worth's unknown although his heights be taken.
Love's not time's fool, though rosy lips and cheeks
Within his bending sickle's compass come;
Love alters not with his brief hours and weeks,
But bears it out even to the edge of doom.
    If this be error and upon me proved,
    I never writ, nor no man ever loved.

WILLIAM SHAKESPEARE

- Work out how the sonnet differs in the way it is arranged from the previous two.
- How are the ideas in the poem developed?

The next sonnet was written by Douglas Dunn after his wife's death.

The Kaleidoscope

To climb these stairs again, bearing a tray,
Might be to find you pillowed with your books,
Your inventories listing gowns and frocks
As if preparing for a holiday.
Or, turning from the landing, I might find
My presence watched through your kaleidoscope,
A symmetry of husbands, each redesigned
In lovely forms of foresight, prayer and hope.
I climb these stairs a dozen times a day
And, by that open door, wait, looking in
At where you died. My hands become a tray
Offering me, my flesh, my soul, my skin.
Grief wrongs us so. I stand, and wait, and cry
For the absurd forgiveness, not knowing why.

DOUGLAS DUNN

- What ideas and feelings is Dunn writing about?
- How do you feel about the poem?
- Does the arrangement of the poem help your understanding and response?

Now have a go at writing your own sonnet.
Here are some hints to help:

- choose a topic;
- decide how to develop your ideas;
- think about your message and a way to conclude the poem;
- experiment with different rhyming arrangements;
- be prepared to fight with the rhythm and the form – you won't find it easy (unless you're a natural genius of a poet, of course).

END OF TIME OUT!

Shakespeare's play *Julius Caesar* is concerned with the death of one famous man. In the first part of the play the 'conspirators' are plotting Caesar's death. In the second part of the play the consequences of killing Caesar are made known.

The assassination of Caesar takes place at the capitol in Rome.

Julius Caesar

Act 3 Scene 1

DECIUS:
  Where is Metellus Cimber? Let him go,
  And presently prefer his suit to Caesar.
BRUTUS:
  He is addressed; press near and second him.
CINNA:
  Casca, you are the first that rears your hand.
CAESAR:
  Are we all ready? What is now amiss
  That Caesar and his senate must redress?
METELLUS:
  Most high, most mighty, and most puissant
  Caesar,
  Metellus Climber throws before thy seat
  An humble heart –
  [Kneeling]
CAESAR:
  I must prevent thee, Cimber.
  These crouchings and these lowly courtesies
  Might fire the blood of ordinary men,
  And turn pre-ordinance and first decree
  Into the law of children. Be not fond

To think that Caesar bears such rebel blood
That will be thawed from the true quality
With that which melteth fools: I mean sweet words,
Low-crooked curtsies, and base spaniel fawning.
Thy brother by decree is banishèd:
If thou dost bend and pray and fawn for him,
I spurn thee like a cur out of my way.
Know, Caesar doth not wrong, nor without cause
Will he be satisfied.
METELLUS:
  Is there no voice more worthy than my own,
  To sound more sweetly in great Caesar's ear
  For the repealing of my banished brother?
BRUTUS:
  I kiss thy hand, but not in flattery, Caesar;
  Desiring thee that Publius Cimber may
  Have an immediate freedom of repeal.
CAESAR:
  What, Brutus?
CASSIUS:
  Pardon, Caesar; Caesar, pardon:
  As low as to thy foot doth Cassius fall,
  To beg enfranchisement for Publius Climber.

CAESAR:
   I would be well moved, if I were as you;
   If I could pray to move, prayers would move me;
   But I am constant as the northern star,
   Of whose true-fixed and resting quality
   There is no fellow in the firmament.
   The skies are painted with unnumbered sparks,
   They are all fire, and every one doth shine;
   But there's but one in all doth hold his place.
   So in the world: 'tis furnished well with men,
   And men are flesh and blood, and apprehensive;
   Yet in the number I do know but one
   That unassailable holds on his rank,
   Unshaken of motion; and that I am he,
   Let me a little show it, even in this,
   That I was constant. Climber should be banished
   And constant do remain to keep him so.
CINNA:
   O Caesar –
CAESAR:
   Hence! Wilt thou lift up Olympus?
DECIUS:
   Great Caesar –
CAESAR:
   Doth not Brutus bootless kneel?
CASCA:
   Speak hands for me!
   [They stab Caesar.]
CAESAR:
   Et tu, Brute? Then fall, Caesar!
   [Dies]

CINNA:
   Liberty! Freedom! Tyranny is dead!
   Run hence, proclaim, cry it about the streets.
CASSIUS:
   Some to the common pulpits, and cry out,
   'Liberty, freedom, and enfranchisement!'
BRUTUS:
   People and senators, be not affrighted.
   Fly not; stand still. Ambition's debt is paid.
CASCA:
   Go to the pulpit, Brutus.
DECIUS:
   And Cassius too.
BRUTUS:
   Where's Publius?
CINNA:
   Here, quite confounded with his mutiny.
METELLUS:
   Stand fast together, lest some friend of Caesar's
   Should chance –
BRUTUS:
   Talk not of standing. Publius, good cheer;
   There is no harm intended to your person,
   Nor to no Roman else. So tell them, Publius.
CASSIUS:
   And leave us, Publius, lest that the people,
   Rushing on us, should do your age some mischief.
BRUTUS:
   Do so; and let no man abide with this deed
   But we the doers.

WILLIAM SHAKESPEARE

TASKS

12   The conspirators (Brutus, Cassius, Metellus) believe Caesar is too proud
     and arrogant. Is there evidence in the passage to support this opinion?

13   Casca tells Brutus to 'Go to the pulpit'. He means that Brutus must go to
     address the crowds, telling them of Caesar's death.
     Write Brutus' speech for him. Bear in mind that he must try to persuade
     the crowd to his side. Remember that Caesar was a popular leader
     among the Romans.
     (There is no need for you to write in Shakespeare's kind of verse
     although some of the more adventurous may well want to try.)

Before Brutus has a chance to speak to the crowds, Mark
Antony arrives at the Capitol. He is Caesar's friend and so
has to be careful about what he says to the conspirators
because his own life may be in danger. However, when he is
left alone with Caesar's body we learn his true feelings.

Julius Caesar

Act 3 Scene 1

ANTONY:

O pardon me, thou bleeding piece of earth,
That I am meek and gentle with these butchers.
Thou art the ruins of the noblest man
That ever lived in the tide of times.
Woe to the hand that shed this costly blood!
Over thy wounds now do I prophesy –
Which like dumb mouths do ope their ruby lips,
To beg the voice and utterance of my tongue –
A curse shall light upon the limbs of men;
Domestic fury and fierce civil strife
Shall cumber all the parts of Italy;
Blood and destruction shall be so in use,
And dreadful objects so familiar,
That mothers shall but smile when they behold
Their infants quartered with the hands of war,
All pity choked with custom of fell deeds;
And Caesar's spirit, ranging for revenge,
With Ate by his side come hot from hell,
Shall in these confines with a monarch's voice
Cry havoc, and let slip the dogs of war,
That this foul deed shall smell above the earth
With carrion men, groaning for burial.

[Enter a SERVANT.]

You serve Octavius Caesar, do you not?

SERVANT:

I do, Mark Antony.

ANTONY:

Caesar did write for him to come to Rome.

SERVANT:

He did receive his letters, and is coming,
And bid me say to you by word of mouth –
O Caesar!

ANTONY:

Thy heart is big; get thee apart and weep.
Passion, I see, is catching, for mine eyes,
Seeing those beads of sorrow stand in thine,
Begin to water. Is thy master coming?

SERVANT:

He lies tonight within seven leagues of Rome.

ANTONY:

Post back with speed, and tell him what
   have chanced.
Here is a mourning Rome, a dangerous Rome,
No Rome of safety for Octavius yet;
His hence, and tell him so. Yet stay awhile,
Thou shalt not back till I have borne this corse
Into the market place. There shall I try
In my oration, how the people take
The cruel issue of these bloody men;
According to the which, thou shalt discourse
To young Octavius of the state of things.
Lend me your hand.

[Exeunt with CAESAR's body.]

WILLIAM SHAKESPEARE

TASKS

14 Explain what Antony's opinions and true feelings are about the death
    of Caesar.

15 Write about what he thinks will be the consequences of the
    assassination.

16 What do you think is added to this scene by the news that the servant
    brings to Antony?

17 Imagine that you are directing this part of the play (ie both the extracts
    we have looked at). How would you make it moving and dramatic?
    You should think about:

    ■ the way in which the actors should speak;

    ■ how they should look and move;

    ■ the scenery and how that can help to create the effect you want.

The word 'assassinate' refers to the sudden death of a public figure; 'murder' refers to a deliberate and unlawful killing. 'Execution' is, however, different. It means the taking of a life lawfully, usually following a trial held by proper authorities (although this is not always the case).

In the year 1649 King Charles I went to his death. Here is how Antonia Fraser describes what happened.

Cromwell: Our Chief of Men

So on the morning of Tuesday, 30 January, Charles Stuart walked with calm dignity and religious resignation from St James' Palace to the designated place of his death at Whitehall. Once arrived, he rested within Whitehall itself, and strengthened himself with a little red wine and a little bread. There was a slight delay, probably because the Commons was even then passing an urgent Act which forbade the proclamation of his successor after his death. They had suddenly taken into account Pride's words on the problems of cutting off the head of an hereditary King, when they had not yet officially abolished monarchy: they would simply find themselves with another sovereign on their hands. It was two o'clock in the afternoon when Charles stepped forth from the Banqueting House windows in front of the enormous, silent crowd. The weather was icy – Charles was secretly wearing two shirts so that he should not shiver and be accused of fear. With him came only his chaplain, Bishop Juxon, for his faithful servant Sir Thomas Herbert who had accompanied him on the mournful march from St James' Palace begged to be excused from the painful task of being a witness. There were the two Colonels, Hacker and Tomlinson, on the scaffold to supervise the execution, and serried troops below, lest even now the King should appeal to his people – or the people perhaps to their King.

To the spectators indeed their King seemed greatly aged, his beard grey and his hair silver. Now they could see that, but his words could only be heard by those very close to him, Bishop Juxon, the two Colonels, and the two masked executioners, for the ban on any form of public appeal remained absolute. To this tiny audience, but every word would be lovingly treasured by his chaplain to reach the audience of the world, he regretted nothing: 'For the people truly I desire their liberty and freedom as much as anybody whatsoever; but I must tell you that their liberty and freedom consists in having government, those laws by which their lives and goods maybe most their own. It is not their having a share in the government; that is nothing appertaining

to them; a subject and sovereign are clean different things....' So the sovereign went to his death at the hands of his subjects, proud and unrepentant on that interpretation of government whose inflexibility had brought about his downfall: those words alone did much to show why Charles died. Yet another of his sayings showed also why another section of his people would always regard him as King Charles the Martyr: 'I go from a corruptible crown to an incorruptible crown,' he told Juxon, 'where no disturbance can be, no disturbance in the world.' And it was Andrew Marvell, very likely present among the crowd, in an ode intended to celebrate Charles's mortal adversary Cromwell, who penned the words which later immortalised the King's courage in his last moments, as he bent his neck in silent submission on to the black-draped block:

> Nor call'd the Gods with vulgar spite
> To vindicate his helpless Right
> But bow'd his comely Head
> Down as upon a Bed.

A minute later the executioner (believed to be the common hangman named Brandon, but with his assistant he had insisted on the utmost precautions being taken to preserve his identity, including a false beard and wig) was holding up the severed head with the traditional cry: 'Behold the head of a traitor!' In less than a quarter of an hour, said the French Ambassador, this whole sad ceremony was over. But from the people watching went up not the raucous cries of the crowd at justice done, not the human response to blood lust of so many public executions; something so deeply shocking had been perpetrated that up from the people went a great deep groan, a groan, said an eye-witness, 'as I never heard before and desire I may never hear again', it was a lament that would be heard as long and as far as the problems of justice and injustice were caused for. For whatsoever could be said of the execution of King Charles I, that it was inevitable, even that it was necessary, it could never be said that it was right.

ANTONIA FRASER

TASKS

18 What impression of King Charles do you get from this extract?

19 Explain what we learn about the way public executions were carried out.

20 What are the writer's opinions about the king's death?

You will find that we have reprinted this extract in your homework book, together with a task which gives you a chance to write imaginatively about this event.

A century or so before Charles I another great Englishman suffered a similar fate. Thomas More was a lawyer, a statesman and a scholar, yet in 1535 he was executed on Henry VIII's orders.

Robert Bolt's play, *A Man for All Seasons*, is about More. Towards the end of the play More is on trial for his life.

A Man for all Seasons

CROMWELL (*backs away. His face stiff with malevolence*):
My lords, I wish to call (*raises voice*)
Sir Richard Rich!
Enter RICH. *He is now splendidly official, in dress and bearing;*

even NORFOLK *is a bit impressed.*
Sir Richard (*indicating* CRANMER).
CRANMER (*proffering Bible*):
I do solemnly swear…

RICH:
> I do solemnly swear that the evidence I shall give before the Court shall be the truth, the whole truth, and nothing but the truth.

CRANMER (*discreetly*):
> So help me God, Sir Richard.

RICH:
> So help me God.

NORFOLK:
> Take your stand there, Sir Richard.

CROMWELL:
> Now, Rich, on 12 March, you were at the Tower?

RICH:
> I was.

CROMWELL:
> With what purpose?

RICH:
> I was sent to carry away the prisoner's books.

CROMWELL:
> Did you talk with the prisoner?

RICH:
> Yes.

CROMWELL:
> Did you talk about the King's Supremacy of the Church?

RICH:
> Yes.

CROMWELL:
> What did you say?

RICH:
> I said to him: 'Supposing there was an Act of Parliament to say that I, Richard Rich, were to be King, would not you, Master More, take me for King?' "That I would," he said, "for then you would be King."'

CROMWELL:
> Yes?

RICH:
> Then he said—

NORFOLK (*sharply*):
> The prisoner?

RICH:
> Yes, my lord. 'But I will put you a higher case,' he said. 'How if there were an Act of Parliament to say that God should not be God?'

MORE:
> This is true; and then you said—

NORFOLK:
> Silence! Continue.

RICH:
> I said 'Ah, but I will put you a middle case. Parliament has made our King Head of the Church. Why will you not accept him?'

NORFOLK:
> Well?

RICH:
> Then he said Parliament had no power to do it.

NORFOLK:
> Repeat the prisoner's words!

RICH:
> He said 'Parliament has not the competence.' Or words to that effect.

CROMWELL:
> He denied the title?

RICH:
> He did.

All look to MORE *but he looks to* RICH.

MORE:
> In good faith, Rich, I am sorrier for your perjury than my peril.

NORFOLK:
> Do you deny this?

MORE:
> Yes! My lords, if I were a man who heeded not the taking of an oath, you know well I need not to be here. Now I will take an oath! If what Master Rich has said is true, then I pray I may never see God in the face! Which I would not say were it otherwise for anything on earth.

CROMWELL (*to* FOREMAN, *calmly, technical*):
> That is not evidence.

MORE:
> Is it probable – is it probable – that after so long a silence, on this, the very point so urgently sought of me, I should open my mind to such a man as that?

CROMWELL (*to* RICH):
> Do you wish to modify your testimony?

RICH:
> No, Secretary.

MORE:
> There were two other men! Southwell and Palmer!

CROMWELL:
> Unhappily, Sir Richard Southwell and Master Palmer are both in Ireland on the King's business. (MORE *gestures helplessly.*) It has no bearing. I have their deposition here in which the Court will see they state that being busy with the prisoner's books they did not hear what was said. (*Hands deposition to* FOREMAN *who examines it with much seriousness.*)

MORE:
> If I had really said this is not obvious he would instantly have called these men to witness?

CROMWELL:
> Sir Richard, have you anything to add?

RICH:
> Nothing, Mr Secretary.

NORFOLK:
> Sir Thomas?

MORE (*looking at* FOREMAN):
  To what purpose? I am a dead man. (*To* CROMWELL.) You have your desire of me. What you have hunted me for is not my actions, but the thoughts of my heart. It is a long road you have opened. For first men will disclaim their hearts and presently they will have no hearts. God help the people whose Statesmen walk your road.

NORFOLK:
  Then the witness may withdraw.

  RICH *crosses stage, watched by* MORE.

MORE:
  I *have* one question to ask the witness. (RICH *stops.*)
  That's a chain of office you are wearing. (*Reluctantly* RICH *faces him.*) May I see it? (NORFOLK *motions him to approach.* MORE *examines the medallion.*) The red dragon. (*To* CROMWELL.) What's this?

CROMWELL:
  Sir Richard is appointed Attorney-General for Wales.

MORE (*looking into* RICH'S *face*: *with pain and amusement*):
  For Wales? Why, Richard, it profits a man

nothing to give his soul for the whole world … But for Wales –!

Exit RICH, *stiff faced, but infrangibly dignified.*

CROMWELL:
  Now I must ask the Court's indulgence! I have a message for the prisoner from the King: (*urgent*) Sir Thomas, I am empowered to tell you that even now –

MORE:
  No no, it cannot be.

CROMWELL:
  The case rests! (NORFOLK *is staring at* MORE.) My lord!

NORFOLK:
  The jury will retire and consider the evidence.

CROMWELL:
  Considering the evidence it shouldn't be necessary for them to retire. (*Standing over* FOREMAN.) Is it necessary?

  FOREMAN *shakes his head.*

NORFOLK:
  Then is the prisoner guilty or not guilty?

FOREMAN:
  Guilty, my lord!

ROBERT BOLT

TASKS

21   Explain how in this extract it is made clear that More is actually innocent.

22   Imagine you are the foreman of the jury. Write your account of what is happening here, your true feelings and why you pronounced More guilty.

TIME OUT TASK!

Colons and semi-colons

There's no getting away from it. The vast majority of you will use full stops and commas in your sentences and that will be all.

Your GCSE examiners will be impressed if you show that you can use the full range of punctuation devices and that includes colons and semi-colons.

You know what they are – ; – :. But do you know when to use them?

Colon

■   If you want to put a list in a sentence then put a colon after the introduction and before the list. For instance –
      'These would include: …'

■   If you want to quote then put a colon after the introduction and before the quotation, which you should start on a new line.

■   If you want to give an example, then again put a colon after your introduction and before you give your example.

Semi-colon

■ Remember, as with full-stops and commas, a semi-colon is a pause and, if we're talking in terms of length, then it is longer than a comma and shorter than a full stop.

An example:

'She was running like mad; her breath was coming in laboured gasps; she felt sick; she was determined that she wouldn't be defeated.'

Those points are all very closely connected and the writer wanted to keep them as closely connected as possible. Commas wouldn't have been enough. Using simple conjunctions would have been repetitive. The semi-colon pauses between each idea and perhaps contributes a little jerkiness to the style which, in this case, would be appropriate.

■ When you are reading look at how semi-colons are used by writers. In your own writing consciously try to use colons and semi-colons.

END OF TIME OUT!

This next extract is from the newsletter of a charitable organisation: 'Let The Children Live!' In it we learn about someone who is set on trying to save the lives of young children.

One-Way Ticket!

In 1982, Peter Walters, a young student for the Anglican priesthood, decided to take a look at Latin American Christianity – there are more Christians in Latin America than in the rest of the world put together, yet in Europe we know so little about them. Colombia became his destination purely by chance. The Colombian national airline was offering the cheapest flights!

Parts tourists rarely reach

Peter landed in the capital Bogota, a vast throbbing city of 3 million people, and made his way to Cartagena, on the Caribbean coast. A city of wonderful churches, good hotels and fine beaches – great for a holiday if you have money. Peter found, to his alarm, that the cut-price ticket – with no return date on it – was not such a bargain after all. The airline could offer him no return flight at the end of his holiday, and he had to stay two weeks longer than he expected. Decisions were necessary – either he could eat reasonably well and sleep on the silvery beaches, or get a cheap hotel room and eat about every other day! And so it was that he found himself in parts of the city the tourist rarely sees.

Helped by children

It was the children he noticed – everywhere – asleep on pavements, some as young as six, roaming around, aimless with nothing to do, approaching strangers with begging hands. He became their target, but as soon as they realised that this tourist who had little Spanish and very little money was going neither to harm them nor be able to help them, they became curious and friendly. They offered him scraps of food they had foraged for themselves, showed him the cheap places to buy it, and trailed around with him, helping him survive like themselves.

Violence and abuse

Peter heard stories he couldn't believe – how they lived on the streets and in the sewers – with nothing to eat or live on but what they could earn, beg or steal. That they had no contact with their parents – in many cases their fathers had been murdered. When policemen appeared, he noticed how they vanished, reappearing when the coast was clear. He saw their scars and heard their accounts of violence and abuse. He watched them polishing shoes, washing car windscreens and hawking sweets, cigarettes, flowers and fruit. These children as young as six, told him of drugs and prostitution, robbery and violence.

Why? Why?

This young student decided to do something – he rang the bell and requested an audience with the Roman Catholic Bishop – who turned out to be an Archbishop! There seemed nothing strange in his request to be seen: the Archbishop was available every morning for anyone at all who would like to talk to him. This saintly man who listened patiently to Peter's faltering Spanish, nodding and confirming that what the children had said was true. 'Then why' demanded this young student, coming to the purpose of his visit, 'Why isn't the Church doing something to help?'

God wants you!

Good bishops have a way of discerning vocations – especially in passionate young men and women burning with righteous zeal or anger. Far from being offended, he told Peter about the various projects the Church runs for the Street-children, and agreed that so much more could be done, given more money and resources. Peter went away thoughtfully, spending more days with the children, but his

heart, mind and prayers were tormented by what he could see. Next week he returned to the Archbishop, to hear him say, 'You came here asking me to do something for the street-children – *maybe God is telling you He wants you to do something!*'

Life-changing visit

So from 1982 to 1993, Fr. Peter, by then an Anglican priest, saved all his money and holidays to go out twice a year to help the children he had found on the streets. His only sorrow and regret? – That, sadly, he never did again meet those little ones from that first life-changing visit of 1982!

In January 1994, Fr. Peter decided the time had come to make a greater commitment. Having founded the charity 'Let The Children Live', to raise funds for the work, he went to live in Medellin, where he is now a Roman Catholic priest working with street children. He and his team occasionally make trips to Britain and North America, speaking in churches, and schools, and to other groups of people willing to help. He can be contacted by writing to 'Let The Children Live!', PO Box 11, Walsingham, Norfolk, NR22 6EH.

TASKS

23 Answer the short questions below which test that you have read the passage with understanding.

   a How did Peter Walters become involved in Colombia?

   b What was the attitude of the Archbishop?

   c What is Peter Walters trying to do in South America?

24 Write a letter to your local newspaper.

   You have just found out about Peter Walters' work and you think that people should support him. Your letter should try to persuade people to this end.

In your homework book you will find a task which will ask you to research and to take these ideas further.

Sometimes death simply makes us sad; at other times it makes us angry.

In *Death in Leamington* John Betjeman tells us of an old woman at the end of her life.

Death in Leamington

She died in the upstairs bedroom
By the light of the ev'ning star
That shone through the plate glass window
From over Leamington Spa.

Beside her the lonely crochet
Lay patiently and unstirred,
But the fingers that would have work'd it
Were dead as the spoken word.

And Nurse came in with the tea-things
Breast high 'mid the stands and chairs—
But Nurse was alone with her own little soul,
And the things were alone with theirs.

She bolted the big round window,
She let the blinds unroll,
She set a match to the mantle,
She covered the fire with coal.

And 'Tea!' she said in a tiny voice,
'Wake up! It's nearly **five**.'
Oh! Chintzy, chintzy cheeriness,
Half dead and half alive!

Do you know that the stucco is peeling?
Do you know that the heart will stop?
From those yellow Italianate arches
Do you hear the plaster drop?

Nurse looked at the silent bedstead,
At the gray decaying face,
As the calm of a Leamington ev'ning
Drifted into the place.

She moved the table of bottles
Away from the bed to the wall;
And tiptoeing gently over the stairs
Turned down the gas in the hall.

JOHN BETJEMAN

Charles Dickens is a writer who not only had stories to tell but messages to get across.

In this extract from *Bleak House* he writes of the death of a boy, Jo. This boy was a cross-sweeper. By keeping a crossing point clean he hoped to earn just enough money to support himself.

Bleak House

Jo is in a sleep or in a stupor today, and Allan Woodcourt, newly arrived, stands by him, looking down upon his wasted form. After a while, he softly seats himself upon the bedside with his face towards him – just as he sat in the law-writer's room – and touches his chest and heart. The cart had very nearly given up, but labours on a little more.

The trooper stands in the doorway, still and silent. Phil has stopped in a low clinking noise, with his little hammer in his hand. Mr Woodcourt looks round with that grave professional interest and attention on his face, and, glancing significantly at the trooper, signs to Phil to carry his table out. When the little hammer is next used, there will be a speck of rust upon it.

'Well, Jo! What is the matter? Don't be frightened.'

'I thought,' says Jo, who has started, and is looking round – 'I thought I was in Tom-all-Alone's agin. Ain't there nobody here but you, Mr Woodcot?'

'Nobody.'

'And I ain't took back to Tom-all-Alone's. Am I, sir?'

'No.' Jo closes his eyes, muttering, 'I'm wery thankful.'

After watching him closely a little while, Allan puts his mouth very near his ear, and says to him in a low, distinct voice,–

'Jo! Did you ever know a prayer?'

'Never knowd nothink, sir.'

'Not so much as one short prayer?'

'No, sir. Nothink at all. Mr Chadbands he was a-prayin wunst at Mr Sangsby's and I heerd him; but he sounded as if he wos a-speakin to hisself, and not to me. He prayed a lot, but *I* couldn't make out nothink on it. Different times there was other genlmen come down Tom-all-Alone's a-prayin; but they all mostly sed as the t'other wuns prayed wrong, and all mostly sounded to be a-talking to theirselves, or a-passing blame on the t'others, and not a-talkin to us. *We* never knowd nothink. *I* never knowd what it wos all about.'

It takes him a long time to say this; and few but an experienced and attentive listener could hear, or, hearing, understand him. After a short relapse into sleep or stupor, he makes, of a sudden, a strong effort to get out of bed.

'Stay, Jo! What now?'

'It's time for me to go to that there berryin-ground, sir,' he returns with a wild look.

'Lie down, and tell me. What burying-ground, Jo?'

'Where they laid him as wos wery good to me. Wery good to me indeed he wos. It's time fur me to go down to that there berryin-ground, sir, and ask to be put along with him. I wants to go there and be berried. He used fur to say to me, "I am as poor as you today, Jo," he ses. I wants to tell him that I am as poor as him now, and have come there to be laid along with him.'

'By-and-by, Jo. By-and-by.'

'Ah! P'raps they wouldn't do it if I wos to go myself. But will you promise to have me took there, sir, and laid along with him?'

'I will, indeed.'

'Thank'ee sir. Thank'ee, sir. They'll have to get the key of the gate afore they can take me in, for it's allus locked. And there's a step there, as I used fur to clean with my broom.—It's turned wery dark, sir. Is there any light a-comin?'

'It is coming fast, Jo.'

Fast. The cart is shaken all to pieces, and the rugged road is very near its end.

'Jo, my poor fellow!'

'I hear you, sir, in the dark, but I'm a-gropin—a-gropin – let me catch hold of your hand.'

'Jo, can you say what I say?'

'I'll say anythink as you say, sir, for I knows it's good.'

'OUR FATHER.'

'"OUR FATHER"—yes, that's wery good, sir.'

'WHICH ART IN HEAVEN.'

'"Art in Heaven" – is the light a-comin, sir?'

'It is close at hand. HALLOWED BE THY NAME!'

'"Hallowed be – thy –"'

The light is come upon the dark benighted way. Dead!

Dead, your Majesty. Dead, my lords and gentlemen. Dead, Right Reverends and Wrong Reverends of every order. Dead, men and women, born with Heavenly compassion in your hearts. And dying thus around us every day.

CHARLES DICKENS

Dylan Thomas also writes forcefully about death in *Do not go Gentle into that Good Night*.

Do not go Gentle into that Good Night

Do not go gentle into that good night,
Old age should burn and rave at close of day;
Rage, rage against the dying of the light.

Though wise men at their end know dark is right,
Because their words had forked no lightning they
Do not go gentle into that good night.

Good men, the last wave by, crying how bright
Their frail deeds might have danced in a green bay,
Rage, rage against the dying of the light.

Wild men who caught and sang the sun in flight,
And learn, too late, they grieved it on its way,
Do not go gentle into that good night.

Grave men, near death, who see with blinding sight
Blind eyes could blaze like meteors and be gay,
Rage, rage against the dying of the light.

And you, my father, there on the sad height,
Curse, bless, me now with your fierce tears, I pray.
Do not go gentle into that good night.
Rage, rage against the dying of the light.

DYLAN THOMAS

TASKS

25 Look at these three pieces of writing and, in groups, discuss their different attitudes to death and the effectiveness of each piece of writing.

26 Write a study of at least two of the pieces, bringing out the similarities and the differences. Remember to write about the effect that these pieces have on you.

27 Undertake some writing of your own; you may write poetry if you wish. Here are some possible titles:
   ◼ An Untimely Death
   ◼ Strange Ending
   ◼ Death and Destruction
   ◼ The Funeral

TIME OUT TASK!

Let's go to the cinema

How often do you go to the cinema? What makes it different from watching television?

The cinema is a particular sort of medium where things are perhaps a little larger than life and where you are one of a large audience watching and reacting together.

Think of the last film which you saw and complete the following:

- Write down the title.
- Explain briefly what it was about.
- Describe what was most effective for you.
- Try to recall and describe the atmosphere in the cinema.
- Explain why it would not have been quite the same watching the film on television.

How would you try to persuade a friend who never goes to the cinema that it is a good experience?

END OF TIME OUT!

A lan Bennett allowed an old woman, Miss Shepherd, to live in a van in his front garden in Camden Town. After about 20 years the day came when Miss Shepherd died.

The Lady in the Van

28 April. I am working at my table when I see Miss B arrive with a pile of clean clothes for Miss Shepherd, which must have been washed for her at the day centre yesterday. Miss B knocks at the door of the van, then opens it, looks inside and – something nobody has ever done before – gets in. It's only a moment before she comes out, and I know what has happened before she rings the bell. We go back to the van where Miss Shepherd is dead, lying on her left side, flesh cold, face gaunt, the neck stretched out as if for the block, and a bee buzzing round her body.

It is a beautiful day, with the garden glittering in the sunshine, strong shadows by the nettles, and bluebells out under the wall, and I remember how in her occasional moments of contemplation she would sit in the wheelchair and gaze at the garden. I am filled with remorse for my harsh conduct towards her, though I know at the same time that it was not harsh. But still I never quite believed or chose to believe she was as ill as she was, and I regret too all the questions I never asked her. Not that she would have answered them. I have a strong impulse to stand at the gate and tell anyone who passes.

Miss B meanwhile goes off and returns with a nice doctor from St Pancras who seems scarcely out of her teens. She gets into the van, takes the pulse in Miss S's outstretched neck, checks her with a stethoscope and, to save an autopsy, certifies death as from heart failure. Then comes the priest to bless her before she is taken to the funeral parlour, and he, too, gets into the van – the third person to do so this morning, and all of them without distaste or ado in what to me seem three small acts of heroism. Stooping over the body, his bright white hair brushing the top of the van, the priest murmurs an inaudible prayer and makes a cross on Miss S's hands and head. Then they all go off and I come inside to wait for the undertakers.

I have been sitting at my table for ten minutes before I realise that the undertakers have been here all the time, and that death nowadays comes (or goes) in a grey Ford transit van that is standing outside the gate. There are three undertakers, two young and burly, the third older and more experienced – a sergeant, as it were, and two corporals. They bring out a rough grey-painted coffin, like a prop a conjuror might use and, making no comment on the surely extraordinary circumstances in which they find it, put a sheet of white plastic bin-liner over the body and manhandle it into their magic box, where it falls with a bit of a thud. Across the road, office workers stroll down from the Piano Factory for their lunch, but nobody stops or even looks much, and the Asian woman who has to wait while the box is carried over the pavement and put in the (other) van doesn't give it a backward glance.

Later I go round to the undertakers to arrange the funeral, and the manager apologises for their response when I had originally phoned. A woman had answered, saying, 'What exactly is it you want?' Not thinking callers rang undertakers with a great variety of requests, I was nonplussed. Then she said briskly, 'Do you want someone taking away?' The undertaker explains that her seemingly unhelpful manner was because she thought my call wasn't genuine. 'We get so many hoaxes these days. I've often gone round to collect a corpse only to have it open the door.'

9 May. Miss Shepherd's funeral is at Our Lady of Hal, the Catholic church round the corner. The service has been slotted into the ten o'clock mass, so that, in addition to a contingent of neighbours, the congregation includes what I take to be regulars: the fat little man in thick glasses and trainers who hobbles along to the church every day from Arlington House; several nuns, among them the 99-year-old sister who was in charge when Miss S was briefly a novice; a woman in a green straw hat like an upturned plant pot who eats toffees throughout; and another lady who plays the harmonium in tan slacks and a tea-cosy wig. The server, a middle-aged man with white hair, doesn't wear a surplice, just ordinary clothes with an open-necked shirt, and, but for knowing all the sacred drill, might have been roped in from the group on the corner outside The Good Mixer. The priest is a young Irish boy with a big, red peasant face and sandy hair, and he, too stripped of his cream-coloured cassock, could be wielding a pneumatic drill in the roadworks outside. I keep thinking about these characters during the terrible service, and it reinforces what I have always known: that I could never be a Catholic because I'm such a snob, and that the biggest sacrifice Newman made when he turned his back on the C of E was the social one.

Yet kindness abounds. In front of us is a thin old man who knows the service backwards, and seeing we have no prayer books he lays down his own on top of his copy of the *Sun*, goes back up he aisle to fetch us some, and hands them round, all the time saying the responses without faltering. The first

hymn is Newman's 'Lead Kindly Light', which I try and sing, while making no attempt at the second hymn, which is 'Kum Ba Ya'. The priest turns out to have a good strong voice, though its tone is more suited to 'Kum Ba Ya' than to Newman and J B Dykes. The service itself is wet and wandering, even more so than the current Anglican equivalent, though occasionally one catches in the watered-down language a distant echo of 1662. Now, though, arrives the bit I dread, the celebration of fellowship, which always reminds one of the warm-up Ned Sherrin insisted on inflicting on the studio audience before *Not So Much a Programme*, when everyone had to shake hands with their neighbour. But again the nice man who fetched us the prayer books shames me when he turns round without any fuss or embarrassment and smilingly shakes my hand. Then it is the mass proper, the priest distributing the wafers to the 99-year-old nun and the lady with the plant pot on her head, as Miss S lies in her coffin at his elbow. Finally there is another hymn, this one by the (to me) unknown hymnodist Kevin Norton, who's obviously reworked it from his unsuccessful entry for the Eurovision Song Contest; and with the young priest acting as lead singer, and the congregation a rather subdued backing group, Miss Shepherd is carried out.

The neighbours, who are not quite mourners, wait on the pavement outside as the coffin is hoisted on to the hearse. 'A cut above her previous vehicle,' remarks Colin H; and comedy persists when the car accompanying the hearse to the cemetery refuses to start. It's a familiar scene, and one which I've played many times, with Miss S waiting inside her vehicle as well-wishers lift the bonnet, fetch leads and give it a jump start. Except this time she's dead.

Only A and I and Clare, the ex-nurse who lately befriended Miss S, accompany the body, swept around Hampstead Heath at a less than funeral place, down Bishop's Avenue and up to the St Pancras Cemetery, green and lush this warm, sunny day. We drive beyond the scattered woods to the furthest edge where stand long lines of new gravestones, mostly in black polished granite. Appropriately, in view of her lifelong love of the car, Miss S is being buried within sight and sound of the North Circular Road, one carriageway the other side of the hedge, with juggernauts drowning the words of the priest as he commits the body to the earth. He gives us each a go with his little plastic bottle of holy water, we throw some soil into the grave, and then everybody leaves me to whatever solitary thoughts I might have, which are not many, before we are driven back to Camden Town – life reasserted when the undertaker drops us handily outside Sainsbury's.

ALAN BENNETT

TASKS

28 Write about the discovery of Miss Shepherd's body. What are the writer's feelings and what are yours?

29 This piece of writing is 'reflective': as we are reading it we are constantly made to think about life and death and some of the odd things that happen.
Explain what it made you think about.

In John Steinbeck's novel *Of Mice and Men* George takes responsibility for Lennie, a big man who is mentally very slow. They are workers on a ranch but they have a dream that one day they will own their own place. Everything goes wrong when Lennie kills the wife of Curley, who is the ranch owner's son. Lennie didn't mean to do it but George knows that it is no good; their dreams are over and Lennie must be spared the pain that is waiting for him.

George finds Lennie and, because Lennie wants to, they start talking about their dream…

Of Mice and Men

Lennie said craftily, 'Tell me like you done before.'

'Tell you what?'

''Bout the other guys an' about us.'

George said, 'Guys like us got no fambly. They make a little stake an' then they blow it in. They ain't got nobody in the worl' that gives a hoot in hell about 'em—'

'*But not us,*' Lennie cried happily. 'Tell about us now.'

George was quiet for a moment. 'But not us,' he said.

'Because—'

'Because I got you an'—'

'An' I got you. We got each other, that's what, that gives a hoot in hell about us,' Lennie cried in triumph.

The little evening breeze blew over the clearing and the leaves rustled and the wind waves flowed up the green pool. And the shouts of men sounded again, this time much closer than before.

George took off his hat. He said shakily, 'Take off your hat, Lennie. The air feels fine.'

Lennie removed his hat dutifully and laid it on the ground in front of him. The shadow in the valley was bluer, and the evening came fast. On the wind the sound of crashing in the brush came to them.

Lennie said, 'Tell how it's gonna be.'

George had been listening to the distant sounds. For a moment he was business-like. 'Look acrost the river, Lennie, an' I'll tell you so you can almost see it.'

Lennie turned his head and looked off across the pool and up the darkening slopes of the Gabilans. 'We gonna get a little place,' George began. He reached in his side pocket and brought out Carlson's Luger; he snapped off the safety, and the hand and gun lay on the ground behind Lennie's back. He looked at the back of Lennie's head, at the place where the spine and skull were joined.

A man's voice called from up the river, and another man answered.

'Go on,' said Lennie.

George raised the gun and his hand shook, and he dropped his hand to the ground again.

'Go on,' said Lennie. 'How's it gonna be. We gonna get a little place.'

'We'll have a cow,' said George. 'An' we'll have maybe a pig an' chickens… an' down the flat we'll have a… little piece alfalfa—'

'For the rabbits,' Lennie shouted.

'For the rabbits,' George repeated.

'And I get to tend the rabbits.'

'An' you get to tend the rabbits.'

Lennie giggled with happiness. 'An' live on the fatta the lan'.'

'Yes.'

Lennie turned his head.

'No, Lennie. Look down there across the river, like you can almost see the place.'

Lennie obeyed him. George looked down at the gun.

There were crashing footsteps in the brush now. George turned and looked toward them.

'Go on, George. When we gonna do it?'

'Gonna do it soon.'

'Me an' you.'

'You… an' me. Ever'body gonna be nice to you. Ain't gonna be no more trouble. Nobody gonna hurt nobody nor steal from 'em.'

Lennie said, 'I thought you was mad at me, George.'

'No,' said George. 'No, Lennie. I ain't mad. I never been mad, an' I ain't now. That's a thing I want ya to know.'

The voices came close now. George raised the gun and listened to the voices.

Lennie begged, 'Le's do it now. Le's get that place now.'

'Sure, right now. I gotta. We gotta.'

And George raised the gun and steadied it, and he brought the muzzle of it close to the back of Lennie's head. The hand shook violently, but his face set and his hand steadied. He pulled the trigger. The crash of the shot rolled up the hills and rolled down again. Lennie jarred, and then settled slowly forward to the sand, and he lay without quivering.

George shivered and looked at the gun, and then he threw it from him, back up on the bank, near the pile of old ashes.

The brush seemed filled with cries and with the sound of running feet. Slim's voice shouted, 'George. Where you at, George?'

But George sat stiffly on the bank and looked at his right hand that had thrown the gun away. The group burst into the clearing, and Curley was ahead. He saw Lennie lying on the sand. 'Got him, by God.' He went over and looked down at Lennie, and then he looked back at George. 'Right in the back of the head,' he said softly.

Slim came directly to George and sat down beside him, say very close to him. 'Never you mind,' said Slim. 'A guy got to sometimes.'

But Carlson was standing over George. 'How'd you do it?' he asked.

'I just done it,' George said tiredly.

'Did he have my gun?'

'Yeah. He had your gun.'

'An' you got it away from him and you took it an' you killed him?'

'Yeah. That's how.' George's voice was almost a whisper. He looked steadily at his right hand that had held the gun.

Slim twitched George's elbow. 'Come on, George. Me an' you'll go in an' get a drink.'

George let himself be helped to his feet. 'Yeah, a drink.'

Slim said, 'You hadda, George. I swear you hadda. Come on with me.' He led George into the entrance of the trail and up toward the highway.

Curley and Carlson looked after them. And Carlson said, 'Now what the hell ya suppose is eatin' them two guys?'

JOHN STEINBECK

TASK

30 Think about three basic questions which we might ask about George's actions.

a Was George right to kill Lennie?

b Do you understand why he killed Lennie?

c What effect will these events have on George?

What are your views?

We have been considering quite a difficult subject in this chapter.

Let us consider some of the vocabulary associated with death:

- death
- murder
- carnage
- slaughter
- assassination
- execution

These are all words associated with the end of life. What other words do you know and what are the differences in meaning between them?

Euphemism

This is a way of saying a difficult or shocking thing so that it does not upset someone too much. Write down as many euphemisms as you can think of for death.

You might start with:

> The old boy has kicked the bucket.

'The future's bright; the future's orange.'

That's the way that a television advertisement, very familiar at the time of writing, has been running for some time. But how bright is the future? For you personally? For the place where you live? For our planet?

In this chapter we shall be looking to the future – sometimes seriously, sometimes lightheartedly.

ENGLISH IN THE NATIONAL CURRICULUM:

Key Skills you will cover in this chapter

- ☑ You will be given the opportunity to develop your ability to write narrative – by drawing on your experience of good fiction; by developing your use of writing techniques and by using the knowledge you have built up of story structure, description of settings, organisation of plot, and means of conveying characters and relationships.
- ☑ You will be encouraged to broaden your understanding of the principles of sentence grammar to help you to organise your writing. You will be invited to reflect on the meaning and clarity of the writing of other people.
- ☑ You will be asked to reflect on writers' presentation of ideas, how they develop plot and character and how they create a real impact on the reader.
- ☑ You will be given the chance to read factual and informative texts so that you can select information from them. You will be asked to compare the information which you have drawn from different texts, so that you can make effective use of this information in your own writing and so that you can evaluate how this information has been presented.
- ☑ You will be expected to take different roles in discussion and to express yourself forcefully and effectively.

In this first extract we read the diary entry of Theodore Faron for 1 January 2021.

The Children of Men

The children born in the year 1995 are called Omegas. No generation has been more studied, more examined, more agonized over, more valued or more indulged. They were our hope, our promise of salvation, and they were – they still are – exceptionally beautiful. It sometimes seems that nature in her ultimate unkindness wished to emphasise what we have lost. The boys, men of 25 now, are strong, individualistic, intelligent and handsome as young gods. Many are also cruel, arrogant and violent, and this has been found to be true of Omegas all over the world. The dreaded gangs of the Painted Faces who drive around the countryside at night to ambush and terrorise unwary travellers are rumoured to be Omegas. It is said that when an Omega is caught he is offered immunity if he is prepared to join the State Security Police, whereas the rest of the gang, no more guilty, are sent on conviction to the Penal Colony on the Isle of Man, to which all those convicted of crimes of violence, burglary or repeated theft are now banished. But if we are unwise to drive unprotected on our crumbling secondary roads, our towns and cities are safe, crime effectively dealt with at last by a return to the deportation policy of the nineteenth century.

The female Omegas have a different beauty, classical, remote, listless, without animation or energy. They have their distinctive style which other women never copy, perhaps fear to copy. They wear their hair long and loose, their foreheads bound with braid or ribbon, plain or plaited. It is a style which suits only the classically beautiful face, with its high forehead and large, widely spaced eyes. Like their male counterparts, they seem incapable of human sympathy. Men and women, the Omegas are a race apart, indulged, propitiated, feared, regarded with a half-superstitious awe. In some countries, so we are told, they are ritually sacrificed in fertility rites resurrected after centuries of superficial civilisation. I occasionally wonder what we in Europe will do if news reaches us that these burnt offerings have been accepted by the ancient gods and a live child has been born.

Perhaps we have made our Omegas what they are by our own folly; a regime which combines perpetual surveillance with total indulgence is hardly conducive to healthy development. If from infancy you treat children as gods they are liable in adulthood to act as devils. I have one vivid memory of them which remains the living icon of how I see them, how they see themselves. It was last June, a hot but unsultry day of clear light with slow-moving clouds, like wisps of muslin, moving across a high, azure sky, the air sweet and cool to the cheek. A day with none of the humid languor I associate with an Oxford summer. I was visiting a fellow academic in Christ Church and had entered under Wolsey's wide, four-centred arch to cross Tom Quad when I saw them, a group of four female and four male Omegas elegantly displaying themselves on the stone plinth. The women, with their crimped aureoles of bright hair, their high bound brows, the contrived folds and loops of their diaphanous dresses, looked as though they had stepped down from the Pre-Raphaelite windows in the cathedral. The four males stood behind them, legs firmly apart, arms folded, gazing not at them but over their heads, seeming to assert an arrogant suzerainty over the whole quad. As I passed, the females turned on me their blank, incurious gaze, which nevertheless signalled an unmistakable flicker of contempt. The males briefly scowled, then averted their eyes as if from an object unworthy of further notice and gazed again over the quad. I thought then, as I do now, how glad I was that I no longer had to teach them. Most of the Omegas took a first degree, but that was all; they aren't interested in further education. The undergraduate Omegas I taught were intelligent but disruptive, ill-disciplined and bored. Their unspoken question, 'What is the point of all this?', was one I was glad I wasn't required to answer. History, which interprets the past to understand the present and confront the future, is the least rewarding discipline for a dying species.

The university colleague who takes Omega with total calmness is Daniel Hurstfield, but then, as professor of statistical palaeontology, his mind ranges over a different dimension of time. As with the God of the old hymn, a thousand ages in his sight are like an evening gone. Sitting beside me at a college feast in the year when I was wine secretary, he said, 'What are you giving us with the grouse, Faron? That should do very nicely. Sometimes I fear you are a little inclined to be too adventurous. And I hope you have established a rational drinking-up programme. It would distress me, on my deathbed, to contemplate the barbarian Omegas making free with the college cellar.'

I said: 'We're thinking about it. We're still laying down, of course, but on a reduced scale. Some of my colleagues feel we are being too pessimistic.'

'Oh, I don't think you can possibly be too pessimistic. I can't think why you all seem so surprised at Omega. After all, of the four billion life forms which have existed on this planet, three billion, nine hundred and sixty million are now extinct. We don't know why. Some by wanton extinction, some through natural catastrophe, some destroyed by meteorites and asteroids. In the light of these mass extinctions it really does seem unreasonable to suppose that *Homo Sapiens* should be exempt. Our species will have been one of the shortest-lived of all, a mere blink, you may say, in the eye of time. Omega apart, there may well be an asteroid of sufficient size to destroy this planet on its way to us now.'

He began loudly to masticate his grouse as if the prospect afforded him the liveliest satisfaction.

P D JAMES

TASKS

1 Answer the following questions.

   a Explain what the world is like in 2021 according to Theodore Faron.

   b What sort of people are the 'Omegas'?

   c What effect would it have on the world if children stopped being born?

2 Write your own story entitled 'Omega Child'. You may write as one of the last people to be born in 1996 if you wish.

TIME OUT TASK!

Writing

Remember that 'writing' is assessed separately at GCSE. You will be expected to write (and speak) in a variety of ways, according to the people you are writing (and talking) to.

Here is one way of practising the art of adjusting your language to suit different occasions. Think of a basic piece of information, eg to do with a hobby or an interest, then prepare three short talks on this subject. The three different audiences at whom you should aim your talks are:

- your 6- or 7-year-old brother or sister
- a friend of your own age
- the judges of a public speaking competition.

Alternatively think about 'Breaking the News'. Write the dialogue which would be fitting to break the following different kinds of news.

- Telling your Mum and Dad you've won the lottery.
- Telling your small brother or sister that a pet they love has died.
- Telling your English teacher you haven't had time to do your homework because of Geography coursework.

You must always try to make your writing suitable for your audience.

END OF TIME OUT!

In *The Day of the Triffids* John Wyndham imagines what would happen if, on one particular night in the future, almost everyone in the world became blind.

His book, set in England, adds the complication of a scourge of plants ('triffids') who were originally grown for their oil but have broken free, attacking people and living off their flesh. A real hazard if you are blind.

Human beings always want to overcome difficulties. In this extract a group of people (a few who can see, the majority of whom are blind) are trying to make a plan of survival.

The Day of the Triffids

'It will not be easy: old prejudices die hard. The simple rely on a bolstering mass of maxim and precept, so do the timid, so do the mentally lazy – and so do all of us, more than we imagine. Now that the organisation has gone, our ready-reckoners for conduct within it no longer give the right answers. We *must* have the moral courage to think and to plan for ourselves.'

He paused to survey his audience thoughtfully. Then he said:

'There is one thing to be made quite clear to you before you decide to join our community. It is that those of us who start on this task will all have our parts to play. The men must work – the women must have babies. Unless you can agree to that there can be no place for you in our community.'

After an interval of dead silence, he added:

'We can afford to support a limited number of women who cannot see, because they will have babies who can see. We cannot afford to support men who cannot see. In our new world, then, babies become very much more important then husbands.'

For some seconds after he stopped speaking silence continued, then isolated murmurs grew quickly into a general buzz.

I looked at Josella. To my astonishment she was grinning impishly.

'What do you find funny about this?' I asked, a trifle shortly.

'People's expressions mostly', she replied.

I had to admit it as a reason. I looked round the place, and then across at Michael. His eyes were moving from one section to another of the audience as he tried to sum up the reaction.

'Michael's looking a bit anxious,' I observed.

'He should worry,' said Josella. 'If Brigham Young could bring it off in the middle of the nineteenth century, this ought to be a pushover.'

'What a crude young woman you are at times,' I said. 'Were you in on this before?'

'Not exactly, but I'm not quite dumb, you know. Besides, while you were away someone drove in a bus with most of these blind girls on board. They all came from some institution. I said to myself, why collect them from there when you could gather up thousands in a few streets round here? The answer obviously was that (a) being blind before this happened they had been trained to do work of some kind, and (b) they were all girls. The deduction wasn't terribly difficult.'

'H'm,' I said. 'Depends on one's outlook, I suppose. I must say, it wouldn't have struck me. Do you- ?'

'Sh-sh,' she told me, as a quietness came over the hall.

A tall, dark, purposeful-looking, youngish woman had risen. While she waited, she appeared to have a mouth not made to open, but later it did.

'Are we to understand,' she inquired, using a kind of carbon-steel voice, 'are we to understand that the last speaker is advocating free love?' And she sat down, with spine-jarring decision.

Doctor Vorless smoothed back his hair as he regarded her.

'I think the questioner must be aware that I never mentioned love, free, bought, or bartered. Will she please make her question clearer?'

The woman stood up again.

'I think the speaker understood me. I am asking if he suggests the abolition of the marriage law?'

'The laws we knew have been abolished by circumstances. It now falls to us to make laws suitable to the conditions, and to enforce them if necessary.'

'There is still God's law, and the law of decency.'

'Madam. Solomon had three hundred – or was it five hundred? – wives, and God did not apparently hold that against him. A Mohammedan preserves rigid respectability with three wives. These are matters of local custom. Just what our laws in these matters, and in others, will be is for us all to decide later for the greatest benefit of the community.

'This committee, after discussion, has decided that if we are to build a new state of things and avoid a relapse into barbarism – which is an appreciable danger – we must have certain undertakings from those who wish to join us.

'Not one of us is going to recapture the conditions we have lost. What we offer is a busy life in the best conditions we can contrive, and the happiness which will come of achievement against odds. In return we ask willingness and fruitfulness. There is no compulsion. The choice is yours. Those to whom our offer does not appeal are at perfect liberty to go elsewhere, and start a separate community on such lines as they prefer.

'But I would ask you to consider very carefully whether or not you do hold a warrant from God to deprive any woman of the happiness of carrying out her natural functions.'

The discussion which followed was a rambling affair descending frequently to points of detail and hypothesis on which there could as yet be no answers. But there was no move to cut it short. The longer it went on, the less strangeness the idea would have.

Josella and I moved over to the table where Nurse Berr had set up her paraphernalia. We took several shots in our arms, and then sat down again to listen to the wrangling.

'How many of them will decide to come, do you think?' I asked her.

She glanced round.

'Nearly all of them – by the morning,' she said.

I felt doubtful. There was a lot of objecting and questioning going on. Josella said:

'If you were a woman who was going to spend an hour or two before you went to sleep tonight considering whether you would choose babies and an organisation to look after you, or adherence to a principle which might quite likely mean no babies and no one to look after you. You'd not really be very doubtful, you know. And after all, most women want babies, anyway – the husband's just what Doctor Vorless might call the local means to the end.'

'That's rather cynical of you.'

'If you really think that's cynical you must be a very sentimental character. I'm talking about real women, not those in the magazine-movie-make-believe world.'

'Oh,' I said.

She sat pensively awhile, and gradually acquired a frown. At last she said:

'The thing that worries me is how many will they expect? I like babies, all right, but there are limits.'

After the debate had gone on raggedly for an hour or so, it was wound up. Michael asked that the names of all those willing to join in his plan should be left in his office by ten o'clock the next morning. The Colonel requested all who could drive a lorry to report to him by 7.00 hours, and the meeting broke up.

Josella and I wandered out of doors. The evening was mild. The light on the tower was again stabbing hopefully into the sky. The moon had just risen clear of the Museum roof. We found a low wall, and sat on it, looking into the shadows of the Square garden, and listening to the faint sound of the wind in the branches of the trees there. We smoked a cigarette each almost in silence. When I reached the end of mine, I threw it away, and drew a breath.

'Josella,' I said.

'M'm?' she replied, scarcely emerging from her thoughts.

'Josella,' I said again. 'Er – those babies. I'd – er – I'd be sort of terribly proud and happy if they could be mine as well as yours.'

She sat quite still for a moment, saying nothing. Then she turned her head. The moonlight was glinting on her fair hair, but her face and eyes were in shadow. I waited, with a hammered, and slightly sick feeling inside me. She said, with surprising calm:

'Thank you, Bill, dear. I think I would, too.'

I sighed. The hammering did not ease up much, and I saw that my hand was trembling as it reached for hers. I didn't have any words, for the moment. Josella, however, did. She said:

'But it isn't quite as easy as that, now.'

I was jolted.

'What do you mean?' I asked.

She said, consideringly: 'I think that if I were those people in there' – she nodded in the direction of the tower – 'I think that I should make a rule. I should divide us up into lots. I should say every man who marries a sighted girl must take on two blind girls as well. I'm pretty sure that's what I should do.'

I stared at her face in the shadow.

'You don't mean that,' I protested.

'I'm afraid I do, Bill.'

JOHN WYNDHAM

TASKS

3 Develop your answers to the following questions.

  a What is the proposal being made here? Do you think it is sensible?

  b 'Morality' is about right and wrong. Discuss what is right or wrong about these proposals.

  c Can you think of other emergencies which can overtake people when the normal rules of right or wrong might be broken? Write briefly about several such emergencies.

  d Take one of these examples and write a statement justifying or criticising the action.

4 Imagine you are Josella in the extract. Write from her point of view, giving her feelings and reactions.

You will find this passage from 'The Day of the Triffids' reprinted in your homework book, together with a rather different task, which allows you to take your thinking forward.

TIME ØUT TASK!

The final approach

Reading

As you know, in GCSE examinations your ability to read and your ability to write are assessed separately.

Here is a type of question which specifically tests that you have read the stimulus material with understanding. It expects you to be able to summarise, to analyse language and to make deductions.

The extract is adapted from an article in *Hi-Fi News and Record Review*.

Hi-Fi News & Record Review

There are many good things to say concerning this amplifier, but there is one area where its ability is so remarkable it deserves pride of place.

Frankly its bass is awesome. KAS-2 fully defines the meaning of the word 'slam' as applied to audio. With the KAS-2, even the fastest, most unimportant bass sounds made by percussion instruments can really sound like a door slamming. You can feel the dynamic bass impact as a physical blow. The edge is fast, the control absolute. Bass can start and stop with amazing precision. When the bass rolls it is like opening the floodgates: a rich, deep power fills the room, a raw, dark force rich in sounds, in harmony without any blurring or booming of those sounds.

Some customers would be prepared to buy the KAS-2 for its bass alone, even if the rest was not significantly better than the fine standard already set by the KSA-300-S, the previous model.

But there's more. That low frequency register, the really deep sound, also has clarity, a superbly extended range of tone (it really feels like a direct current amplifier), very good differentiation between bass and tune playing.

So it is not just the bass. Compared with the current KAS series of amplifiers to which I have already referred, this new KAS amplifier shows much more delicacy in the mid and high treble ranges of notes, with very little imperfect sound and substantially greater clarity and purity. Backgrounds are quieter and more low level detail can be heard clearly.

In the middle ranges of sounds the KAS-2 has a hint of 'solidity', just a hint of a rather flat sound – I hesitate to use the word which we sometimes use, 'glare', because it is very well controlled and so mild comp-ared with the usual supporting electronics. KAS-2 high treble sounds are very fine, with excellent definition and a free-dom from either becoming too quiet and soft or from wavering around.

This amplifier gives a highly stable sound from very low to very high levels, from very easy to more difficult loads on speakers. And can it play loud! The whole range of sound, from very quiet to incredibly loud, can be used and I would never have dreamt how perfectly clean sounding the whole range would be, a very real tribute to the KAS-2.

Flat out drive is no effort at all. All the panel lights and indicators come on and yet there is no fluctuation; everything is rock solid and you can hear the sound of every instrument no matter what other sounds are also there. A flute solo can gently pick its way through a thundering bass line and still be heard perfectly.

When using two loudspeakers to listen to stereo, the sound remains excellent.

So, if we weigh up these points about this new amplifier, my sound rating for the KAS-2 is very high indeed, much higher than almost any other amplifier. It is one of the best.

Its design doesn't disappoint us at all and, in fact, the KAS-2 is a remarkable solid-state amplifier. The company which produces it, Krell, has pushed its own high standards even higher. It is an effortless power house.

Always remember that it is in the bass notes that it best demon-strates its absolute quality. It sounds as if an extra range of clean powerful bass has been added to your system: it repro-duces tracks containing heavy fast bass lines with unprec-edented power and accuracy. Test results are first class.

With stunning bass, genuinely high power, and very fine sound overall, the new KAS-2 joins the very best group of amplifiers at the top of the market. It's not cheap but it's superb.

The writer of the Hi-Fi article is very enthusiastic about the KAS-2 amplifier. How does he set out to convey that enthusiasm to you and persuade you to his point of view? You should consider:

■ the facts and ideas which are presented
■ the kind of language the writer uses
■ the kind of audience the writer is writing for

END OF TIME OUT!

W hen considering the future it may occur to you that some people might not have a future. Health problems, accidents, natural disasters, all these things can take away the future.

Printed on the following pages are two leaflets, which you could pick up in any doctor's surgery, which give information about how you may be able to give someone else a future.

Life – don't keep it to yourself

Organ donation can be a difficult subject to think or talk about.

Most people do not want to contemplate their own death. Nor do bereaved relatives find it easy to decide on the donation of the organs of a loved one who has just died. The same goes for the doctors and nurses who may have fought to save the patient's life.

Medicine has developed so rapidly over the past 20 years that transplant surgery is now an established and successful method of treatment – one that not only saves lives in the short run but which can allow the patient receiving the organ to live a full life for many years to come. But far more patients could be saved if there were more donor organs available.

By allowing your organs to be used for transplant after your death, you will be giving someone else their life back.

This leaflet aims to answer some of the most commonly asked questions about organ donation.

What is organ donation?
It means making it clear that you agree that after your death, organs from your body may be used for transplantation to help other people. In many cases, this will save lives. In others, it will allow blind people to see again. Or it will free patients from other forms of long and painful treatment, such as spending hours a week on a kidney machine.

What organs can be donated?
The major donor organs are the kidneys, heart, lungs, liver and pancreas. In addition, heart valves, other muscular tissue and, above all the cornea – the front part of the tough outer shell of the eyeball – can all be used for transplantation. **This means that one donor can help many other patients.**

Who will receive the organs?
Recipients are chosen on the grounds of need and by blood group and, if necessary, by tissue characteristics. There is a waiting list for organ transplants because the demand exceeds the supply.

Who can be an organ donor?
Anyone could be a donor. But, for the major organs, it is only those people who have suffered serious accidents (mostly head injuries) who actually become donors.

Will the fact that I am a known donor affect the treatment I receive in hospital?
Definitely not. The doctors involved in your treatment will not be the ones interested in organ donation. In any case, the prime concern of all doctors and nurses is for their living patients and they will make every attempt to save their patients' lives. Only after they are satisfied that nothing more can be done will the question of organ donation be raised.

Will I really be dead when they remove my organs?
Yes. Before a donor organ is removed from a patient, doctors establishes death has taken place with a series of tests to ensure the brain stem does not function. These are carried out twice by two senior doctors, acting independently from one another, who work under a strict code of practice and who are not involved in the transplant process. The time of death is the time of the second set of tests.

The brain stem is nerve tissue that makes up the lowest part of the brain and connects with the spinal cord. It is a highway for messages travelling between the brain and the rest of the body through the spinal cord and it controls the basic workings of the body as a whole. When the brain stem stops functioning, a person cannot be regarded as alive.

What happens after the tests?
Once doctors are sure that brain stem death has occurred, the donating patient is kept on a 'ventilator' which keeps the heart beating in order to circulate oxygen. This maintains the organs in a healthy condition until they are removed.

Will all the organs be used?
All healthy organs are normally used. It will be up to the doctors responsible to decide whether or not – and which – organs can be successfully

transplanted to another patient. In most cases, organs can be used despite advanced age and previous illness. If you have suffered from certain illnesses, this could rule out the donation of some organs but not others.

Will the organs be used for research?
In the rare cases when organs cannot be placed with a recipient, if the relatives have given prior permission, the organs may be used for research. No organs will be used for experimentation unless you have decided to leave your body to medical science and made the proper arrangements.

Will my body be damaged by organ donation?
When any organs are removed, it is done by a skilled operating team. The body is treated with respect and dignity throughout. And once the operation is over, there will be no sign that any organs have been removed.

Will the funeral by delayed?
No. Arrangement for the funeral can be made as in any case of death. The body can be viewed after the organs have been removed, and the funeral need not be delayed in any way.

How can I become an organ donor?
Simply complete this organ donor card and carry it with you at all times so that should it become necessary your wish to donate your organs to help others will be known to your doctors.

Even if you register on the NHS Organ Donor Register you should still inform your relatives who will be asked for permission to remove organs in the event of your death.

BUT PLEASE DISCUSS YOUR DECISION WITH YOUR RELATIVES.

Please also fill in the form in this leaflet and send it to the NHS Organ Donor Register. This confidential Register will give doctors and nurses a more efficient method of discovering whether a deceased person wanted to donate their organs. There is no need to complete this form if the DVLA has printed on your driving licence that you are registered as an organ donor.

Must my relatives be involved?
If you carry a donor card and/or your name is on the NHS Organ Donor Register, technically your organs may be used for transplantation without consulting anyone else. But in practice, doctors will not remove organs if your relatives object.

Once a patient has been certified brain stem dead, the relatives will be asked to agree to organ donation. This has to be done within hours because the organs must be removed very soon if they are to be used for transplantation.

SO, TO BE SURE THAT YOUR ORGANS ARE DONATED AFTER YOUR DEATH, PLEASE DISCUSS THE SUBJECT WITH YOUR RELATIVES AS SOON AS YOU DECIDE TO BECOME AN ORGAN DONOR.

Will my relatives know who receives my organs?
Strict confidentiality is maintained throughout the donation and transplantation process. However, your relatives will normally be told how your organ donation was used and the outcome of the transplant operations.

Why is it necessary to discuss organ donation with my relatives so soon after my death?
For medical reasons, a decision on organ donation cannot be left too long. So, while it may be a difficult subject for relatives to handle, if they know that the deceased definitely wished to be an organ donor, then the burden of a decision to allow organ donation to proceed will be much less.

What is more, organ donation can often help relatives deal with their own feelings in a positive way if they know that, by giving their consent, they are helping to give life to another person. And that, therefore, they could be sparing another family the grief that they themselves are experiencing.

You too could save a life …
become a bone marrow donor

How do bone marrow transplants save lives?
In a bone marrow transplant the patient's diseased marrow is destroyed by chemotherapy and/or radiation. Healthy donor marrow is then infused into the patient's bloodstream. The new bone marrow travels to the cavities of the large bones and, if engraftment is successful, begins producing normal, healthy blood cells.

What is bone marrow?
Bone marrow, found in the centre of all large bones, is the factory where new blood cells are

made. Without it our bodies would be unable to produce the white cells needed to fight infection, the red cells needed to carry oxygen to and remove waste products from organs and tissues, and platelets which are needed to stop bleeding.

How are donors and patients matched?

Just as there are several different red cell groups known as blood groups, white blood cells carrying genetic markers, sometimes termed 'genetic finger-prints', can also be categorised into groups known as 'tissue-types'. Unlike red cell blood groups, there are enormous numbers of possible tissue-types and it takes an extremely large register of unrelated donors to find an exact 'tissue-type' match for every patient. In spite of access to over two million donors worldwide some searches are still not successful.

What does the donor initially do?

Volunteers are required to complete an application form including medical details. If deemed to be suitable on medical grounds the donor is asked to attend his/her doctor for a small blood sample to be taken and sent to our laboratories for tissue-typing. The results are placed on a confidential computer record.

What sort of donors are needed?

Male donors of any ethnic background – for a variety of clinical reasons male donors are usually preferred.

Donors from ethnic minorities within the UK eg African, African-Caribbean, Asian, Chinese, Jewish, Eastern European, Mediterranean as well as volunteers of mixed ethnic background. 'Tissue-types' and inherited characteristics, and it is these that are used in matching donors and patients. The likelihood, therefore, of finding a matching donor will be considerably greater in donors from the same ethnic background as the patient.

What is The Anthony Nolan Trust?

The Anthony Nolan Bone Marrow Trust manages the world's first and largest fully independent Register of potential bone marrow donors with over a quarter of a million volunteers. The Trust was started in 1974 by Shirley Nolan in a vain attempt to save the life of her son Anthony. He sadly died in 1979, aged 7, of an immune deficiency disease without a matching donor being found.

Why do people need bone marrow transplants?

Every year thousands of people with bone marrow diseases such as leukaemia, aplastic anaemia and inborn metabolic and immune deficiency conditions reach a stage when only a bone marrow transplant can possibly save them.

Why are unrelated donors needed?

Family members, particularly brothers and sisters, can be the best matches. Due to the average family size only approximately 30% of patients have a suitable family donor.

What happens next?

Requests from all over the world to search our Register are received at a rate of over 3,000 each year. When a patient search is referred to us, the patient's tissue type is entered onto the computer and searched against donor tissue-type listed. Possible matching donors will be asked to provide further blood samples to help select the donor who matches best for that particular patient. A volunteer may be approached on several occasions to provide blood samples for further more detailed tests. This can occur soon after registering or over a period of a number of years.

How is the bone marrow removed?

The donor is given a general anaesthetic under operating theatre conditions and marrow, which looks like blood, is withdrawn from the hip bones using needle and syringe. No surgical incision is required. The marrow replaces itself within 21 days.

Does it hurt?

The marrow is taken from the donor under general anaesthetic and therefore no pain is experienced during the operation. The donor my feel some post-operative tenderness and discomfort in the lower back; general weakness and tiredness is inevitable for a few days afterwards and the general recovery period is 10 – 14 days.

What are the risks for the donor?

As with any procedure requiring a general anaesthetic, there is a small but definite risk. This is no different from any other minor operation. The donor has to undergo a thorough medical examination beforehand to ensure that he/she is fit to proceed.

Where would I donate?

The medical procedure for obtaining donor marrow is called a harvest. If you are asked to donate marrow you would be required to attend a specialist harvest centre in the UK – usually in London. Under normal circumstances you would be hospitalised for two nights.

Is a transplant a definite cure?

Unfortunately the field of bone marrow transplantation is complex and a number of patients still die of complications despite the best medical care. Over the past five years increasing numbers of successful transplants have been carried out using matched unrelated donors. Donors can only be assured that they will offer the hope of a future to patients whose disease would almost certainly otherwise prove fatal.

Can I change my mind?

The Trust appreciates that the circumstances of our volunteers may change over time and of course you can remove your name from the register whenever you wish. It should nevertheless be remembered that this is a commitment and serious thought should be given to the full implications of being a donor before you give your first blood sample.

What are the criteria to join the Register?

If you are:

- aged between 18–40 (after joining it is possible to donate up to age 55)
- in excellent health
- weigh at least 8 stone (51 kgs)
- prepared to undergo a general anaesthetic and suffer some short-term discomfort to try to save the life of another person
- permanently resident in the UK and likely to be so for at least the next 2–3 years
- prepared to take time to give several blood samples as and when required
- prepared and able to take time off work or from your normal duties if required to donate marrow

TASKS

5 Either in groups or as a class discuss the issues which are raised in these leaflets.

It is almost certain that different members of the class will have different views and you should listen carefully, as well as putting your own view.

6 Imagine that you are very keen to participate in these schemes but other members of your family have doubts.

In the form of a play script, write the discussion which takes place around the dinner table when you mention the idea.

(Use information from both leaflets to provide material for the discussion.)

You will find another leaflet referred to in your homework book which, perhaps in a different way, talks about giving people a future.

The poet Louis MacNeice paints a bleak picture of the future in his poem *Prayer Before Birth*.

Prayer Before Birth

I am not yet born; O hear me.
Let not the bloodsucking bat or the rat or the stoat
*   or the clubfooted ghoul come near me.*

I am not yet born; console me.
I fear that the human race may with tall walls wall me,
with strong drugs dope me, with wise lies lure me,
on black racks rack me in, in blood-baths roll me.

I am not yet born; provide me
With water to dandle me, grass to grow for me, trees to talk
to me, sky to sing to me, birds and a white light
in the back of my mind to guide me.

I am not yet born; forgive me
For the sins that in me the world shall commit, my words
when they speak me, my thoughts when they think me,
my treason engendered by traitors beyond me,
my life when they murder by means of my
hands, my death when they live me.

I am not yet born; rehearse me
In the parts I must play and the cues I must take when old men lecture me,
bureaucrats hector me, mountains
frown at me, lovers laugh at me, the white
waves call me to folly and the desert calls
me to doom and the beggar refuse
my gift and my children curse me.

I am not yet born; O hear me,
Let not the man who is beast or who thinks he is God
come near me.

I am not yet born; O fill me
With strength against those who would freeze my
    humanity, would dragoon me into a lethal automaton,
        would make me a cog in a machine, a thing with
            one face, a thing, and against all those
                who would dissipate my entirety, would
                    blow me like thistledown hither and
                        thither or hither and thither
                            like water held in the
                                hands would spill me
Let them not make me a stone and let them not spill me.
Otherwise kill me.

LOUIS MACNEICE

TASKS

7 Answer the following questions.
   a What are the main thoughts in this poem?
   b Has the unborn child really got so much to fear, do you think?
8 Write a poem to balance this one: call it something like 'The Joys to Come'.

Several times in this book we have asked you to develop your skills of comparison. Comparing involves looking at:

■ contents and ideas
■ the way these are shaped or developed
■ the ways the language used creates effects
■ mood, tone and feelings
■ your own reactions and responses

Printed below is another poem, *5 Ways to Kill a Man* by Edwin Brock.

5 Ways to Kill a Man

There are many cumbersome ways to kill a man:
you can make him carry a plank of wood
to the top of a hill and nail him to it. To do this
properly you require a crowd of people
wearing sandals, a cock that crows, a cloak
to dissect, a sponge, some vinegar and one
man to hammer the nails home.

Or you can take a length of steel,
shaped and chased in a traditional way,
and attempt to pierce the metal cage he wears.
But for this you need white horses,
English trees, men with bows and arrows,
at least two flags, a prince and a
castle to hold your banquet in.

Dispensing with nobility, you may, if the wind
allows, blow gas at him. But then you need
a mile of mud sliced through with ditches,
not to mention black boots, bomb craters,
more mud, a plague of rats, a dozen songs
and some round hats made of steel.

*In an age of aeroplanes, you may fly
miles above your victim and dispose of him by
pressing one small switch. All you then
require is an ocean to separate you, two
systems of government, a nation's scientists,
several factories, a psycopath and
land that no one needs for several years.*

*These are, as I began, cumbersome ways
to kill a man. Simpler, direct, and much more neat
is to see that he is living somewhere in the middle
of the twentieth century, and leave him there.*

EDWIN BROCK

TASK

9 Compare *Prayer Before Birth* with *5 Ways to Kill a Man*.

The future might not be so terrifying if only we could find out in advance what will happen. Human beings have made claims to have this skill. 'Telling fortunes' and reading horoscopes are two popular pastimes.

TASKS

10 Do some research and find out about some forms of telling the future and how they are supposed to work.
   Prepare a presentation about this for your class.
11 Collect your own horoscopes from different places over a period of time.
   Report back to the class on similarities and differences between the various horoscopes.
   Was there any truth in them?

Here is a selection of horoscopes from two magazines – *Company* and *Elle*. They are taken from the same month, April 1995.

Horoscopes

Tanya Obreza reveals what's in your stars for April

Aries 21 March – 20 April
New developments that occur this month will help you achieve important ambitions and discover exciting options and interests, but be prepared to face deeper personal issues, and watch out for emotional dramas mid-month. Work is fast-paced and demanding, but at last it feels like you're really beginning to get somewhere. If you make new business contacts you could be rewarded with a promotion, and a long-held wish may suddenly come true. Lucky work day: 18th.

Taurus 21 April – 21 May

You really value your freedom and independence, but you may be asked to sacrifice it this month to help friends and family deal with their problems. At work, steaming ahead and pursuing ambitions is still your top priority, but prepare yourself for new, exciting challenges. This is an excellent time to make that career move you've been aiming for, so make the most of any opportunities that come your way. Lucky career day: 5th.

Gemini 22 May – 21 June

This looks set to be an emotional month, leaving you confused and uncertain, and looking for support from friends and colleagues, but your cries for help won't be heard unless you stop hiding your feelings. You're approaching a major turning point in your life, so give yourself the time and space to sort out those deeper needs and emotions. And remember, the lessons learned now will prove invaluable in the years to come. Lucky love day: 4th.

Cancer 22 June –22 July

Relationships continue to be a major issue, but your emotions have settled down since recent upheavals. It's a good time to take control of professional matters – more money and a better lifestyle is what Cancerians should be aiming for right now. Give free reign to your imagination and creativity and show off your talents. Expect to work hard, but for tremendous rewards. Lucky career day: 25th.

Leo 23 July – 23 August

The difficulties you've experienced over recent months seem long gone. You've survived some major personal dramas and learned how to stay calm and collected. It's not in your nature to be constantly down, and few can match your great sense of humour. Bring back the fun and laughter to your life by contacting neglected friends who have been missing you. After the 17th, expect a financial bonus as you begin to reap the rewards of brave career moves made earlier this year. Lucky love day: 3rd.

Virgo 24 August – 23 September

You're a perfectionist who doesn't like to break promises and once committed, it's impossible for you to do anything half-heartedly. But the standards you set are often too high, so don't be hard on yourself if you can't reach them – just remember to judge your efforts as well as the results. What you really need now is reassurance and sympathy, and friends will be going out of their way to please and comfort you with all the compassion and understanding you need. Lucky love day: 12th.

Libra 24 September – 23 October

Many Librans will be in the mood for love this month, so brace yourself for some sizzling surprises. Turn on the charm and you'll soon be meeting exciting, interesting new friends… and maybe lovers. But even if new romance is somewhat short-lived, the wonderful memories you'll be left with will last a lifetime. At work, be prepared to change plans at short notice, as something you've been quietly hoping for could suddenly materialise – golden opportunities are on their way. Lucky work day: 13th.

Scorpio 24 October – 22 November

Make the best of the brilliant opportunities that look set to occur after the 21st. There are some significant and positive lifestyle changes on the way, so get ready to embark on a journey of self-discovery. But before taking that first step, think back to events that happened a couple of years ago and don't let history repeat itself. You're determined to outshine the competition, and a proposed trip could prove much more rewarding than originally thought. Lucky love day: 13th.

Sagittarius 23 November – 21 December

Financial shocks and setbacks continue to restrict your spending power in early April. If you're in a dead-end job, start planning your great escape right now, but keep long-term goals in mind and don't just plan for tomorrow. Get ready to capitalise on unexpected offers from new friends and colleagues after the 15th, but resist the temptation to turn a professional relationship into something more passionate. Lucky love day: 11th.

Capricorn 22 December – 20 January

You always make the best of any opportunity, and this month is no exception. It's likely there will either be financial gains or losses, but either way you'll turn the situation to your advantage. Make the most of new business contacts, but sort out potential pitfalls before making long-term commitments. If friends start to burden you with their problems, resist the temptation to deal with situations they should sort out themselves. A relative may decide this is a good month to visit you, so be warned! Lucky love day: 8th.

Aquarius 21 January – 18 February

Just when you think it's safe to put your feet up and relax, you'll be thrown back into a hectic social scene. Be patient early on in the month, when your plans may change time and time again. The pace will be tough, but the end result will be well worth all the upheaval. Money will be in short supply, but try not to get too frustrated – it's a short-term situation that will sort itself out sooner rather than later. Lucky work day: 26th.

Pisces 19 February – 20 March

A major commitment or goal will eclipse everything else in your life this month and you could end up completely worn out. Watch out for new responsibilities that may sap all your energy, leaving you weepy and on edge. There will be lots to organise that requires attention to detail, so take your time and be methodical. When things get too much, make a dash for freedom and take some time off to relax and unwind. Lucky career day: 3rd.

Horoscopes

For March 9 – April 12

Aries *Mar 21 – April 20*

In the next few weeks, 1995 which has brought you virtually nothing so far, starts to work in your favour. There is contact between your own planet Mars and the great, beneficent Jupiter on March 9, and again on April 12. In between these two dates nothing seems to move much, but somehow everything improves. It's all very strange. Think of the first date as the time when your situation stops getting worse, and the second as the time when it starts getting better. It's simply a question of attitude, but it works.

Taurus *April 21 – May 21*

This month sees one of the biggest celestial events for many years: a change of signs by mighty Uranus, taking place at one of the most sensitive and important places in your horoscope – the topmost point, the career angle. Some sort of change in the direction of your professional life is therefore inevitable. Since Uranus takes months to complete its moves, you can, if you wish, tell yourself that you needn't worry about it just yet. But while this is true, postponing something doesn't mean it disappears.

Gemini *May 22 – June 21*

The time to prove yourself is at hand. You are well aware that the tasks you have taken on are not simple, but you are still confident that you have what it takes. Unfortunately not everyone agrees, on account of some of your recent actions. Your apparent unwillingness to face a problem head on, while examining all the options, has created rumours about your intentions and abilities. Your were wise to wait, but a further delay at this point will work against you. Act decisively now and take control of the situation.

Cancer *June 22 – July 22*

You are in a state of flux, which often bothers the cautious Cancerian more than it should. Change, after all, is natural, and there is no evidence that is necessarily for the worse. This month's New Moon, high in the chart, shows opportunities for a new role or position in your professional life. This, coupled with the improvements in your financial position indicated by other planets, could be the start of something much larger than you think – something that gives you a completely different view of your future.

Leo *July 23 – Aug 23*

You can no longer ignore the warning bells in your private affairs. For too long you have been telling yourself that the problem will solve itself, bit it is showing no sign of doing so. Patience is a fine virtue, but is your apparent forbearance really an unwillingness to start an argument in case you lose it and look small? Perhaps this is truer than you are prepared to admit. Whatever the reasons, you have now run out of time. You must accept that your present situation is unworkable. Anything – win or lose – would be better.

Virgo *Aug 24 – Sept 22*

Sometimes you are too sympathetic and understanding for your own good. Virgo has a strong need to serve, and you are more than willing to inconvenience yourself for the sake of others, but they are taking shameless advantage of you and have no intention of giving you similar service in return. As they go forwards, with your help, you are in fact going backwards – and it is time for all this to stop. You must rethink the way you work. It cannot be done overnight but it must be done for your own long-term happiness.

Libra *Sept 23 – Oct 23*

This is a tense and difficult time in your emotional affairs. It is made no easier by the fact that your partner appears to want one thing one day and something else the next. This makes it difficult for you to balance your response with his needs, but the truth of the matter is that he is having a worse time of it than you are, and what you both need most is a little space. It may well be possible – and desirable – to build the relationship in a different way, so that you can both be more self-sufficient and less dependent on each other.

Scorpio *Oct 24 – Nov 22*

At last you can make a fresh start. Your new agenda was drawn was drawn up at the end of last year but circumstances beyond your control conspired to fill your time with less important things. This continues for most of March, but once Mars changes direction on the 24th it should be possible to put a lot of last year's leftovers behind you and make progress towards the real business of 1995 and the future. What takes place around April 4 is important: you can then see what to aim for and how you are going to afford it.

Sagittarius *Nov 23 – Dec 23*

Jupiter, your ruling planet, pauses in its headlong rush through the sign at the end of March, giving you time to assess your position. Although your rate of progress will slow down as a result, remember that speed isn't everything. You need time to make sure you are doing everything thoroughly along the way, so that you are not forced to come back later and finish things properly. Don't worry that you might not reach your goals – your present run of good fortune lasts right through until the start of 1996.

Capricorn *Dec 24 – Jan 20*
Uranus leaves Capricorn at the end of March – its departure means that the period of upheaval and reorganisation that has been going on for so long is now coming to an end. Usually it is the presence rather than the absence of a planet in a sign that is seen as an indicator of events but when as in this case, a large and powerful planet has been your constant companion for seven years, losing its influence can have quite a noticeable effect. Believe it or not, the future is beginning to look more stable.

Aquarius *Jan 21 – Feb 18*
The event you have been waiting for all your life takes place on April 1, when Uranus, Aquarius'

ruler, returns to the sign for the first time since 1920. It will be with you until 2003. Obviously such a long-term influence will take time to make its presence and purpose felt, but it is nonetheless important to be aware of it. If you have wondered whether you would ever find your niche in life, or a direction you could follow wholeheartedly, then this period will provide it. Your time starts now.

Pisces *Feb 19 – Mar 20*
Your affairs are very finely balanced at the moment. You know what you ought to do but you wish somehow that it could be easier for you and less painful for everyone else involved. You wish that the crisis you fear would miraculously disappear but you know that this is unlikely to happen. These things have to be faced. Your own mind is firmly made up but others may be unable – or unwilling – to match your commitment. Be ruthless in your approach to them, and be prepared to act alone if need be.

TASKS

12 Working in pairs, discuss the similarities and differences between the two sets of horoscopes.

13 Look at the way they are written. What do you notice about their language?
Write a short passage explaining the language of the horoscopes and saying why you think they are written in this way.

14 Write a page of horoscopes of your own. Remember that you really do have to try to make people believe them!
Then compare your horoscopes with those in magazines or newspapers you read.

15 Interview a cross-section of people and write a report about their opinions on horoscopes.

H ere's a girl who has a future! And she is concerned about our future as well.

Debbie pulls it off

DEBBIE SIMMONS has seen the future and it is filthy, unless she and her 800 child delegates can get their hands on it. Later this month, they fly in from all over the world to a conference in Eastbourne. She will be chairing it. She is 13 years old. **Jessica Berens** *reports.*

On 23 October, 800 children aged between 10 and 12 will travel from more than 50 countries to stay in hotels along the seafront at Eastbourne. They will assemble at the Devonshire Park Centre where why will present projects on the environment and formulate a charter to take back to their respective governments.

Delegates include Dominique Godino from the Philippines who has seen the waterfalls of Hinulugang Taktak ruined by refuse and who is spearheading a campaign to rehabilitate the area; Sulmaan Khan, from Pakistan, illuminating the plight of endangered wildlife, in particular the houbbara bustard, the snow leopard and the Himalayan brown bear; and Ibrahim Alex Bangura, from Sierra Leone, who, through Peace Child International, has planted 10,000 trees in areas eroded by deforestation. Things have come a long way since recycling meant making models of Dougal out of old Fairy Liquid bottles, the days when a 'meeting' was an egg sandwich in a tent in the garden.

The International Children's Conference on the Environment – with its slogan LEAVE IT TO US – is the first of its kind, inspired by children, run for children and with the key decision-making remaining in the hands of children. Workshops, to be held in the afternoons, offer a sophisticated range. Subject include the Internet ('discover the potential of global communication'), conference radio ('learn how to use the media to communicate your ideas'), and enviroscoping, DNA fingerprinting and bio-diversity.

The driving force behind it all is Debbie Simmons, a 13-year-old British girl. Debbie, despite her wide, disarming smile and her dynamic plans for world improvement, is not the sinister dwarf of Hollywood lore. At home, she has a collection of carved owls, and is saving up to buy a flute. She is 'not good at PE'. She used to be quite shy. When she first joined the junior board of Drusillas Park – a private zoo near Eastbourne – at the age of eight, she 'found it difficult to speak out'. Now, as chairperson of the International Children's Conference on the Environment, she has found herself with responsibilities.

Meetings of the junior board are held at Drusillas Park on Saturday afternoons. Once in the boardroom, Debbie becomes a focused individual with a bulging A4 folder and a firm and articulate manner. Pavel, who is from Russia, is 12 and has run straight from school. Rebecca, 12, and Anna, 11, both have bobs and are business-like; Ben, 11, is quiet; Dermot, 12, is absent because he is at a Liverpool match. 'Dermot's favourite word is 'patronising'. Debbie tells me this before the meeting. 'He doesn't like children's presenters because they are patronising.'

Michael Ann and his wife, Kitty, both directors of the zoo, have always felt that, since children are their main customers, it is children who are likely to have the most pertinent ideas about the zoo. The junior board, launched in 1989, began by initiating schemes for the zoo – dustbins in the shape of animals, a play area for toddlers – but raised the idea of an international conference on the environment three years ago. A second group of children was then selected to organise the conference after letters were sent to local schools asking teachers to nominate candidates. Debbie, as a long-term member of the original junior board, was co-opted as chair-person. 'The children felt that there was so much more that they could be doing', says Kitty Ann, 'all they needed was a voice and some encouragement.'

The project has involved argument, compromise, patience, endless telephone calls, faxes and letters, long days for the Anns (who organised backing and sponsorship) and stalwart commitment from Debbie and her team who meet twice a month. Finance has been provided by British Airways (who, acting as sponsors, are giving free flights to delegates – 600 of whom are from overseas) as well as organisations such as East Sussex County Council, Eastbourne Borough Council, the English Tourist Board and the United Nations Environment Programme. Delegates will pay a fee of £94 and for their accommodation (at subsidised rates); most have been sponsored by their schools and local environmental organisations. A number of the children will present projects, chosen after hundreds of applications were examined by a conference sub-committee and the junior board, whose brief was to find inter-esting ideas from a wide geographical spread.

Thus the junior board has learned much of the specifics involved in the democratic process (the importance of voting, for instance) and Debbie can claim a working knowledge of how power works. The adults, meanwhile, may be credited with helping to realise what is, in essence, a child's fantasy.

'If you have one person saying "I think you should do this", no one is going to take any notice,' says Debbie. 'But if you have 800 children standing there saying "We think you should do this because you are ruining the world," then governments and the media might listen'. She hopes that the event will 'make people aware that children know what is going on'.

Debbie is most reluctant to see herself as a heroine. Does she feel proud? 'Yes,' she says, 'in a way. You come up with a small idea and it grows … but it wasn't actually me, it was the whole board.' She is not precocious or bossy, feeling only 'a bit annoyed' when she sees someone dropping litter in the street. She would not dream of accosting the offender. 'Even if you did', she says, 'it wouldn't make any difference.'

Debbie was born in Eastbourne. Her father, Anthony, is a solicitor and her mother, Joanne, an occupational therapist. The family live in a street full of gabled mock-Tudor houses. Debbie remembers a time when their garden stretched into fields in which there were sheep. Now there is a main road. The reduction of space is a tangible experience; a generation has grown up with a deterioration from which it has been impossible to escape. 'The world', she says simply, 'is turning into a tip.'

Debbie's mother had watched *Blue Peter* as a child and had saved milk bottle tops for Guide Dogs for the Blind, a task familiar to anyone who grew up with John Noakes and his nice dog, Shep. 'I don't throw things away' she says. 'I just never have. But it was from the children that we got the recycling. Boxes go to the school; tin cans go to Drusillas for the rainforest.' She had been a Girl Guide and, as a mother, took Debbie and her younger sister, Emma, on the pond-dipping expeditions that she had enjoyed when young. These helped to foster Debbie's love of animals and concern for their welfare, as did the school plays in which Debbie took part. The *Bumble Snouts* featured aliens who appeared on earth and were horrified by what they saw. In *Ocean World*, which addressed the endangerment of whales, she played the part of a coral reef, wearing a white catsuit decorated with fabric paints; and at ten, she appeared in *Save the Human*, in which society was run by animals and the humans faced extinction. These, she says, 'made us more aware'.

Joanne worries sometimes that Debbie will be agitated by the pressures of the limelight but thinks that, in general, she copes very well. 'She knows I am here, but it is her thing and I let her do it.'

The junior board settles down to address its business. An official conference song must be chosen, but songs sent in by hopeful contenders all sound like 'We Are The World'. Things liven up considerably, however, when the subject of lunch is broached. The board is particularly sensitive to the problems that may be encountered by visiting children unfamiliar with the English language and English food. Kitty Ann wonders how 800 people are going to eat at once. The talk is of buffets and roasts and cards you can fill in, like the ones you get in hospitals. Kitty Ann delivers the disheartening news that there will probably only be packed lunch.

'What kind of sandwiches do you have in Russia, Pavel?' she asks. He shrugs. 'Fish.' 'Ugh,' says Rebecca, 'I hate fish.' 'Egg mayonnaise?' suggests Ben, speaking for the first time. 'I like tuna salad sandwiches as long as they don't have mayonnaise,' says Anna. Marmite attracts a unanimous verdict: 'Really gross.' The subject flows swiftly on to crisps and soft drinks before suddenly arriving at Frank Bruno. Some people wish that he could come to the conference. Frank Bruno, you see, is not gross. And he is not patronising.

TASKS

16 Using information from the article, write a character study of Debbie Simmons. You should refer to:

- her family
- her early life
- her involvement with the zoo
- her school life
- her hopes for the future

17 You are a newspaper reporter from the local Eastbourne paper. You have been sent to 'cover' the conference.
Use information from the passage and write your report, which your editor has told you must not exceed 400 words.

18 You will be going to the conference as one of the delegates. Write about your hopes for what might be achieved.

You will find this article reprinted in your homework book, together with a further task involving you as a delegate.

n *Macbeth* Banquo asks the witches about the future.

'If you can look into the seeds of time
And say which grain will grow, and which will not,
Speak then to me...'

This is at the beginning of the play.

After Macbeth has become king and been responsible for two
murders he goes to the witches to find out what is going to
happen to him in the future.

Macbeth

Act 4 Scene 1
Thunder. FIRST APPARITION, *an armed head*
MACBETH:
  Tell me, thou unknown power –
1 WITCH:
  He knows thy thought.
  Hear his speech, but say thou nought.
1 APPARITION:
  Macbeth, Macbeth, Macbeth! beware Macduff.
  Beware the Thane of Fife. Dismiss me. Enough.
                                    (*Descends*)
MACBETH:
  Whate'er thou art, for they good caution thanks.
  Thou hast harped my fear aright. But one word
    more –
1 WITCH:
  He will not be commanded. Here's another,
  More potent than the first.
Thunder. SECOND APPARITION, *a bloody child*
2 APPARITION:
  Macbeth, Macbeth, Macbeth!
MACBETH:
  Had I three ears, I'd hear thee.
2 APPARITION:
  Be bloody, bold and resolute. Laugh to scorn
  The power of man, for none of woman born
  Shall harm Macbeth.   (*Descends*)
MACBETH:
  Then live Macduff, what need I fear of thee?
  But yet I'll make assurance double sure
  And take a bond of fate. Thou shalt not live,
  That I may tell pale-hearted fear it lies,
  And sleep in spite of thunder.
Thunder. THIRD APPARITION, *a child crowned with a
tree in his hand*
  What is this,

That rises like the issue of a king,
And wears upon his baby brow the round
And top of sovereignty?
ALL:
  Listen, but speak not to't.
3 APPARITION:
  Be lion-mettled, proud and take no care
  Who chafes, who frets, or where conspirers are.
  Macbeth shall never vanquished be until
  Great Birnam wood to high Dunsinane hill
  Shall come against him.   (*Descends*)
MACBETH:
  That will never be.
  Who can impress the forest, bid the tree
  Unfix his earth-bound root? Sweet bodements,
    good!
  Rebellious dead, rise never till the wood
  Of Birnam rise, and our high-placed Macbeth
  Shall live the lease of nature, pay his breath
  To time and mortal custom. Yet my heart
  Throbs to know one thing: tell me, if your art
  Can tell so much, shall Banquo's issue ever
  Reign in this kingdom?
ALL:
  Seek to know no more.
MACBETH:
  I will be satisfied. Deny me this,
  And an eternal curse fall on you. Let me know...
  Why sinks that cauldron, and what noise is this?
                                    (*hautboys*)
1 WITCH:
  Show!
2 WITCH:
  Show!
3 WITCH:
  Show!

ALL:
Show his eyes, and grieve his heart,
Come like shadows, so depart.

A show of eight kings, the last with a glass in his hand, BANQUO *following*

MACBETH:
Thou art too like the spirit of Banquo. Down!
Thy crown does sear mine eyeballs, and
    thy hair,
Thou other gold-bound brow, is like the first …
A third is like the former … Filthy hags,
Why do you show me this? A fourth? Start, eyes!
What, will the line stretch out to the crack
    of doom?
Another yet … A seventh? I'll see no more.
And yet the eighth appears, who bears a glass,
Which shows me many more, and some I see
That twofold balls and treble sceptres carry.

Horrible sight!… Now I see 'tis true,
For the blood-boltered Banquo smiles upon me,
And points at them for his. What, is this so?

1 WITCH:
Ay sir, all this is so. But why
Stands Macbeth thus amazedly?
Come sisters, cheer we up his sprites,
And show the best of our delights.
I'll charm the air to give a sound,
While you perform your antic round,
That this great King may kindly say,
Our duties did his welcome pay,
(*Music. The* WITCHES *dance and vanish*)

MACBETH:
Where are they? Gone? Let this pernicious hour
Stand aye accursed in the calendar.

WILLIAM SHAKESPEARE

TASK

19 Answer the following questions

   a Explain exactly what Macbeth has found out here.

   b How do you think Macbeth will be affected by what he has heard?

   c What do you notice about the form and the words which make up the apparitions?

I f you look at *Macbeth* in detail you will discover that after this visit Macbeth's fortunes do not improve. In the last act of the play, after he has been deserted by many of his followers and his wife has died, he utters these words:

Macbeth

Act 5 Scene 5
MACBETH:
  She should have died hereafter.
  There would have been a time for such a word.
  Tomorrow, and tomorrow, and tomorrow
  Creeps in this petty pace from day to day,
  To the last syllable of recorded time,
  And all our yesterdays have lighted fools

  The way to dusty death. Out, out, brief candle!
  Life's but a walking shadow, a poor player
  That struts and frets his hour upon the stage
  And then is heard no more. It is a tale
  Told by an idiot, full of sound and fury,
  Signifying nothing.

          WILLIAM SHAKESPEARE

TASK

20 How does Macbeth feel now about the future?

   How has the mood of these lines been created by Shakespeare?

   Write your own version capturing Macbeth's thoughts and feelings.

TIME OUT TASK!

The final approach – revising a literature text

The importance of structured revision during the run-in to your examinations cannot be stressed too highly.

Literature revision – a schedule

- Read the text again. It is vital that the text is as fresh in your mind as possible.
- A number of examination boards allow you to take your annotated texts into the examination room. If you cannot remember the significance of an annotation then it is worse than useless – it is in fact distracting.
- Look through everything you have ever written about the text – essays, notes etc. Summarise this work on a couple of sides of A4 paper.

- Make sure that these notes cover the fundamental elements of:
  - characters   - style
  - plot   - your opinion
  - structure
- If necessary, rearrange your summarised notes into a sensible order.
- You should now have your revision condensed to:
  a the usefully annotated text
  b a couple of sides of comprehensive notes

Apply this schedule to all of your literature texts.

END OF TIME OUT!

One of the concerns of the modern world is about atomic and nuclear power. Put simply, human beings now have the power to destroy themselves and life on the planet.

The dropping of the first atomic bomb on Hiroshima in 1945 showed us something of what could be involved.

Peter Porter has written a poem about an imminent nuclear attack. It is called *Your Attention Please*.

Your Attention Please

The Polar DEW has just warned that
A nuclear rocket strike of
At least one thousand megatons
Has been launched by the enemy
Directly at our major cities.
This announcement will take
Two and a quarter minutes to make,
You therefore have a further
Eight and a quarter minutes
To comply with the shelter
Requirements published in the Civil
Defence Code – section Atomic Attack.
A specially shortened Mass
Will be broadcast at the end
Of this announcement –
Protestant and Jewish services
Will begin simultaneously –
Select your wavelength immediately
According to instructions

in the Defence Code. Do not
Take well loved pets (including birds)
Into your shelter – they will consume
Fresh air. Leave the old and bed
ridden, you can do nothing for them.
Remember to press the sealing
Switch when everyone is in
The shelter. Set the radiation
Aerial, turn on the geiger barometer.
Turn off your Television now.
Turn off your radio immediately
The Services end. At the same time
Secure explosion plugs in the ears
Of each member of your family. Take
Down your plasma flasks. Give your
*   children*
The pills marked one and two
In the C.D. green container, then put
Them to bed. Do not break

311

The inside airlock seals until
The radiation All Clear shows
(Watch for the cuckoo in your
perplex panel), or your District
Touring Doctor rings your bell.
If before this, your air becomes
Exhausted or if any of your family
Is critically injured, administer
The capsules marked 'Valley Forge'
(Red pocket in No. I Survival Kit)
For painless death. (Catholics
Will have been instructed by their priests
What to do in this eventuality.)
This announcement is ending.

Our President
Has already given orders for
Massive retaliation – it will be
Decisive. Some of us may die.
Remember, statistically
It is not likely to be you.
All flags are flying fully dressed
On Government buildings – the sun
  is shining.
Death is the least we have to fear.
We are all in the hands of God,
Whatever happens happens by His Will.
Now go quickly to your shelters.

PETER PORTER

TASKS

21 Answer the following questions.
   a Summarise the main instructions given by this announcement.
   b What are the main problems being addressed here?
   c How difficult would people find it to carry out these instructions?
22 Write your own 'reply' to this poem, in prose or verse. You could call it:
    'The day I heard that announcement'.

Another poet, Edwin Muir, has written a poem called *The Horses*.

The Horses

Barely a twelvemonth after
The seven days war that put the world to sleep,
Late in the evening the strange horses came.
By then we had made our covenant with silence,
But in the first few days it was so still
We listened to our breathing and were afraid.

On the second day
The radios failed; we turned the knobs; no answer.
On the third day a warship passed us, heading north,
Dead bodies piled on the deck. On the sixth day
A plane plunged over us into the sea. Thereafter
Nothing. The radios dumb;

And still they stand in corners of our kitchens,
And stand, perhaps, turned on, in a million rooms
All over the world. But now if they should speak,
If on a sudden they should speak again,
If on the stroke of noon a voice should speak,
We would not listen, we would not let it bring
That bad old world that swallowed its children quick
At one great gulp. We would not have it again.
Sometimes we think of the nations lying asleep,
Curled blindly in impenetrable sorrow,
And then the thought confounds us with its strangeness.

The tractors lie about our fields; at evening
They look like dank sea-monsters crouched and waiting.
We leave them where they are and let them rust:
'They'll moulder away and be like other loam.'
We make our oxen drag our rusty ploughs,
Long laid aside. We have gone back
Far past our fathers' land.
                              And then, that evening
Late in the summer the strange horses came.
We heard a distant tapping on the road,
A deep drumming; it stopped, went on again
And at the corner changed to hollow thunder.
We saw the heads
Like a wild wave charging and were afraid.
We had sold our horses in our fathers' time
To buy new tractors. Now they were strange to us
As fabulous steeds set on an ancient shield
Or illustrations in a book of knights.
We did not dare go near them. Yet they waited,
Stubborn and shy, as if they had been sent
By an old command to find our whereabouts
And that long-lost archaic companionship.
In the first moment we had never a thought
That they were creatures to be owned and used.
Among them were some half-a-dozen colts
Dropped in some wilderness of the broken world,
Yet new as if they had come from their own Eden.
Since then they have pulled our ploughs and borne our loads,
But that free servitude still can pierce our hearts.
Our life is changed; their coming our beginning.

EDWIN MUIR

TASKS

23 Explain why you think we have chosen this poem to accompany *Your Attention Please.*

24 This poem could be put very effectively into story form.
Work with one or two people to create such a story.

25 Explain in detail the general mood of this poem.

26 Explain why the horses are so important to the whole idea of the poem.

27 Write about the poems you have been studying, which have been about nuclear war.
Concentrate on:

- concerns people have in the second half of the twentieth century
- the way countries with nuclear weapons behave
- fears for the spread of nuclear weapons
- the way people organise themselves to express their opinions

N ovelists have written about nuclear wars too. The next two extracts are concerned with beginnings and endings.

Robert Swindell's novel, *Brother in the Land,* describes a nuclear war.

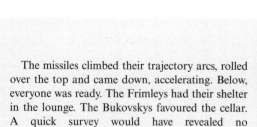

Brother in the Land

East is East and West is West, and maybe it was a difference of opinion or just a computer malfunction. Either way, it set off a chain of events that nobody but a madman could have wanted and which nobody, not even the madmen, could stop.

There were missiles.
Under the earth.
In the sky.
Beneath the waves.
Missiles with thermo-nuclear warheads, enough to kill everybody on earth.
Three times over.

And something set them off; sent them flying, West to East and East to West, crossing in the middle like cars on a cable-railway.

East and West, the sirens wailed. Emergency procedures began, hampered here and there by understandable panic. Helpful leaflets were distributed and roads sealed off. VIPs went to their bunkers and volunteers stood at their posts. Suddenly, nobody wanted to be an engine-driver anymore, or a model or a rock-star. Everybody wanted to be one thing: a survivor. But it was an overcrowded profession.

The missiles climbed their trajectory arcs, rolled over the top and came down, accelerating. Below, everyone was ready. The Frimleys had their shelter in the lounge. The Bukovskys favoured the cellar. A quick survey would have revealed no overwhelming preference, worldwide, for one part of the house over the others.

Down came the missiles. Some had just the one warhead, others had several, ranging from the compact, almost tactical warhead to the large, family size. Every town was to receive its own, individually-programmed warhead. Not one had been left out.

They struck, screaming in with pinpoint accuracy, bursting with blinding flashes brighter than a thousand suns. Whole towns and city-centres vapourised instantly; while tarmac, trees and houses thirty miles from the explosions burst into flames. Fireballs, expanding in a second to several miles across, melted and devoured all matter that fell within their diameters. Blast-waves, travelling faster than sound, ripped through the suburbs. Houses disintegrated and vanished. So fierce were the flames that they devoured all the oxygen around them, suffocating those people who had sought refuge in deep shelters. Winds of a hundred-and-fifty miles an hour, rushing in to fill the vacuum, created fire-storms that howled through the streets, where temperatures in the thousands cooked the subterranean dead. The very earth heaved and shook as the warheads rained down, burst upon burst, and a terrible thunder rent the skies.

For an hour the warheads fell, then ceased. A great silence descended over the land. The Bukovskys had gone, and the Frimleys were no more. Through the silence, through the pall of smoke and dust that blackened the sky, trillions of deadly radioactive particles began to fall. They fell soundlessly, settling like an invisible snow on the devastated earth.

Incredibly, here and there, people had survived the bombardment. They lay stunned in the ruins, incapable of thought. Drifting on the wind, the particles sifted in upon them, landing unseen on clothing, skin and hair, so that most of these too would die, but slowly.

Most, but not all. There were those whose fate it was to wander this landscape of poisonous desolation. One of them was me.

ROBERT SWINDELL

Robert O'Brien wrote about surviving a nuclear war in *Z for Zachariah*.

Anne Burden is the only survivor in her family. She learns to cope. But one day an intruder arrives in her valley. Many problems arise between them, until finally the book ends with their parting of ways.

Z for Zachariah

August 8th

From the start the interview did not go as I had planned. Mr Loomis came on the tractor at top speed, with gun across his lap. I shouted to him to *Stop*, to *Halt*; but he did not even slow the tractor. Instead, he came on. I thought perhaps he could not hear me over the sound of the engine and in desperation I fired my rifle into the air, but if he heard the shot he ignored it. He drove the tractor to the very top of Burden Hill, just opposite my hiding place. He jumped down and began to scan the road towards Ogdentown.

My heart was pounding and I did not know what to do. His back was towards me, but I could not shoot. I was not ever sure I could speak, but I tried and my voice came out reasonably firm.

'Drop your gun,' I said.

Instantly he whirled and fired in the direction of my voice. He had not yet seen me but I was no more than 25 feet away. I knew it was the end. I was sixteen and I had worked so hard to keep things going and now I was going to die. A wave of disappointment swept over me, disappointment so bitter it wiped out even my fear. I stood up and faced him. I do not know why he did not shoot me. Instead he saw the safe-suit and began to shout:

'It's *mine*. You know it's mine. Take it off!'

'No,' I said, 'I won't.'

He aimed the gun at me. I stood still. I could not think what to do, so that when words came from my mouth even I was surprised and not conscious of having thought. I realise now they probably saved my life.

'Yes,' I said, 'you can kill me ... the way you killed Edward.'

He stared at me. Then he shook his head, as if he had heard it wrong, or not heard the words at all. Yet he lowered the gun and stepped back.

'No,' he said, 'you don't know that. ...' His voice was weak.

'You told me when you were sick,' I said. 'You told me how you shot him in the chest. You had to patch the bullet holes in the suit.'

Now Mr Loomis turned away from me. For a moment he just stood there; I was not sure but I thought that his shoulders were trembling. After a time he spoke quietly.

'He tried to steal the suit ... the way you are stealing it now.'

'I have no choice,' I said. 'I didn't want to die, and you wouldn't give me anything. During the winter I would have starved on the hillside. I don't want to live with you hunting me as if I were an animal, and I will never agree to be your prisoner.' I felt reassured by my own voice and talked on:

'I'll search for a place where there are other people, people who will welcome me. To stop me you will have to kill me, too.'

'It's wrong,' he said, but he knew that I meant it, and his tone was frightened and bewildered. I thought he was going to cry.

'Don't go,' he said. 'Don't leave me. Don't leave me here alone.'

I spoke carefully:

'If you shoot me you will really be alone. You searched for months and found no one else. There may not be anyone else. But if I should find people I will tell them about you, and they may come. In the meantime you have food. You have the tractor and the store. You have the valley.'

There was bitterness in my voice. And suddenly, feeling near tears myself:

'You didn't even thank me for taking care of you when you were sick.'

So my last words were childish.

That was all. I adjusted the mask so that it fitted tightly over my face, and cool air from the tank flowed into my mouth. I turned my back on him. I waited for the jar and the sharp pain of a bullet, but it did not come. I went into the deadness. I heard Mr Loomis calling after me, but the mask covered my ears, so that his voice seemed garbled and far away, and I could not understand. I walked on. Yet suddenly his voice came clearly to me, and I realised he was calling my name. There was something in his tone that made me stop and look back up the hill. He was standing at the very edge of the deadness. He was pointing to the west and he seemed to shout the same thing over and over. Then I heard him.

'Birds,' he said, 'I saw birds … west of here … circling. They went away and I couldn't find the place. I saw them.'

I raised my hand to him to let him know that I had understood. Then I forced myself to turn and walk away.

Now it is morning. I do not know where I am. I walked all afternoon and almost all night until I was so tired I could not go on. Then I did not bother to put up the tent, just spread my blanket by the roadside and lay down. While I was sleeping the dream came, and in the dream I walked until I found the schoolroom and the children. When I awoke the sun was high in the sky. A stream was flowing through the brown grass, winding west. The dream was gone, yet I knew which way to go. As I walk I search the horizon for a trace of green. I am hopeful.

ROBERT O'BRIEN

TASKS

28 In groups or in class discuss these two extracts. What are their strengths and weaknesses as a beginning and an ending of a story?

29 Danny is one of those 'whose fate it was to wander this landscape of poisonous desolation'.
   Using the first extract, write about the problems Danny will face.

30 In the second extract Anne and Mr Loomis can no longer stay together. Describe your feelings as you read this extract.

A rtists express their visions in different ways and the picture printed below shows one such expression. Few of us are art critics but we can all have a go at interpreting what we see.

TASK

31 Explore the picture in your own writing. (Don't just describe the picture but let your ideas take off into the future with fantastic machines, space suits...)

And finally…

The sea has affected many people and inspired many thoughts.

In *Dover Beach*, written by Matthew Arnold in 1867, the poet's thoughts range back and forth over time and the history of humankind.

Dover Beach

The sea is calm tonight.
The tide is full, the moon lies fair
Upon the straits; – on the French coast the light
Gleams and is gone; the cliffs of England stand,
Glimmering and vast, out in the tranquil bay.
Come to the window, sweet is the night-air!
Only, from the long line of spray
Where the sea meets the moon-blanch'd land,
Listen! you hear the grating roar
Of pebbles which the waves draw back, and fling,
At their return, up the high strand,
Begin, and cease, and then again begin,
With tremulous cadence slow, and bring
The eternal note of sadness in.
Sophocles long ago
Heard in on the Aegean, and it brought
Into his mind the turbid ebb and flow
Of human misery; we
Find also in the sound a thought,
Hearing it by this distant northern sea.

The Sea of Faith
Was once, too, at the full, and round
  earth's shore
Lay like the folds of a bright girdle furl'd.
But now I only hear
Its melancholy, long, withdrawing roar,
Retreating, to the breath
Of the night-wind, down the vast edges drear
And naked shingles of the world.

Ah, love, let us be true
To one another! for the world, which seems
To lie before us like a land of dreams,
So various, so beautiful, so new,
Hath really neither joy, nor love, nor light,
Nor certitude, nor peace, nor help for pain;
And we are here as on a darkling plain
Swept with confused arms of struggle and flight,
Where ignorant armies clash by night.

MATTHEW ARNOLD

TASK

32 Write your own study of this poem.
    Consider carefully:
    ▪ the images and pictures it creates
    ▪ the thoughts inspired by the sea
    ▪ what the poet is saying to his wife in the last verse
    ▪ the feelings inspired in you by the poem

INDEX